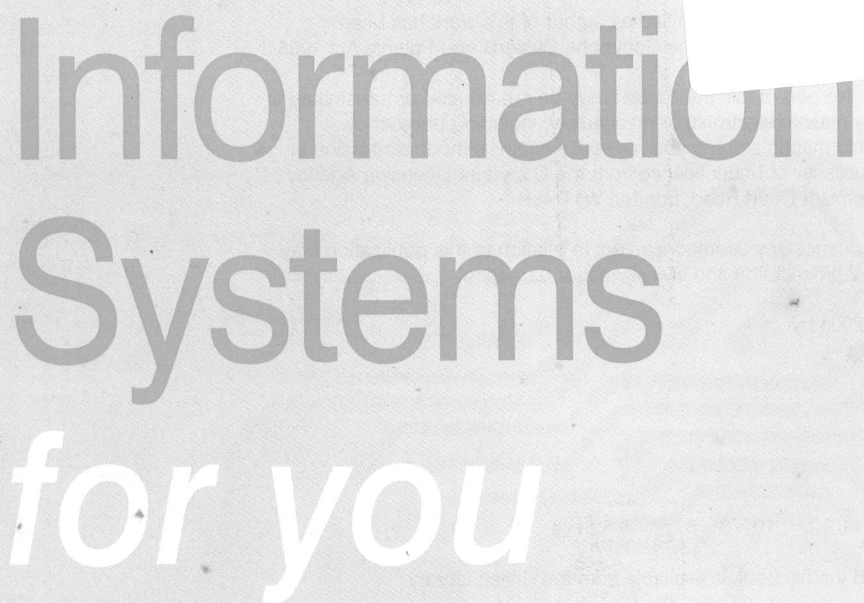

Information Systems *for you*

SKILLBUILDER

Office XP Edition

Stephen Doyle

First published in 2003 by:
Nelson Thornes Ltd
Delta Place
27 Bath Road
CHELTENHAM
GL53 7TH
United Kingdom

03 04 05 06 07 / 10 9 8 7 6 5 4 3 2 1

A catalogue record for this book is available from the British Library

ISBN 0 7487 7278 2

Cartoons by Shaun Williams, Jane Cope
Page makeup by GreenGate Publishing Services

Printed and bound in Italy by Canale

Acknowledgements
The author and publisher wish to thank Robert Penrose for his considerable input and advice during the development of this resource.

Microsoft Office screenshots are reprinted with permission from Microsoft Corporation. Microsoft and its products are registered trademarks or trademarks of Microsoft Corporation in the United States and/or other countries.

Contents

Introduction

Why use this book?

All the GCSE ICT syllabuses, both the full and short courses, require students to produce coursework that contributes 60% of the total marks for the subject. This book has been designed to be used in parallel with the core text, *GCSE Information Systems For You*.

The primary aims of the book are:

- to build up gradually the skills needed for GCSE ICT coursework by working through a series of simple exercises in Microsoft Office (Word, Excel and Access); to encourage students to solve problems themselves, there are lots of questions spread throughout each chapter
- to give instructions about designing, implementing and documenting an information technology system
- to build up practical experience that will be tested by questions in the theory paper
- to help students produce the best coursework by providing examples, tasks, tips, sample documentation, ideas, etc.

Here are a few comments about coursework, taken from Chief Examiners' Reports:

- 'Many candidates produced a large quantity of paper with little or no structure.'
- 'Many portfolios from candidates were similar in nature and were structured and directed with little variation in marks.'
- 'The modelling strand was poorly addressed by the majority of candidates. Modelling was poorly understood. No evidence of "what if ... ?", with the forming and testing of hypotheses as a central element.'
- 'Many candidates provided no evidence for the measuring and control strand.'
- 'Candidates should be encouraged to adopt a systems analysis approach to the development and design of a system.'
- 'Candidates should be encouraged to develop systems for others to use.'

This book seeks to address these problems and will help students to learn the skills needed to use software to develop new and original solutions to ICT problems.

Students are able to work through this book by themselves. There are many activities for them to try and they involve solving interesting problems.

Which software is covered?

This book covers Microsoft Office XP, in particular, the following:

- Word XP, the wordprocessing package
- Excel XP, the spreadsheet package
- Access XP, the database package.

Microsoft Office XP Professional includes all the above packages and some additional ones. The Small Business Edition of Microsoft Office XP includes Excel and Word, but not Access.

Can the book be used with earlier software such as Office 2000 or Office 97?

Word XP and Excel XP are very similar to the older versions and there is little difference for the parts of the packages that we will look at. Students will therefore be able to use the book to learn about these packages.

There is a greater difference between Access XP and earlier versions of Access, so some screens will look different. This can cause some problems, but it is still possible to use this section successfully with earlier versions of Access.

How does this book fit in with *Information Systems For You*?

The two books can be used together. *Information Systems For You* covers the theory, with some practical material. This book covers the Microsoft Office skills needed to complete the coursework needed for GCSE.

To the student

How do I use the book?

In order to gain sufficient skills in using each package you will need to work through everything in a particular chapter. You must do the exercises, activities and questions, as they will help you build up your skills and consolidate them.

Here are some of the main features of the book and how to use them.

Test Yourself
These are short snappy questions to help you build your knowledge.

Exercises
For the exercises you will be required to use a computer in conjunction with Microsoft Office (i.e. the software) and a suitable operating system (Windows XP, Windows 2000, Windows NT, etc.)

You have to work through the exercises and carefully follow a series of steps. These steps will guide you through doing a particular task using the software. These skills can then be applied to the tasks the book asks you to solve, or your coursework.

IT Tasks
IT tasks are tasks that you do for yourself. In most cases you will be given a problem to solve using some of the skills developed in the exercises. You are also left to consider the design of a solution. It is important to do these IT tasks, because they will give you practice for doing your coursework.

Questions
Questions have been included within the text to help you understand concepts as you come to them. In this way you do not have to wait until the end of a chapter before testing your understanding.

What do I do when I have worked through the book?

When you have worked through this book, you will be a fairly proficient user of Microsoft Office. However, this book can only touch the surface of the software. Office is a very big package and if you are interested in finding out more about what you can do with it than you can use reference manuals or the on-line help facility.

Coursework, where you have to develop solutions to problems, accounts for up to 60% of the final mark for the GCSE. It is therefore a very important part of the course.

After working through the chapters you will have learnt how to solve problems using the software. You will now have to solve problems identified by other people and fully document them. You should keep referring back to the chapter on coursework to check that you are working correctly.

I hope you enjoy working through the book. Good luck with your coursework and exams.

Introduction to Spreadsheets

What is a spreadsheet?

Here is a list of numbers to add up:

12, 23, 14, 87, 34, 8, 90, 32, 15, 67.

There are only ten numbers in this list and it would be possible to add them in your head. Imagine that you had one hundred such numbers to add up. An easy task you might say, but you would probably ask for a calculator. Even on a calculator the task is not easy. A moment's lapse of concentration and you could enter the same number twice or forget where you were up to.

If you entered these numbers into a spreadsheet you could add the numbers up instantly by giving a simple instruction (or formula). If one or more of the numbers were to change, you could simply amend the list and the total would be recalculated automatically. This is a very simple example. Spreadsheets can do a lot more than just add up lists of numbers. Here is another example which shows the power of spreadsheet software.

Years ago, people such as accountants who used figures and calculations a lot, used to write them on a piece of paper, as in Figure 1.1. This paper was called a ledger.

The paper was already marked with a grid which kept the numbers in neat lines.

	Mortgage (home loan)	*£45,000*			
	Interest rate	*6.25%*			
	Number of monthly payments	*240*			
	Monthly payment				

Figure 1.1 *Part of a traditional ledger*

Calculations were performed in your head or by a calculator. In this case there is a complicated formula to calculate the monthly payments and once this has been applied, the answer could be added to the grid. If any of the quantities (such as the amount of the mortgage) needed changing then the whole thing would be calculated again from scratch.

Using spreadsheet software, once you have input the amount borrowed, the length of the mortgage and the interest rate, the spreadsheet does the quite complicated calculation to work out the monthly repayments. Any changes can be made on the screen and the spreadsheet software immediately comes up with the recalculated payments.

The same task performed using spreadsheet software would produce the following screen.

Microsoft Excel - Chapter 1 spread 1

File Edit View Insert Format Tools Data Windo

Arial 10 B I U

	A	B	C
1			
2	Mortgage (Home Loan)	£45,000	
3	Interest rate	6.25%	
4	Number of monthly payments	240	
5			
6	Monthly Payment	£328.92	
7			
8			
9			
10			
11			
12			
13			
14			
15			
16			

The good thing about the spreadsheet is that you can change numbers without having to do the calculation again. As soon as any figures are changed, the computer works out the answer.

Introduction to spreadsheet software

Although spreadsheets are perfect for doing repetitive calculations, you can also use them for manipulating text, producing graphs and even drawing maps. By the time you have learnt some of these software skills you will be a competent user who can apply these skills to new and often novel situations. Eventually you will be able develop your own solutions to problems and build applications using Microsoft Excel, which you can then use as coursework for your GCSE exam.

Spreadsheets: the basics

Before we start with the software, let's look at a few basic things about spreadsheets.

The grid into which you put your own data is often referred to as a worksheet. The worksheet is the working area of the spreadsheet and is arranged as follows:

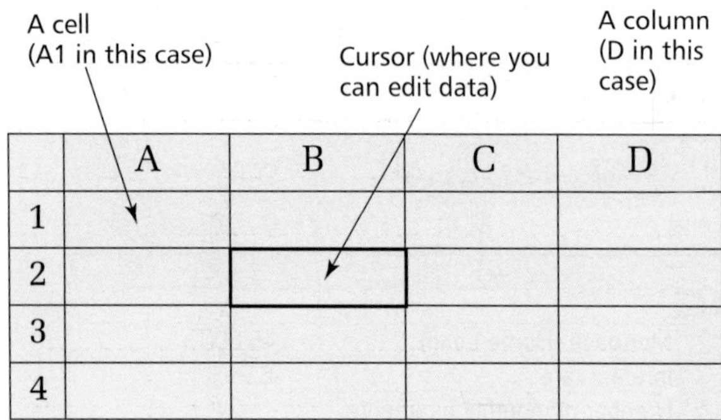

Figure 1.2 *The essential features of a spreadsheet*

Cells

As we have seen in Figure 1.2, the small rectangles produced by the crossed lines of columns and rows are called cells. A particular cell is referred to using the column letter followed by the row number. Cell C3 is the cell where column C intersects row 3. Hence S4 is a proper cell reference whereas 4S is not.

Figure 1.3 below shows the cell references for several columns and rows.

	A	B	C	D
1	Cell A1	Cell B1	Cell C1	Cell D1
2	Cell A2	Cell B2	Cell C2	Cell D2
3	Cell A3	Cell B3	Cell C3	Cell D3
4	Cell A4	Cell B4	Cell C4	Cell D4

Figure 1.3 *Cell references*

As well as referring to individual cells, we also refer to columns and rows. Column B would be the column with the column heading B and all the cell references would start with the letter B. Rows are referred to by their numbers. Row 3 contains those cells ending with the number 3 whatever letter precedes the 3.

Rows and columns

What is a row?

A row is a straight line of cells going across the worksheet. Rows are located by numbers. In the worksheet shown below, row 6 has been highlighted.

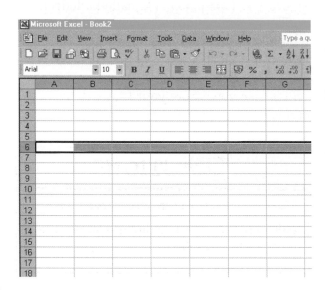

What is a column?

A column is a vertical line of cells going down the worksheet. Columns are located by letters.

In the worksheet shown below, column C has been highlighted.

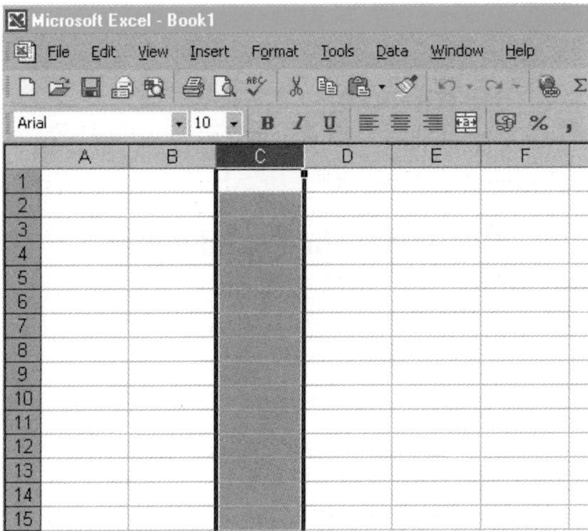

Putting data into cells

If you type in data (numbers, text or a formula), it goes into the cell where the cursor is positioned. The cursor may be moved around from one cell to another using the mouse (or the cursor keys). When you have finished entering data into a cell, check to see if it is correct and then enter it into the worksheet by pressing the Enter key.

Loading the software

Your teacher will show you how to load the spreadsheet program Microsoft Excel. If you need to keep your work on a floppy disk then your teacher will show you how to do this. If you are working on a network your teacher will advise you where your files will be stored.

QUESTIONS

It is important that you are able to load Excel.

Write down a set of brief instructions to remind yourself how to do this.

QUESTIONS

Have you got the hang of cell references? Answer the following questions to prove it.

1 Here is a spreadsheet grid.

	A	B	C	D
1				
2		Cell B2		
3				
4				
5				
6				

Copy the worksheet above into your book and mark on your diagram the following cell positions. The first one has been done for you.

(a) Cell B2
(b) Cell B4
(c) Cell D3
(d) Cell C6

2

	A	B	C	D	E
1	(a)			↑	
2				│	
3				│	
4				│	
5		(b)		(d)	
6				│	
7				│	
8				│	(c)
9				│	
10	←		(e)	↓	→

Using the words cell, column and row, describe fully the cell references of (a), (b), (c), (d) and (e).

Using Excel

Excel is the most popular spreadsheet software package in use and is provided either separately or as part of the integrated software package Microsoft Office. The version used in these chapters is Excel XP or Office XP.

Excel is ideal if you want to produce tables (Microsoft Word will also do this). Quite apart from doing repetitive sums, Excel is also excellent for producing graphs and charts from a set of data.

Using a spreadsheet for the first time

If you have already used a spreadsheet this will be useful revision.

When you load Excel the screen below appears.

The top part of the spreadsheet is the command area where commands to do certain things are issued.

The large area in the middle is the working area of the spreadsheet and it is in this area that you enter data. This area is commonly called the worksheet.

Can you spot the cursor? It is the bold rectangle around cell C7. You can move this cursor (sometimes also called the active cell) by using the mouse or the cursor keys.

Using the mouse

Here are a few reminders concerning using the mouse.

Click or click-click; single and double mouse clicks

As with all Windows software, you make selections using the mouse.

Single click – this is where you press the mouse button once. (Use the left button if there is more than one.)

Double click – here the mouse button is pressed twice in quick succession.

Dragging

Dragging the mouse is when you click and then keep the mouse button pressed down.

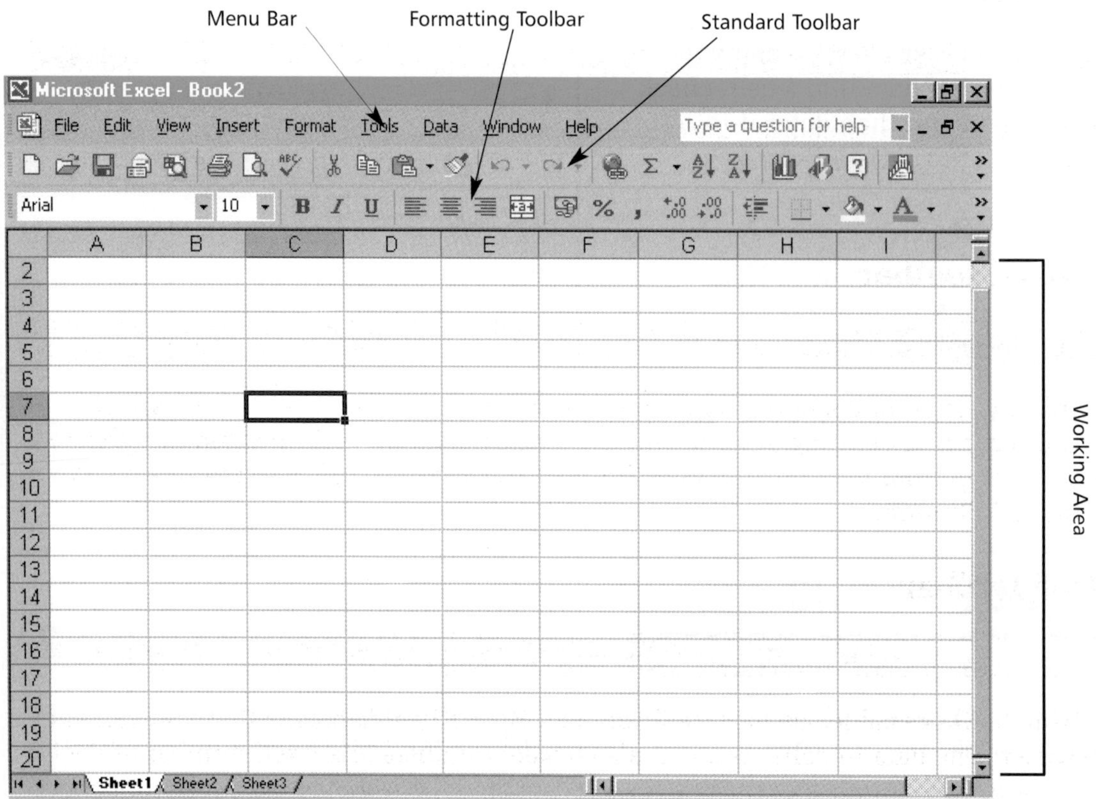

Dragging the mouse!

Toolbars

Toolbars appear at the top of your worksheet. Their purpose is to make it easy for you to find and issue the commands that tell the spreadsheet what to do.

The menu bar

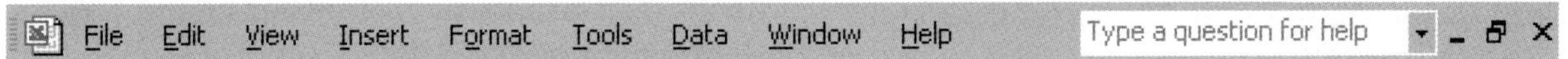

The menu bar is a special toolbar where you can select menus such as Print, Edit and View. Clicking on any item in the menu bar pulls down a list from which further selections can be made.

The standard toolbar

The standard toolbar contains buttons for open, save, print, cut, paste, etc. There are also buttons to sort data in ascending and descending order, to add up cells, produce graphs and even produce a map from your data. Notice the button at the end with the question mark on it. This is the help button.

Formatting toolbar

The formatting toolbar enables cells to be formatted. Basically, this means that you can alter the appearance of the data in cells. You can also format numbers to a fixed number of decimal places. It also allows you to use borders and colour to give the worksheet greater impact.

Mathematical operators

You will not find the divide sign (÷) or the multiplication sign (×) on the computer keyboard. Instead * is used for multiply and / for divide. Mathematical operators are summarised in the following table.

Table 1.1 *Mathematical operators used in spreadsheets*

Operator	Use
+	addition
–	subtraction
*	multiplication
/	division
%	percentage

The order of doing calculations

If a calculation involves only addition and subtraction, it does not matter in which order the operations are done. Similarly, if a calculation involves only multiplication and division then the order does not matter. If part of a calculation is in brackets, then the part within the brackets must be done first. If a calculation involves a mixture of addition, subtraction, multiplication and division, then the multiplication and division must be done before any addition or subtraction.

Here are some examples. Make sure you understand how the rules described above have been followed in each of these examples.

12 – 8 + 5 = 9

4*5/10 = 20/10 = 2

12 – (2+4) = 12 – 6 = 6

2 + 7*3 = 2 + 21 = 23

4*5 – 3*4 = 20 – 12 = 8

20/5 + 6*8 = 4 + 48 = 52

(5 + 3 + 9 + 10 + 7 + 11)/9 = 45/9 = 5

QUESTIONS

What are the answers to the following?

(a) 12/4

(b) 3*8

(c) 2*4*6

(d) 24/6/4

(e) 4*3/12

(f) 2+4*5

(g) 3*4–3*2

What can be put into a spreadsheet cell?

You can put any of the following types of data into a spreadsheet cell.

Numbers

These must be proper numbers (such as 12.45 or 1879) and not telephone numbers like 0151 – 220 – 1121 (which contain dashes) or numbers with other characters in them, such as A121X.

Text

Text means any of the keys on the keyboard. This includes numbers, letters, punctuation marks and any special symbols.

Formulae

If you type in a formula to add two cells together (like C3 + C4) the spreadsheet will just enter C3 + C4 in the cell where the cursor is. It will treat any such entry as text. In order to distinguish between text and formulae the equals symbol (=) needs to be typed in first.

Here are some calculations and what they do. Notice that you can use upper or lower case (capital or small) letters.

=C3+C4	adds the numbers in cells C3 and C4 together
=A1*B4	multiplies together the numbers in cells A1 and B4
=3*G4	multiplies cell G4 by three
=sum(b1:b10)	adds up all the cells from b1 to b10 inclusive
=C4/D1	divides the number in cell C4 by the number in cell D1
=30%*A2	finds 30% of cell A2

Test Yourself

Test yourself constructing formulae

You have to write a formula to do each of the following.

1. Add together cells A6 and B6.
2. Subtract cell F17 from cell G14.
3. Add together cells A1, A2, A3, A4 and A5.
4. Divide cell A6 by cell B3.
5. Add together cells A5, A7 and A9.
6. Divide cell A3 by 100.
7. Add together cells B3 and B4 and then divide the result by 50.
8. Find the average of cells C1, C2, C3, C4 and C5. (Hint: you will need to add the cells together and then divide by the number of cells.)
9. Find the average of cells A2, B2, C2 and D2.
10. Multiply cell B4 by itself.
11. Find 15% of cell A4.
12. Find 17.5% of cell C6.

Questions

Here are some examples of data. You have to decide whether they are text, numbers, currencies, dates or formulae. Copy out the table and fill in the last column. The first question has been done for you.

Description of data	Data	Type
Order number	1000900X	Text
Price	10.95	
Volume	0.897	
Telephone number	0161–282–4135	
VAT	=B2*17.5%	
Discount	3%	
Total	£164.25	
Date	12/04/00	
Total	=sum(B2:B5)	

Spreadsheets and worksheets; what's the difference?

A spreadsheet is a piece of software. It is the program that produces the grid and allows the user to make use of all the special features that help handle the data.

A worksheet is the single grid/matrix into which you enter data. When you have finished entering data and formulae the work is saved as a worksheet. In some questions, you may see the words spreadsheet and worksheet and they are often used interchangeably.

Exercise 1.1

Your first spreadsheet

In this spreadsheet you will learn to:

- **enter data into a worksheet**
- **enter a formula into a cell.**

Here is a simple spreadsheet for you to try. You will need to follow the instructions very carefully and in sequence. If you make a mistake, simply type over it or delete it using the delete button.

1 Load the spreadsheet software Excel.

You should now see a screen like this.

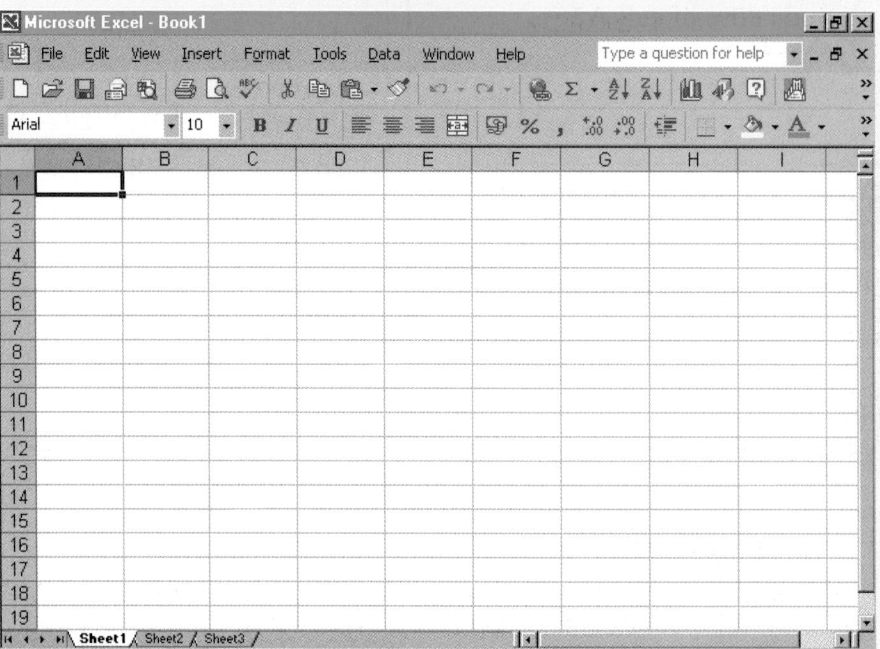

You are now ready to enter some data.

2 Move the mouse to position the cursor (the small black rectangle) on cell A2.

Type **Car** into this cell. When you have checked it, press Enter.

Because **Car** contains letters, it is text.

3 Move the cursor to cell B2 and enter the number **56**. Check and then enter the data by pressing Enter. Notice that numbers move to the right of the cell whereas text moves to the left.

4 Move the cursor to cell A3 and then enter **Rent**. (By 'enter **Rent**' we mean type in the data and then press Enter.)

5 Move the cursor to cell B3 and enter the amount for the rent which is **33**.

6 The rest of the data needs to be entered into the worksheet in the same cells as in the following screen shot.

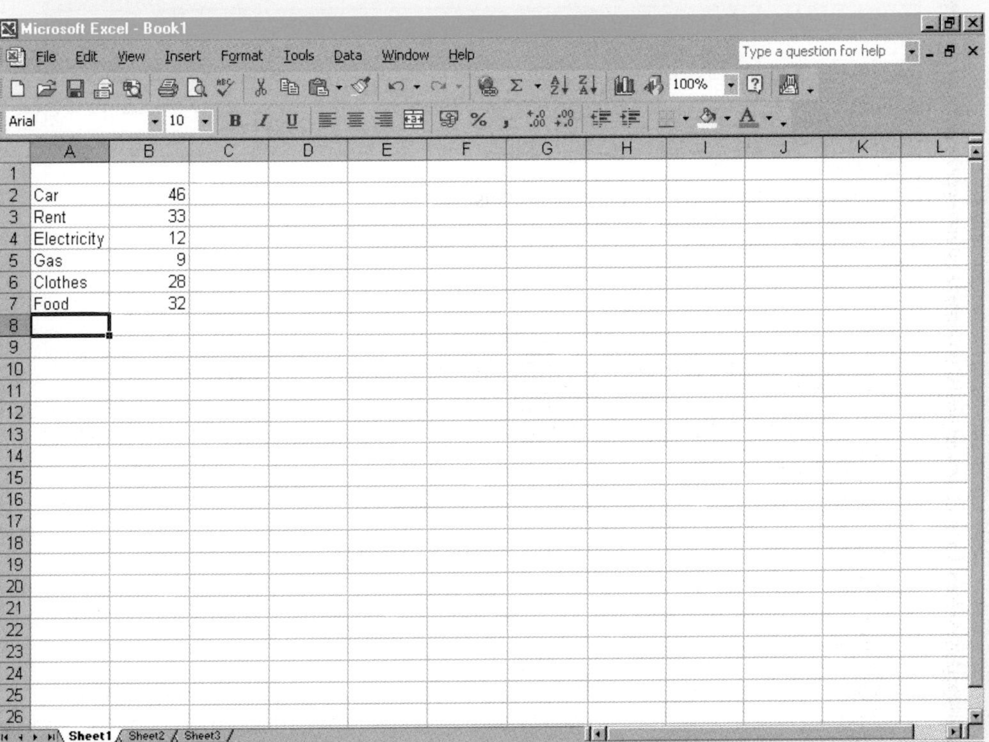

7 Enter the text **Total** into cell A8.

8 The numbers in column B represent the weekly amounts spent on each item. We now need to add up the cells from B2 to B7 and put the result in cell B8.

There are several ways this can be done. For the moment we will move the cursor to cell B8 and enter the following formula in cell B8:

=B2+B3+B4+B5+B6+B7 Enter

Remember to press the Enter key. Notice that the formula starts with an equals sign. All formulae in Excel start with an equals sign.

The result of the calculation automatically appears in cell B8; check that this is 170.

9 Now suppose a mistake has been made for the weekly car amount. Change the contents of cell B2 from 56 to 46. To do this move the cursor onto the cell and simply type the new value over the old one. Press Enter to enter the new amount.

Notice that the total in cell B8 automatically decreases by ten.

If we change a number in any of the cells from B2 to B7, the spreadsheet automatically recalculates the new total. This is one of the chief advantages in using a spreadsheet.

10 Quit the spreadsheet without saving. To do this click on the cross at the top right, which closes the worksheet.

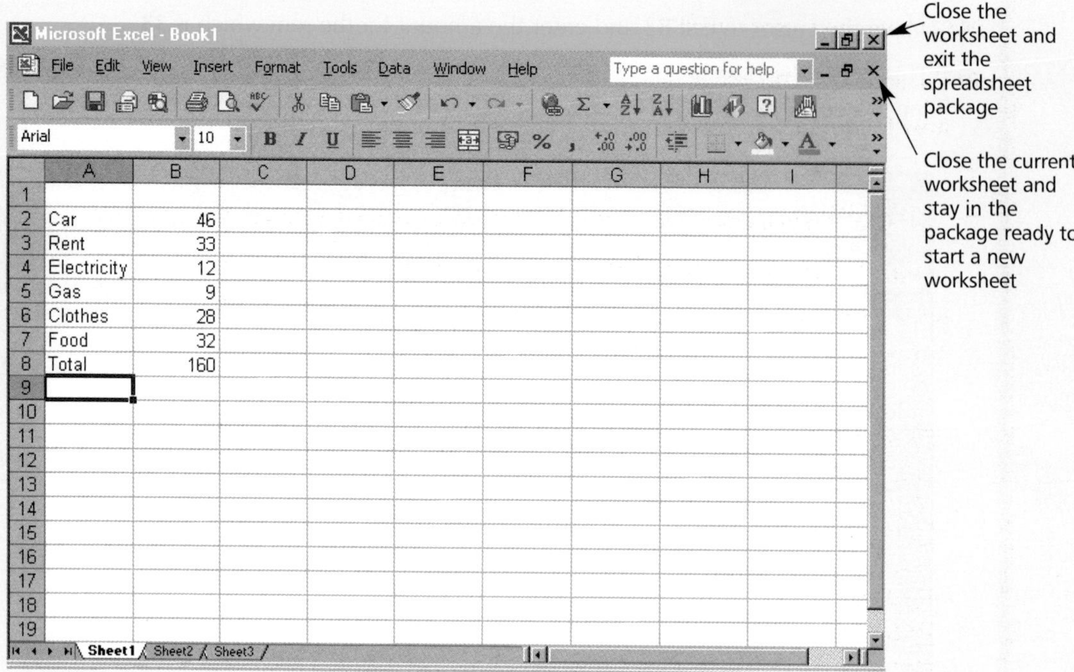
Close the worksheet and exit the spreadsheet package
Close the current worksheet and stay in the package ready to start a new worksheet

There are two ways to leave the worksheet. Clicking the upper cross means you will exit the spreadsheet software, while clicking the lower cross allows you to close the worksheet but stay in the spreadsheet package.

The following menu will appear asking you if you want to save your work.

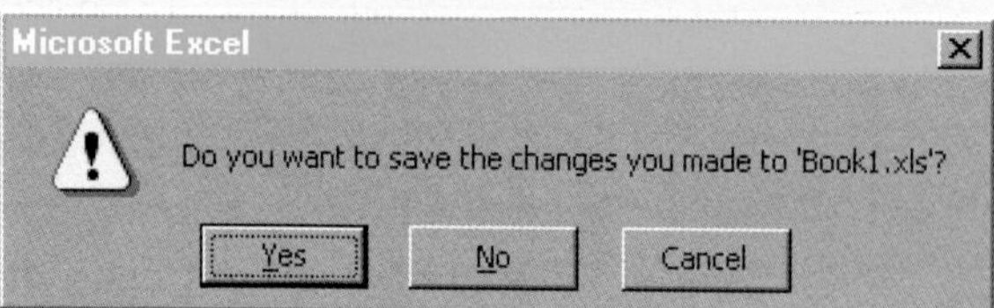
Microsoft Excel
Do you want to save the changes you made to 'Book1.xls'?
Yes
No
Cancel

Click on No. You will now have left the spreadsheet package without saving your work.

Your second spreadsheet

In this exercise you will learn

- **how to widen columns.**

1 Load the spreadsheet software and start a new worksheet.

2 The data you will enter concerns the preferences of a class for certain flavours of crisp.

Put the headings **Variety** and **Pupils** in cells A2 and B2 respectively.

Now enter the crisp flavours in cells A3 to A6. Do not worry that they spill into the next column. This will be corrected in the next step.

	A	B	C	D	E	F	G
1							
2	Variety	Pupils					
3	Salt and Vinegar						
4	Cheese and Onion						
5	Plain						
6	Prawn						
7							
8							

Your screen will now look identical to the one shown above.

3 In this step we will widen column A to accommodate the largest line of text in the column.

Move the cursor to the letter of the column you want to widen, A in this case, and click on it. It will change to a cross and the column will be highlighted. As you move the cursor to the line separating the two columns you will notice that it changes to a vertical line with a double-headed arrow. When you see this, drag your mouse to the right until you are happy with the new width. The same method can be used to make a column narrower.

Make the column wide enough to enable the longest crisp name to just fit in.

Your worksheet will now look like the one below.

	A	B	C	D	E	F
1						
2	Variety	Pupils				
3	Salt and Vinegar					
4	Cheese and Onion					
5	Plain					
6	Prawn					
7						
8						
9						

4 Now quit the spreadsheet without saving.

In this spreadsheet you will learn

- **how to format numbers to a certain number of decimal places.**

Load Excel and start a new worksheet.

Type the data into the spreadsheet in exactly the same places as in the screen shot shown below. To input the data you will need to position the cursor (the small rectangle) by moving the mouse to the correct cell.

If you make a mistake, don't worry. You can simply delete what you have typed in by pressing the backspace key (i.e. the large key with the arrow pointing to the left in the row containing the numbers).

The manager of an Indian takeaway uses a spreadsheet to help him estimate the sales of meals. A section of the spreadsheet used is shown.

	A	B	C	D	E
1	Dish	Price	Qty Sold	Takings	
2	Chicken Madras	5.95	12		
3	Prawn Korma	5.5	8		
4	Chicken Tandoori	6.25	10		
5	Pilau Rice	1.5	25		
6	Boiled Rice	1.3	9		
7	Poppadom	0.4	14		
8	Sheek Kebab	2.1	8		
9	Onion Bhaji	1.9	15		

1 Enter the data into the worksheet. You will need to widen column A to enable the text to fit in.

2 You will need to put a formula in cell D2 to work out the takings. The formula will multiply the quantity sold by the price. Refer back to page 6 for the operator table and look for the symbol that means multiply.

The formula is =C2*B2. It is very important to enter the equals sign at the start of every formula.

3 Now put in the formula to work out the takings for the rest of the column (i.e. for cells from D3 to D9). There is a quick way to do this by copying the formula, which will be looked at later.

4 Enter the text **total takings =** into cell C11. Widen column C to accommodate the width of this text. Put the formula to calculate the total takings into cell D11. The formula needs to add up all the numbers in cells D2 to D9.

You could use

=D2+D3+D4+D5+D6+D7+D8+D9

but a much quicker formula is

=SUM(D2:D9)

which adds up all cells in the range from D2 to D9.

5 We need to make sure that numbers representing money are set to two decimal places.

Increases decimal places

Decreases decimal places

Microsoft Excel - Takeaway1

File Edit View Insert Format Tools Data Window Help

Type a question for help

Arial 10

	A	B	C	D	E	F	G	H
1	Dish	Price	Qty Sold	Takings				
2	Chicken Madras	5.95	12	71.4				
3	Prawn Korma	5.5	8	44				
4	Chicken Tandoori	6.25	10	62.5				
5	Pilau Rice	1.5	25	37.5				
6	Boiled Rice	1.3	9	11.7				
7	Poppadom	0.4	14	5.6				
8	Sheek Kebab	2.1	8	16.8				
9	Onion Bhaji	1.9	15	28.5				
10								
11			Total Takings =	278				
12								
13								
14								
15								
16								
17								
18								
19								

Sheet1 Sheet2 Sheet3

Move the cursor to the first cell that needs to be formatted (cell B2) and click once. Keeping the mouse button down, move the mouse down until the column of numbers is highlighted. Then take your finger off the mouse button and move to the formatting toolbar. There are two relevant buttons on this toolbar: one to increase the number of decimal places shown, the other to decrease them. Experiment with this and set the entire column of numbers to two decimal places. Now repeat the process for the takings column. For the single cell showing total takings we can simply move to the cell and then click on the button to increase the number of decimal places.

6 Check that your final spreadsheet looks like this.

	A	B	C	D	E
1	Dish	Price	Qty Sold	Takings	
2	Chicken Madras	5.95	12	71.40	
3	Prawn Korma	5.50	8	44.00	
4	Chicken Tandoori	6.25	10	62.50	
5	Pilau Rice	1.50	25	37.50	
6	Boiled Rice	1.30	9	11.70	
7	Poppadom	0.40	14	5.60	
8	Sheek Kebab	2.10	8	16.80	
9	Onion Bhaji	1.90	15	28.50	
10					
11			Total Takings =	278.00	
12					

QUESTIONS

1 Set up the following spreadsheet and enter the data in cells from A1 to C4.

	A	B	C
1	6	9	
2	5	3	
3	12	6	
4	36	3	

(a) What formula needs to be placed in C1 to add the contents of A1 and B1?

(b) What formula needs to be placed in C2 to subtract the contents of cell B2 from cell A2?

(c) What formula needs to be placed in C3 to multiply the contents of cell A3 by the contents of cell B3?

(d) What formula needs to be placed in C4 to divide the contents of cell A4 by the contents of cell B4?

Correcting mistakes

What happens if you make a mistake and enter the wrong data into a cell? There are three ways to correct mistakes.

1 You can delete the contents of a cell (text, number or formula) by moving to the cell and using the backspace key.
2 You can simply type over what is already there.
3 You can highlight those cells whose contents need deleting, then go to Edit then Clear and finally All.

Correcting a command

It is quite easy to issue a command and the wrong menu appears. If this happens, you can just press the Esc (Escape) key to get rid of it.

Aligning cells

When you enter data into a cell the program automatically aligns (i.e. positions) the data according to the following:

- numbers are aligned to the right
- text is aligned to the left.

Do not put any spaces in front of numbers in order to align them as this will make it impossible for the spreadsheet to use the numbers in calculations.

If you want to align the data differently, you can use the special alignment buttons in the formatting toolbar. Using this method, you can align data to the left, right or centre.

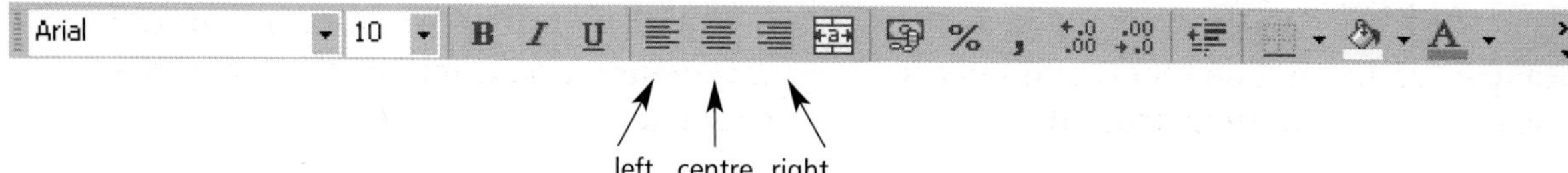

Tips when using a spreadsheet for the first time

1 Do not work out any of the calculations using a calculator. The whole point of the spreadsheet is to avoid having to do this yourself.
2 Use formulae wherever possible. This means that if you change any of the cells the spreadsheet will automatically recalculate to take account of the values.
3 Make sure that any formulae you enter start with an = sign and that you press Enter to confirm entry.
4 You may need to widen the columns. If the result of a calculation appears like this – ####### – it means that the number is too big to fit in the current width. You can correct this by widening the column.
5 Plan the layout of the spreadsheet first on paper. It is easier to get it right than to try to change it later.
6 Do not worry too much about the appearance of the spreadsheet. It is more important that it works. You will learn about improving the appearance of a spreadsheet later on.

Saving your work

If you want to come back to your work at a later date, or if you want to print it out, you will need to save it. You will usually save the work on a floppy disk or on the hard disk. It is important to save your work before printing, in case there is something wrong with the printer. If the computer cannot print the work it sometimes 'freezes' and the only option is to switch it off and start again. If this is done without saving your work, you will lose everything done since you last saved.

There are several ways to save work.

1 You can press the save button on the standard toolbar .
2 You can go to the File menu and choose one of the Save options from the list.

Saving for the first time

When you save a worksheet for the first time you will be asked to give it a name. You can use long names that explain what the spreadsheet does. Remember that you might have to find the spreadsheet a few months or years later, so spreadsheet titles such as 'spreadsheet 1' are not very helpful. Spreadsheet names such as 'Favourite_Crisps.xls' or 'Weekly_Budget.xls' are much better.

To save a worksheet for the first time follow this sequence.

1 Click on the File menu and then on Save As. This will open up a box where you can do several things:
   (a) You can change where the worksheet will be saved. In many cases you will want to store your worksheets on the A drive (i.e. the floppy disk).
   (b) You can type in the filename you are giving to the worksheet.

   Now check everything in this box is correct and then click on the Save button at the bottom of the box (see the screen at the top of the next page).
2 When you have saved your work once it is easy to save it again because the computer will remember what you called it and where you last stored it. You just go to Save in the File menu. If you intend to change the name or where you want to store your worksheet, you will need to go back to the Save As option in the File menu where you can make changes as described in step 1.

Closing Excel without saving

Sometimes you may just want to do a quick calculation using the spreadsheet and then exit the package without saving your work. To do this you go to the File menu on the menu bar and then select Exit from the list of options. You will be asked if you want to save your work. Click on No to exit the package.

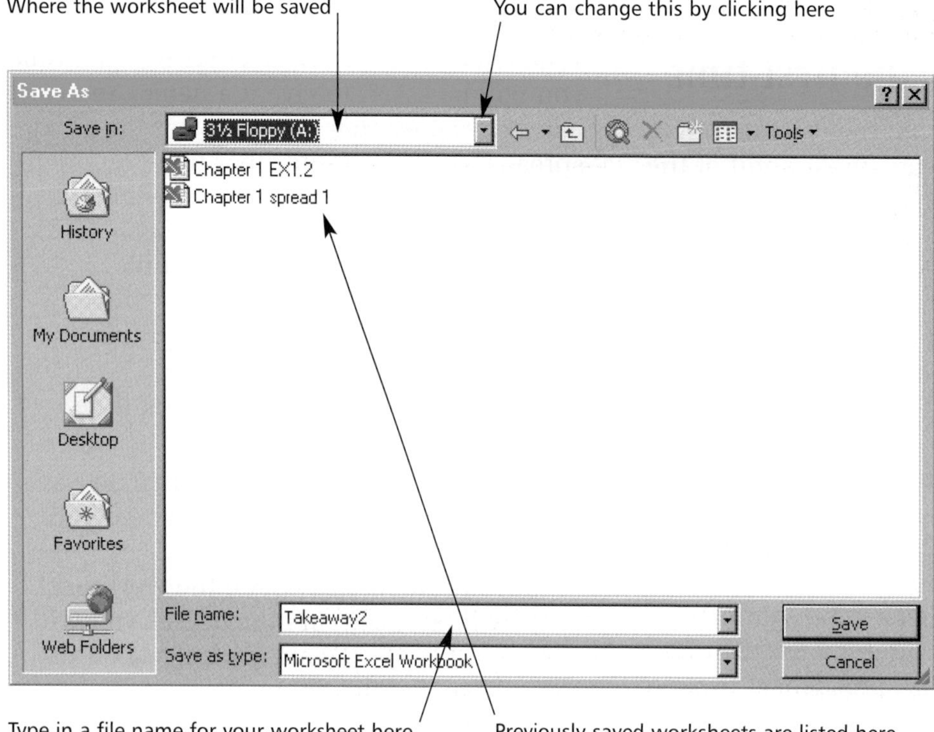

Printing out your work

Things to remember before printing:

- Carefully spell check and proof read your work. Printing takes time and costs money (paper, electricity, toner/ink cartridges, etc.) so make sure your worksheet is correct before you print it.
- Use the print preview option (it comes up under File) to check the layout.
- Check the printer setup and page setup and make sure they are correct.
- Save your work before printing.
- Check that the computer you are using is connected to a printer.
- Check that the printer has paper, is switched on and is on-line.

Opening a previously saved worksheet

When you save a worksheet it will most likely be stored on the hard disk or on a floppy disk. If you need to come back to the worksheet you will need to load it from the disk and put it into the active memory of the computer. This process is called opening a worksheet. There are several ways to open a previously saved worksheet.

One way is to use the Open button on the standard toolbar.

Another way is to click on File and then select Open from the menu.

The following menu then appears:

Click here to look in different places for your file.
You can use this to select the A drive (the one with the floppy disk in it).

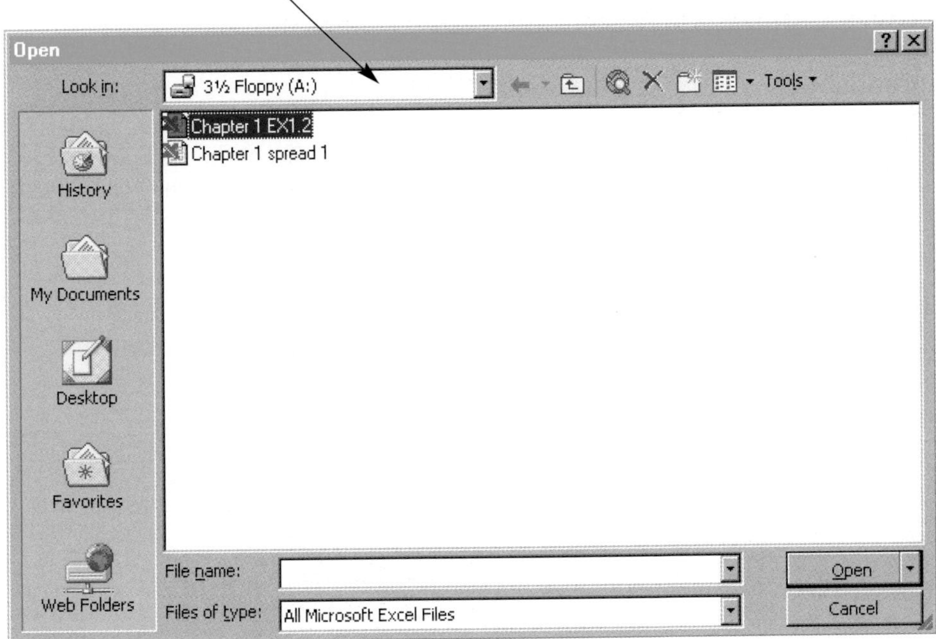

When you see the name of the file you need to open, select it by clicking on it and then pressing the Open button.

QUESTIONS

1 Here is a simple spreadsheet to calculate wages.

	A	B	C
1			
2	Hours worked	40	
3	Wages per hour	£4.75	
4	Pay	£190.00	

The contents of cell B4 are calculated.

We could use either of these formulae for this:

- =B2*B3
- =40*4.75

They both give the right answer, but one is much better than the other. Which one is best and why?

2 Explain the following terms used in spreadsheets:
(a) row
(b) column
(c) cell.

3 Briefly explain what types of information can be typed into a cell.

4 Explain how you would:
(a) add the contents of two cells together
(b) add up a column of figures
(c) multiply the contents of two cells together
(d) divide one cell by another.

IT TASKS

Design your own spreadsheet

One of your younger relatives is having trouble doing their maths. The problem is that they do not know their 'times tables' very well. You have been asked to supply them with a copy of a grid that they can refer to when doing their sums.

You should use formulae to calculate the tables.

One such design might be as follows but feel free to design your own.

	A	B	C	D	E	F	G	H	I	J	K	L	M
1		1	2	3	4	5	6	7	8	9	10	11	12
2	1												
3	2												
4	3												
5	4												
6	5												
7	6												
8	7												
9	8												
10	9												
11	10												
12	11												
13	12												

Once you are happy with the worksheet, save it with the name 'Multiplication table' and then print out a copy.

Saving Time Using Spreadsheets

Features of spreadsheets that save you time

There are many features of spreadsheets that save you time. For example, if you need to apply a formula to a column or row of cells it is only necessary to type it in once. You can then copy the formula down the column or across the row. Slight changes in formulae are made automatically unless you instruct the spreadsheet otherwise. Some of these features save you only a little time while others save a lot of time. In this chapter we look only at those features you will find of most use when you create spreadsheets of your own. Features of spreadsheets which save time include the ability to:

- edit cells
- undo commands
- insert rows and columns
- delete cells, rows, columns or blocks of cells
- copy formulae
- show all the formulae used so they can be checked.

Editing cells

If you notice a small mistake in the data or formula in a cell, you can change it without retyping the whole thing. This process is called 'editing' a cell. In the case of data (text and numbers) you simply move to the cell, using the mouse, then position the cursor (a flashing vertical line) and correct the mistake. When you are happy that the contents are correct, simply press Enter.

If you move to a cell containing a formula (such as cell E2 in the worksheet here) you will notice that the result of the calculation (a number) is shown. To see the actual formula you need to double click on the mouse. The formula will be shown and you can now edit it. When you are happy with the alterations, just press Enter.

The cell mentioned in the formula has a blue border round it

Microsoft Excel - Book3

File Edit View Insert Format Tools Data Window Help

	A	B	C	D	E
1		Price	V.A.T.	Price inc V.A.T.	DM
2	Digital Cameras	£599.00	£104.83	£703.83	=B2*2.85
3	Inkjet Printers	£259.00	£45.33	£304.33	738.15 DM
4	Scanners	£69.00	£12.08	£81.08	196.65 DM

Sheet1 / Sheet2 / Sheet3

Double click on the cell to see the formula

Using Undo

It is easy to issue the wrong command with the result that the spreadsheet does something you did not expect it to. It is also possible to press the wrong buttons by accident. Some keys, when used together, issue commands and you might do this by mistake. Suddenly something happens or the screen goes blank. What can you do if this happens?

First thing is don't panic! You can undo the last command in this way:

1 Click on Edit in the menu bar and then select Undo from the list.
2 If more than one command has been issued you can use step 1 several times.

Undo is also very useful if you delete something by mistake.

Inserting rows and columns

When you are designing spreadsheets of your own, you may find you need to insert a column between two columns that already contain data. Alternatively you may need to insert an extra row.

To insert a column, take these steps:

1. Use the mouse to position the cursor on any cell in the column to the right of where you want the column to be inserted.
2. Click on Insert in the main menu bar and select Columns from the list.
3. Check that the column has been inserted in the correct place. Notice that insertion of the column pushes all the data on the right of the cell the cursor is on to the right. Any formulae in these cells will be automatically adjusted.

To insert a row, take these steps:

1. Place the cursor on any of the cells in the row below where the new row needs to be inserted.
2. Click on Insert in the main menu bar and select Rows from the list.
3. Check that the row has been inserted in the correct place.

Deleting a row or a column

1. Move the cursor to the row or column that you want to delete.
2. Select Edit from the menu bar and then choose Delete.
3. The following box will appear (this is called a dialogue box).

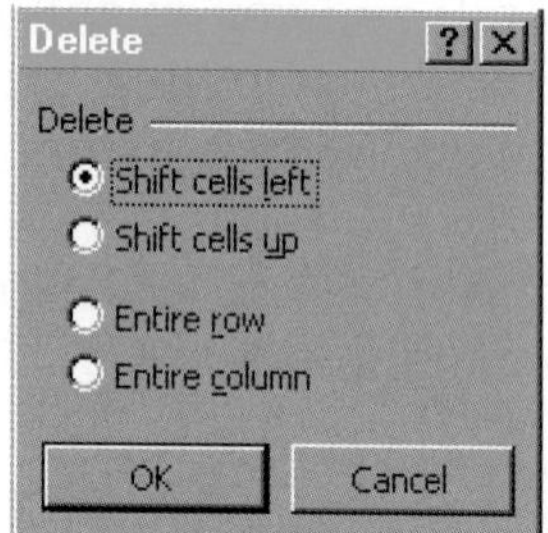

4. Select either the Entire row or Entire column and click on OK.

If a column is being deleted, those cells in columns to the left will move and fill the gap.

If a row is being deleted, those cells in the rows below the one being deleted will move up to fill the gap.

Deleting groups of cells

First, select the group of cells you want to delete, next choose Edit and then Delete. A box will appear where you can select the way in which the remaining cells are selected to fill the gap.

A note about deleting cells

You have to be quite careful about deleting cells because the remaining cells are shifted to fill the gap. This can cause unexpected results, so remember you can use the Edit and then Undo to undo an unwanted action.

If you just have a couple of cells to delete, then you are best using the backspace key (the key at the top with the arrow pointing to the left). Another way is to use the Del key when the cursor in positioned on the cell.

QUESTIONS

Explain how you would:

(a) delete the contents of a single cell
(b) delete the contents of an entire column
(c) delete the contents of a block of cells.

Copying formulae

The best way to understand how to copy formulae is to set up a spreadsheet in which many formulae need to be copied. This is the purpose of the following exercise.

In this spreadsheet exercise you will learn:

- **how to copy formulae**
- **how to set up a spreadsheet to work out a certain percentage of a number in a cell**
- **how to format a group of cells so that pound signs are included (i.e. set to currency format).**

Vale Wood Products Ltd is a small business that makes and sells a variety of wooden garden products such as bird nest boxes, feeders, etc. They intend to use a spreadsheet to help them with their business and part of it is shown below.

Microsoft Excel - Wood product spread 1

	A	B	C	D	E	F	G	H
1	Product	Cost of	Cost of	Total	Desired profit	Selling price	Number of items	Potential monthly
2	Description	Materials	Labour	Cost	per unit	per unit	made per month	profit
3	Large bird table	23.75	15.25					
4	Small bird table	15.25	10.95					
5	Tit nest box	7.5	3.75					
6	Robin nest box	8.25	4.1					
7	Bat box	8.65	4.3					
8	Owl box	12.9	8.9					
9	Squirrel feeder	4.5	2.55					
10	Peanut feeder	3.5	1.75					
11	Seed hopper	2.9	1.2					
12	Windmill	19.5	16.75					
13	Small bridge	65.5	27.35					
14	Large bridge	125	34.95					
15								
16								
17								
18								
19								
20								
21								

1 Set up a spreadsheet exactly as it is shown here. Notice that the numbers are not all set to two decimal places. Do not worry about this as it is easy to format the entire spreadsheet at the end, so that all the numbers are to two decimal places.

2 We need to add together cells B3 and C3 using a formula. This formula is placed in cell D3 to give the total cost.

Enter the formula **=B3+C3** into cell D3.

3 This formula needs to be copied down column D. We do this by moving the cursor to the cell containing the formula. Now click on the bottom right-hand corner of the cell and you should get a black cross shape. Hold the left mouse button down and move the mouse down the column until cell D14 is reached. You will see a dotted rectangle around the area where the copying is to take place. Now take your finger off the button and all the results will be inserted. This is called relatively copying because the formulae are changed slightly to take account of the changed positions of the two numbers which are to be added together.

Check with this screen shot to make sure that your totals are the same.

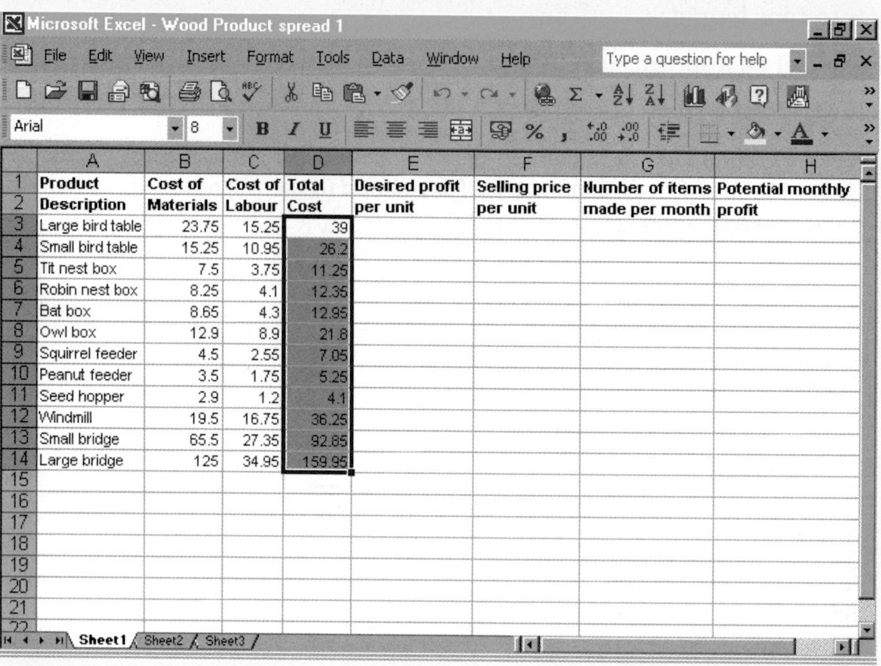

	A	B	C	D	E	F	G	H
1	**Product**	**Cost of**	**Cost of**	**Total**	**Desired profit**	**Selling price**	**Number of items**	**Potential monthly**
2	**Description**	**Materials**	**Labour**	**Cost**	**per unit**	**per unit**	**made per month**	**profit**
3	Large bird table	23.75	15.25	39				
4	Small bird table	15.25	10.95	26.2				
5	Tit nest box	7.5	3.75	11.25				
6	Robin nest box	8.25	4.1	12.35				
7	Bat box	8.65	4.3	12.95				
8	Owl box	12.9	8.9	21.8				
9	Squirrel feeder	4.5	2.55	7.05				
10	Peanut feeder	3.5	1.75	5.25				
11	Seed hopper	2.9	1.2	4.1				
12	Windmill	19.5	16.75	36.25				
13	Small bridge	65.5	27.35	92.85				
14	Large bridge	125	34.95	159.95				

4 The manager has decided that the desired profit per unit is to be 25% of the total cost of each product. We therefore have to find 25% of each of the numbers in column D.

We do this by placing the formula **=D3*25%** in cell E3. This is then copied relatively down the column in the same way as in step 3.

Your spreadsheet should now look like this.

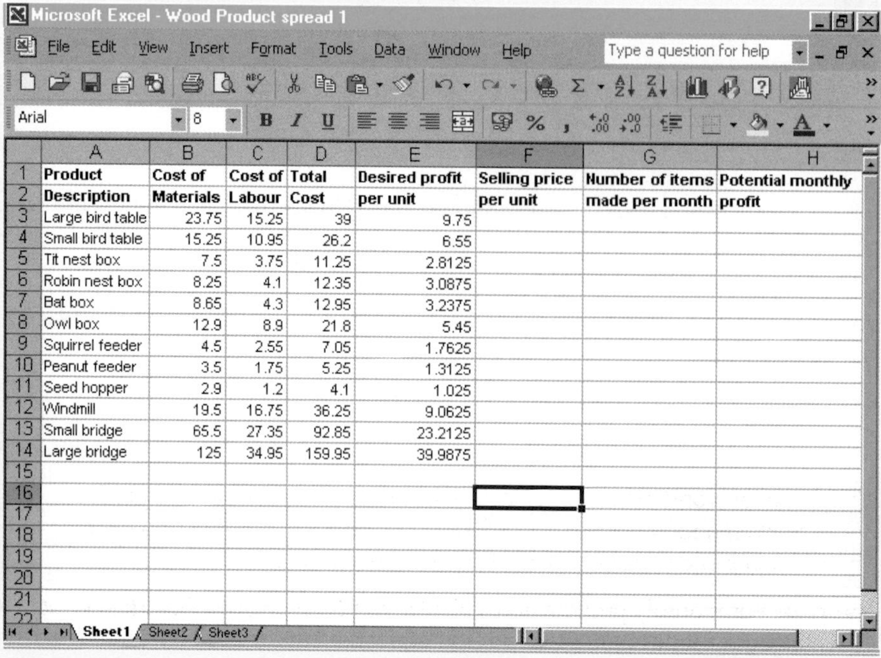

	A	B	C	D	E	F	G	H
1	**Product**	**Cost of**	**Cost of**	**Total**	**Desired profit**	**Selling price**	**Number of items**	**Potential monthly**
2	**Description**	**Materials**	**Labour**	**Cost**	**per unit**	**per unit**	**made per month**	**profit**
3	Large bird table	23.75	15.25	39	9.75			
4	Small bird table	15.25	10.95	26.2	6.55			
5	Tit nest box	7.5	3.75	11.25	2.8125			
6	Robin nest box	8.25	4.1	12.35	3.0875			
7	Bat box	8.65	4.3	12.95	3.2375			
8	Owl box	12.9	8.9	21.8	5.45			
9	Squirrel feeder	4.5	2.55	7.05	1.7625			
10	Peanut feeder	3.5	1.75	5.25	1.3125			
11	Seed hopper	2.9	1.2	4.1	1.025			
12	Windmill	19.5	16.75	36.25	9.0625			
13	Small bridge	65.5	27.35	92.85	23.2125			
14	Large bridge	125	34.95	159.95	39.9875			

5 Next the selling price column is filled in. This is produced by adding together the cells generated in the two previous steps. You have to decide on the formula and then copy it relatively down the column.

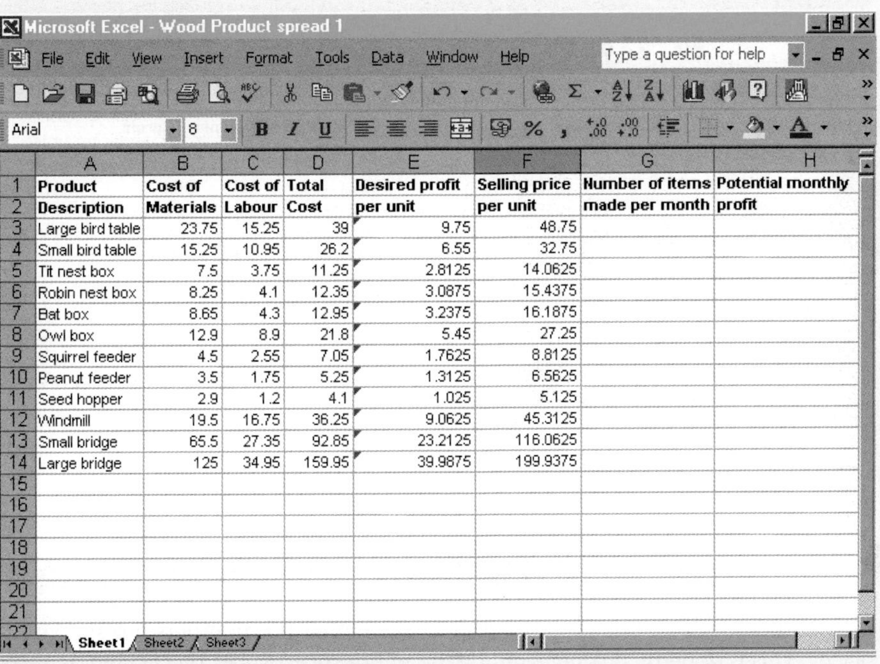

Microsoft Excel - Wood Product spread 1

	A	B	C	D	E	F	G	H
1	Product	Cost of	Cost of	Total	Desired profit	Selling price	Number of items	Potential monthly
2	Description	Materials	Labour	Cost	per unit	per unit	made per month	profit
3	Large bird table	23.75	15.25	39	9.75	48.75		
4	Small bird table	15.25	10.95	26.2	6.55	32.75		
5	Tit nest box	7.5	3.75	11.25	2.8125	14.0625		
6	Robin nest box	8.25	4.1	12.35	3.0875	15.4375		
7	Bat box	8.65	4.3	12.95	3.2375	16.1875		
8	Owl box	12.9	8.9	21.8	5.45	27.25		
9	Squirrel feeder	4.5	2.55	7.05	1.7625	8.8125		
10	Peanut feeder	3.5	1.75	5.25	1.3125	6.5625		
11	Seed hopper	2.9	1.2	4.1	1.025	5.125		
12	Windmill	19.5	16.75	36.25	9.0625	45.3125		
13	Small bridge	65.5	27.35	92.85	23.2125	116.0625		
14	Large bridge	125	34.95	159.95	39.9875	199.9375		

6 Check that you have done step 5 correctly by comparing the results with the screen shot above. Also type into column G the figures for the 'Number of items made per month' as shown in this column.

G
Number of items
made per month
89
121
234
56
31
34
45
251
344
45
39
51

7 The potential monthly profit is calculated by multiplying the desired profit per unit by the number of items made per month. The formula to do this is **=E3*G3** and this is placed in cell H3. The formula is then copied relatively down the column.

8 The potential monthly profit is now calculated. Put the words 'Potential Monthly Profit' in cell G18. Now put the formula **=sum(H3:H14)** in cell H18.

The spreadsheet will look like this.

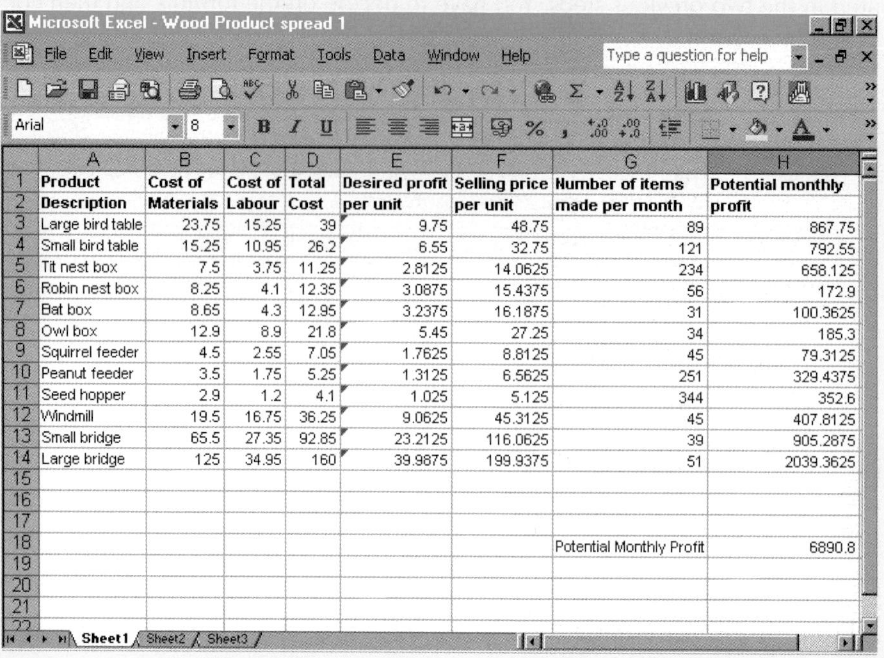

	A	B	C	D	E	F	G	H
1	Product	Cost of	Cost of	Total	Desired profit	Selling price	Number of items	Potential monthly
2	Description	Materials	Labour	Cost	per unit	per unit	made per month	profit
3	Large bird table	23.75	15.25	39	9.75	48.75	89	867.75
4	Small bird table	15.25	10.95	26.2	6.55	32.75	121	792.55
5	Tit nest box	7.5	3.75	11.25	2.8125	14.0625	234	658.125
6	Robin nest box	8.25	4.1	12.35	3.0875	15.4375	56	172.9
7	Bat box	8.65	4.3	12.95	3.2375	16.1875	31	100.3625
8	Owl box	12.9	8.9	21.8	5.45	27.25	34	185.3
9	Squirrel feeder	4.5	2.55	7.05	1.7625	8.8125	45	79.3125
10	Peanut feeder	3.5	1.75	5.25	1.3125	6.5625	251	329.4375
11	Seed hopper	2.9	1.2	4.1	1.025	5.125	344	352.6
12	Windmill	19.5	16.75	36.25	9.0625	45.3125	45	407.8125
13	Small bridge	65.5	27.35	92.85	23.2125	116.0625	39	905.2875
14	Large bridge	125	34.95	160	39.9875	199.9375	51	2039.3625
15								
16								
17								
18							Potential Monthly Profit	6890.8
19								
20								
21								

9 We can now format the whole worksheet so that all the numbers are shown to two decimal places. This is done by first highlighting the entire spreadsheet by clicking on the cell at the top left-hand corner of the spreadsheet. All the cells, except the active cell are highlighted. Now click on Format and select Cells. You will see a screen like the one shown in the diagram. In the category box, highlight Currency. Notice that the decimal places are automatically set at two and a pound sign is automatically included. Also notice that commas have been inserted into the large numbers. Click on OK and the final worksheet is produced.

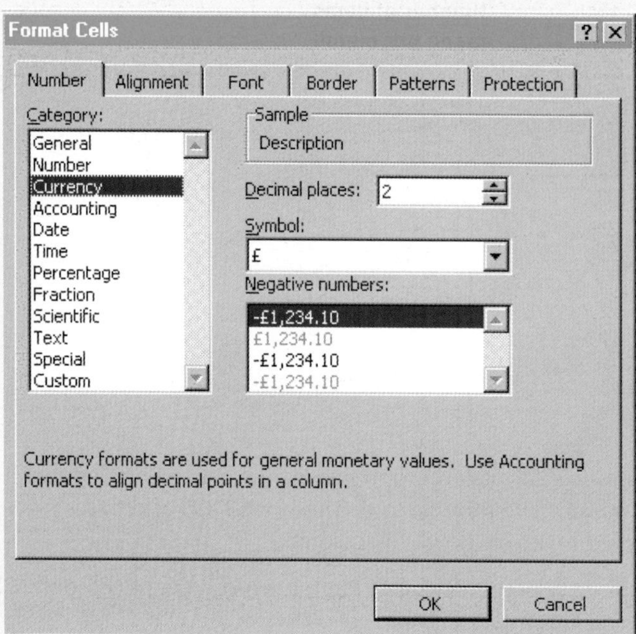

Your worksheet will now look like this.

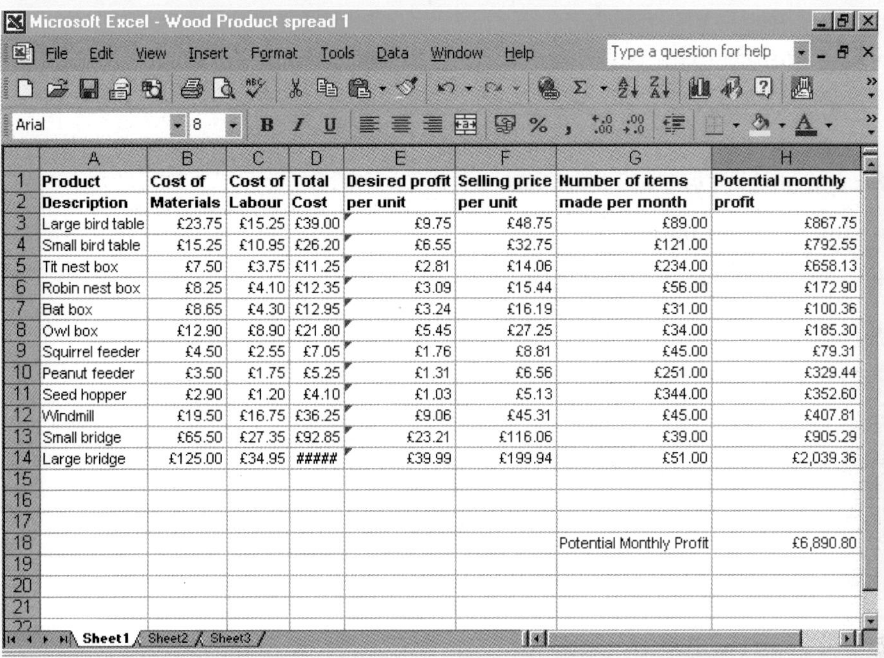

Microsoft Excel - Wood Product spread 1

	A	B	C	D	E	F	G	H
1	Product	Cost of	Cost of	Total	Desired profit	Selling price	Number of items	Potential monthly
2	Description	Materials	Labour	Cost	per unit	per unit	made per month	profit
3	Large bird table	£23.75	£15.25	£39.00	£9.75	£48.75	£89.00	£867.75
4	Small bird table	£15.25	£10.95	£26.20	£6.55	£32.75	£121.00	£792.55
5	Tit nest box	£7.50	£3.75	£11.25	£2.81	£14.06	£234.00	£658.13
6	Robin nest box	£8.25	£4.10	£12.35	£3.09	£15.44	£56.00	£172.90
7	Bat box	£8.65	£4.30	£12.95	£3.24	£16.19	£31.00	£100.36
8	Owl box	£12.90	£8.90	£21.80	£5.45	£27.25	£34.00	£185.30
9	Squirrel feeder	£4.50	£2.55	£7.05	£1.76	£8.81	£45.00	£79.31
10	Peanut feeder	£3.50	£1.75	£5.25	£1.31	£6.56	£251.00	£329.44
11	Seed hopper	£2.90	£1.20	£4.10	£1.03	£5.13	£344.00	£352.60
12	Windmill	£19.50	£16.75	£36.25	£9.06	£45.31	£45.00	£407.81
13	Small bridge	£65.50	£27.35	£92.85	£23.21	£116.06	£39.00	£905.29
14	Large bridge	£125.00	£34.95	#####	£39.99	£199.94	£51.00	£2,039.36
18							Potential Monthly Profit	£6,890.80

10 On looking at the spreadsheet we notice that something is wrong. In column G there is the 'Number of items made per month'. Clearly this should be a whole number (properly called an integer) and should certainly not have a pound sign. We need to change the format of column G by highlighting it, clicking on Format, and selecting Cells. In the box that pops up change the format to Number and alter the decimal places to 0.

Your final worksheet should now look like this.

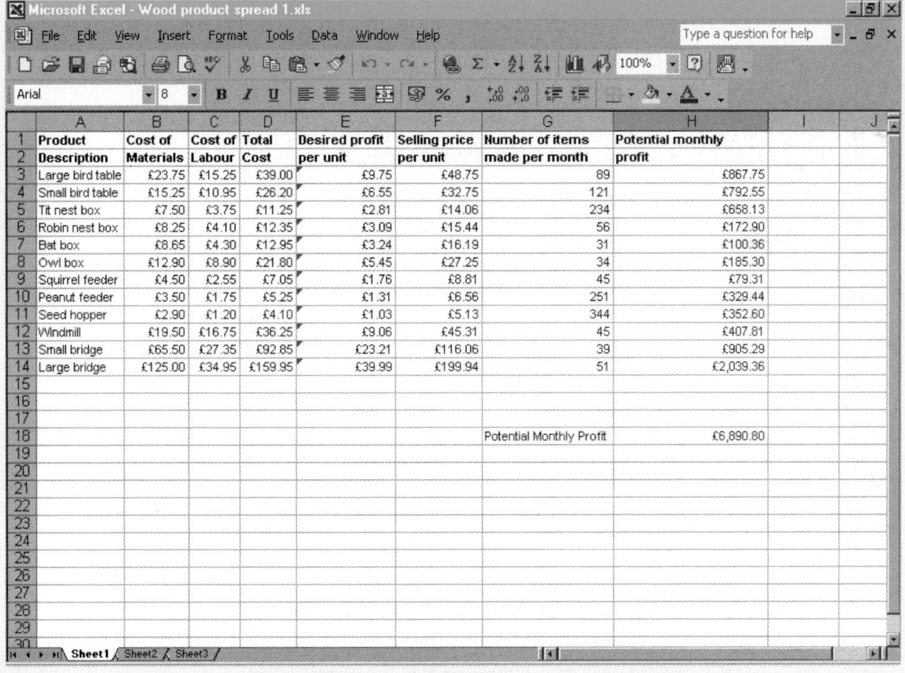

Microsoft Excel - Wood product spread 1.xls

	A	B	C	D	E	F	G	H
1	Product	Cost of	Cost of	Total	Desired profit	Selling price	Number of items	Potential monthly
2	Description	Materials	Labour	Cost	per unit	per unit	made per month	profit
3	Large bird table	£23.75	£15.25	£39.00	£9.75	£48.75	89	£867.75
4	Small bird table	£15.25	£10.95	£26.20	£6.55	£32.75	121	£792.55
5	Tit nest box	£7.50	£3.75	£11.25	£2.81	£14.06	234	£658.13
6	Robin nest box	£8.25	£4.10	£12.35	£3.09	£15.44	56	£172.90
7	Bat box	£8.65	£4.30	£12.95	£3.24	£16.19	31	£100.36
8	Owl box	£12.90	£8.90	£21.80	£5.45	£27.25	34	£185.30
9	Squirrel feeder	£4.50	£2.55	£7.05	£1.76	£8.81	45	£79.31
10	Peanut feeder	£3.50	£1.75	£5.25	£1.31	£6.56	251	£329.44
11	Seed hopper	£2.90	£1.20	£4.10	£1.03	£5.13	344	£352.60
12	Windmill	£19.50	£16.75	£36.25	£9.06	£45.31	45	£407.81
13	Small bridge	£65.50	£27.35	£92.85	£23.21	£116.06	39	£905.29
14	Large bridge	£125.00	£34.95	£159.95	£39.99	£199.94	51	£2,039.36
18							Potential Monthly Profit	£6,890.80

11 Save your work using a suitable file name and then print a copy.

Printing formulae

When you print out a worksheet, it will always print out the results of any formulae along with any text or numbers. It is useful to be able to see these formulae so that they can be checked. Here is a simple exercise to show how to display the formulae on the screen and then print them out.

Exercise 2.2

In this spreadsheet you will learn how to:

- **use the AutoSum button**
- **show the formulae in the worksheet.**

1 Set up a worksheet and enter the following data:

	A	B	C	D	E	F
1	Item	June	July	August	September	Total
2	Swimwear	600	150	142	112	
3	Ski-Wear	50	35	60	98	
4	Shorts	85	87	82	50	
5	Golf Clubs	104	69	75	82	
6	Football	20	32	146	292	
7	T-Racquets	85	90	50	80	
8	Totals					

2 Total column B and put the result in cell B8. The quick way to do this is to press the AutoSum button on the toolbar with the cursor on cell B8. The AutoSum button can be found on the standard toolbar and looks like Σ .

Be careful how you use AutoSum. Check that the cell range indicated by the dotted rectangle is correct. If it does not work as expected, just type in the formula instead.

3 Total row 2 and put the result in cell F2. Again this may be done by positioning the cursor on cell F2 and then pressing the AutoSum button.

4 Copy the formula in cell F2 down the column to cell F7.

5 Copy the formula in cell B8 across the row to cell F8.

Your worksheet should now look like this.

	A	B	C	D	E	F
1	Item	June	July	August	September	Total
2	Swimwear	600	150	142	112	1004
3	Ski-Wear	50	35	60	98	243
4	Shorts	85	87	82	50	304
5	Golf Clubs	104	69	75	82	330
6	Football	20	32	146	292	490
7	T-Racquets	85	90	50	80	305
8	Totals	944	463	555	714	2676

6 Now let's insert formulae wherever there are calculations.

Select the Tools menu and then click on Options.

The following screen will appear:

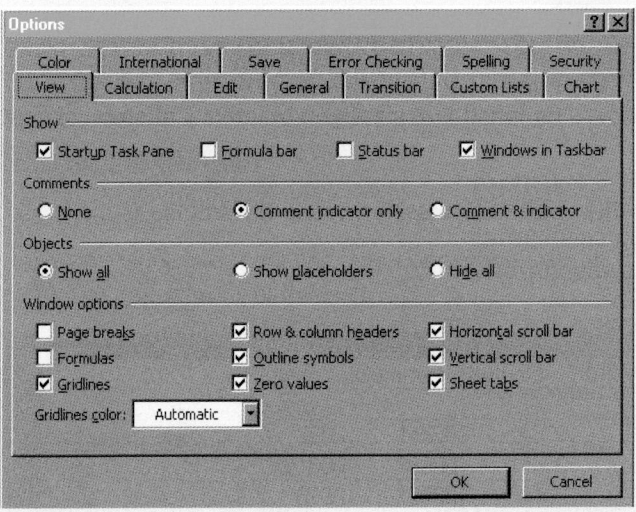

7 Towards the bottom of the above screen you will see a box marked Formulas. Click on this box and a tick will appear indicating that the formulae will be displayed. The following screen containing the formulae now appears.

	A	B	C	D	E	F
1	Item	June	July	August	September	Total
2	Swimwear	600	150	142	112	=SUM(B2:E2)
3	Ski-Wear	50	35	60	98	=SUM(B3:E3)
4	Shorts	85	87	82	50	=SUM(B4:E4)
5	Golf Clubs	104	69	75	82	=SUM(B5:E5)
6	Football	20	32	146	292	=SUM(B6:E6)
7	T-Racquets	85	90	50	80	=SUM(B7:E7)
8	Totals	=SUM(B2:B7)	=SUM(C2:C7)	=SUM(D2:D7)	=SUM(E2:E7)	=SUM(F2:F7)

8 When you try to display the formulae, they often require more space than the current column width so you may need to widen columns. Do this and save, then print a copy of the worksheet containing the formulae on a single sheet. To do this click on File and then Page Setup ... and make sure that the settings are the same as those shown on this screen.

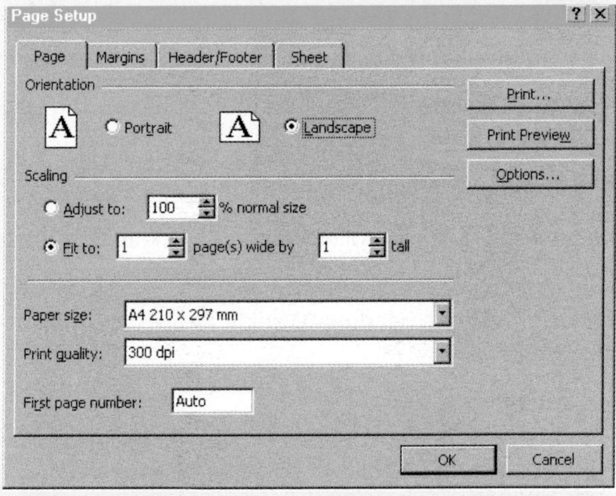

Notice that Landscape has been selected and also Fit to 1 page. Click on OK.

IT TASKS

A school sets up its own savings bank for the pupils. Each pupil is encouraged to save a small amount of money every week. Form teachers need to keep a record of how much each pupil saves that month. At present teachers keep records on paper and the sheet used is shown below.

Name	Week 1	Week 2	Week 3	Week 4	Total
Claire	2.25	3.10	1.20	1.50	
Jane	3.15	1.50	1.00	0.75	
Joseph	2.00	1.00	1.00	1.00	
Amy	3.50	0.50	0.50	1.00	
Suzanne	5.00	1.00	0.00	1.00	
Ian	4.00	1.00	1.00	1.00	
Harry	1.00	2.00	1.00	1.00	
John	3.00	2.50	1.00	1.00	
Joanne	4.50	1.50	1.00	1.00	
Kevin	3.00	1.00	1.00	1.50	
Peter	0.75	1.25	3.00	1.00	

The teacher fills in the above form and calculates the total, then passes the form to the school secretary along with the money for banking.

You have suggested that your form teacher could construct a spreadsheet for this. Set up the spreadsheet in the following way.

1 Set up a new worksheet and enter all the data shown. After entering the data carefully proof read the data to ensure you have not made any mistakes. This is a form of verification. Verification means making sure that you have not made any mistakes inputting the data.

2 Using a formula, calculate the total amount collected for Claire that month. Check the accuracy of the result by adding the numbers together manually or on a calculator.

3 Copy the formula relatively down the totals column. Again, check that this has been done correctly.

4 The form teacher also needs to check the amount actually collected each week against the total amount on the worksheet.

Produce a row at the bottom of the worksheet with the heading 'Weekly Totals' (you may need to widen the first column to accommodate the title).

5 Save and produce a printout of your worksheet.

Understanding referencing

There are two ways in which you can make reference to another cell. They are not the same and it is important to know the difference if you want to copy or move cells.

An absolute reference always refers to the same cell.

A relative reference refers to a cell that is a certain number of rows and columns away. When a cell is copied or moved to a new position, any cell to which the reference is made, will also change position so it remains the same number of columns and rows away, i.e. in the same relative position.

To understand the difference let's look at two examples.

The first example shows relative referencing with cell B4 containing a relative reference to cell A1. This reference tells the spreadsheet that the cell to which it refers is three cells up and one cell to the left of cell B4. If cell B4 is copied to another position, say E5 then the reference will still be to the same number of cells up and to the left, so the reference will now be to cell D2.

With absolute cell referencing, if cell B4 contains a reference to cell A1, then if the contents of B4 are copied to a new position, then the reference will not be adjusted and it will still refer to cell A1.

In most cases we want to use relative cell references and the spreadsheet will assume that ordinary cell references are relative. Sometimes we want to refer to the same cell even when the formula referring to the cell is copied to a new position.

In this case we must make sure the formula contains an absolute cell reference. To do this a dollar sign is placed in front of the column and row number.

Cell B6 is a relative cell reference. To change it to an absolute cell reference we add the dollar signs to give $B$6.

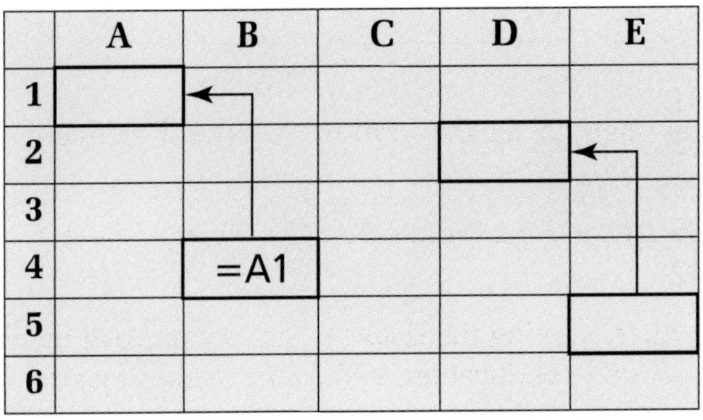

	A	B	C	D	E
1					
2					
3					
4		=A1			
5					
6					

Example 1: Relative cell referencing in a spreadsheet

	A	B	C	D	E
1					
2					
3					
4		=$A$1			
5					
6					

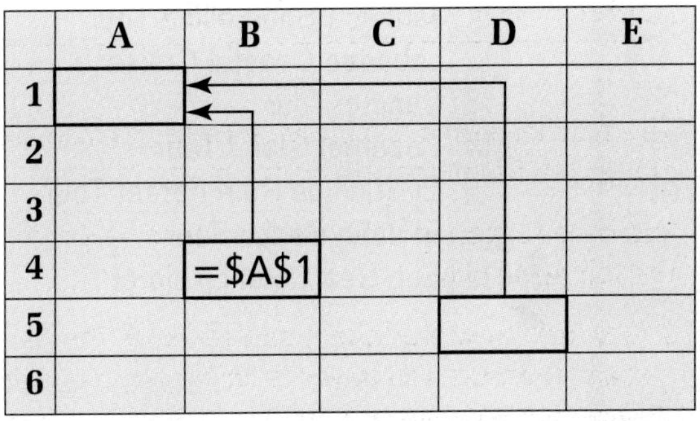

Example 2: Absolute cell referencing in a spreadsheet

In this spreadsheet you will learn to:

- **use relative cell references**
- **use absolute cell references**
- **clear the contents of cells (as an alternative to deleting).**

Here is a list of the shore excursions on a Caribbean cruise. Notice that because the cruise ship is American, prices are given in US dollars. It is quite hard for British passengers to work out the equivalent prices in pounds so the excursion manager has decided to set up a spreadsheet. Because the exchange rate between dollars and pounds changes daily, the prices in pounds will also change. The manager has asked that the exchange rate should be shown on the spreadsheet and this is the only figure that should need retyping each day. All other figures will be calculated automatically from this figure.

1 Load the spreadsheet software and set up the data in a spreadsheet exactly as it is here. Make sure that rows 1 to 4 are left blank. You will need to widen column A so that the destinations fit.

	A	B
5	**Excursions**	**Dollars**
6	Seven Mile Beach Break	14
7	Grand Cayman Flightseeing	64
8	Dunn's River Falls	29
9	San San Luxury Yacht Cruise	63
10	Beach Horseback Riding	79
11	Jamaica Snorkelling Tour	31
12	Labadee Coastal Cruise	20
13	Cancun Tour	31
14	Cozumel Island Tour	39
15	El Yunique Rain Forest Tour	29
16	St John Beach Tour	35
17	Sub-Sea Coral Explorer	42

2 Embolden (i.e. make bold) the headings in row 5. This is done by moving to the desired cell, then pressing the **B** button on the formatting toolbar.

3 In cell A3 type in **Exchange rate (pounds to dollars)**.

In cell B3 type in the exchange rate, **1.58**. This means that there are 1.58 dollars to each pound on this particular day (see the worksheet opposite).

4 In this step we see what happens if we use relative (i.e. ordinary) cell references in the formula. To convert a price in dollars to a price in pounds, we divide by the exchange rate. On this particular day there are 1.58 dollars to each pound so we have to divide by 1.58 to get the price in pounds.

Enter the formula **=B6/B3** in cell C6.

5 Now copy the formula relatively down column C from cell C6 to C17.

Look at the result; clearly something has gone wrong.

Let's find out what has happened.

Move the cursor to cell C7. The formula is =B7/B4. What should it be? It should be =B7/B3. Move the cursor to cell C8. The formula here is =B8/B5. It should be =B8/B3. This has happened because relative cell references have been used for both cells. It is correct to have a relative cell reference for the cells from B6 to B17 but cell B3 needs to stay the same.

6 Highlight all the cells from cell C6 to C17. Now go to Edit and then Clear and select All from the menu. This will remove the cell contents of all the highlighted cells. The Clear command is slightly different to Delete because none of the remaining cells are moved to fill in the gaps left when cells are deleted.

7 We will now enter the correct formula into cell C6. Move the cursor to cell C6 and enter the formula: **=B6/$B$3**.

B6 is a relative cell reference and $B$3 an absolute cell reference. If this cell is copied to cell C7 it will become =B7/$B$3. Notice that cell B3 stays the same in the formula no matter where it is copied to. This is always the case with an absolute cell reference.

8 Copy this formula down the column and check that the results are correct.

9 On one particular day the exchange rate is 1.60. Make this change.

Notice that by changing this one figure, all the equivalent prices of the excursions in pounds automatically change.

10 Save your spreadsheet with filename **Shore excursions**.

11 Print two copies, one should be the Shore excursions worksheet, the other the same worksheet but with all the formulae shown. Refer back to page 27 to remind yourself how to show formulae.

	A	B	C
1			
2			
3	Exchange rate (Pounds to Dollars)	1.58	
4			
5	**Excursions**	**Dollars**	**Pounds**
6	Seven Mile Beach Break	14	
7	Grand Cayman Flightseeing	64	
8	Dunn's River Falls	29	
9	San San Luxury Yacht Cruise	63	
10	Beach Horseback Riding	79	
11	Jamaica Snorkelling Tour	31	
12	Labadee Coastal Cruise	20	
13	Cancun Tour	31	
14	Cozumel Island Tour	39	
15	El Yunique Rain Forest Tour	29	
16	St John Beach Tour	35	
17	Sub-Sea Coral Explorer	42	

The screen after Step 3

Sorting data in spreadsheets

It is easy to sort data into numerical or alphabetical order in a spreadsheet. The following exercise will show how this is done.

Exercise 2.4

In the following spreadsheet you will learn to:

- **sort data into alphabetical order**
- **sort data into numerical order.**

Here are the names of some European countries and their capitals. They have been set up in a spreadsheet but the countries have not been put into any particular order. When finding items it is helpful to have entries in the worksheet sorted into some kind of order.

1 Enter the following data shown into a worksheet. Make the headings bold and widen the columns to allow the data in both columns to be seen.

	A	B
1		
2	**Country**	**Capital**
3	Iceland	Reykjavik
4	Sweden	Stockholm
5	Denmark	Copenhagen
6	Netherlands	Amsterdam
7	Belgium	Brussels
8	France	Paris
9	Spain	Madrid
10	Portugal	Lisbon
11	Italy	Rome
12	Poland	Warsaw

2 We will now sort the data into ascending alphabetical order (i.e. A to Z) according to the name of the country. Click on any item of data in the column you want to base your sort on. In this case you can click on any of the names of the countries.

The button used to sort into ascending and descending order can be seen on the standard toolbar.

Sort ascending

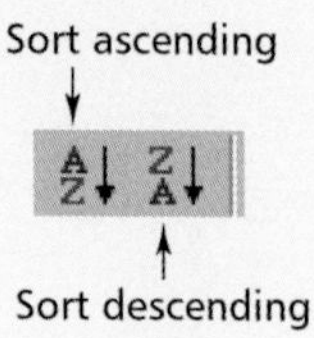

Sort descending

Click on the Sort ascending button.

3 To sort the data in ascending alphabetical order according to capital, click on the column containing the capital data, then select the sort ascending button on the standard toolbar.

4 Next we add some numerical data to the worksheet. Here are the populations you need to type in. Do not worry about the order being the same as that shown in the screen shot.

	A	B	C
1			
2	**Country**	**Capital**	**Population**
3	Iceland	Reykjavik	255000
4	Sweden	Stockholm	8523000
5	Denmark	Copenhagen	5141000
6	Netherlands	Amsterdam	14927000
7	Belgium	Brussels	9881000
8	France	Paris	56342000
9	Spain	Madrid	39322000
10	Portugal	Lisbon	10434000
11	Italy	Rome	57461000
12	Poland	Warsaw	38064000

5 Sort the countries into descending order according to population by clicking on any of the data cells in the population column, then selecting the sort descending button on the standard toolbar.

Your worksheet should look like this:

	A	B	C
1			
2	**Country**	**Capital**	**Population**
3	Italy	Rome	57461000
4	France	Paris	56342000
5	Spain	Madrid	39322000
6	Poland	Warsaw	38064000
7	Netherlands	Amsterdam	14927000
8	Portugal	Lisbon	10434000
9	Belgium	Brussels	9881000
10	Sweden	Stockholm	8523000
11	Denmark	Copenhagen	5141000
12	Iceland	Reykjavik	255000

6 Quit the spreadsheet without saving.

Who has won the premiership?

In the following exercise you will practise skills learnt in the other exercises in Chapter 2. These skills include:

- **copying formulae**
- **inserting columns**
- **sorting into numerical and alphabetical order**
- **sorting using more than one sort key.**

1 Here is a spreadsheet showing the results for the premiership football league for the 1998/99 season. Type in the data exactly as it appears here.

	A	B	C	D	E	F	G	H	I	J	K
1		**HOME**					**AWAY**				
2		**Win**	**Drawn**	**Lost**	**Goals For**	**Goals Against**	**Win**	**Drawn**	**Lost**	**Goals For**	**Goals Against**
3	Arsenal	14	5	0	34	5	8	7	4	25	12
4	Aston Villa	10	3	6	33	28	5	7	7	18	18
5	Blackburn	6	5	8	21	24	1	9	9	16	27
6	Charlton	4	7	8	20	20	4	5	10	21	36
7	Chelsea	12	6	1	29	13	8	9	2	28	17
8	Coventry	8	6	5	26	21	3	3	13	13	30
9	Derby	8	7	4	22	19	5	6	8	18	26
10	Everton	6	8	5	22	12	5	2	12	20	35
11	Leeds	12	5	2	32	9	6	8	5	30	25
12	Leicester	7	6	6	25	25	5	7	7	15	21
13	Liverpool	10	5	4	44	24	5	4	10	24	25
14	Man United	14	4	1	45	18	8	9	2	35	19
15	Middlesbro	7	9	3	25	18	5	6	8	23	36
16	Newcastle	7	6	6	26	25	4	7	8	22	29
17	Nottm Forest	3	7	9	18	31	4	2	13	17	38
18	Sheff Wed	7	5	7	20	15	6	2	11	21	27
19	Southampton	9	4	6	29	26	2	4	13	8	38
20	Tottenham	7	7	5	28	26	4	7	8	19	24
21	West Ham	11	3	5	32	26	5	6	8	14	27
22	Wimbledon	7	7	5	22	21	3	5	11	18	42

Check that your data are exactly the same as those shown above.

Notice that there are the same column headings for HOME and AWAY.

Make bold the titles HOME and AWAY, and the column headings. You can highlight them and then press the bold button in the formatting toolbar.

2 We now need to work out the points as follows:

win home or away = three points

draw home or away = one point.

Enter the column title **Points** into cell L2.

In cell L3 enter a formula to work out the points. Remember this formula needs to calculate the points for the home and away games and then add them all together.

3 Check that the formula is correct by working it out manually. If the formula is OK copy it down the column for the other teams.

4 Some teams could have the same number of points. To determine the places in the league for these teams the goal difference is considered. The goal difference is the total of the 'goals for' minus the total of the 'goals against'.

Exercise 2.5

Enter the column title **Goal Difference** into cell M2.

In cell M3 enter a formula to work out this goal difference. Negative results are possible since these just mean that a team has had more goals scored against them than for them.

5 Check that the formula in cell M3 is correct by working it out manually. If it is OK then copy the formula down the column to show the goal differences for all teams.

6 At the end of the football season all teams will have played the same number of games. This may be calculated by adding the number of games won, lost and drawn both home and away.

It has been decided that the number of games played should be placed in column B. There is already data in this column so a column needs to be inserted and the rest of the data shifted to the right.

Insert a new column between columns A and B, heading this column **Played** (it should be placed in B2). Now enter the formula for the total of the games played into cell B3. Copy this formula down the column for all the other teams. If the formula is correct all the teams should have played a total of 38 games.

There is a mistake for Nottingham Forest. According to the figures they have played only 34 games. Totals like this are an important check. The original results table showed that they have seven home draws not three. Make this alteration to your worksheet.

7 As it stands all the data is arranged in alphabetical order according to the team name.

It now makes sense to have teams arranged in order of points gained.

Click on any cell containing data in the points column and then go to the button Z to A (sort into descending order) on the toolbar.

All the data will now be in order of points.

8 If you look at the points you will notice that some teams have got the same number. When this is the case the goal difference is taken into account. For two teams with the same number of points, the one with the higher goal difference will be above the other in the table.

We need to sort on points first (in descending order) and then sort on goal difference (in descending order).

To sort according to two criteria (points and goal difference), follow these steps.

Move the cursor onto an item of data in the points column.

Select Data and then Sort.

The following box will appear.

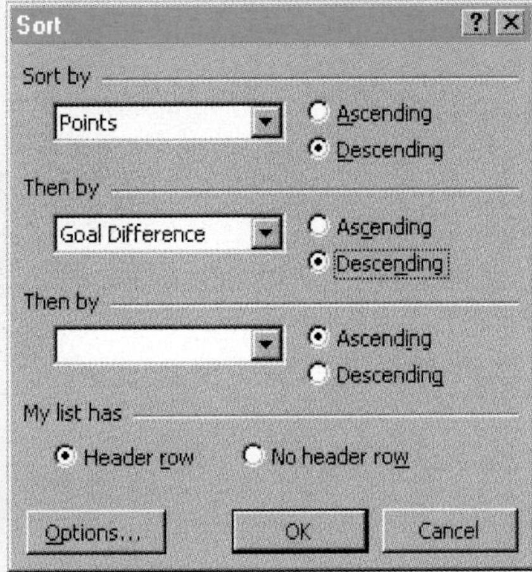

'Sort by' is the first field on which the data is to be sorted. In this case we want the points to be sorted into descending order (i.e. the greatest number of points placed first).

Then we need to sort by goal difference and this also needs to be in descending order.

Fill in the appropriate boxes (check against the screen shot above) and when everything is correct, click on OK.

You should now check that those clubs with the same number of points have also been ordered according to their goal differences.

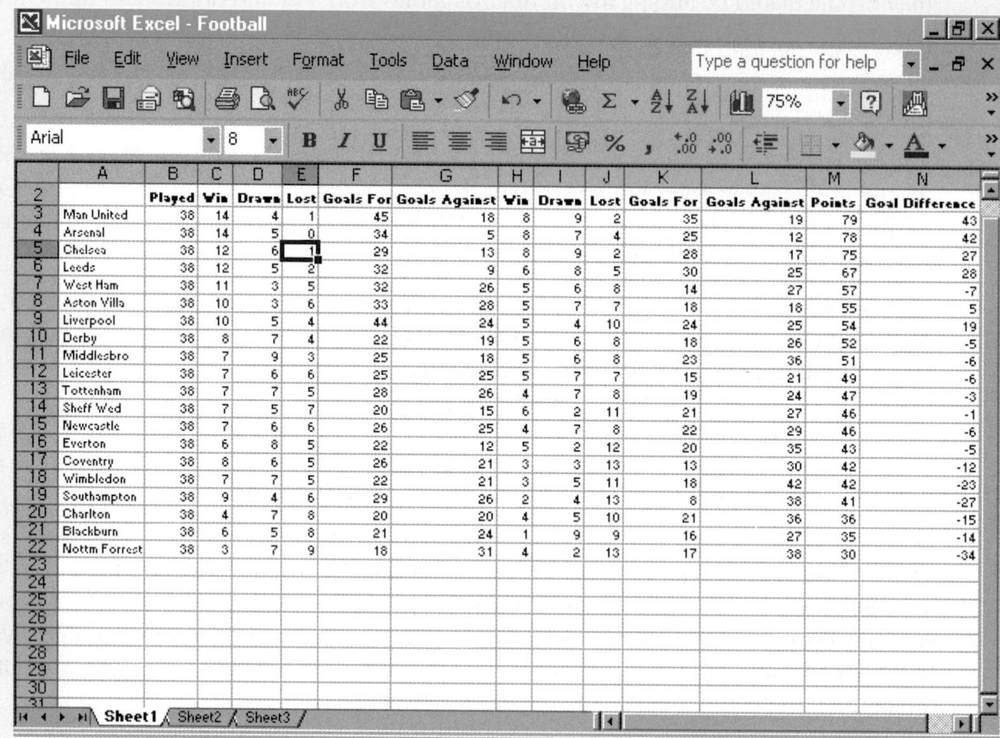

	Played	Win	Drawn	Lost	Goals For	Goals Against	Win	Drawn	Lost	Goals For	Goals Against	Points	Goal Difference
Man United	38	14	4	1	45	18	8	9	2	35	19	79	43
Arsenal	38	14	5	0	34	5	8	7	4	25	12	78	42
Chelsea	38	12	6	1	29	13	8	9	2	28	17	75	27
Leeds	38	12	5	2	32	9	6	8	5	30	25	67	28
West Ham	38	11	3	5	32	26	5	6	8	14	27	57	-7
Aston Villa	38	10	3	6	33	28	5	7	7	18	18	55	5
Liverpool	38	10	5	4	44	24	5	4	10	24	25	54	19
Derby	38	8	7	4	22	19	5	6	8	18	26	52	-5
Middlesbro	38	7	9	3	25	18	5	6	8	23	36	51	-6
Leicester	38	7	6	6	25	25	5	7	7	15	21	49	-6
Tottenham	38	7	7	5	28	26	4	7	8	19	24	47	-3
Sheff Wed	38	7	5	7	20	15	6	2	11	21	27	46	-1
Newcastle	38	7	6	6	26	25	4	7	8	22	29	46	-6
Everton	38	6	8	5	22	12	5	2	12	20	35	43	-5
Coventry	38	8	6	5	26	21	3	3	13	13	30	42	-12
Wimbledon	38	7	7	5	22	21	3	5	11	18	42	42	-23
Southampton	38	9	4	6	29	26	2	4	13	8	38	41	-27
Charlton	38	4	7	8	20	20	4	5	10	21	36	36	-15
Blackburn	38	6	5	8	21	24	1	9	9	16	27	35	-14
Nottm Forrest	38	3	7	9	18	31	4	2	13	17	38	30	-34

9 Save your worksheet with the filename 'Premier league results 98/99'.

10 Print a copy of your worksheet. To do this follow these instructions.

When File and then Print are selected the following box appears:

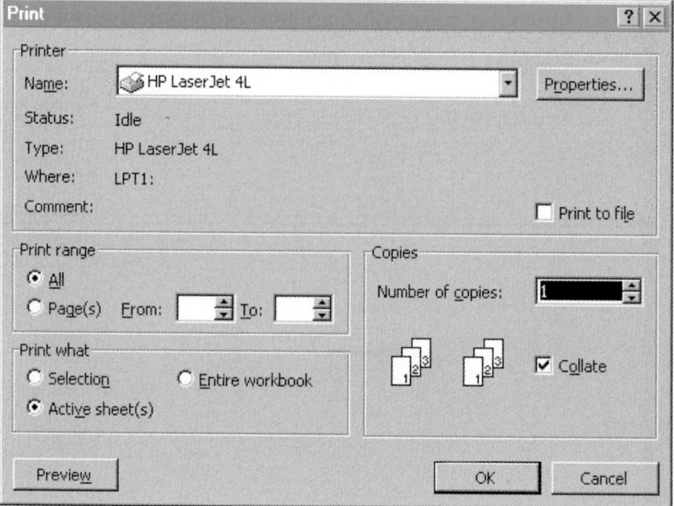

When the Properties button is pressed the following box appears:

You need to make sure that the A4 paper size has been selected.

Notice that you can decide to print in either portrait or landscape format. Normally portrait is used, in which the length of the paper is greater than the width. With spreadsheets, there may be too many columns to fit on a single portrait page. By changing the orientation to landscape you may be able to fit the whole worksheet on one page. It makes reading data from a spreadsheet much easier if the columns are on a single page. Select A4 paper and landscape orientation, then click on OK.

Extra step

It would be nice if we could have a column containing the position of the team in the league. Is there any way you can do this automatically without numbering 1,2,3, manually? Try to do this and produce a brief explanation on how you went about it.

Finding Your Way Around Excel

Excel is a very big software package and contains many features. In this book we cover just some of the most used features. It is thought that 80% of users utilise only around 20% of the available capabilities of any software. Often, users do not employ the features because they do not know they exist. You should try to learn as much as you can about the package and remember to experiment. After you have finished the exercises in each chapter you should spend some time experimenting. It is a good idea to experiment on a copy of your work rather than the original and remember that you can always use Undo if something unexpected happens.

You will eventually use the spreadsheet software to build your own worksheet and solve a problem. To do this you will need to be quite skillful with the software. Although this book teaches you many of the skills you need, there are still many features you may find useful that the book does not have the space to cover.

There are many other ways you can find out about the software:

- use a reference manual
- use the on-line help
- get an experienced user to sit down with you for a couple of hours
- there are many useful tutorials on the Internet.

Use a reference manual

Many reference manuals are expensive and are complicated and therefore not user-friendly. But they can be useful if there is something you know the package can do but you don't know how to do it. Finding an experienced user with time to spare is not that easy. This leaves using the on-line help.

Using the on-line help facility

The help facility is provided as part of the software package and is therefore free (once you have bought the software). The idea of help is to supply the user in many different ways with help to perform a task. It basically saves having to wade through thick manuals to find something out. Also, if the on-line help is called up while you are working on something, the screen splits into two parts. One part contains your work, and the other help on the topic you have requested. This means you can apply the help directly to your own work because you can see both at the same time. In the past you would have had to flick from a screen containing the help to the screen containing your work and so had to remember or print the help.

In Excel XP the on-line help is called the Office Assistant.

Using the Office Assistant you can:

- obtain a new tip every time the software is loaded
- get it to answer your questions
- learn how to do things more quickly and easily.

How do I use the Office Assistant?

Load Excel and then start a new worksheet.

1. As soon as the blank worksheet is loaded, you will see the Office Assistant. If the Office Assistant does not appear, click on Help and then on Show the Office Assistant. It is the paperclip and piece of paper most of the time although you can change its appearance.
2. Click anywhere on the Office Assistant and a screen appears asking you what you would like to do. This screen is called a dialogue box because the software is able to ask you questions and you can type in your replies.

3 You type in your question in ordinary English and then click on search. Suppose we want some help on widening columns. Type 'Widening columns' into the dialogue box and click on Search.
The next window appears asking you 'What would you like to do?' You are now presented with a list of options.

4 Click on the second option, 'Change column width' and the instructions on how to do this are displayed.
Notice that the screen splits in two so that you can read the help instructions and apply them to the worksheet at the same time. This saves trying to remember the instructions in your head or having to print them out. Notice the arrows on this screen. Using these you can move backwards or forwards through the help screens. Notice also the icon showing the printer. If you want to print out the help details, then click on this.

Tasks to try

Here are a few things you might want to do using the spreadsheet package. By using the Office Assistant find out how to do them.

- Use coloured text in the spreadsheet.
- Delete a column of cells.
- Sort a list of numbers into ascending order.
- Put a border around a group of cells.
- Insert subtotal values into a list.
- Insert a comment into a cell.

Exercise 3.1

Finding out about the Office Assistant

In this exercise you will learn to

- **use the Office Assistant to avoid the need to refer to manuals or ask someone else.**

On-line help is a very important and useful tool that you can use to find out about the software for yourself. Reference books are expensive and finding what you want in them is not that easy. Follow these steps to see how easy the Office Assistant is to use.

1 Click on the picture of the Office Assistant.

A menu will appear where you can type in a series of words to describe what help you want.

In this case we need to find out about the Office Assistant itself.

Type in the word 'Office Assistant' as a brief description, then click on Search.

2 You will now see a menu from which you can make a choice:

Click on 'About tips and messages from the Office Assistant'. A screen appears on the right of the screen containing your original worksheet.

Notice the list of items is in blue and each is underlined. You can access the information by clicking on them.

By clicking on the icon of the printer, obtain a printout of the instructions on 'About tips and messages from the Office Assistant'.

Read through the printout; it describes how the Office Assistant can give you answers to your questions, offer tips and provide help.

Now answer the following questions.

QUESTIONS

1 Sometimes when the Office Assistant is being used, a light bulb appears. If this light bulb is clicked what happens?

2 Find out how to customise the Office Assistant. Explain briefly to someone who has not done this before, what you can do.

Moving the Office Assistant

The Office Assistant usually sits at the top right-hand part of the screen. Sometimes it covers an icon or some text. You can move the Office Assistant by first moving the cursor onto it. Hold the left mouse button down, drag the Office Assistant to another part of the screen.

To hide the Office Assistant click the right mouse button and then select Hide from the menu that appears. To get it back you click on Help in the menu toolbar and select Show the Office Assistant.

Help with toolbar buttons

There are many buttons you can click on the toolbars. You can usually figure out what they do by the small pictures or icons on them. For example the picture of a pair of scissors means cut and the diagram of the brush means paste. If you move the cursor using the mouse onto any of these icons, after a moment the name of the icon will appear in a box. The screen shot below shows what happens when the cursor is positioned over one such button.

Using Help on the menu bar

If you look at the menu bar, you will see that there is a menu for Help. Clicking on this brings down the menu.

One very useful feature of Help is the 'What's This?' option. If you click on this option the cursor becomes an arrow with a thick black question mark attached. This can be moved to any item on the screen about which you require help. For example, if it is moved to the Bold icon on the formatting toolbar and the mouse is clicked, a screen appears telling you about the icon.

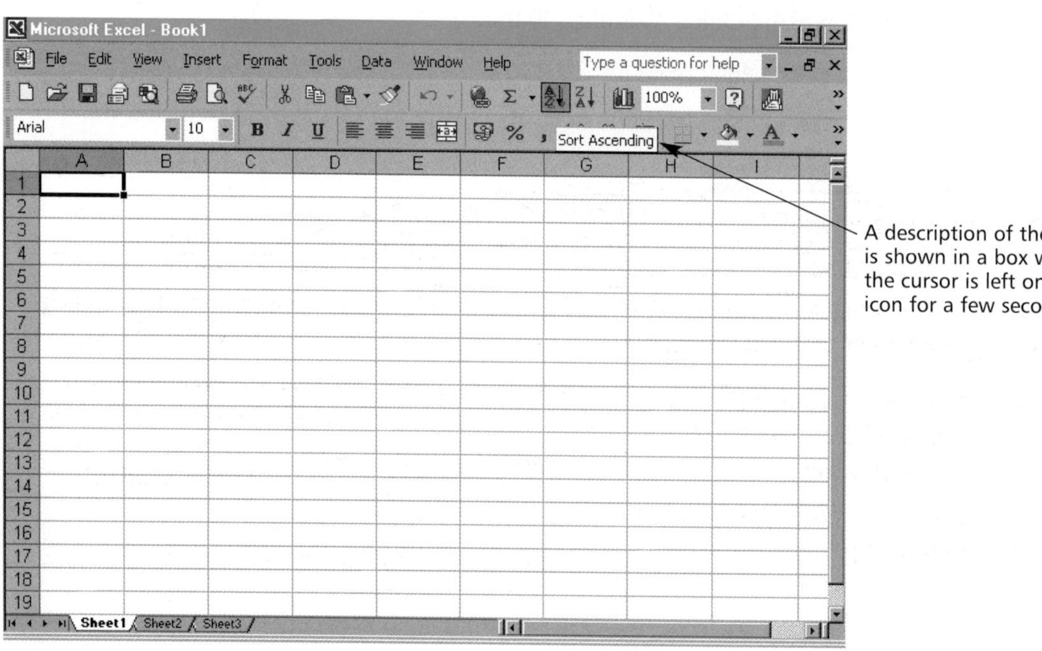

A description of the icon is shown in a box when the cursor is left on the icon for a few seconds.

Exercise 3.2

Customising your Office Assistant

In this exercise we look at how the Office Assistant can be changed to suit you. For example, you might not want the standard paper clip to appear. The package gives you the option of altering certain things.

1 Click on the Office Assistant using the **right** mouse button.

A menu with the following options appears:

Hide

Options...

Choose Assistant

Animate!

2 Click on Choose Assistant. Here there are several other Office Assistants to choose from if you get fed up with the paper clip.

Follow the instructions on the screen. Can you find a better one than the paper clip?

3 Now click on the Options tab. You are now presented with lots of options to choose from to customise your help facility.

You can see from the options screen that there are many ways to build up your knowledge of the package using help. Notice that the Office Assistant can even make a guess as to what you might need help on. For instance, if you were trying to construct a formula then it would know you had been trying to do this and would offer help on this topic.

Notice also that you can ask for a tip of the day. This is quite useful for a novice user since it builds up your skills gradually, almost without you knowing.

Click on Cancel to get rid of the menu.

4 For a bit of entertainment, when you get bored, you can even get your Office Assistant to start moving.

Click on the Office Assistant with the right mouse button and then choose Animate! from the menu.

Click Animate again and it will do a different movement.

QUESTIONS

1 There are many ways you can learn about a new piece of software. These include:

(a) reading a manual
(b) experimenting (what will happen if I do this?)
(c) getting an experienced user to help you learn
(d) using the on-line help facility.

For each one above, write down the method's advantages and disadvantages.

Most people use a combination of approaches. Which one or ones do you prefer and why?

2 Find an on-line tutorial for Excel XP using the Internet. Use this tutorial to see if it could be of use to you. Write a short piece (called an evaluation) on how good you found the tutorial.

3 Using the What's This? option, point to ten icons or menus that you have not used before and write down what they do.

Improving the Appearance of Your Worksheets

Once you have designed, set up and tested your worksheet thoroughly, you can start to think about improving its appearance. Before you do this, you need to think about the use to which the sheet will be put. If you are the only person using it, is it worth spending time improving the appearance? If others are to use it, appearance is very important and it is worth presenting the worksheets in an interesting and visually appealing way.

In this chapter we will look at altering the appearance of the spreadsheet using different fonts and font sizes, styles such as bold and underline, colour, alignment of data in cells and the angle of headings.

Bold, italics and underline

Select the characters, words, sentences and numbers that you want to stand out by clicking on them and keeping the left mouse button pressed down. You can now drag the mouse to highlight your choice and then remove your finger from the button. Next move to the desired icon in the formatting toolbar and click on it. You will now see the formatting applied.

An example of bold text *An example of text in italics* An example of underlined text

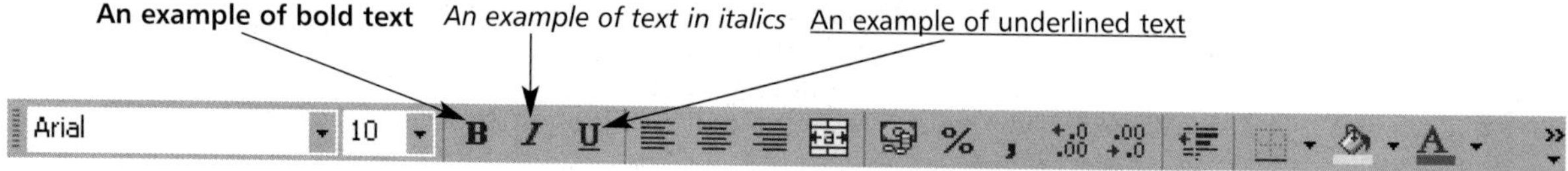

Choosing the shape of the letters (called fonts)

If you don't like the font that the computer has automatically chosen (called the default font) you can change it. To do this select the text you want to change and then click on the font box in the formatting toolbar.

Be careful about using too many different fonts in the same document. Like many of the formatting features in this chapter, you need to be careful in their use. Experiment to find out which fonts work well and which don't. Some fonts take up more space in a cell than others of the same size so check to make sure that all the data in the columns are shown. If some data are missing then increasing the column size will reveal them.

Click on here to see the menu of fonts; click on one of them to make your selection

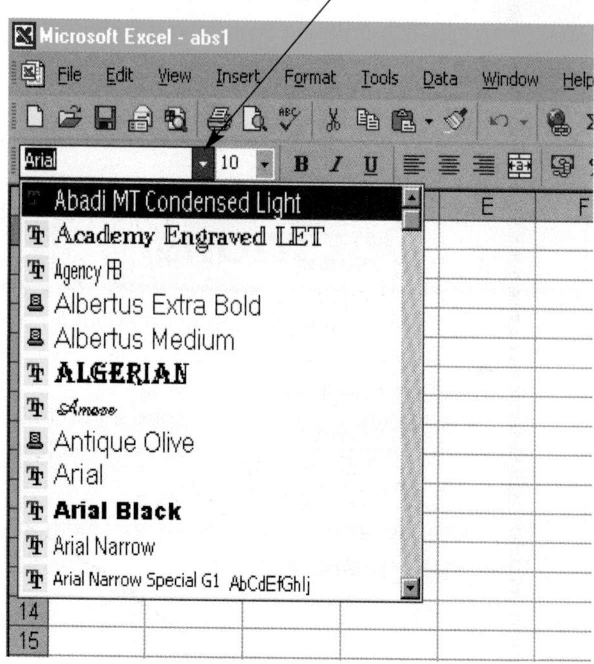

Choosing the font size

The size of a font is usually set at a value of 10 or 12 (this is its height in 'points') but this can be changed. Click on the font size in the formatting toolbar and a menu of font sizes will be displayed from which you can choose. If you alter a font size, you will probably need to alter the width of the columns so that all the data will fit..

Positioning data in cells

Data in cells is normally positioned according to the following:

- numbers are aligned to the right of a cell
- text is aligned to the left of a cell.

By selecting a cell, or group of cells, you can alter the position of data therein. Once the cells have been highlighted click on one of the icons shown below.

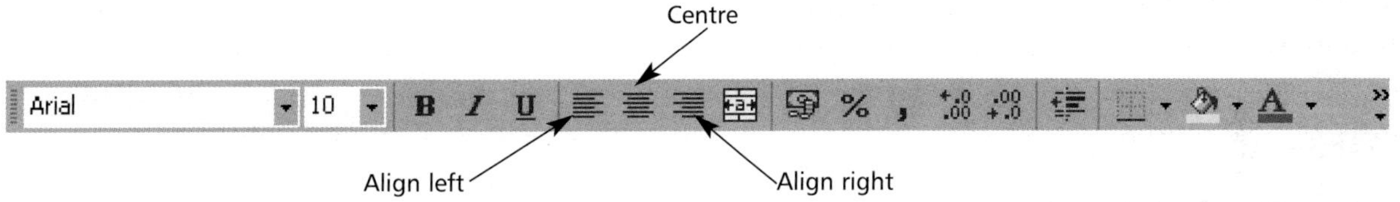

Exercise 4.1

Using simple formatting techniques

In this exercise you will learn to:

- **centre data within cells**
- **alter font style and font size**
- **use bold, italics and underline to format cells**
- **merge cells and centre.**

1 Load the spreadsheet, set up a new worksheet and input the following data. Make the headings bold by clicking on them and then on the bold icon in the formatting toolbar.

	A	B
1	**Subject**	**Examination mark**
2	English Language	67
3	English Literature	45
4	History	71
5	Geography	55
6	Science	46
7	Mathematics	62
8	Information Technology	70
9	PE	82
10	Drama	83

2 The title 'Examination mark' is quite wide and this means the column also needs to be wide. The numbers in cells are right aligned and this has caused them to look too far to the right. To correct this, we can centre them in their cells.

Highlight cells from B2 to B10 and then click on the centre icon.

Your worksheet will now look like this:

	A	B
1	**Subject**	**Examination mark**
2	English Language	67
3	English Literature	45
4	History	71
5	Geography	55
6	Science	46
7	Mathematics	62
8	Information Technology	70
9	PE	82
10	Drama	83

See how much better the worksheet looks just by making this simple change.

3 It is decided that a heading is needed to show to whom the marks refer and the year of the results. Insert a row at the top of the worksheet by clicking on cell A1 then go to Insert on the menu bar and select Rows. All the data will be shifted down a row, leaving a blank row at the top.

4 Type in the heading **Marks for J Hughes June 2000**. Do not worry about it going into the adjacent cell.

5 Alter the font of this heading by highlighting it and then selecting Times New Roman from the font style menu.

6 Highlight the heading again and alter the font size to two greater than the font used for the rest of the data (i.e. if the rest of the worksheet is in 10 point use 12 point for the heading).

7 Highlight the title again and make it bold, in italics and underlined by clicking on the respective icons. The worksheet will now look like this:

	A	B
1	***Marks for J Hughes June 2000***	
2	**Subject**	**Examination mark**
3	English Language	67
4	English Literature	45
5	History	71
6	Geography	55
7	Science	46
8	Mathematics	62
9	Information Technology	70
10	PE	82

Exercise 4.1

8 It is possible to centre the heading across the two columns. This is done using the 'merge cell and centre' icon on the formatting toolbar. Highlight the cells containing the heading and then click on the 'merge cell and centre' icon. Your worksheet will now look like this:

	A	B
1	***Marks for J Hughes June 2000***	
2	**Subject**	**Examination mark**
3	English Language	67
4	English Literature	45
5	History	71
6	Geography	55
7	Science	46
8	Mathematics	62
9	Information Technology	70
10	PE	82
11	Drama	83

9 Close the worksheet without bothering to save.

Adding colour

The use of colour can improve the appearance of your spreadsheet considerably. However, you need to bear in mind the use to which the information is to be put. If you are simply going to use the information yourself, it is not worth going to the trouble. If you are using your data to back up a talk to several people, it may repay the effort involved.

Some tips when working with colour

- Do not add colour unless you are printing in colour. The main reason for this is that when a coloured piece of work is printed in black and white, it becomes very hard to read unless the colours have been chosen carefully.
- Do not overdo the colour. Selecting colours is just like selecting clothes to go on a night out! A particular combination can be attractive… or it can be tasteless.
- Do not spend too much time on appearance at the expense of content. What this means is that you can spend a lot more time on the appearance and not enough time thinking about the problem and how to solve it in the best way possible.

Adding borders

To add borders around a cell, or group of cells, highlight the cells, click on Format and then select Cells. The following formatting menu appears:

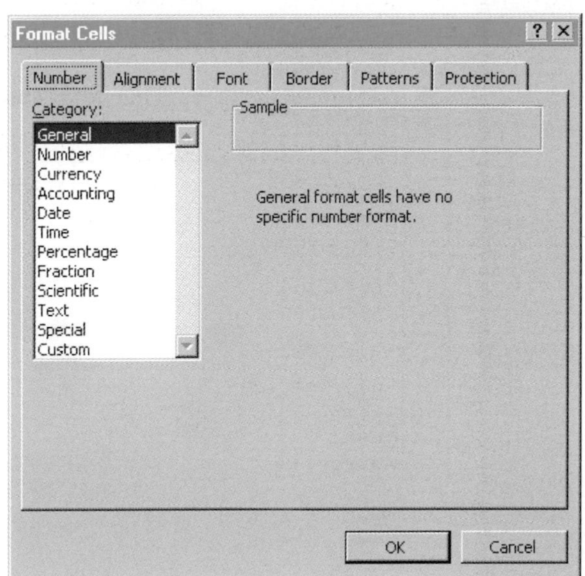

Click on Border in the above menu and the menu below appears.

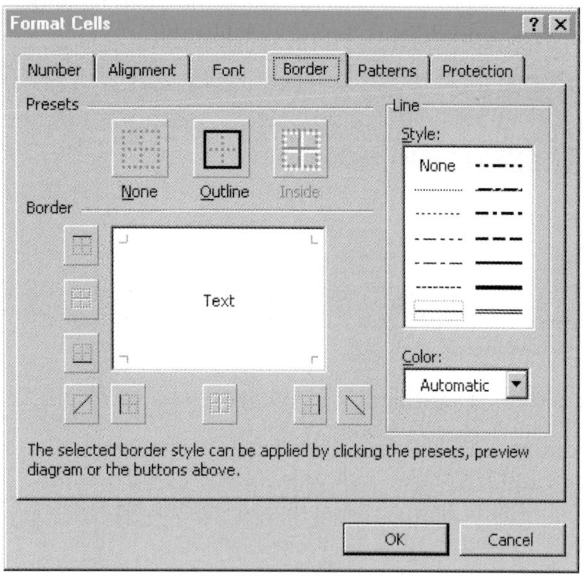

You can now decide on the border around the cells.

First go to the line part of this menu and select the type of lines to make up the border.

The thick black lines and the double line are quite useful to make part of a spreadsheet stand out. The colour of the border can be selected here.

The preset menu is then selected where you can say whether you just want a border around the cells you have selected or if you want a border outside as well as inside. Notice that you can also select just part (or parts) of a border and also that you can have diagonal lines across borders.

Exercise 4.2

Borders around cells

In this exercise you will learn to:

- **select the type of lines for a border**
- **select the colour of a border**
- **alter the font size and colour**
- **alter the fill colour (i.e. the colour behind the cell).**

1 Type in data exactly as it appears here, but make sure that you put in formulae in cells D4 to D8 to work out the wage, rather than just copying the numbers.

	A	B	C	D	E	F
1	**A spreadsheet to work out John's total wages for the six weeks fruit picking.**					
2						
3	Fruit	Quantity picked (kg)	Rate per kg (£)	Wage (£)		
4	Strawberries	30.50	£2.25	£68.63		
5	Blackcurrants	10.75	£4.45	£47.84		
6	Grapes	25.50	£0.60	£15.30		
7	Apples	45.00	£0.25	£11.25		
8	Raspberries	12.75	£3.10	£39.53		
9						
10						
11						
12	**Fruit**	Apples	Blackcurrants	Grapes	Raspberries	Strawberries
13	**Rate per kg**	£0.25	£4.45	£0.60	£3.10	£2.25

Exercise 4.2

2 The title needs to be in a bigger font than the characters in the rest of the worksheet.

Highlight the title by clicking on cell A1 and then dragging to cell E1. Now go to the formatting toolbar and change the font size from 10 to 12 point.

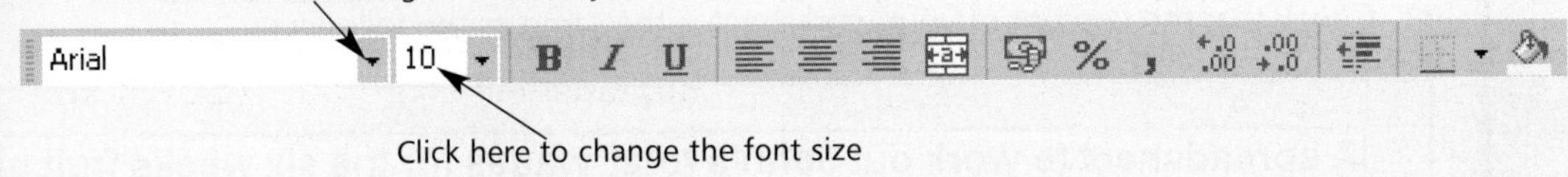

3 We will now place this title in a box to make it stand out even more. Highlight the title again. Go to Format, then Cells and then select Border. Select the double line in the Line part of this menu and also the Outline in the Presets part of the menu.

4 The area of the spreadsheet containing the rates for picking the different types of fruits in cells A12 to F13 needs highlighting and a thick blue border placing around it.

5 The part of the spreadsheet with the amounts and types of fruit along with the payments, should now be highlighted. This is from cell A3 to D8. We now need a blue border and the cells inside need to have a border around them.

When this is done, the content of your worksheet should look like this:

	A	B	C	D	E	F
1	**A spreadsheet to work out John's total wages for the six weeks fruit picking.**					
2						
3	Fruit	Quantity picked (kg)	Rate per kg (£)	Wage (£)		
4	Strawberries	30.50	£2.25	£68.63		
5	Blackcurrants	10.75	£4.45	£47.84		
6	Grapes	25.50	£0.60	£15.30		
7	Apples	45.00	£0.25	£11.25		
8	Raspberries	12.75	£3.10	£39.53		
9						
10						
11						
12	**Fruit**	Apples	Blackcurrants	Grapes	Raspberries	Strawberries
13	**Rate per kg**	£0.25	£4.45	£0.60	£3.10	£2.25
14						

6 Make bold all the text in cells A3, B3, C3 and D3. When you do this, you may have to widen some of the columns since bold text takes up slightly more space than plain.

7 Change the colour of the text for the fruits in cells A4 to A8. Do this by highlighting them first and then selecting the font colour icon in the formatting toolbar. When this icon is clicked a palette of colours appears. Click on red.

The selected text will now be red.

8 Repeat step 7 and change all the text for the fruits in cells B12 to F12 to red.

Exercise 4.2

9 The background colour (called the fill colour by Excel) can now be changed for some of the cells. Select cells A1 to F1 and then click on the fill colour icon (the small picture in the formatting menu with the spilled paint pot on it) and select yellow.

10 Select cells A3 to D3 and give them a yellow fill colour.

11 Check that the content of your worksheet is the same as the following:

	A	B	C	D	E	F
1	**A spreadsheet to work out John's total wages for the six weeks fruit picking.**					
2						
3	**Fruit**	**Quantity picked (kg)**	**Rate per kg (£)**	**Wage (£)**		
4	Strawberries	30.50	£2.25	£68.63		
5	Blackcurrants	10.75	£4.45	£47.84		
6	Grapes	25.50	£0.60	£15.30		
7	Apples	45.00	£0.25	£11.25		
8	Raspberries	12.75	£3.10	£39.53		
9						
10						
11						
12	**Fruit**	Apples	Blackcurrants	Grapes	Raspberries	Strawberries
13	**Rate per kg**	£0.25	£4.45	£0.60	£3.10	£2.25
14						

12 Save your worksheet under the filename 'Formatted Fruit Picking Worksheet'. Notice how a longer filename can be used to more easily identify the worksheet in the future.

Exercise 4.3

Improving the appearance of a worksheet

In this exercise you will learn to:

- **fill in cells with a colour**
- **work out and enter formulae**
- **put borders around groups of cells**
- **import clip art into the worksheet**
- **size and position imported clip art.**

This exercise uses a spreadsheet to work out customer bills for a specialist car hire company who hire out expensive sports cars. The cars are hired on a day-to-day basis for special occasions and promotional activities.

The mileage on the clock when the car is given to the customer is called the 'miles out' figure; when the customer returns the car in the evening, the mileage figure, called 'miles in' is also recorded. There is a daily charge for the hire of the car plus a rate per mile.

1 Start a new worksheet and set up the worksheet shown at the top of the next page.

Make sure that your spreadsheet is identical to the one shown.

	A	B	C	D	E	F
1						
2						
3						
4	Prestige Car Hire Ltd (Specialists in the hiring of prestigious sports cars)					
5						
6	Reference	PY1298				
7	Date	12/03/01				
8						
9	Car Model	Ferrari F355 Berlinetta			Daily Rate	£165.00
10	Car Registration	FER 23			Mileage Rate	£0.25
11	Miles Out	21980			Mileage Charge	
12	Miles In	22329				
13	Miles Covered					
14						
15						
16		Charge for day				
17		VAT				
18		Total charge for day's hire				

2 Enter a suitable formula in cell B13 to work out the miles covered.

Enter a suitable formula to work out the mileage charge (Hint: you will need to multiply the miles covered by the mileage rate) and enter it into cell F11.

Enter a formula into cell C16 to work out the charge for the day, by adding the mileage charge to the daily rate.

Enter a formula into cell C17 to work out the VAT; this is 17.5% of cell C16.

Enter a formula into cell C18 to work out the total charge by adding the VAT to the charge per day.

If your formulae are correct your spreadsheet will look like this:

	A	B	C	D	E	F
1						
2						
3						
4	Prestige Car Hire Ltd (Specialists in the hiring of prestigious sports cars)					
5						
6	Reference	PY1298				
7	Date	12/03/01				
8						
9	Car Model	Ferrari F355 Berlinetta			Daily Rate	£165.00
10	Car Registration	FER 23			Mileage Rate	£0.25
11	Miles Out	21980			Mileage Charge	£87.25
12	Miles In	22329				
13	Miles Covered	349				
14						
15						
16		Charge for day	£252.25			
17		VAT	£44.14			
18		Total charge for day's hire	£296.39			

3 The spreadsheet needs to have its appearance improved since the customer will see the screen.

Sometimes it works well if all the empty cells on the sheet are a colour other than white. A pastel colour such as a light yellow can be chosen as the fill colour.

Fill in all the cells not containing any data with a light yellow.

4 Put thick black borders around the groups of information as shown in the screen shot below.

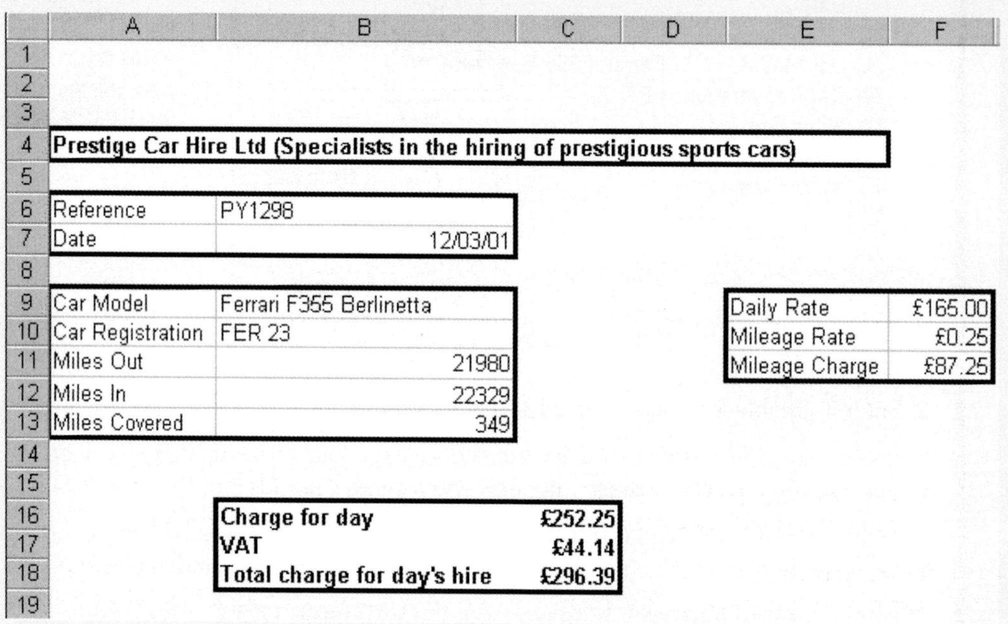

	A	B	C	D	E	F
1						
2						
3						
4	**Prestige Car Hire Ltd (Specialists in the hiring of prestigious sports cars)**					
5						
6	Reference	PY1298				
7	Date	12/03/01				
8						
9	Car Model	Ferrari F355 Berlinetta			Daily Rate	£165.00
10	Car Registration	FER 23			Mileage Rate	£0.25
11	Miles Out	21980			Mileage Charge	£87.25
12	Miles In	22329				
13	Miles Covered	349				
14						
15						
16		**Charge for day**	**£252.25**			
17		**VAT**	**£44.14**			
18		**Total charge for day's hire**	**£296.39**			
19						

5 To complete the design we will import a piece of clip art into the worksheet. To do this click on Insert then Picture and then Clip Art.

Your teacher may need to help you at this stage or the clip art catalogue may just appear. In either case choose your picture.

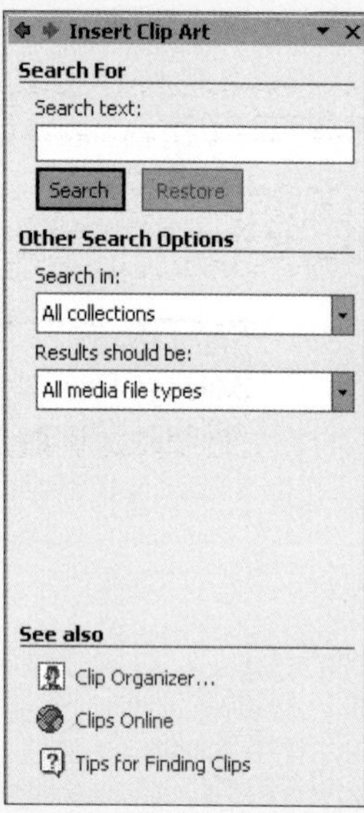

What we are looking for is a picture of an expensive sports car. You can type the words 'sports car' into the section at the top of the catalogue and then click on 'Search'.

Insert Clip Art
Search For
Search text:
Sports car
Search Restore

When you see a picture you like, click on the picture. The piece of clip art will be placed into the worksheet but you may need to size it and move it to the correct position.

To move the piece of clip art, click anywhere on the picture and handles will appear (small rectangles around the picture). If you move to the centre of the picture a four headed arrow will appear. Click on the diagram and drag it to the required position. You can also alter the shape (i.e. length and height) and overall size by clicking on the handles. You should experiment until you are happy with the result.

Your final result will look something like this:

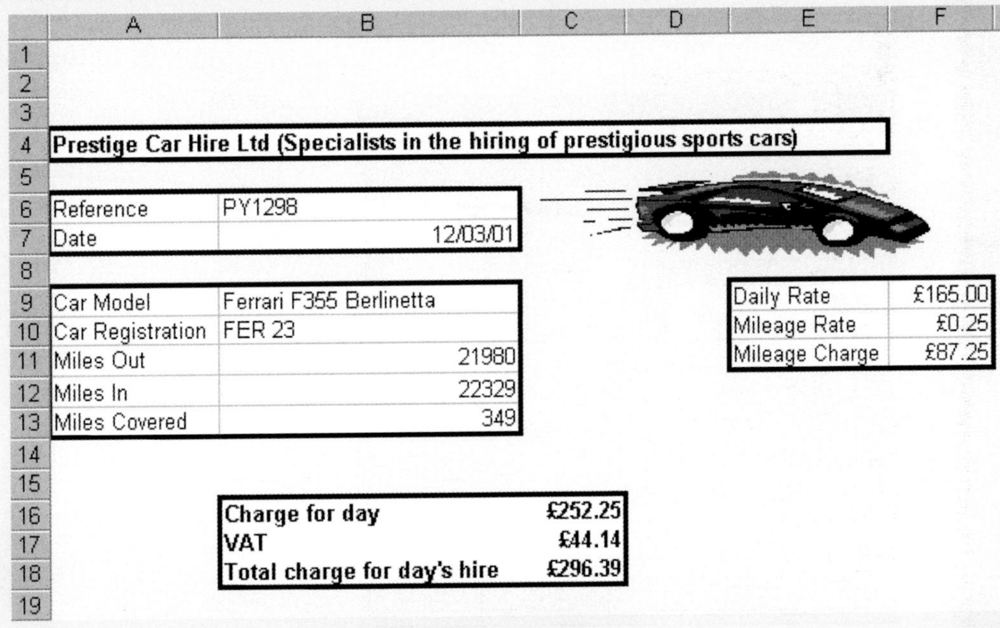

	A	B	C	D	E	F
1						
2						
3						
4	Prestige Car Hire Ltd (Specialists in the hiring of prestigious sports cars)					
5						
6	Reference	PY1298				
7	Date	12/03/01				
8						
9	Car Model	Ferrari F355 Berlinetta			Daily Rate	£165.00
10	Car Registration	FER 23			Mileage Rate	£0.25
11	Miles Out	21980			Mileage Charge	£87.25
12	Miles In	22329				
13	Miles Covered	349				
14						
15						
16		**Charge for day**	**£252.25**			
17		**VAT**	**£44.14**			
18		**Total charge for day's hire**	**£296.39**			
19						

Rotating headings

It is usually preferable to try to get as much data as you can on a single page. Sometimes you cannot do this because the column headings are wider than the data below them. If you look at the worksheet below you can see that 'Registration Group' is a very wide heading for data that is only a single character wide. One solution may be to rotate the heading, as described in Exercise 4.4.

	A	B	C	D	E	F	G
1	**Surname**	**Forename**	**Gender**	**Date of Birth**	**Year Group**	**Registration Group**	**Admission Number**
2	Hughes	Stephen	M	19/12/84	11	L	121221
3	Chaudrey	Saleha	F	17/12/87	8	F	110900
4	Robinson	Peter	M	18/09/87	9	G	110899
5	Green	Amy	F	11/06/86	9	H	150078
6	Roberts	Darren	M	18/11/84	11	L	121897
7	Harman	Paul	M	11/05/85	10	I	138988
8	King	Jason	M	11/07/85	10	I	138971
9	Scott	Susan	F	04/06/89	6	A	140087
10	Adams	Victoria	F	03/04/89	6	B	140075
11	Wilson	Pamela	F	01/02/88	7	C	149999
12	Mason	Veronica	F	03/08/89	6	B	140090
13	Wiliams	Paul	M	01/02/84	11	L	121223
14	Ferris	Jack	M	09/07/89	6	B	140091
15	Corkhill	Kylie	F	01/02/89	11	L	121223
16	Furlong	John	M	01/05/89	11	K	121200

Exercise 4.4

Rotating headings

1 Start a new worksheet and just type a couple of rows of the above worksheet. Make the first row (the headings) bold.

2 Highlight the first row containing the column headings (cells A1 to G1).

3 Click on Format and then Cells. In the Format Cells menu click on Alignment.

The screen should now look like this:

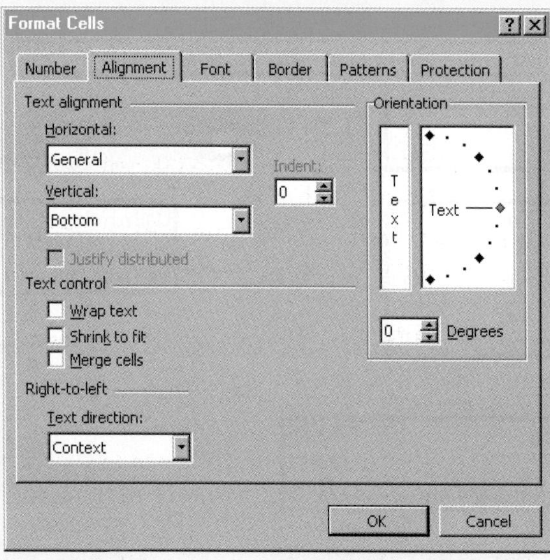

Click on the device that looks a bit like a protractor. You can move the pointer to change the angle of the text. Use the cursor to move the pointer up until an angle of 60° is reached. Click on OK.

4 You will notice that although the headings have been rotated correctly, part of them is missing. This is because the cell height is too small to accommodate the text. The cell height is increased by clicking on the line between the rows (in this case the line between the two row numbers 1 and 2) and dragging until a suitable height is reached.

5 You are now able to reduce the widths of the columns so that more columns can be fitted onto a single page. Go to the line between the column letters and click twice to autofit the column width to the width of the data.

Your finished sheet will look like the one below.

	A	B	C	D	E	F	G
1	Surname	Forename	Gender	Date of Birth	Year Group	Registration Group	Admission Number
2	Hughes	Stephen	M	19/12/84	11	L	121221
3	Chaudrey	Saleha	F	17/12/87	8	F	110900
4	Robinson	Peter	M	18/09/87	9	G	110899
5	Green	Amy	F	11/06/86	9	H	150078
6	Roberts	Darren	M	18/11/84	11	L	121897
7	Harman	Paul	M	11/05/85	10	I	138988
8	King	Jason	M	11/07/85	10	I	138971
9	Scott	Susan	F	04/06/89	6	A	140087
10	Adams	Victoria	F	03/04/89	6	B	140075

One for you to try: a school barbecue for charity

A school wants to raise some money for charity so it is decided to hold a barbecue. Pupils intend to hire a large barbecue, some party lights and a disco unit from a local hire firm. They need to be sure that they will make a profit as well as enjoy themselves, so before they go ahead with the project they produce a spreadsheet. The spreadsheet enables them to see how much profit they will make.

The spreadsheet will show:

- Expenditure – things they have to pay out for (hiring equipment, food, drink, etc.)
- Income – money coming in from the sale of tickets, drinks, etc.

Tickets will cost £5 each which includes admission and the cost of the food. Although pupils think that this is quite expensive, they reckon that people will be prepared to spend this much if it goes to a good cause.

Thinking about the problem

The whole point of this exercise is to make sure that the proposed barbecue will make a profit. If expenditure is greater than income, a loss will be made which would be a great embarrassment to the organisers.

Accounts are normally organised with the income first and expenditure below.

Some of the items in the income and expenditure depend on the number of people attending the barbecue. The number of people who it is hoped will attend the event, needs to appear on the spreadsheet. It is estimated that 200 will attend.

Food has been estimated to cost £1.50 a head, so food for 200 would cost £300.

The cost of the equipment hire does not depend on the number of people attending, so this is a definite cost.

Exercise 4.5

Look at the proposed worksheet below. Write a list of the categories of income and expenditure that will depend on the number of pupils attending the event. For each one, briefly explain why that item depends on the number of pupils attending.

1 Enter the data into a new worksheet exactly as shown below.

	A	B	C	D	E
1	**Year 10 and 11 Proposed Barbecue For Charity**				
2	**Estimated Income/Expenditure**				
3	Total No of tickets sold	200		Ticket price	£5.00
4					
5	**INCOME**				
6	Ticket sales				
7	Drink sales				
8	Raffle ticket sales			Total income	
9				Total expenditure	
10	**EXPENDITURE**			Profit	
11	Hire of party lights	£27.00			
12	Hire of disco unit	£35.00			
13	Hire of barbecue	£45.00			
14	Barbecue fuel	£14.00			
15	Fire lighters	£4.00			
16	Food	£300.00			
17	Printing of tickets	£27.50			
18	Cases of soft drink (240 cans)	£60.00			
19	Raffle prizes	£50.00			
20					

2 Put a formula in cell B6 to work out the income from ticket sales. The total number of tickets sold needs to be multiplied by the ticket price. (Note: the number of tickets sold and the ticket price are put on the spreadsheet because we may want to experiment by changing these.)

3 If all the drinks are sold, then the income from the sale of drinks will be £96. Enter this value into cell B7.

4 We will assume that all 200 people buy a raffle ticket (some may buy none whilst others may buy several). Each raffle ticket costs £0.50, so the income from the sale of raffle ticket will be £100. Enter this value into cell B8.

5 Enter a formula into cell E8 to add up the total income.

6 Enter a formula into cell E9 to calculate the total expenditure.

7 The profit from the barbecue can be worked out by subtracting the total expenditure from the total income. Enter a formula to do this into cell E10.

Exercise 4.5

8 Now check carefully that all your numbers are identical to those shown below.

	A	B	C	D	E
1	**Year 10 and 11 Proposed Barbecue For Charity**				
2	**Estimated Income/Expenditure**				
3	Total No of tickets sold	200		Ticket price	£5.00
4					
5	**INCOME**				
6	Ticket sales	£1,000.00			
7	Drink sales	£96.00			
8	Raffle ticket sales	£100.00		Total income	£1,196.00
9				Total expenditure	£562.50
10	**EXPENDITURE**			Profit	£633.50
11	Hire of party lights	£27.00			
12	Hire of disco unit	£35.00			
13	Hire of barbecue	£45.00			
14	Barbecue fuel	£14.00			
15	Fire lighters	£4.00			
16	Food	£300.00			
17	Printing of tickets	£27.50			
18	Cases of soft drink (240 cans)	£60.00			
19	Raffle prizes	£50.00			

9 Save a copy of the spreadsheet under the filename 'Proposed Barbecue Estimated Income/Expenditure'. This spreadsheet will be used again in a later chapter on modelling.

10 Now you have the chance to improve the appearance of the spreadsheet.

The spreadsheet is to be presented to the Head of Business Studies and also the Headteacher so it will impress them if it looks good. See what you can do, and remember to save each copy of your alterations under a different file name (e.g. BBQ1, BBQ2 etc.) as you go along. (Do not use the filename in step 9 again, since we need to keep this worksheet so it will be identical for everyone when used again.)

11 When you are happy with the final result, save your preferred version and print it out (preferably in colour).

Backing up a worksheet

Sooner or later most computer users will experience some loss of data for a variety of different reasons. It usually happens at the most inconvenient time, such as the day before your GCSE project work has to be handed in.

There are many reasons why data is lost and these include the following:

- virus attack
- hardware fault
- a bug (error) in the software
- operator error
- loss of an important disk.

It is, therefore, important to keep a separate copy of your work, called a 'backup copy'. The process of copying your work onto another disk is called backing up your data. Backup copies should be taken regularly and kept in a safe place away from the computer and also away from where you normally keep your disks.

I always save my work on the hard disk and then on a floppy at regular intervals (usually every half an hour).

QUESTIONS

1 Why should you never keep your backup copy in the same place as the disk containing the original?

2 There is a facility with Microsoft Office called Autosave. Use the help menu to find out what it is and how it can be useful to you. Write a short paragraph about it when you have found out.

Procedures for taking a backup copy

When you are working on a spreadsheet you should periodically take a copy of your work. If you simply save then the latest version of the worksheet will replace the previous version. If you mess up a spreadsheet and save it you cannot easily go back to the previous version. Instead of using Save you can use Save As (click on File to see this) and use different version numbers for each save. For example you could have 'Car Hire 1', 'Car Hire 2' etc. When you are happy with the final version you can go back and delete the earlier versions.

Keeping copies of your work under different names is useful if you need to go back to a previous version

5 Functions

What is a function?

A function is simply a specialised calculation that Excel has memorised. There are many functions (around 200) built into Excel and they can do lots of different things. In this chapter just a few of them will be mentioned since many demand specialist knowledge for their use (e.g. accountancy, statistics, advanced maths and so on).

We have already come across simple mathematical functions (e.g. add, subtract, multiply and divide). There are other functions you might find useful and some of the main ones are outlined here.

Like a formula, a function needs to start with an equals sign and you also need to tell the spreadsheet which cells you want to use it with. A cell range from A1 to A13 would be written as (A1:A13). Here are some of the most popular, simple functions. Notice they all start with an equals sign followed by the name of the function and then the range of cells the function is to be applied to. The range is put inside a pair of brackets.

Average

=AVERAGE(A1:A10) gives the average of all the numbers in the cells from A1 to A10 inclusive.

Maximum

=MAX(E4:E11) displays the largest number from all the cells from E4 to E11 inclusive.

Minimum

=MINIMUM(B2:B12) displays the smallest number from all the cells from B2 to B12 inclusive.

Count

Suppose we want to count the number of numeric entries in the range C3 to C30.
We can use =COUNT(C3:C30)
Any blank lines or text entries in the range are not counted.

Counta

To count a number of items or names of people (not numeric entries, as above) we need to be able to count text entries. To do this we can use =COUNTA(C3:C30). You need to make sure that headings are not included in the range so that they are not counted as well. Again, blank lines are not counted.

The IF function

The IF function is very useful because you can use it to test a condition and then choose between two actions based on whether the condition is true or false.
The IF function makes use of something called relational operators. You may have come across these in your mathematics lessons but it is worth going through what they mean.

Relational operators
(=, <, >, <>, <=, >=)

The most popular operator by far is the equals sign, but sometimes a comparison needs to be made between two items of data. For example, we may need to find a list of employees whose salaries are greater than a certain amount.

Operators can also be used with characters or character strings, so one character can be compared with another and since each character has a binary code (ASCII) associated with it, the computer can work out that A comes before B and so on.

You can also test to see if the contents of a certain cell have a certain word in them. For example, you could test to see IF B6="Yes".

The IF function is structured like this:

=IF(condition, value if true, value if false)

The value can either be a number or a message. If the values are messages, then they need to be enclosed inside double quote marks (e.g. "High"). The commas within the brackets are essential to separate the different parts.

Symbol	Meaning	Examples
=	equals	5 + 5 = 10
>	greater than	5*3 > 2*3
<	less than	–6 < –1 or 100 < 200
<>	not equal to	"Red" <> "White" or 20/4 <> 6*4
<=	less than or equal to	"Adam" <= "Eve"
>=	greater than or equal to	400 >= 200

Exercise 5.1

Choosing between two postage charges

In the following spreadsheet you will learn to:

- **test a cell with an IF function and then to print a number dependant on whether the test is true or false.**

Suppose a mail order company has two charges for postage. If the order is £500 or over then the charge is £25, otherwise the charge is £15.

In the worksheet shown, a column has been left blank so that the postage charge can be added.

1 Set up your worksheet so that it is exactly the same as shown below.

	A	B
1	£350.45	
2	£450.21	
3	£34.98	
4	£56.76	
5	£789.90	
6	£1200.00	
7	£12.55	

2 An IF function is needed to test the value in cell A1 to see if it is £500 or over. We express this condition in maths as greater than or equal to 500. This is written in mathematical language as >=500.

Put the following IF function in cell B1:

=IF(A1>=500,25,15)

Basically this formula means that if the charge is £500 or over then £25 will be placed in column B for the postage and if not then £15 is put in.

Note: Do not put the £ signs into the formula as it will no longer work properly if anything other than numerals are present.

Your worksheet will now look like this.

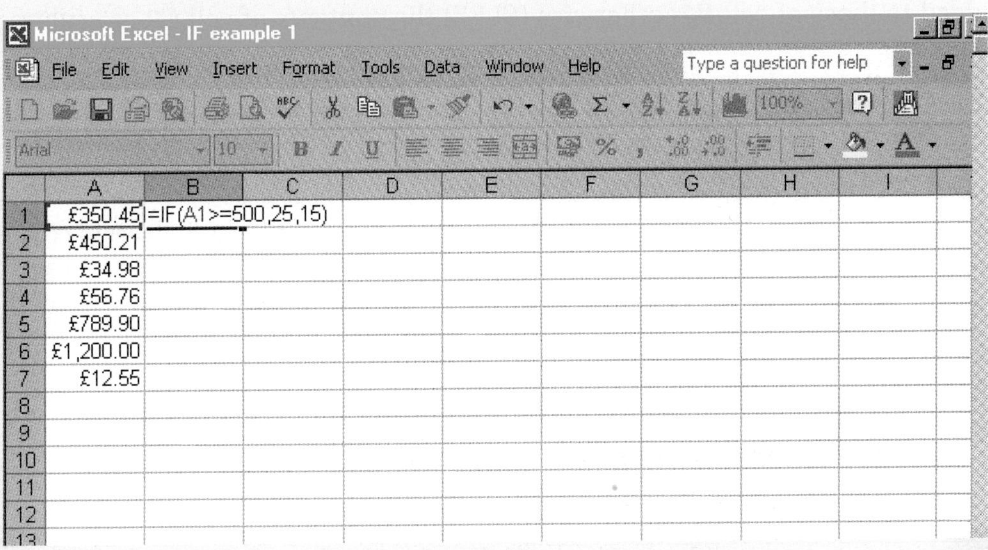

3 This formula is now copied relatively down the rest of the column.

4 Your worksheet will now look like this:

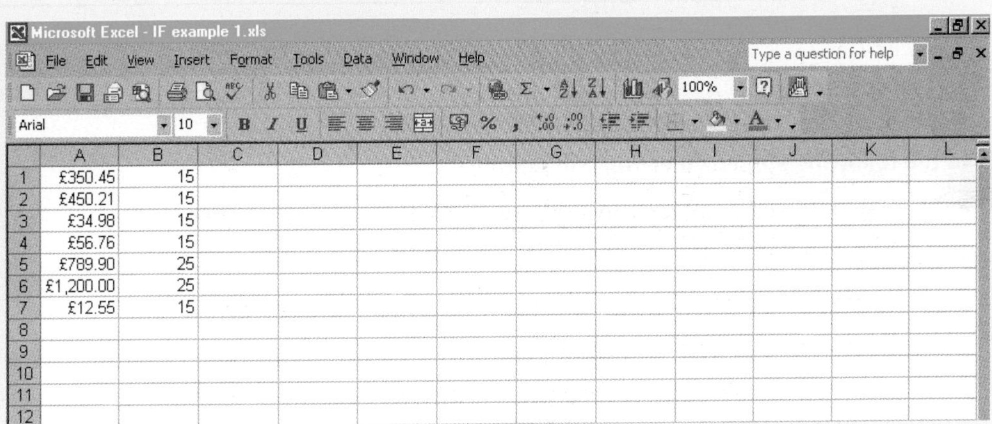

5 Notice that the delivery charges do not have a £ sign. Now format this column so that these numbers are set to currency with the pound sign included.

Extra tasks

6 In column C, add the invoice amount to the delivery charge. This is done by adding together the pairs of numbers in columns A and B.

7 Produce suitable headings for each column. Note you will need to insert a row to do this.

Making sense of IF … THEN … ELSE statements

Look at the following expression:

=IF(A3>5,A6+B2,A6–C2)

This means that IF the number in cell A3 is greater than five THEN the contents of cell A6 will be added to those of cell B2, otherwise (ELSE) the contents of cell C2 are subtracted from those in cell A6.

QUESTIONS

Here is a worksheet containing some numerical data:

	A	B	C	D
1				
2			12	
3	6	4		
4				
5				
6	20			

The expression =IF(A3>5,B3+C2,A6–C2) is entered into cell C6.

1 (a) What number will appear in cell C6?
(b) If the number in cell A3 is changed from six to three and the expression in cell C6 is the same as in (a), what number now appears in cell C6?

2 Explain as simply as you can, what each of the following expressions will do:
(a) =IF(A2>=200,"5% discount given","No discount given")
(b) =IF(T<0,"Below zero","Zero or above")
(c) =IF(A2>=200,A2*0.95,A2)

Exercise 5.2

Teacher's markbook: using a range of functions

In the following spreadsheet you will learn to:

- **test a pupil's mark and then print 'Pass' or 'Fail' using an IF function**
- **print the average mark, the highest mark and the lowest mark for each group**
- **use the COUNTA function to count the number of pupils in each group.**

A teacher teaches two advanced level mathematics groups. Both groups have just taken a test and the teacher records the names and marks for each group in her mark book. The marks are all expressed as percentages.

The headteacher has asked the teacher to set up a spreadsheet according to her instructions. You have to set up the spreadsheet following these instructions.

1 Load Excel and enter the data as follows:
- in cell A1 enter **Group A**
- in cell D1 enter **Group B**
- since these are both headings, increase the font size to 14 and embolden them
- in cell A2 enter **Name**
- in cell B2 enter **Marks**
- repeat this in cells D2 and E2 respectively
- now embolden all of this.

2 Now enter all the names of the pupils and their marks in exactly the same places as in the following worksheet.

	A	B	C	D	E
1	**Group A**			**Group B**	
2	**Name**	**Marks**		**Name**	**Marks**
3	Hughes,J	65		Harrison,B	98
4	Turnpike,A	71		Ross,J	60
5	Smith,E	49		Davies,A	86
6	Daulby,A	61		Arnold,P	90
7	Evens,C	85		Edwards,S	41
8	Jacobs,E	34		Cannon,L	55
9	Doyle, A	27		Jenkins,P	74
10	Prescott,S	45		Denning,J	21
11	Harris,P	49			

After entering the data you should verify it. This means making sure it is correct by comparing what you have typed with the data shown above. This method of verification is called proof reading. Remember that the data is the exam marks so it must be correct.

3 The pass mark for the examination was 55%. A message needs to be displayed next to the marks to indicate whether the pupil has passed or failed.

In cell C3 enter the following formula:

=IF (B3>=55,"Pass","Fail")

Copy this formula relatively for the other pupils down column C.

Now enter a similar formula (yes, you have to devise this for yourself!) and again copy it relatively, down column F.

Check that your worksheet looks identical to the one below.

	A	B	C	D	E	F
1	**Group A**			**Group B**		
2	**Name**	**Marks**		**Name**	**Marks**	
3	Hughes,J	65	Pass	Harrison,B	98	Pass
4	Turnpike,A	71	Pass	Ross,J	60	Pass
5	Smith,E	49	Fail	Davies,A	86	Pass
6	Daulby,A	61	Pass	Arnold,P	90	Pass
7	Evens,C	85	Pass	Edwards,S	41	Fail
8	Jacobs,E	64	Pass	Cannon,L	55	Pass
9	Doyle, A	27	Fail	Jenkins,P	74	Pass
10	Prescott,S	45	Fail	Denning,J	21	Fail
11	Harris,P	49	Fail			

4 So that the performance of both groups can be compared, we will work out the following: the average mark, the highest mark and the lowest mark for each group.

In cells A13 and D13 enter the text **Average=**

In cell B13 enter the following formula to work out the average:

=Average(B3:B11)

Enter a similar formula in cell E13 to work out the average for group B.

In cells A15 and D15 enter the text **Highest mark=**

In cell B15 enter the formula to work out the highest mark:

=MAX(B3:B11)

In cell E15 enter a similar formula, but remember that there is one less pupil in group B.

In cells A16 and D16 enter the text **Lowest mark=**

In cell B16 enter the formula to work out the lowest mark:

=MIN(B3:B11)

Enter a similar formula in cell E16.

5 As a check, to make sure that all the required pupils have been included, the headteacher has specified that the total number of pupils in each group should be shown.

Enter the text **Number of pupils=** into cells A20 and D20.

Now enter the formula into cell B20 to work out the number of pupils. Since we are going to count the names (i.e. text) we use the COUNTA function in the following way:

=COUNTA(A3:A11)

Now use a similar formula to count the number of pupils in group B and place the answer in cell E20.

If you have done everything correctly, your worksheet will look like this:

	A	B	C	D	E	F
1	**Group A**			**Group B**		
2	**Name**	**Marks**		**Name**	**Marks**	
3	Hughes,J	65	Pass	Harrison,B	98	Pass
4	Turnpike,A	71	Pass	Ross,J	60	Pass
5	Smith,E	49	Fail	Davies,A	86	Pass
6	Daulby,A	61	Pass	Arnold,P	90	Pass
7	Evens,C	85	Pass	Edwards,S	41	Fail
8	Jacobs,E	64	Pass	Cannon,L	31	Fail
9	Doyle, A	27	Fail	Jenkins,P	74	Pass
10	Prescott,S	45	Fail	Denning,J	21	Fail
11	Harris,P	49	Fail			
12						
13	Average =	57.33		Average =	62.63	
14						
15	Highest mark =	85		Highest mark =	98	
16	Lowest mark =	27		Lowest mark =	21	
17						
18						
19						
20	Number of pupils =	9		Number of pupils =	8	

The Lookup function

Lookup functions are very useful; they work as follows. When you enter data the spreadsheet looks through a table until it finds a match along with other important data. For example, if each product in a shop is given a unique number, we can store this number along with a description of the product, price, etc. in a table in another part of the spreadsheet. If we then type in a product number in another part of the spreadsheet, the spreadsheet searches through the table until it locates the product number and related details.

This sounds quite complicated, so let's look at an example.

There are two parts to the worksheet below. The table contains the reference data at the bottom of the sheet (cells A10 to C14) while the working part of the data is at the top (cells A4 to B6).

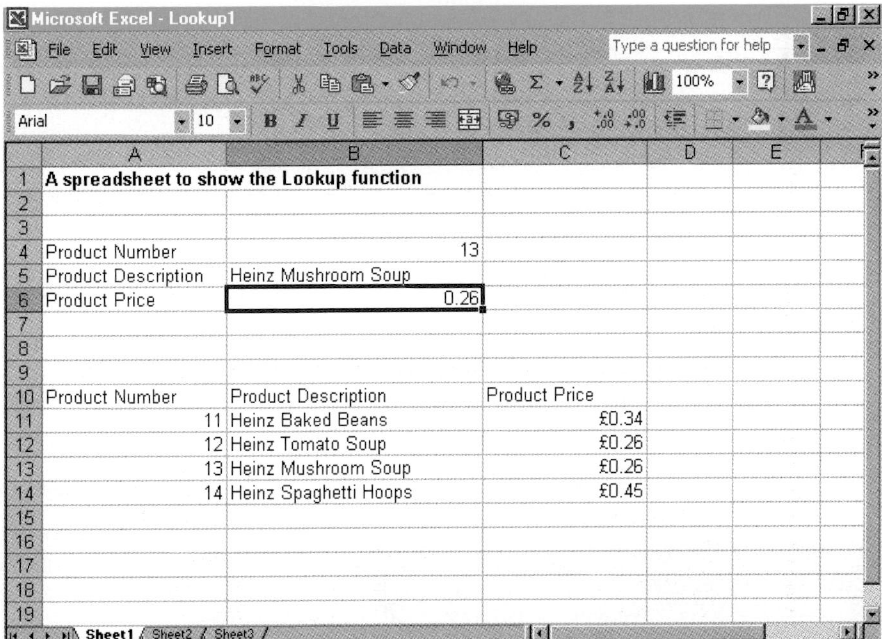

	A	B	C
1	A spreadsheet to show the Lookup function		
2			
3			
4	Product Number	13	
5	Product Description	Heinz Mushroom Soup	
6	Product Price	0.26	
7			
8			
9			
10	Product Number	Product Description	Product Price
11	11	Heinz Baked Beans	£0.34
12	12	Heinz Tomato Soup	£0.26
13	13	Heinz Mushroom Soup	£0.26
14	14	Heinz Spaghetti Hoops	£0.45

Exercise 5.3

Creating a lookup table: supermarket products and prices

In the following spreadsheet you will learn to:

- **create a lookup table and use the VLOOKUP function.**

1 Key in the data exactly as it is shown in the screen above. Do not type in the values for the cells B5 and B6 as these contain formulae that will be entered later.

2 Check that all the data is in the same position as the screen shown and that all the values are the same.

3 Cells B5 and B6 contain formulae. In cell B5 type the following formula:

=VLOOKUP(B4,A11:C14,2,FALSE)

and in cell B6 type the following formula:

=VLOOKUP(B4,A11:C14,3,FALSE)

In order to use the LOOKUP function we have to understand how it works.

Looking at the formula in cell B5, =VLOOKUP(B4,A11:C14,2,FALSE).

Exercise 5.3

B4 is where the data is entered to match a value held in the table of data. In this case we are matching product number 13. A11:C14 is the range of cells where the table of data is located. The number '2' then tells the computer it has to look at the second column in this table to find the data it needs to put into the cell where the formula is.

In cell B6 we have the formula =VLOOKUP(B4,A11:C14,3,FALSE) which is the same as the formula in B5 except for the '3' since the data for the product description is in the third column of the table.

Notice that as soon as the formulae are typed in, the data appears automatically.

4 You should now test your worksheet fully. Test this by entering other values for the item number and see if it produces the correct results. Also, you should test it by entering a product number that is not in the table. What happens?

5 Save your worksheet using a suitable filename and print out two copies, one of the results of the worksheet and the other containing the formulae used.

The two types of LOOKUP function

There are two types of lookup function, called VLOOKUP and HLOOKUP. Which to use depends on whether the data in the table is arranged vertically or horizontally. We have already used a vertical table with the headings at the top of the columns. In the next exercise a worksheet will be constructed.

IT TASKS

Here is a list of the interest rates offered by a leading building society. As you can see, the more money you invest, the higher the interest rate you are offered.

Interest rates applicable to various savings totals

Amount	Interest rate (%)
£10,000	6.70
£20,000	6.80
£40,000	6.95
£100,000	7.10

1 Use a lookup table that will enable you to type in a sum of money and have the correct interest rate appear.

2 Add the following features to your worksheet:
   (a) When you enter the sum of money, the actual amount of interest gained in one year is shown.
   (b) Some people may use a large sum of money to provide them with a monthly income. Include on your worksheet a calculation that will display this. You will need to divide the yearly interest by 12.

An example of the HLOOKUP function: fruit picking

In the following spreadsheet you will learn to:

- **use the HLOOKUP function.**

John has a job over the summer holidays picking fruit. The job is to last six weeks and a variety of fruit will be picked during this period.

John is paid by the number of kilograms of each fruit he picks. The rate per kilogram depends on the type of fruit, according to the following table.

Fruit	Strawberries	Raspberries	Blackcurrants	Grapes	Apples
Rate per kg	£2.25	£3.10	£4.45	£0.60	£0.25

John wants to be able to enter the type of fruit and the weight he has picked for each of the above, and thus work out how much money he will get at the end of the six weeks.

The table above will form the basis of the lookup table. Because this table is arranged horizontally we will need to use the HLOOKUP function.

Before putting the data into a lookup table in the worksheet it will have to be altered slightly. The rates per kilogram must be put into the lookup table in ascending order. The table will not work properly if you do not do this.

1 Open a worksheet and input the data exactly as shown on the screen shot, except do not put the numbers into column C as these will be obtained later.

Microsoft Excel - Book2

	A	B	C	D	E	F	G	H
1	**A spreadsheet to work out John's total wages for the six weeks fruit picking.**							
2								
3	**Fruit**	**Quantity picked (kg)**	**Rate per kg (£)**	**Wage (£)**				
4	Strawberries	125.5	2.25					
5	Blackcurrants	56.75	4.45					
6	Grapes	78.25	0.6					
7	Apples	235.25	0.25					
8	Raspberries	89.5	3.1					
9								
10								
11								
12	Fruit	Apples	Blackcurrants	Grapes	Raspberries	Strawberries		
13	Rate per kg	£0.25	£4.45	£0.60	£3.10	£2.25		
14								
15								
16								

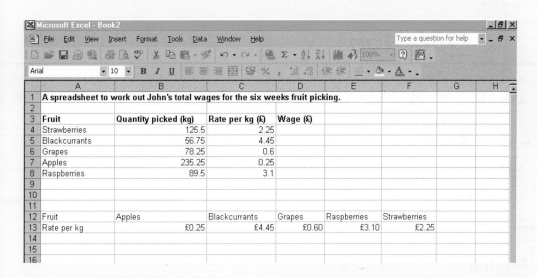

2 In cell C4 enter the following formula:

=HLOOKUP(A4,B12:F13,2,FALSE)

This works by looking for a match between the contents of cell A4 and the data in the cell range from B12 to F13. When a match is found (i.e. it finds 'Strawberries' in the horizontal lookup table), the 2 tells the computer that the data to be inserted is to be found in row 2 of the table. The FALSE part of the function makes sure that if the fruit is not found in the lookup table an alternative will not be used.

Exercise 5.4

3 You now need to produce a similar formula for each of the cells from C5 to C8 inclusive and enter them into the worksheet. Check that these formulae are correct by making sure that the correct data is being picked from the lookup table. Note that you cannot replicate the formula. Each of these has to be typed in separately as each formula will be slightly different.

4 Now enter a formula in cell D4 to calculate the wage. The wage is obtained by multiplying the quantity picked by the rate per kilogram.

Check that this formula gives the right result and then copy the formula relatively down the rest of the column. Again, check the results.

5 John needs to work out the sum of money he will receive for the entire six weeks' work.

In cell C10 place the text **Total wage** and in cell D10 put in a formula to calculate this.

6 The numbers in the spreadsheet now need to be formatted. Weights are formatted to two decimal places. All currency amounts need to be set to two decimal places and also have a pound sign added. Make these adjustments.

7 Save your worksheet and print out a copy on a single page using landscape orientation.

Extra step

Are there any adjustments you can make to this worksheet? Make any such adjustments, save the worksheet and produce a printout.

Questions

1 Mr Einstein, the physics teacher, has just given his class a test. The marks expressed as a percentage are as follows:

Class physics marks

Name of pupil	Mark (%)	Comment
V Adams	63	
S Cohen	49	
B Blackwell	32	
R Theckston	55	
A Prescott	61	
P Doyle	98	
G Williams	41	
D Hughes	25	

Set up a spreadsheet showing the pupils' names and marks and also (using an IF function) a message that will display PASS if their mark is 55% or more and FAIL if they get less than 55%. The messages should be displayed in the comment column.

2 A local quarry supplies rockery stone to garden centres. The table below shows the load size in tonnes. You are required to set up a simple worksheet and then, in the column next to the load size, say whether a large truck or a small truck is needed. A small truck is used for loads of under 1.5 tonnes and a large truck is used for loads of 1.5 tonnes and over.

Rockery stone; load sizes

Load size in tonnes	Truck size
1.50	
3.50	
0.75	
4.50	
1.25	

Calculations using dates

Suppose we want to work out the number of days between two dates. We can do this provided we have entered the date in the format dd/mm/yy. This means that the date 20th December 1999 is entered as 20/12/99. Similarly, 1st April 2001 becomes 01/04/01.

If, as a video library, we wanted to determine quickly what fine should be charged when a video is brought back late, we can subtract the date the video was borrowed from today's date using a formula containing the date function.

Suppose the video was borrowed 20/12/99 and returned 13/01/00, the calculation would be entered as:

=“13/01/00”–“20/12/99”

Notice that the later (i.e. ‘bigger’) date comes first.

Exercise 5.5

Subtracting dates to work out fines in a video library

In the following spreadsheet you will learn to:

- **find the number of days that have elapsed between two dates**
- **change the format of a cell to the number format.**

Let's look at how we can use this. In a video library they need to be able to calculate fines. Using the borrowing and returning dates, the spreadsheet can calculate the number of days late and then multiply this by the fine per day to give the total fine.

1 Load Excel and select New from the file menu.

2 Enter the data exactly as it appears here.

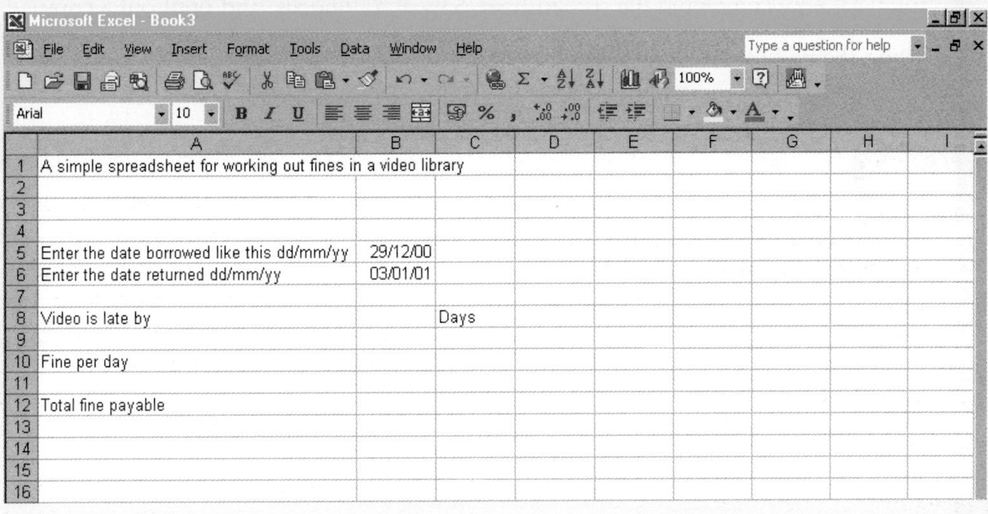

3 In cell B8 enter the formula to subtract the two dates. Remember the latest date comes first. The formula is:

=B6 – B5

When you enter this something unexpected happens. You need to format the cell to give you a number. Go to the format menu on the toolbar and select **cells**.

The following menu (called the format menu) will appear:

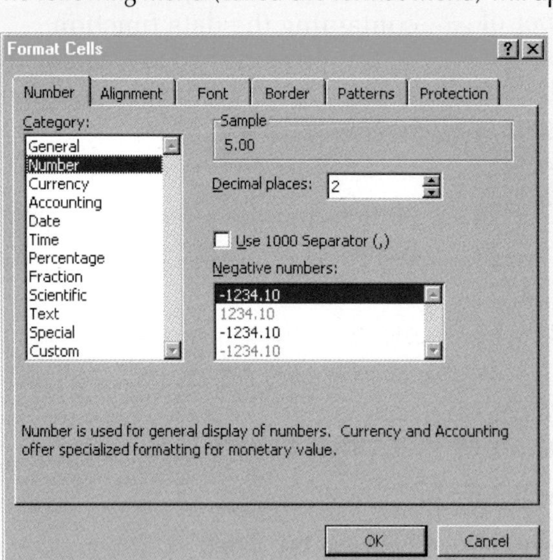

We need to change the format of the result to Number and also to change the decimal places (normally set at two) to zero by clicking on the downward pointing arrow. Click on OK and the result of the calculation will be displayed.

4 Enter **£1.75** as the fine per day into cell B10.

5 Enter the calculation **=B8*B10** into cell B12. This calculates the total fine by multiplying the number of days late by the fine per day.

You have now completed the spreadsheet. Save it as 'fine.xls' and print out a copy.

Check that your worksheet is identical to the one shown below.

	A	B	C
1	A simple spreadsheet for working out fines in a video library		
2			
3			
4			
5	Enter the date borrowed like this dd/mm/yy	29/12/00	
6	Enter the date returned dd/mm/yy	03/01/01	
7			
8	Video is late by	5	Days
9			
10	Fine per day	£1.75	
11			
12	Total fine payable	£8.75	
13			

6 Try changing the return date to the following and write down the answers for the number of days late and the total fine payable:
(a) 31/12/00 (b) 12/01/01
(c) 01/02/01 (d) 04/03/01

7 Video rental prices have increased to £4.00 per night and the fines are normally half of this. Change the fine per day to £2.00 and then use the spreadsheet to calculate the total fine payable for the dates above.

IT TASKS

How many days have elapsed since you were born?

Think about working this out manually. What would you need to know? These same facts will be the inputs to the system.

Also, think about the calculation that would be needed.

As a rough estimate you could try multiplying your age in years by 365. What inaccuracies will there be in doing this?

One problem is that some of the years will be leap years with 366 days. To do the task accurately you would need to take account of this. Two dates would be needed: today's date and your date of birth. If you were doing the task manually you would need to know the numbers of days in each month and also that February contained 29 days in a leap year.

However, the task is very simple for a spreadsheet to perform. For a start it knows what today's date is because the computer contains a calendar from which it also knows which years are leap years. As we have already seen, we are able to subtract two dates to find the number of days between them.

IT TASKS

Produce a spreadsheet to work out the number of days between your date of birth and today's date.

Hint: use the '=Now() date' function to let the spreadsheet know today's date.

Also remember that the cell in which the number of days is calculated will have to be changed from date format to number format.

Another useful function

Suppose you want to borrow some money, perhaps for a new hi-fi, a holiday or a motorcycle. Here are some things you will need to consider:

- How much money need you borrow?
- How long you want to repay the money (called the period of the loan). This is usually expressed in months.
- What is the interest rate (different banks and building societies offer different rates)?

There is a function in Excel to work out the monthly payment, provided you supply the spreadsheet with the above information. The formula is quite simple to enter, but complicated in what it does. We don't need to understand the actual formula as long as we know how to use it.

The essential information has been entered below.
The formula to work out the monthly payment is:

=PMT(B2/12,B3,–B1)

	A	B	C
1	Amount of loan	£2500	
2	Interest rate	11%	
3	Period in months	24	
4			
5	Monthly payment		

This is put in cell B5.

Once the formula has been entered, the monthly payment is automatically displayed.

QUESTIONS

1

	A	B
1	Cost of items	Discount %
2	£500.00	
3	£250.75	
4	£375.60	
5	£130.15	

In the above spreadsheet a discount of 5% is shown in column B if the item in column A is £300 or over, otherwise a discount of 2% is displayed.

In order to do this, what formula needs to be placed in cell B2? You will need to produce a formula to do this.

2 Mr Hughes likes the cars that appear below. He has set up a worksheet containing the names of the cars along with their prices. He cannot pay more than £5000 for a car. Construct a formula containing the IF function so that the messages 'Too expensive' or 'Possible' are displayed next to the cars based on his criterion.

	A	B	C
1	Car	Price	
2	Vauxhall Astra	£4995	
3	Ford Mondeo	£6500	
4	Fiat Bravo	£4775	
5	Nissan Primera	£5750	

3 Look at this worksheet.

	A	B
1	100	Yes
2	125	Yes
3	99	No
4	250	Yes

Using the answers in column B, can you work out an IF function that could have been placed in cell B1 and then copied relatively down the column?

4 The owner of a software company that produces computer games wants to compare the sales of a particular game with the previous year. The value of the sales from the games is shown in the part of the spreadsheet shown here:

	A	B	C	D	E
1	Year 2002	Value of sales	Year 2003	Value of sales	
2	Jan	£23900	Jan	£18980	
3	Feb	£12756	Feb	£13089	
4	Mar	£13098	Mar	£11187	
5	Apr	£20320	Apr	£12908	
6	May	£17200	May	£16352	
7	Jun	£10900	Jun	£12008	
8	Jul	£10050	Jul	£10100	
9	Aug	£13210	Aug		
10	Sep	£26034	Sep		
11	Oct	£30121	Oct		
12	Nov	£40560	Nov		
13	Dec	£53900	Dec		
14					
15	Total sales				
16	Average monthly sales				

(a) (i) Give the formula that would be put in cell B15 to work out the total value of the sales for year 2002.

(ii) Give the formula that would be put in cell B16 to work out the average monthly value of sales for 2002.

(b) It is August 2003 and the owner has just entered the figures for July 2003. She quickly looks over the figures and compares them to the previous year.

She would like to add a message 'UP' or 'DOWN' in column E depending on whether the sales for each month are up or down compared to the previous year.

Describe what she would need to do to display these messages for all the months shown.

(c) The owner would like to be able to predict the value of the sales for the whole year.

(i) Explain how she might do this using the spreadsheet shown.

(ii) Explain why this is an example of modelling.

(iii) In what way could this model be unreliable?

Spreadsheet problems for you to solve

The following problems can be solved using simple spreadsheets and the knowledge and skills you have built up in chapters 1–5.

IT TASKS

Problem 1

Here are the share prices of ten popular shares for two consecutive days. Notice that the prices of some shares have risen whilst others have fallen.

1 Set up a worksheet with the following data:

	A	B	C
1			
2			
3	**Share**	**Day 1**	**Day 2**
4	Abbey National	£12.33	£11.10
5	Halifax	£7.01	£6.84
6	ICI	£6.95	£7.06
7	BT	£10.75	£10.79
8	Tesco	£1.64	£1.63
9	Asda	£2.19	£2.20
10	Prudential	£8.80	£8.90
11	P&O	£9.80	£9.78
12	Alliance and Leic	£8.25	£8.23
13	Utd Utills	£7.80	£7.84

2 In column D work out the difference between the two prices for each share. To do this you subtract the Day 2 price from the Day 1 price.

3 How can you see from these numbers which shares have risen in value and which have fallen?

4 In column E work out the percentage rise/fall. You will need to enter a formula that divides the difference worked out in column D by the original price of the share (the Day 1 price) and then multiply this by 100.

5 We need to draw attention to those shares that have fallen or risen. Devise a function that will work this out from the difference in column D and put the appropriate message 'Risen' or 'Fallen' in column F.

(Hint: test whether the number in column D is positive or negative.)

6 Try to improve the presentation of this worksheet.

7 Save and print a copy of your worksheet.

IT TASKS

Problem 2

The headteacher is asking you for help!

The headteacher of your school has a problem. There is to be a special prize (or prizes) at the annual 'Prize Giving' to be given to the pupil (or pupils) with the best GCSE results in the school.

The headteacher has a list of all the GCSE results for each pupil arranged as shown below.

Example from headteacher's GCSE results list

E Richards		S Spencer	
English Language	C	English Language	D
English Literature	C	English Literature	C
Maths	D	Maths	B
Single Science	C	Single Science	B
French	E	Spanish	F
History	D	History	E
Art	A	IT	C
CDT	B	Geography	D
RE	E	Home Economics	G

His problem is how to tell which of these two pupils has done better? He thinks about this problem and comes up with the following solution. He will use a points system where each grade is allocated a certain number of points and the points for each pupil added up to give the total for all subjects. It should then be possible to put the pupils into an order and spot those who have done the best.

He decides to allocate the following numbers of points to each GCSE grade:

A* = 10	D = 6
A = 9	E = 5
B = 8	F = 4
C = 7	G = 3

Your task

Hint: You will need to use a LOOKUP table to do the following tasks.

1 Set up a spreadsheet and key in the results of the two pupils shown above.

2 Make the next column a points column with the points for each grade.

3 Use formulae to add up the points to give the total for each pupil.

4 Use your spreadsheet to decide which of the two pupils did best in their results.

What we have done here is to create a model and use this model to help the headteacher make a decision. This is a simple model but later we will be looking at more sophisticated ones.

Advanced Spreadsheet Features

By now you will have developed skills in many of Excel's features; this chapter looks at some of the more advanced features. You may need some of these when developing your GCSE coursework.

Using logic in your spreadsheets

In Chapter 5 you saw that you can use the spreadsheet to make simple logical decisions. For example =IF(A2<0,"Account overdrawn","Account in credit") tests cell A2 to see if it is less than 0. If true the message 'Account overdrawn' appears, if false the message is 'Account in credit'. The use of these can be extended by combining them with the logical expressions AND and OR so that more than one condition is tested.

Combining conditions with AND

If you want to perform a calculation or produce a message only when two conditions are true, then you can use the AND() function.

The following exercise uses the AND() function.

Exercise 6.1

Using the AND() function

In the following exercise you will learn how to:

- **use the AND() function with two conditions to determine which of two messages is displayed.**

The worksheet below shows a list of candidates for a job. To get an interview the candidate must have GCSEs in both English and mathematics at grade C or above.

1 Start a new worksheet and enter the data exactly as it appears below.

	A	B	C
1			
2	**Name of candidate**	**English GCSE (C and above)**	**Maths GCSE (C and above)**
3	Hepworth, G	Yes	No
4	Hughes, A	Yes	Yes
5	Adams, G	No	No
6	Jones, D	No	Yes
7	Carrington, A	No	Yes
8	Larkhill, B	Yes	Yes
9	Hardaker, H	Yes	Yes
10	Pillans, N	Yes	No
11	Quayle, M	Yes	Yes
12	Williams, A	Yes	No
13	Woods, J	Yes	Yes
14	Forrest, Y	Yes	Yes
15			

▶▶

2 In cell D3 we need the message 'Yes' to appear if the data in cells B3 and C3 are both Yes. The formula to do this is as follows:

=IF(AND(B3="Yes",C3="Yes"),"Yes","No")

Notice how this formula works. The innermost brackets contain the two conditions to be tested. In this case we are checking to see if both cells have Yes in them. After these brackets is placed (in inverted commas) the message to be printed if the conditions in the brackets are true. After this comes the message for the false condition (i.e. "No").

Enter the above formula into cell D3.

This is what the formula looks like.

	A	B	C	D
1				
2	**Name of candidate**	**English GCSE (C and above)**	**Maths GCSE (C and above)**	
3	Hepworth, G	Yes	No	=IF(AND(B3="Yes",C3="Yes"),"Yes","No")
4	Hughes, A	Yes	Yes	
5	Adams, G	No	No	
6	Jones, D	No	Yes	
7	Carrington, A	No	Yes	
8	Larkhill, B	Yes	Yes	
9	Hardaker, H	Yes	Yes	
10	Pillans, N	Yes	No	
11	Quayle, M	Yes	Yes	
12	Williams, A	Yes	No	
13	Woods, J	Yes	Yes	
14	Forrest, Y	Yes	Yes	
15				

3 Copy this formula relatively down column D for all the other candidates.

Your worksheet should now look like the one shown.

	A	B	C	D
1				
2	**Name of candidate**	**English GCSE (C and above)**	**Maths GCSE (C and above)**	**Interview?**
3	Hepworth, G	Yes	No	No
4	Hughes, A	Yes	Yes	Yes
5	Adams, G	No	No	No
6	Jones, D	No	Yes	No
7	Carrington, A	No	Yes	No
8	Larkhill, B	Yes	Yes	Yes
9	Hardaker, H	Yes	Yes	Yes
10	Pillans, N	Yes	No	No
11	Quayle, M	Yes	Yes	Yes
12	Williams, A	Yes	No	No
13	Woods, J	Yes	Yes	Yes
14	Forrest, Y	Yes	Yes	Yes

IT TASKS

A cosmetics company sells cosmetics to customers via agents. The agents are entitled to a free weekend holiday for two people if either they have been with the company for five years or more or have had orders to a total value of £6000 in the previous twelve months.

The worksheet below shows a table of the agents' names, how long they have been agents and the value of their orders over the previous twelve months. To save time, the names are the same as those used in the last exercise so you can just delete parts of the worksheet not needed.

	A	B	C
1			
2		**Number of years as an agent**	**Value of orders in last 12 months**
3	Hepworth, G	12	£6,000
4	Hughes, A	2	£1,298
5	Adams, G	1	£4,598
6	Jones, D	5	£6,004
7	Carrington, A	28	£12,320
8	Larkhill, B	13	£14,982
9	Hardaker, H	25	£4,781
10	Pillans, N	30	£5,934
11	Quayle, M	24	£10,093
12	Williams, A	1	£14,500
13	Woods, J	4	£9,761
14	Forrest, Y	4	£4,921

Using an OR() function, in a similar way to the AND() function in the last exercise, devise a formula and a spreadsheet to determine if the agents in the table are entitled to a free holiday or not.

Important note: when testing to see if the value of the orders in the last twelve months is greater than or equal to £6000, do not include the £ sign in the expression, even though it appears in the worksheet.

A simple expert system

Expert systems are programs that mimic the intelligence of a human expert in a specific field of knowledge. It is quite easy to develop a very simple expert system using a spreadsheet.

Exercise 6.2

Developing a simple expert system

In the following spreadsheet you will learn to:

- **use the AND() function to test many conditions**
- **thoroughly test a solution to a problem.**

1 Load the spreadsheet and input the data as shown below.

	A	B	C	D	E
1	A very simple expert system				
2					
3	Is the weather going to be nice today?				Yes
4	Do I have school today?				No
5	Do I have over £10?				Yes
6	Is my friend free today?				Yes
7					

2 Enter the following formula into cell E9:

=IF(AND(E3="Yes",E4="No",E5="Yes",E6="Yes"),"Go to the beach","Stay at home")

3 When the formula is entered the message 'Go to the beach' will appear.

4 Alter the answer to the question 'Is the weather going to be nice today' to 'No' in cell E3. Check that the message in cell E9 changes to 'Stay at home'.

5 Thoroughly test the solution by using other combinations of Yes and No for cells from E3 to E6.

IT TASKS

Produce a spreadsheet to act as a simple expert system to troubleshoot printer problems.

Here is a list of the common problems:

- power is not switched on
- cable between the printer and the computer missing or not connected properly
- a paper jam has been left by the previous user.

Cell comments

Many people have to produce spreadsheets for others to use. It is therefore important to make these spreadsheets easy to use. Cell comments are useful because they allow you to add comments to data or calculations in the spreadsheet. These comments can be used to add background information.

Exercise 6.3

Adding comments to a spreadsheet

In the following spreadsheet you will learn to:

- **add a cell comment to a cell**
- **view a cell comment**
- **edit a cell comment.**

A large electrical store sets targets for their sales staff. At the end of each month they review the actual sales with the targeted sales for each member of staff.

1 You first need some data. Set up a new worksheet and enter the data shown at the right. Embolden each of the headings as shown.

	A	B	C	D	E
1	**Sales targets and actual sales for sales staff at LowPrice Electricals**				
2	**For November 2002**				
3					
4	**Salesperson**	**Sales target**	**Actual sales**		
5	Jenny Hughes	£20,000	£25,876		
6	John Jeffries	£30,000	£30,545		
7	Mark Doyle	£18,000	£17,420		
8	Rachel Smith	£30,000	£40,564		
9	Joan Jackson	£25,000	£35,900		
10	Amy Lee	£18,000	£20,890		
11					

2 Amy Lee was off work for a fortnight during this month. The sales manager wants to put a comment into this worksheet to remind her of this.

Move to the cell containing Amy's actual sales (i.e. cell C10).

3 Click on Insert in the menu bar and then select Comment.

4 A comment box with your name in (showing who is making the comment) appears. You should change the name to your own, if necessary.

Exercise 6.3

	A	B	C	D	E
1	Sales targets and actual sales for sales staff at LowPrice Electricals				
2	For November 2002				
3					
4	Salesperson	Sales target	Actual sales		
5	Jenny Hughes	£20,000	£25,876		
6	John Jeffries	£30,000	£30,545		
7	Mark Doyle	£18,000	£17,420		
8	Rachel Smith	£30,000	£40,564		
9	Joan Jackson	£25,000	£35,900	Stephen Doyle:	
10	Amy Lee	£18,000	£20,890		
11					
12					
13					
14					

5 You now type the following comments into the box:

This figure is only for two weeks' sales as Amy was off sick for a fortnight.

Your comments will appear in the box like this:

	A	B	C	D	E
1	Sales targets and actual sales for sales staff at LowPrice Electricals				
2	For November 2002				
3					
4	Salesperson	Sales target	Actual sales		
5	Jenny Hughes	£20,000	£25,876		
6	John Jeffries	£30,000	£30,545		
7	Mark Doyle	£18,000	£17,420		
8	Rachel Smith	£30,000	£40,564		
9	Joan Jackson	£25,000	£35,900	Stephen Doyle: This figure is only for two weeks' sales as Amy was off sick for a fortnight.	
10	Amy Lee	£18,000	£20,890		
11					
12					
13					

Notice the red comment indicator at the corner of the cell. This shows that there is a comment for this cell.

6 Click anywhere on the worksheet outside the comment box and the comment box will disappear.

7 To view a cell comment, move the cursor to the cell containing the comment (cell C10 in this case). The cell comment is automatically displayed.

8 The sales manager wants to add some further information in the comment box. To edit the comment box, move to cell C10 and then click on Insert in the menu bar and then on Edit Comment. The comment box now appears and you are able to type in further information.

£35,900	Stephen Doyle: This figure is only for two weeks' sales as Amy was off sick for a fortnight.	
£20,890		

Type in the following:

Must congratulate her on this performance.

Exercise 6.3

Your comment box will now look like this:

£35,900
£20,890
This figure is only for two weeks sales as Amy was off sick for a fortnight. Must congratulate her on this performance.

9 Click on another part of the worksheet.

Now move the pointer to the cell containing the comment (i.e. cell C10).

The comment now appears but not all of it is shown.

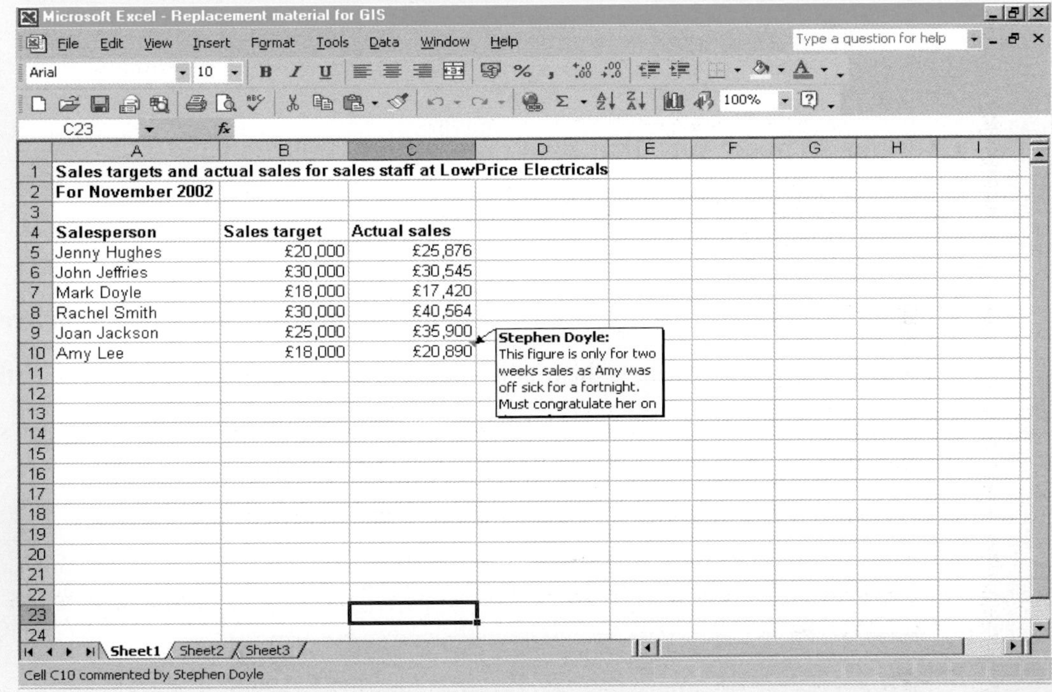

We need to make the comment box bigger.

To do this click on cell C10 and then click on Insert in the menu bar and then on Edit Comment. The comment box appears.

10 Notice the small circles around the box. Click on a circle at the corner and drag to re-size the box until all the text is shown like this.

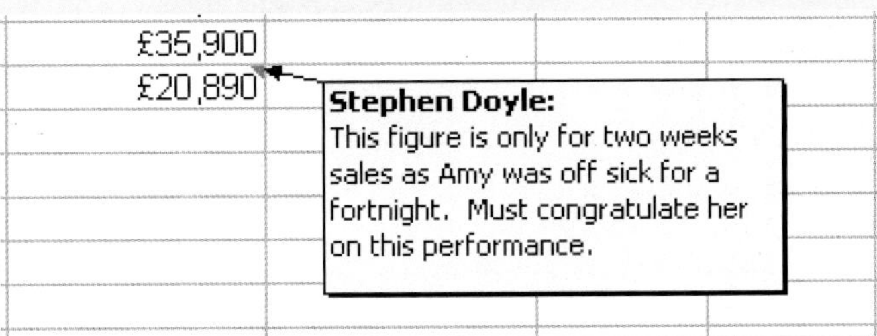

Check that the comment box works.

Data validation

With many spreadsheets, the final user has to type in some data. An example of this might be a spreadsheet to work out loan repayments. The user types in the amount of the loan required and the period over which the money is to be repaid.

It is important that only valid data is entered. For example, you might not be able to borrow money over a period greater than five years or an amount greater than £10 000.

Validation checks are used to restrict the user in some way when entering data. Validation checks are used to make sure that data that is completely incorrect is not processed.

Exercise 6.4

Checking to make sure that data entered into cells is valid

In this exercise you will learn how to:

- **put a validation check into a cell**
- **produce a message to inform the user about the type of data that is allowable in a certain cell**
- **produce a message that alerts the user if they try to enter data that breaks the validation rules.**

1 Open a new worksheet and move the cursor to cell A2. This is the cell where a pupil's age is to be entered.

Click on Data and then Validation. The following data validation menu appears:

Data Validation
Settings | Input Message | Error Alert
Validation criteria
Allow:
Any value
Ignore blank
Data:
between
Apply these changes to all other cells with the same settings
Clear All | OK | Cancel

2 Click on the pulldown menu for Allow and the following menu appears. Here you can pick the type of data that you will allow to be put into the cell.

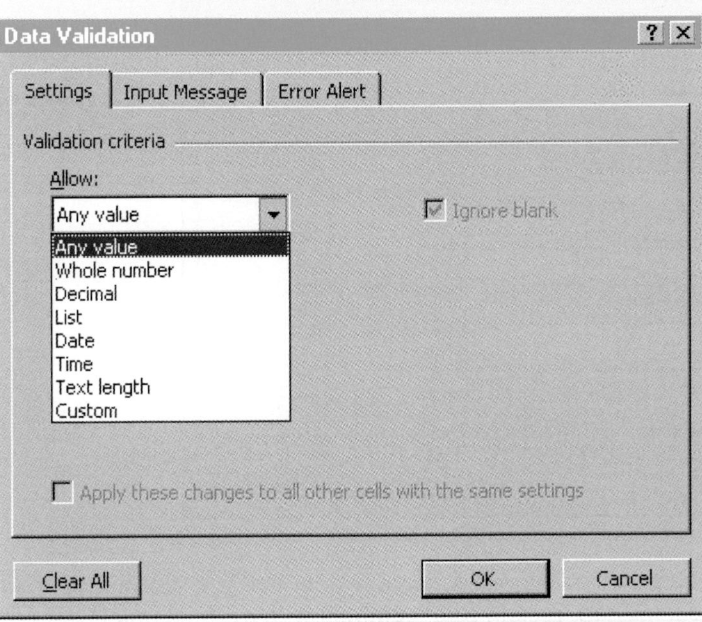

3 Select Whole number from this menu and then click on the pulldown menu for Data.

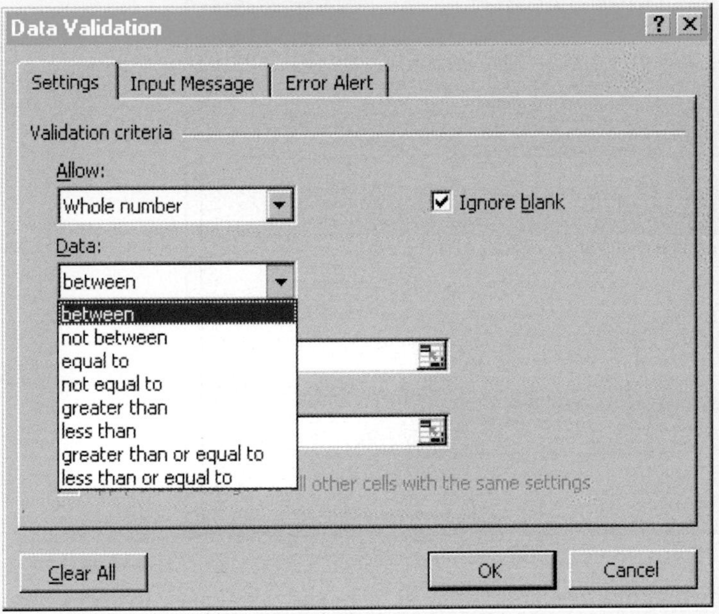

4 We want to validate the age so that only whole numbers between 11 and 19 can be entered into cell A2.

Enter **11** in the Minimum section and **19** in the Maximum section, then click on OK.

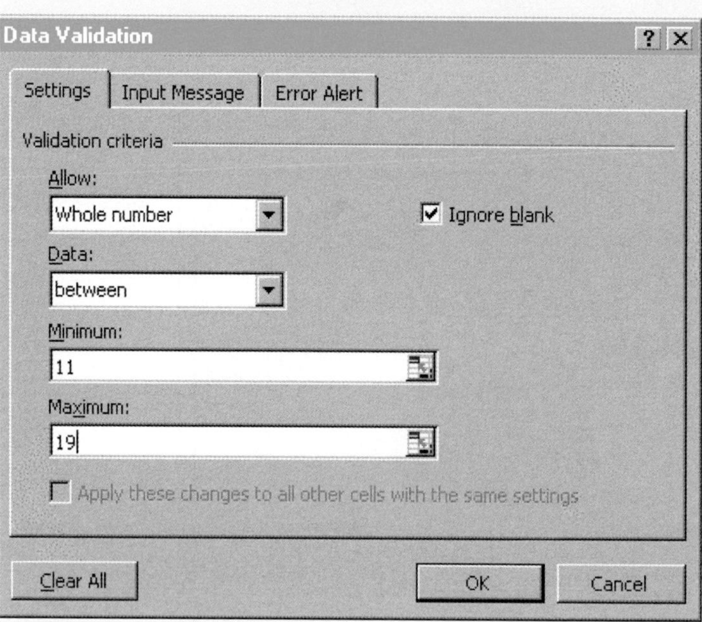

5 Click on Input Message in the Data Validation menu. In the Title section type in **Enter a whole number**. In the Input message section type **Numbers with decimal points are not allowed for this cell**.

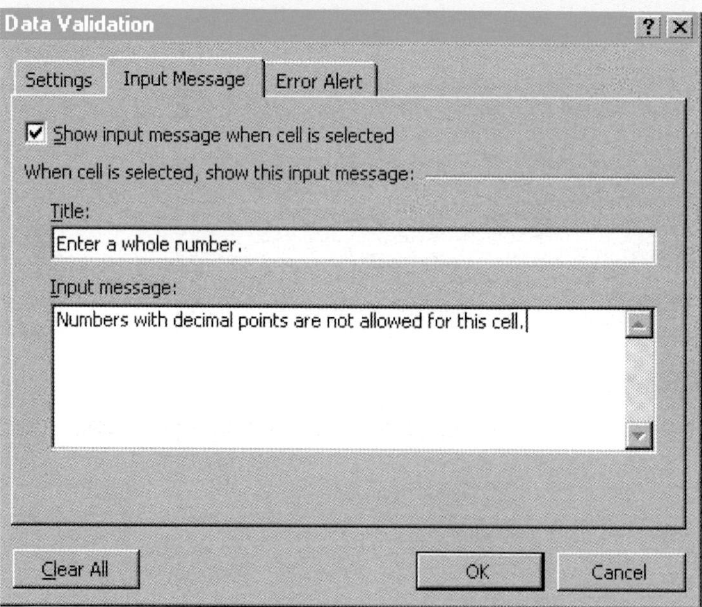

6 Check that the title and message are displayed by moving the cursor to cell A2. You should see the following message to guide the user:

'**Enter a whole number.** Numbers with decimal points are not allowed for in this cell!'

7 Now enter too high a number (above 19) into cell A2. The following menu appears. Click on Retry and then enter a number too low (below 11). The same menu should appear. If you type in a number between 11 and 19, it should be accepted.

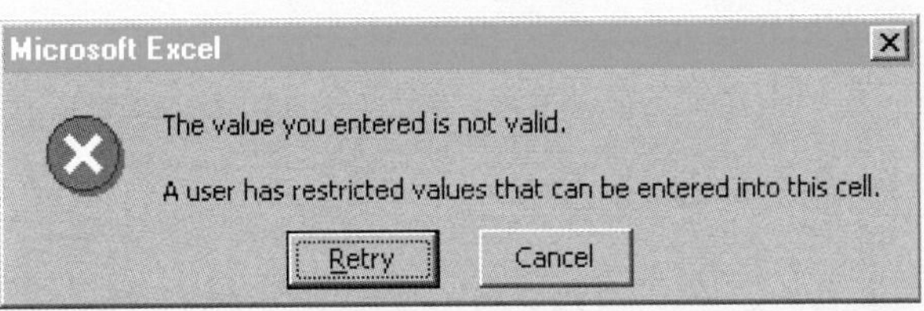

8 Go back to the Data Validation menu. Select Error Alert. Enter the following into the Title section: **A whole number must be entered**.

In the Error message section type in the following: **This cell must have a whole number entered into it. Please re-enter**.

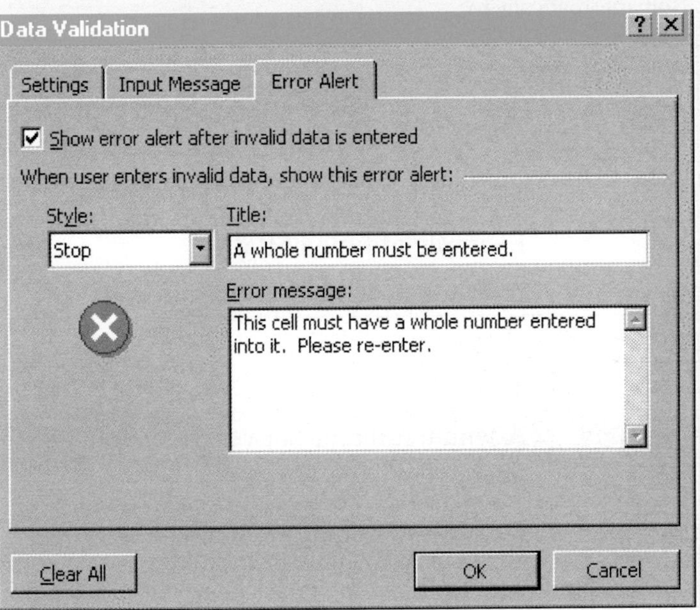

9 Now enter invalid data into cell A2 and make sure that the following message is displayed.

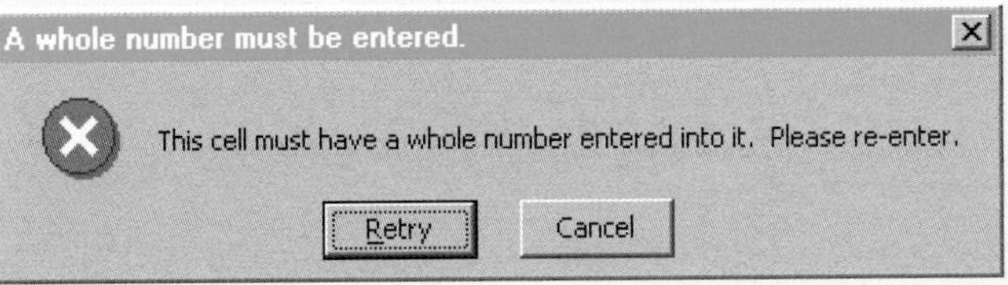

Exercise 6.5

Checking data used for calculating course fees

In this exercise you will:

- **practise creating validation checks for different types of data**
- **test the validation checks.**

This screen shows a spreadsheet used by a college for their part-time courses to calculate the fee that each student should pay.

	A	B	C	D
1	**Course fee calculation**			
2				
3	Enrolment Number			
4	Forename			
5	Surname			
6	Date of birth			
7				
8	Number of hours study			
9	Rate per hour			
10				
11	Total fee payable			

1 Set up the spreadsheet exactly as it is shown here. Increase to 16 point the font size of the title 'Course fee calculation' and embolden it. Notice that the cell height adjusts itself automatically to accommodate the larger text.

2 The example data that is to be entered into the cells in this worksheet is shown below.

Data	Example of type of data
Student number	A five digit whole number (e.g. 94523)
Surname	Text
Forename	Text
Number of hours study	A whole number between one and 16
Rate per hour	£3.35
Total fee payable	Less than or equal to £53.60

Using the table as a guide, produce suitable validation checks for the cells B3, B4, B5, B6, B8, B9 and B11. Enter the checks and fill in the Input Message and Error Alert boxes.

3 Thoroughly test your solutions by entering some data which is valid and some which is invalid for each of the cells mentioned above.

QUESTIONS

1 (a) Explain the purpose of a validation check.

(b) Here are some of the main types of checks you can use with the spreadsheet Excel:

- Character type check – used to make sure that the right sorts of characters are entered.
- Range checks – used to make sure that numbers are within a certain range.

What other checks may be performed on the data entered into a spreadsheet?

Displaying your Data Pictorially

Thus far we have improved the presentation of data by using borders, different type sizes and fonts. Although the data may look more presentable, it is still just figures and text.

If you look at the way newspapers and magazines present data, they nearly always do so pictorially, using graphs and charts.

Figure 7.1 shows some of the many ways in which data is presented pictorially. Can you name these types of chart?

Using Excel you can produce many attractive charts and graphs. To do this you need some data. The data can either be set up specially or you can use data from an existing worksheet.

In this chapter you will learn some of the skills needed to set up charts. Creating charts is a bit like producing a picture, since you can always improve them in some way. To find out more than this chapter covers, you will need to experiment and also use the help menu.

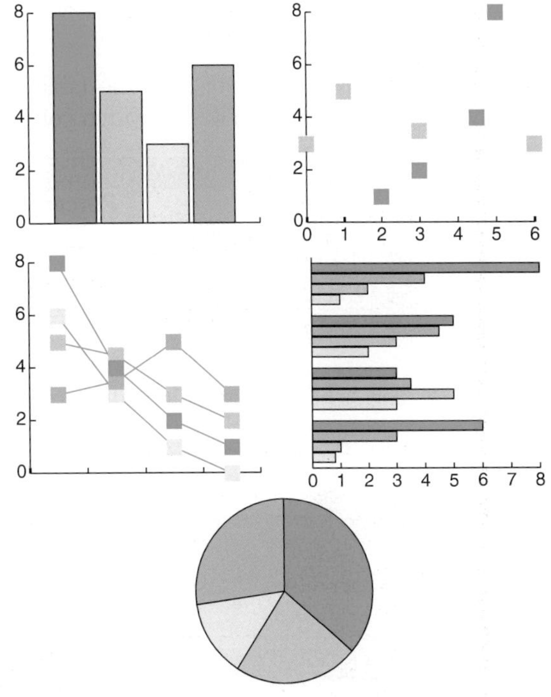

Figure 7.1 *Data is often presented in graphical form*

Exercise 7.1

Producing a pie chart: smoking habits of young girls

In this exercise you will learn how to:

- **select data to produce a chart**
- **use the chart wizard**
- **produce a pie chart**
- **size and move a chart.**

A magazine contains an article on teenage smoking. The writer of the magazine article was particularly concerned about smoking by young girls. A survey was carried out among 11–12-year-old girls the data from which is shown below.

Response	Percentage of 11–12-year-old-girls
Have never smoked	75.2
Used to smoke	21.5
Would like to give up	3.1
Don't want to give up	0.4

Notice that the figures in the table do not add up to 100 because they have been rounded to one decimal place. Do not worry about this as it often happens when working out percentages for pie charts.

When there are only a few items of data, it is often best to present the data as a pie chart. Pie charts are chosen when we want to show what makes up a whole something. In this case the 'whole something' is all the 11–12-year-old girls questioned.

Producing the pie chart

1 First type the data from the table on the previous page into a worksheet exactly as shown below. You will need to widen columns A and B to accommodate the titles.

	A	B
1	**Response**	**Percentage of 11-12 year-old girls**
2	Have never smoked	75.2
3	Used to smoke	21.5
4	Would like to give up	3.1
5	Don't want to give up	0.4

2 Highlight all the data including the titles.

3 Click on the Chart Wizard icon, [icon], on the standard toolbar.

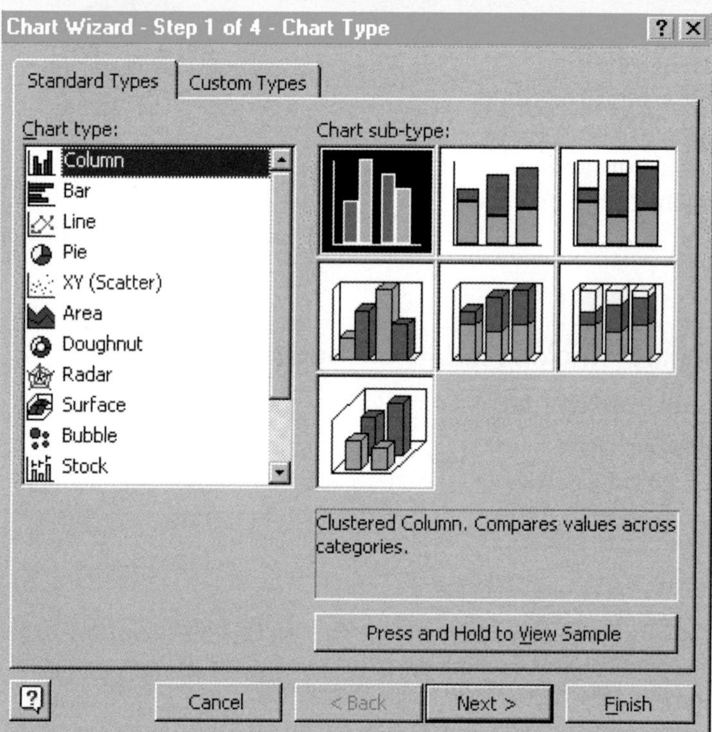

The above menu pops up. Choose Pie from the Chart type menu.

4 From the following menu, showing a variety of different pie charts, choose a sub-type.

Click on the one highlighted to select a pie with a 3D visual effect. Notice that when you click on Pie in the Chart type menu, on the right of the screen a new menu appears called the Chart

sub-type menu. This menu allows you to choose a particular type of pie chart (3D, exploded etc.)

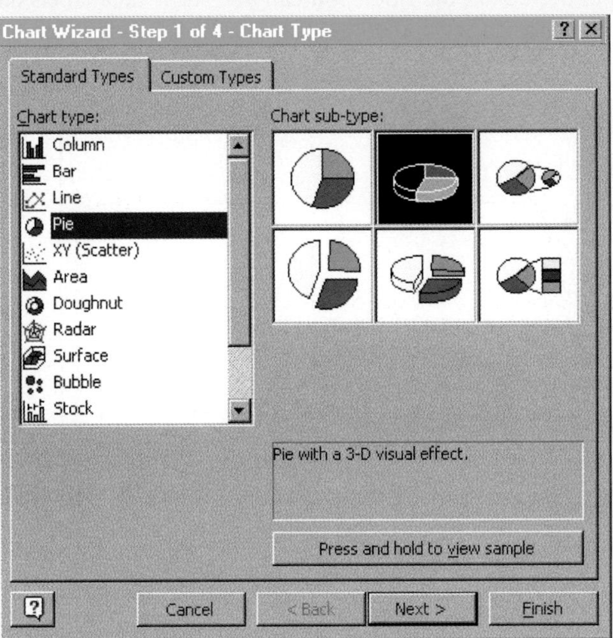

Click on the button 'Press and hold to view sample' and keep the button held down. Now you can see what the pie chart will look like. You can of course change your mind at this stage and choose one of the other pie chart designs to see which looks the best.

When you are happy, click Next>.

5 The following menu appears:

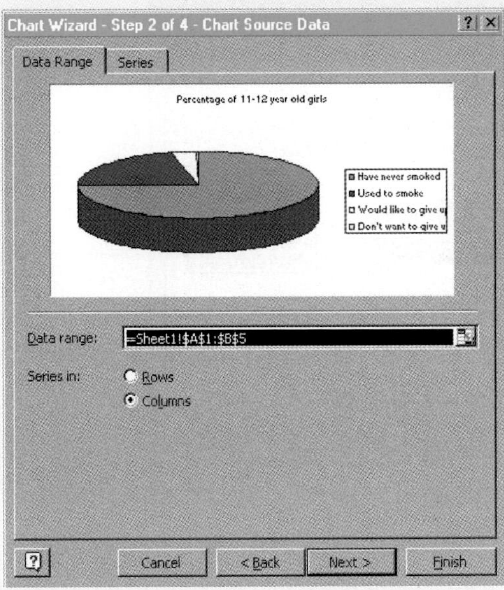

Check that the pie chart is OK and then click on Next>.

Exercise 7.1

6 The menu below now appears, in which you are able to make changes to the title of the chart and also to the legend (the legend is the explanation of what each sector of the pie chart represents and this is shown in the box at the side). You can also show data labels (i.e. the actual values of the data or percentages) by clicking on the Data Labels tab at the top of the screen.

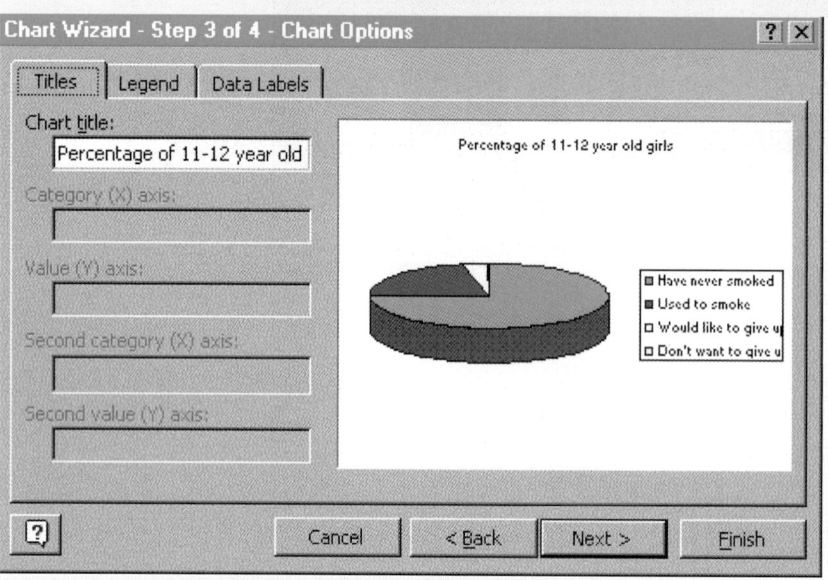

Click Data Labels and the following screen appears.

Choose Show value (since the data is already expressed as a percentage).

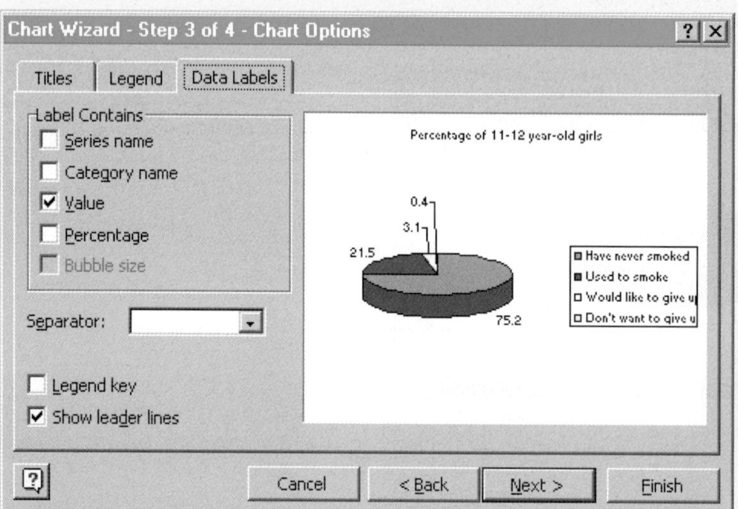

You can try experimenting with some of the options on this menu. Notice that if you choose Percentage the figures are displayed with a percentage sign and also that the values are shown to the nearest whole number. Under this setting, using the number 0.4 will result in 0 being displayed as a data value which is not suitable for this pie chart.

7 Now click on Next>.

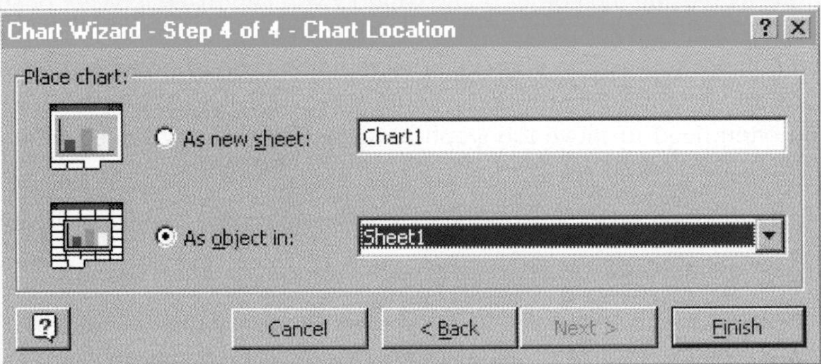

We can either save the chart in its own sheet or put it into the sheet containing the data. When in its own sheet the pie chart will appear on its own. When the chart is put in the same sheet as the data a box is produced near the data for the chart to be drawn in.

We will put it with the data.

Now click on Finish.

8 The pie chart now appears alongside the data in the table. Your worksheet should now look like this:

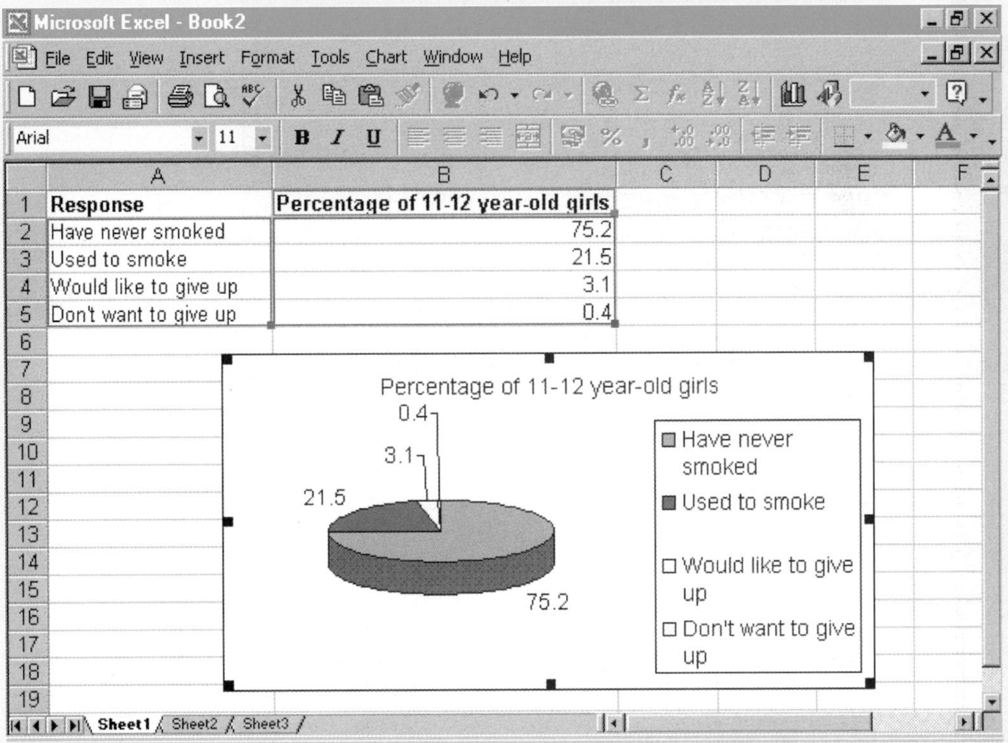

Sizing and moving the graph

9 To size the graph, click on the corner of the main box and you should see a double-headed, diagonal arrow. By moving the corner of the window you can make it bigger or smaller. If you want to move the entire graph, click inside the window and you will see a four headed arrow and a dotted outline. You can now move the dotted rectangle to position the graph by using handles which are the small squares at the corners and in the middle of the edges of the box selected. You often need to move the graph because it is covering some of the data in your worksheet.

10 Check the chart and then save the worksheet under the filename 'Smoking Survey Pie Chart'.

11 Print out a copy of the worksheet on a single page in landscape orientation.

12 Now print a copy of just the chart. To do this double click anywhere in the white background of the chart. Click on the Properties tab and the following screen appears:

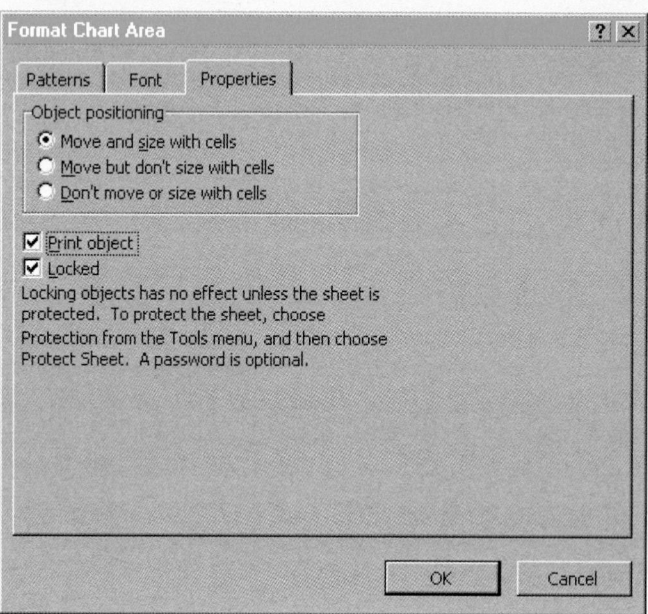

13 Make sure that there is a tick in the Print object box and click on OK.

14 Now print in the usual way and just the chart will be printed.

Producing a 3-D bar chart: garden centre sales

In this exercise you will learn how to:

- **enter the data in a suitable way for a 3-D bar chart**
- **set up the 3-D bar chart**
- **place the 3-D bar chart in its own sheet rather than with the data.**

The following worksheet contains data concerning sales in the various departments of a garden centre for the four seasons of the year.

	A	B	C	D	E
1		Spring	Summer	Autumn	Winter
2					
3	Seasonal	9800	14500	15600	21900
4	Plants	21800	36900	14500	2800
5	Tools	8900	12700	6400	3900
6	Compost/Fertiliser	10900	12300	6100	1900

The data looks a bit dry and needs to be livened up for an important meeting. The best way to do this is to present it pictorially. We could use a 3D bar chart with four bar charts representing the sales for each of the departments for the four seasons. Thus it will be four groups of four bar charts.

1 Load the spreadsheet software and enter the data above into the worksheet exactly as it appears.

2 Highlight all the data in the worksheet (including all the row and column headings). In this case you need to highlight those cells from A1 to E6.

3 Click on the chart wizard icon in the standard toolbar. Select the chart type bar and the chart sub-type clustered bar with a 3-D visual effect.

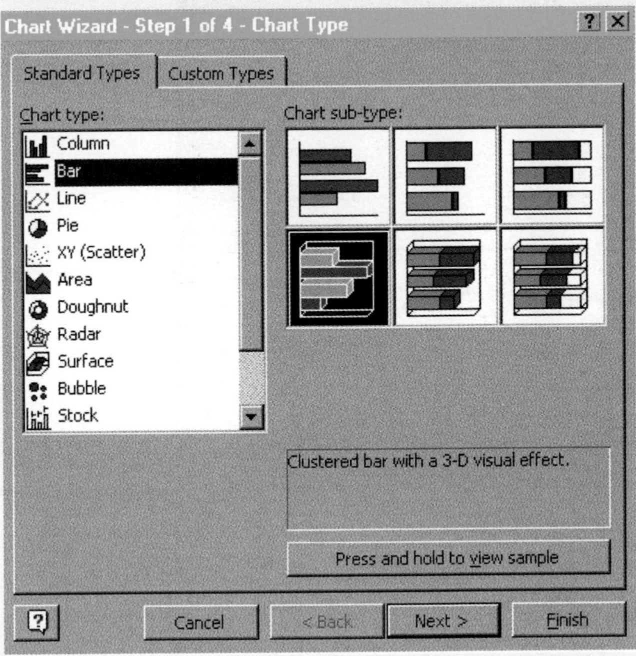

Check that your screen looks the same as the screen on the previous page. You can view the chart by clicking on the button marked Press and hold to view sample.

Click on Next > to move on to the next step.

4 Click on Series: in Rows in step 2 of the chart wizard (see the screen below). This tells Excel that we want to group the data according to the rows. Since the seasons (spring, summer, etc.) represent the rows, the products will be grouped according to the seasons.

If you chose Series: in Columns, the data would be grouped under the departments (Seasonal, Plants etc.)

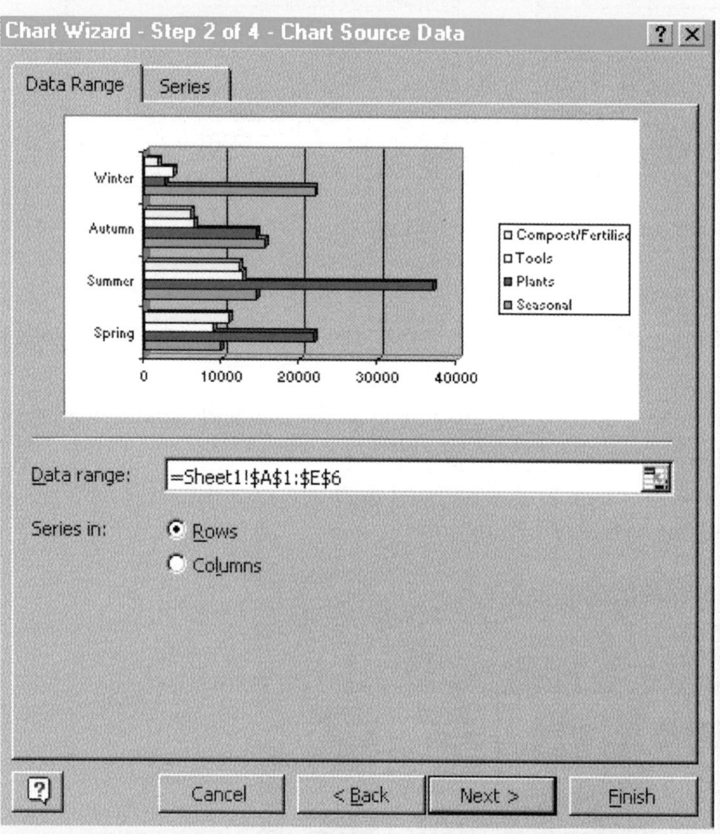

Now click on Next >.

5 The step 3 menu for the chart wizard now appears as shown at the top of the next page.

You can now add a title for your chart. Type in **Department sales by season for 1999** as the title for the chart.

Also, for the Category (X) axis, type in the following name **Value of sales in £**. This will tell the reader what the numbers along the horizontal axis represent.

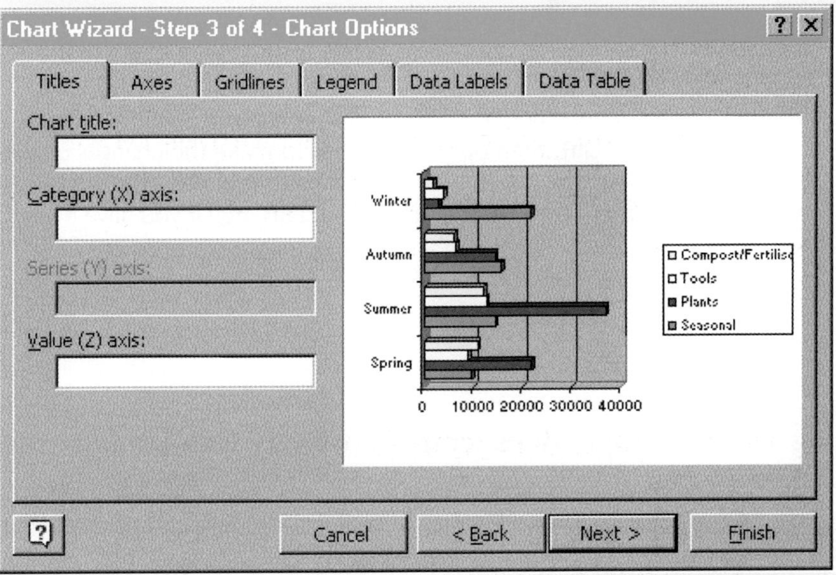

Notice that these changes appear on the diagram so you can check them.

Click on Next.

6 Instead of putting the chart with the data, we will put it in its own sheet. This means the chart will appear on a new worksheet on its own.

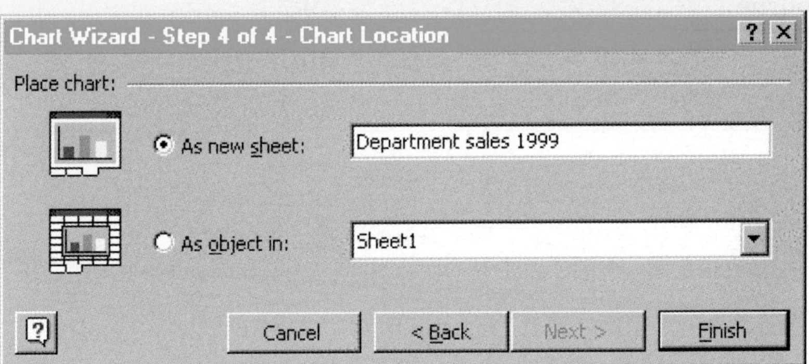

Click on As new sheet and enter the title of this new sheet as **Department sales 1999** into the space as shown above.

7 Save your chart and then print out a copy.

IT TASKS

There are many ways in which the appearance of charts, including this one, can be improved. Click once to select any relevant sections of the chart, then open the menus to make the changes or double click for the menu options to open. By changing options in these menus you should be able to improve the chart's appearance. Many of the options refer to the colour (background, bars etc.) If you have a colour printer see which colours go best together.

Exercise 7.3

Producing a scatter graph: does temperature vary with latitude south of the equator?

Here is a list of some cities in Australia along with their latitude south of the equator and their annual mean temperature.

City	Latitude (°S)	Annual mean temperature in degrees Celsius
Sydney	33.9	21.4
Adelaide	34.9	22.4
Hobart	42.8	16.7
Perth	32.0	23.1
Brisbane	27.4	25.4
Melbourne	37.7	19.7
Darwin	12.3	32.3
Canberra	35.3	19.3

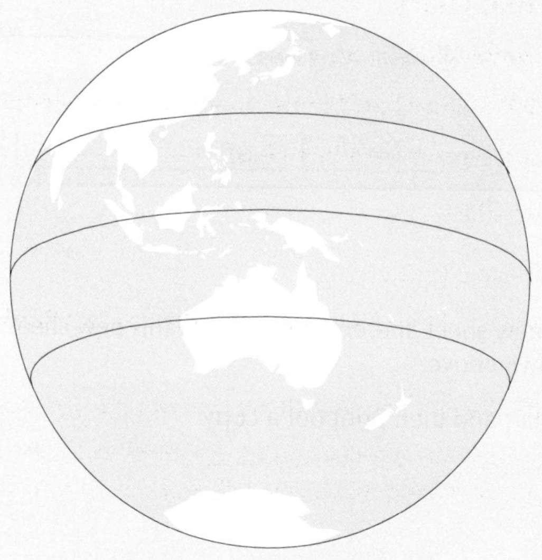

Exercise 7.3

Hypothesis: the further south you go in the southern hemisphere, the lower the temperature as you go further from the equator and nearer the South Pole

Rather than trying to see a trend in the data in the table, it is easier to plot a scatter graph and see whether our hypothesis looks right.

1 Key the above data into your worksheet.

2 Select the two last columns (including titles).

3 Click on the chart wizard icon (the one with a bar chart on it) on the standard toolbar. You can now select the chart type.

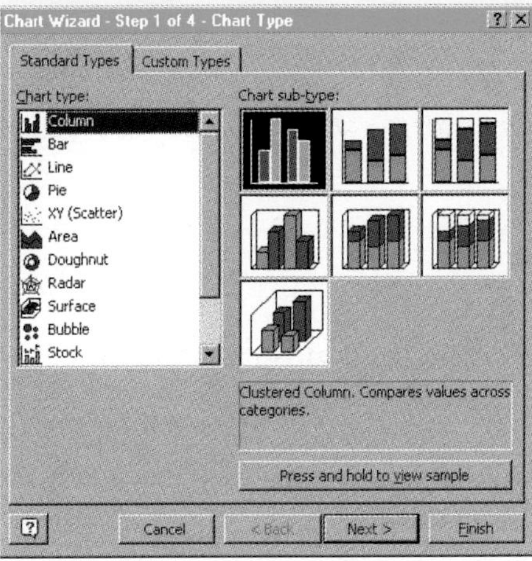

4 Choose XY(Scatter) from this menu and click on Next>.

5 What does the scatter graph you have produced show?

Exercise 7.4

Producing a line chart

In this exercise you will learn how to:

- **use the AutoFill feature to fill in the months of the year automatically**
- **set up the data to produce a line chart**
- **produce a line chart.**

1 Start with a new worksheet.

2 Across the first row of the worksheet enter the heading **Book sales each month for 2000–2001**. Make this bold.

3 In cell A2 enter the heading **Month** and in cell B2 enter the heading **Sales**.

4 In cell A3 enter **Jan**. We use the AutoFill facility to fill in all other months automatically. To do this click on cell A3 to make it the active cell. You should now see a bold rectangle around this cell.

Move the cursor to the bottom right-hand corner of the bold rectangle and position it over the outer fill handle; you will see that the cursor changes to a cross. Keeping your left mouse button pressed down, drag down the column and you will see the months change as you do this. Stop when you get to December and take your finger off the mouse button and all the months will be inserted. AutoFill is a really useful feature and can save a lot of unnecessary typing.

Your worksheet should now look like this.

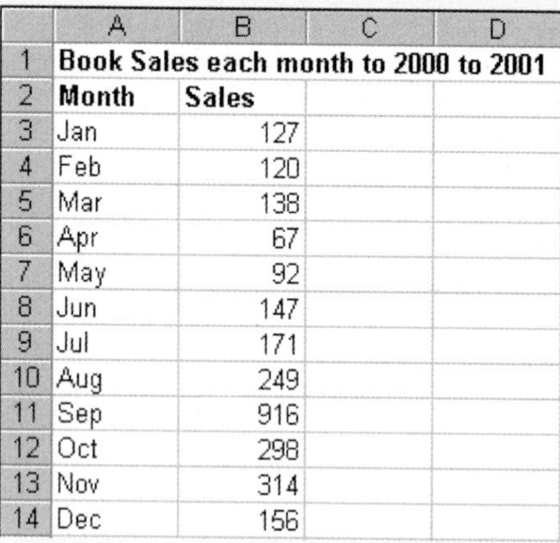

	A	B	C	D
1	**Book Sales each month to 2000 to 2001**			
2	**Month**	**Sales**		
3	Jan	127		
4	Feb	120		
5	Mar	138		
6	Apr	67		
7	May	92		
8	Jun	147		
9	Jul	171		
10	Aug	249		
11	Sep	916		
12	Oct	298		
13	Nov	314		
14	Dec	156		

5 A line chart is now drawn to show how the sales change over a year. With a line chart, the x-axis (the horizontal one) contains the equally spaced intervals (in this case the months) and the numbers (in this case sales) are plotted vertically against these.

Highlight the column headings and the data to be plotted from cells A2 to B14 and then click on the chart wizard icon.

6 Choose Line as the chart type in step 1 of the chart wizard and then select the simple line from the chart sub-types as shown below.

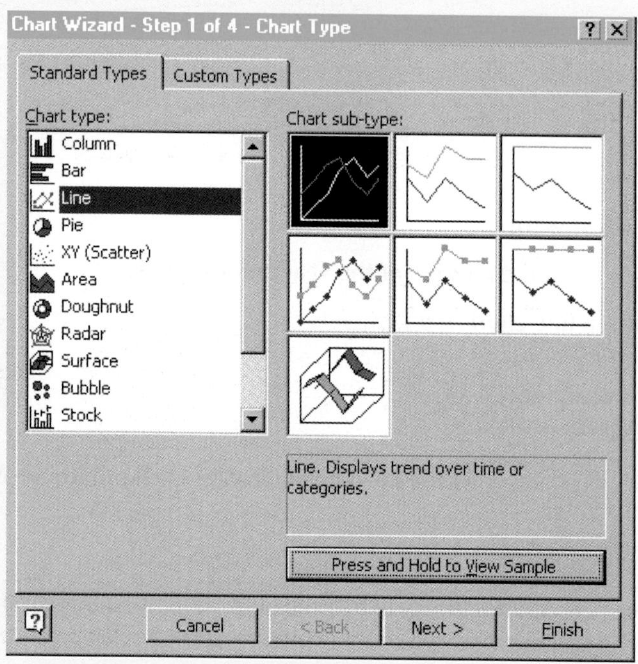

Exercise 7.4

7 For step 2 of the chart wizard just click on Next>.

8 For step 3 of the chart wizard enter the chart title **Book sales each month for 2000–2001**. Also add the value (Y) axis as **Sales (copies)**.

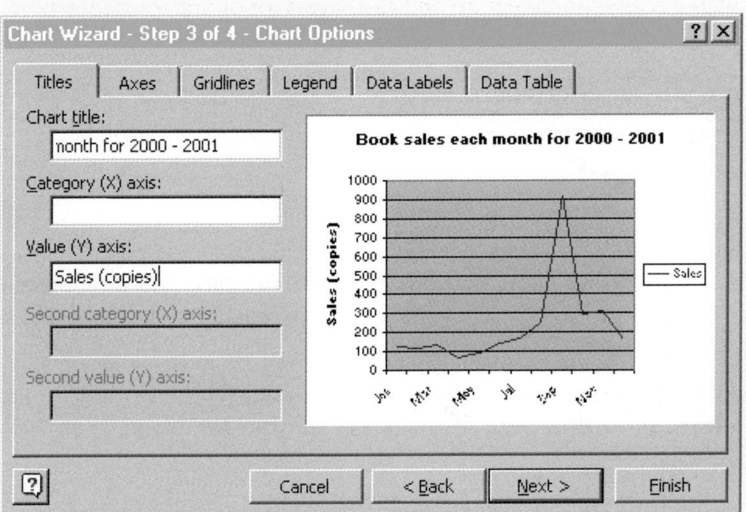

9 In step 4 of the chart wizard, choose to put the chart with the data in the same worksheet and then size the chart by clicking on the corners to get the handles.

Your worksheet should now look like the one shown below.

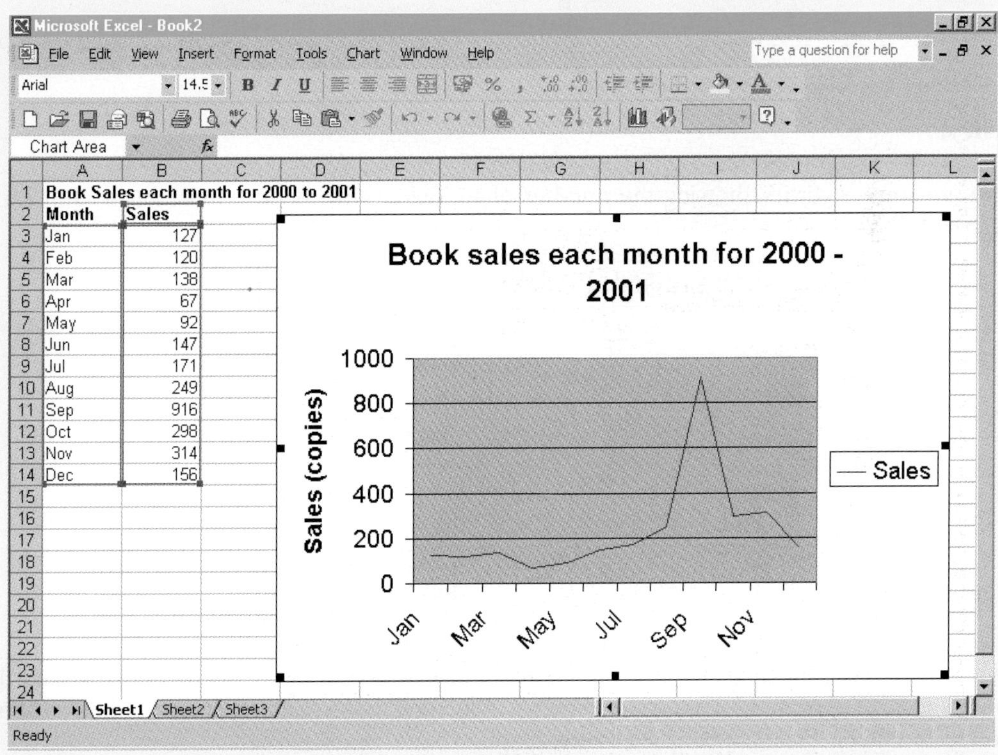

Here is a variety of tasks for you to try; they make use of some of the skills you have learnt in this chapter.

IT TASKS

Task 1

One member of your class says that taller people have bigger feet. The class needs to either prove or disprove this statement. One way to do this would be to measure the height of all the members of the class and record this along with their shoe size.

Set out the results in a worksheet using suitable headings. Using the data in your worksheet, produce a scatter graph, save and print a copy. What does your scatter graph tell you? Write your brief explanation next to the graph.

IT TASKS

Task 2

Here are some statistics showing the number of serious accidents on bonfire night and the number of organised displays.

Organised displays	Serious injuries
85	58
169	41
277	30
410	28
432	19
458	13
496	11

A local authority is thinking about organising more displays. They have asked you to present the information in the table as a chart for a meeting. You have decided that a scatter graph would be most appropriate. Produce a suitably titled and labelled scatter graph.

What conclusion can you draw from your scatter graph?

IT TASKS

Task 3: how using a mobile phone may affect you

Here are some results from a study conducted in Scandinavian countries about use of mobile phones. The table below shows the health problems associated with using these phones with their risk factors. A risk factor of one is the normal risk factor of these symptoms occurring even if you never use a mobile phone.

Side Effect	**Risk Factor:** two to four calls per day	**Risk Factor:** five or more calls per day
Memory loss	1.4	1.5
Discomfort	2.4	1.6
Fatigue	1.8	2.3
Tingling/tightness	1.2	2.4
Concentration loss	2	2.5
Burning skin	1.4	2.9
Dizziness	2.5	3.1
Headaches	2.1	3.7
Warmth behind the ear	1.8	4.6
Warmth on the ear	2.2	5.1

1 Put the data in the above table into a worksheet.

2 Format the figures to one decimal place (if they aren't already so formatted.)

3 Now use the data in the worksheet to produce a side-by-side bar chart. This chart needs to be on the same worksheet as the original data.

4 Add the title **How using a mobile phone may affect you** to the chart.

5 Move and size the bar chart on the spreadsheet so that you can see the original data.

6 Save your work and then print a copy of the whole worksheet.

Extra steps

7 Can you import a piece of clip art to suitably illustrate some place in the worksheet? Again, save and print your work.

8 Add formatting to the worksheet to improve the presentation.

IT TASKS

Task 4: producing a pictogram

To make your worksheets more attractive, you can add pictures. You can also construct pictograms using pictures of your choice. In this task, a bar chart is produced made up from graphics imported from a clip art disk. See if you can find out (maybe using Help) how to do this.

IT TASKS

Task 5

Looking through the holiday brochures you often see a comparison of the average daily maximum temperature in London with that in a particular resort.

Here is just such a comparison for the Costa del Sol in Spain, and London.

Month	Av. maximum temp. London (°F)	Av. maximum temp. Costa del Sol (°F)
April	55	70
May	63	73
June	65	80
July	68	83
August	68	82
September	65	80
October	60	72

Produce a side-by-side bar chart to compare easily the temperatures in the two places for the months in the table.

Give your graph a suitable title and remember to label the vertical axis (the y-axis).

Check that your chart is correct, then save it under an appropriate file name and print a copy.

IT TASKS

Task 6

A recording company chief, Mr Fatcheck, wants a breakdown of the cost of a £12.99 CD. You have been asked for this information and have decided to produce it as a 3D pie chart. The sales and marketing department have supplied you with the data shown in the table.

Item	Cost
VAT	£1.93
Shop profit	£2.68
Distribution cost	£3.39
Royalty to artists	£4.20
Cost of making	£0.79

You are free to produce your own design for the worksheet.

Think about the following before you start:

- Do you intend to produce a single worksheet containing the data and the chart or are you going to put them in separate worksheets?
- What can be done to make the data in the spreadsheet more eyecatching (e.g. use borders, colours, different font sizes and styles etc.)?
- What can be done to make the chart more eyecatching?
- What titles need to be given?
- What data needs to be on the sectors (slices)?

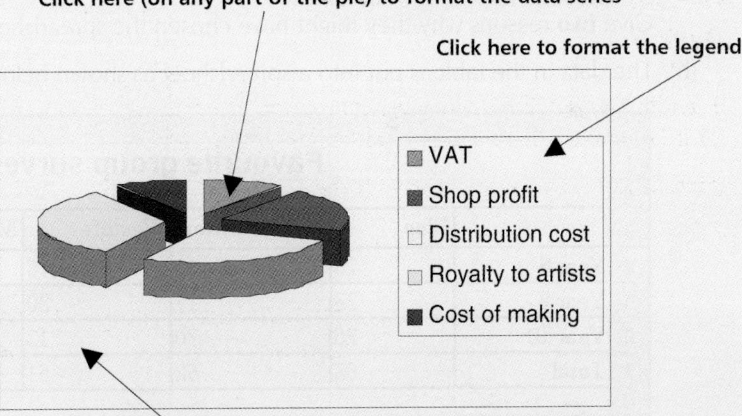

There are many alterations you can make to the pie chart shown above. By clicking on parts of the chart you can call up menus using which you can do all sorts of things.

Do not be afraid to experiment.

By double clicking certain areas on the chart you can make the menus to the right appear and thus alter the appearance of your chart. Remember the Edit Undo option if you want to undo an effect you don't like.

If you are not sure how to do something, then use the help menu.

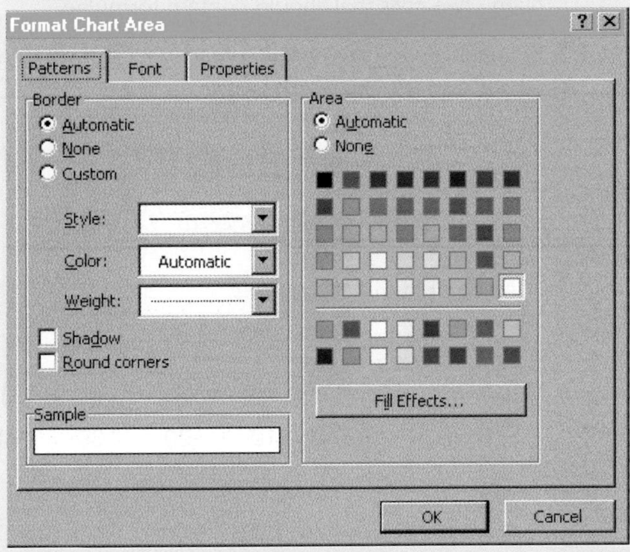

QUESTIONS

1 The students in year 11 did a survey on boy/girl bands in their school. The results of the survey are to be analysed and the conclusions put into the school magazine. The results of the survey are shown below:

	Blue	Atomic Kitten	Westlife	Mystique
Year 8	20	15	18	18
Year 9	23	17	20	5
Year 10	25	30	13	8
Total	68	62	51	31

(a) What is the name of the form on which the data can be manually recorded? The teacher has given the students the choice of using a spreadsheet or a database to record and then analyse the results. After some discussion, the students decide to use a spreadsheet.

Give **two** reasons why they might have chosen the spreadsheet rather than the database.

(b) The data in the table is put into a spreadsheet as shown below:

	A	B	C	D	E	F
1			Favourite group survey			
2						
3		Blue	Atomic Kitten	Westlife	Mystique	
4	Year 8	20	15	18	18	
5	Year 9	23	17	20	5	
6	Year 10	25	30	13	8	
7	Total	68	62	51	31	
8						
9						

Name two cells that should contain formulae.

(c) By making reference to the spreadsheet shown above, explain how the chart below could be produced.

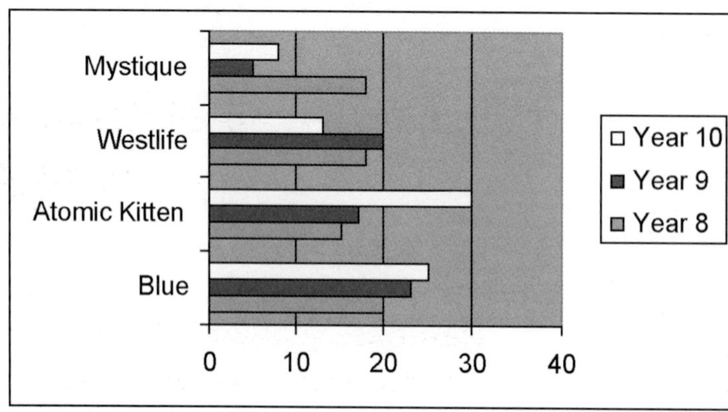

Creating Databases using Excel

Simple databases can also be created using the spreadsheet package Excel. Instead of using the spreadsheet to perform calculations and produce results, here the database has the main purpose of storing data from which information can be extracted.

There is little difference between creating an ordinary worksheet and a database. When creating a database in Excel you must type in the field names in the top row of the worksheet. Examples of fields include surname, street, date of birth, postcode. Each column is then used to store all the details for that particular field. All the rows, apart from the first row, are used to hold the records. A record is the detail about one particular thing or person. The personal details about one person (surname, forename, date of birth, street, town, postcode) represent a record.

Before using Excel as a database you need to ask yourself if you might be better off using a specialist database package, such as Microsoft Access, which is provided as part of the Microsoft Office Professional integrated package.

The two types of databases: flat file and relational databases

The database in Excel is what is called a flat file database and with this type of database you can only access a single file at a time. This means that if you were trying to build a database for a video library using Excel, you would need to enter the customer, video and rental details, each time a video is borrowed. This is a lot of work. There is another more powerful type of database, called a relational database, in which many database files (or tables as they are called) can be accessed at the same time. This means that you can have one file to hold customer details, one file to hold video details and another to hold the details of the rentals. To rent a video you need only to enter the date, the number of days borrowed, the video number and the customer number. Using the customer number and video number, which are unique, the database gets the information from the other database files. This saves a lot of typing and also reduces the likelihood of errors being made.

When is it appropriate to use Excel?

It is appropriate to use Excel rather than a specialist database package in the following circumstances:

- if you only have Excel and you do not want to go to the expense of buying Access
- if only a simple database is needed and you don't have time to learn how to use Access, which can be quite complicated
- if you need to solve a problem that can be expressed in mathematical terms (i.e. there are lots of calculations).

Fundamentals of databases

Here are some of the terms you are likely to encounter when developing databases using Excel.

Database (called a list in Excel)

A database is a collection of related information. For example, a pupil list would contain all the data about every pupil in a school.

Field

A field is single type of data such as surname, date of birth, telephone number, etc. In Excel a field would be a column in the list.

Record

A record is a set of related information about a thing or individual. Records are subdivided into fields. For example, a pupil record in a school would contain all the data relating to a single pupil.

Planning a simple database

It is much easier to get the database right before you start setting it up on the computer. Although it is possible to insert or move columns, this all takes time. Take some time to plan what you are trying to do. You will have to do this when you come to your GCSE coursework and also need to write about what you have done.

You should get into the habit of planning your solution on paper before starting the work on the computer.

Here are some things to think about.

- Decide whether you need a flat file database (e.g. Excel) or a relational database (e.g. Access).
- Think about what you need to extract from a database.
- Think about the data you will need to enter into the database to get the information out.
- Think about any calculations you need to perform.
- Decide on the names for the fields you intend to use.
- Plan the order in which the fields will appear. Usually, the most important and unique fields should appear first.
- Decide what searches will be needed and ask yourself if you have the data suitably stored to do these.
- Think about the order in which the data will appear. You can easily change the order by performing a sort.

Exercise 8.1

Setting up a database in Excel

In this spreadsheet you will learn to:

- **set up the data so that the spreadsheet package can recognise it as a database**
- **enter data into a database**
- **create a form which may be used to enter data into the database or perform searches**
- **set up searches to find specific data**
- **use operators (<,<=, >,>= and =) in search criteria.**

1 Enter the data into the database exactly as it is shown. The first row contains the field names and subsequent rows the pupil records. Important note: Do **not** leave any blank rows between the data. When setting up a database in Excel, always make sure that the field names are in neighbouring cells along the first row.

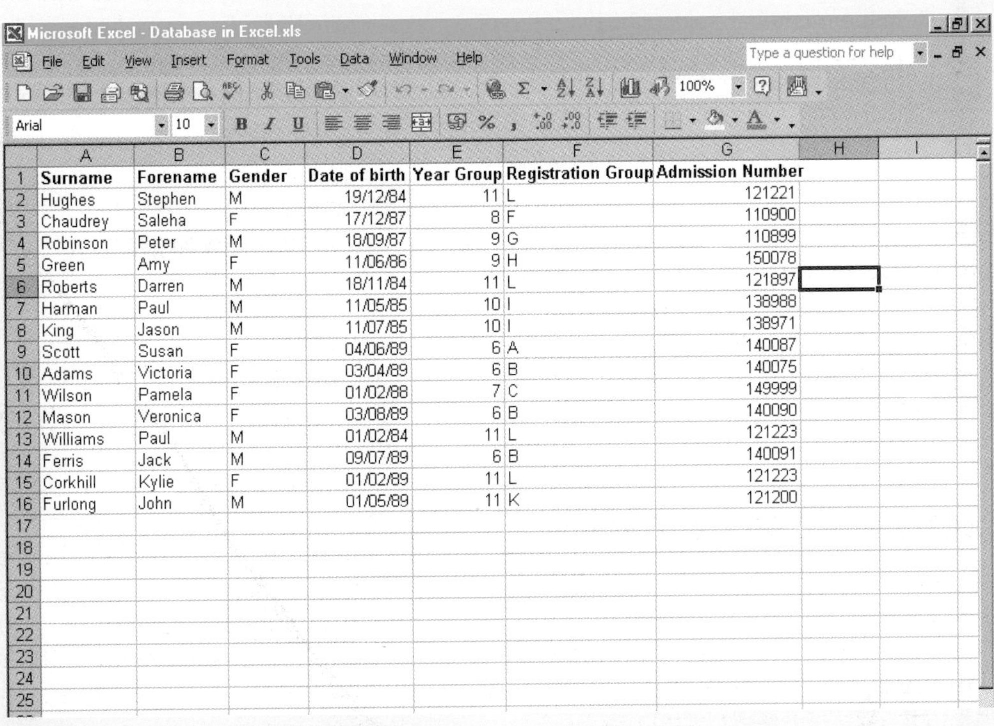

Microsoft Excel - Database in Excel.xls

Surname	Forename	Gender	Date of birth	Year Group	Registration Group	Admission Number
Hughes	Stephen	M	19/12/84	11	L	121221
Chaudrey	Saleha	F	17/12/87	8	F	110900
Robinson	Peter	M	18/09/87	9	G	110899
Green	Amy	F	11/06/86	9	H	150078
Roberts	Darren	M	18/11/84	11	L	121897
Harman	Paul	M	11/05/85	10	I	138988
King	Jason	M	11/07/85	10	I	138971
Scott	Susan	F	04/06/89	6	A	140087
Adams	Victoria	F	03/04/89	6	B	140075
Wilson	Pamela	F	01/02/88	7	C	149999
Mason	Veronica	F	03/08/89	6	B	140090
Williams	Paul	M	01/02/84	11	L	121223
Ferris	Jack	M	09/07/89	6	B	140091
Corkhill	Kylie	F	01/02/89	11	L	121223
Furlong	John	M	01/05/89	11	K	121200

2 The next step is to create a data form that can then be used to add new records, edit existing records or delete records.

To create a form, you have to select (i.e. highlight) the row containing the field names and a sample row of data. Your worksheet should now look like the screen below when you have highlighted the field names and one row of data.

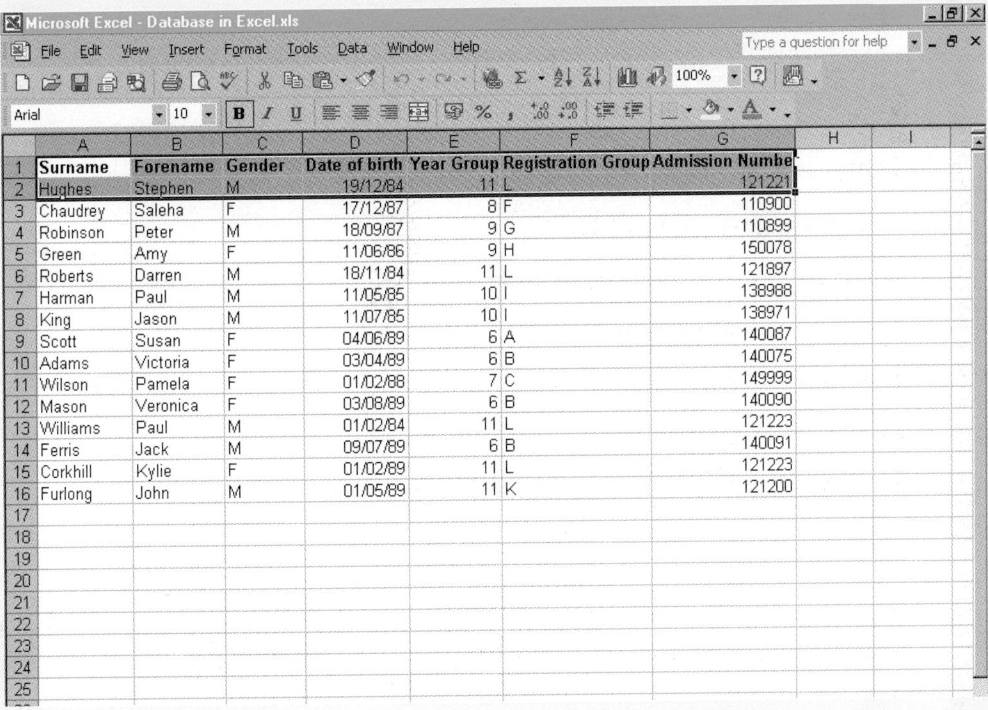

Microsoft Excel - Database in Excel.xls

Surname	Forename	Gender	Date of birth	Year Group	Registration Group	Admission Number
Hughes	Stephen	M	19/12/84	11	L	121221
Chaudrey	Saleha	F	17/12/87	8	F	110900
Robinson	Peter	M	18/09/87	9	G	110899
Green	Amy	F	11/06/86	9	H	150078
Roberts	Darren	M	18/11/84	11	L	121897
Harman	Paul	M	11/05/85	10	I	138988
King	Jason	M	11/07/85	10	I	138971
Scott	Susan	F	04/06/89	6	A	140087
Adams	Victoria	F	03/04/89	6	B	140075
Wilson	Pamela	F	01/02/88	7	C	149999
Mason	Veronica	F	03/08/89	6	B	140090
Williams	Paul	M	01/02/84	11	L	121223
Ferris	Jack	M	09/07/89	6	B	140091
Corkhill	Kylie	F	01/02/89	11	L	121223
Furlong	John	M	01/05/89	11	K	121200

Exercise 8.1

3 In the menu bar, select Data and then Form. You will not see Form straight away but if you wait a couple of seconds a further menu will drop down with it on. Alternatively you can click on the double arrows at the bottom of the initial menu and this further menu will be displayed immediately.

You will now see the following form over your spreadsheet.

The field names have been inserted down the left of the form with the variable data in the boxes.

Notice the buttons on the right-hand side of the form. The form can now be used to create a new record, delete records, browse records (i.e. go from one to another looking at them) and also to search for certain records using search criteria.

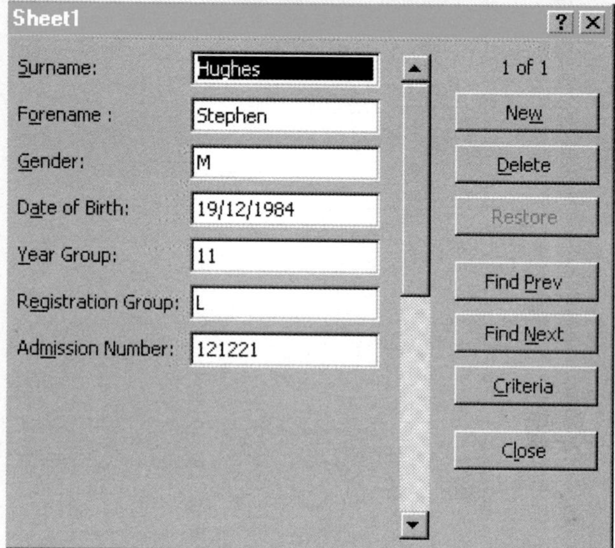

4 Now search for the record for Harman. To do this it is necessary to go back to the worksheet and select the field surname and the data (i.e. from cells A1 to G16). When this is done, the screen will look like this:

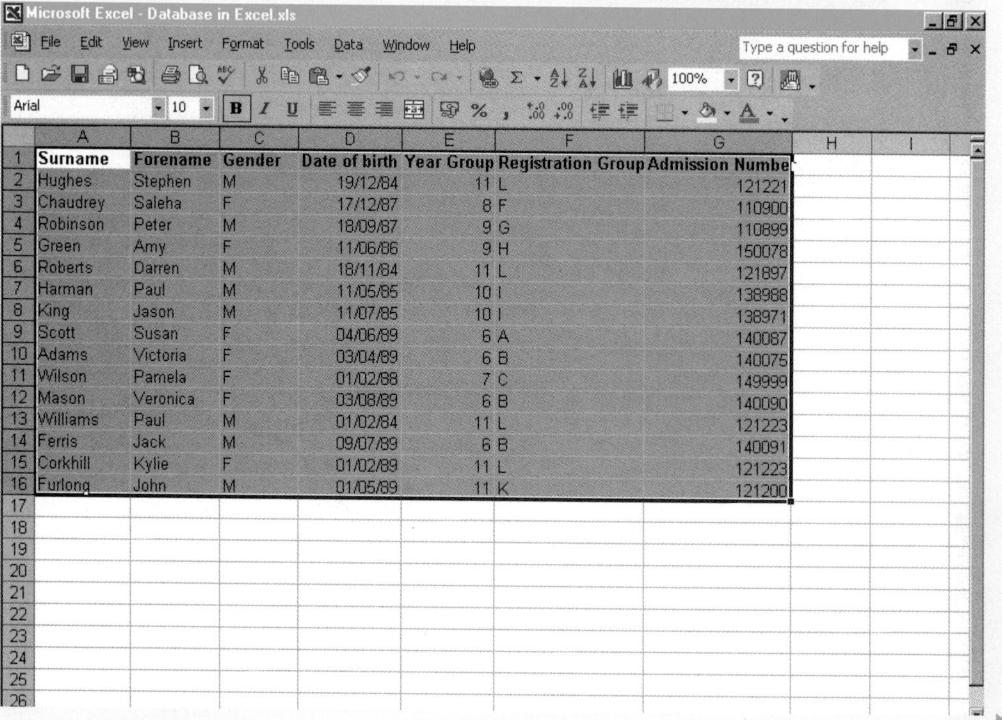

	A	B	C	D	E	F	G
1	Surname	Forename	Gender	Date of birth	Year Group	Registration Group	Admission Numbe
2	Hughes	Stephen	M	19/12/84	11	L	121221
3	Chaudrey	Saleha	F	17/12/87	8	F	110900
4	Robinson	Peter	M	18/09/87	9	G	110899
5	Green	Amy	F	11/06/86	9	H	150078
6	Roberts	Darren	M	18/11/84	11	L	121897
7	Harman	Paul	M	11/05/85	10	I	138988
8	King	Jason	M	11/07/85	10	I	138971
9	Scott	Susan	F	04/06/89	6	A	140087
10	Adams	Victoria	F	03/04/89	6	B	140075
11	Wilson	Pamela	F	01/02/88	7	C	149999
12	Mason	Veronica	F	03/08/89	6	B	140090
13	Williams	Paul	M	01/02/84	11	L	121223
14	Ferris	Jack	M	09/07/89	6	B	140091
15	Corkhill	Kylie	F	01/02/89	11	L	121223
16	Furlong	John	M	01/05/89	11	K	121200

Now get the form on the screen by selecting Data and then Form and then click on the Criteria button. You will now get a blank form. Enter the surname Harman into the surname box and then click on Find Next and the whole record for Harman will be shown.

Enter one or more search criteria in this box

Click on Find Next to display the whole record

You can also add to your search criteria operators chosen from this table.

Operator	Meaning
=	Equal to
>	Greater than
<	Less than
<=	Less than or equal to
>=	Greater than or equal to
<>	Is not equal to

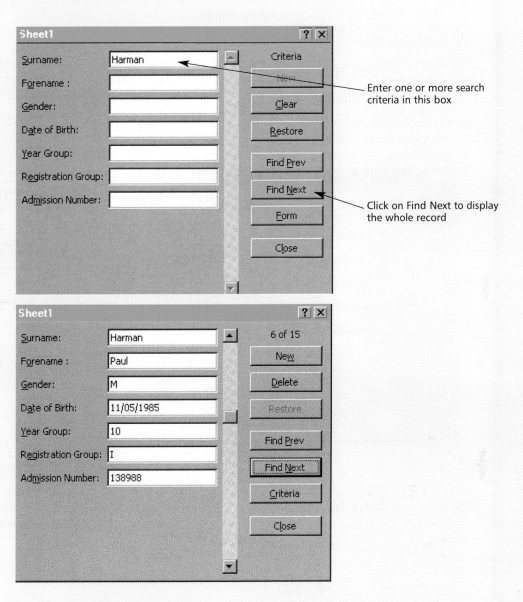

Exercise 8.1

Try the following searches:

(a) In the Date of Birth field on the form enter >01/09/87. This will select the pupils with dates of birth after 1 September 1987. Only one record will be shown at a time, so you will have to use the Find Next button to see the others.

(b) Clear the previous form by clicking on Clear.

Suppose we want to look the details of those pupils who are in Year Group 11 and Registration Group L. If we fill in these details, the spreadsheet will link them automatically with AND, so only those pupils satisfying both criteria will be picked. Enter the details as shown below.

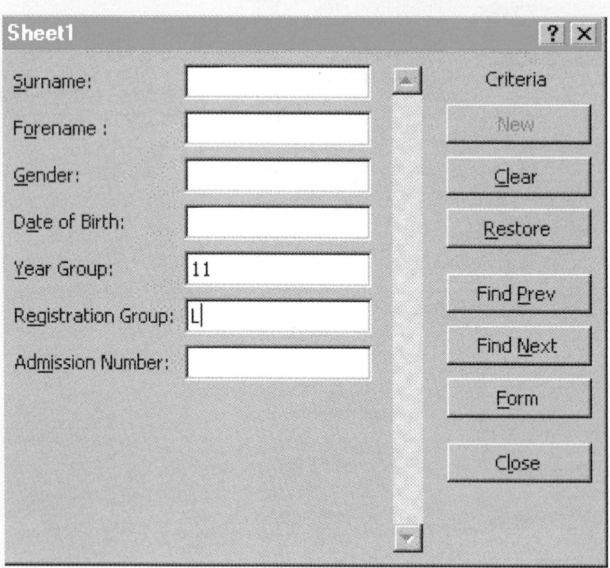

To find the records of those pupils whose details match the search criteria, click on Find Next. To see each record in turn, just click on Find Next. You will see that four records match the search criteria.

Toggling between the form and search criteria

The screen shot below shows the screen.

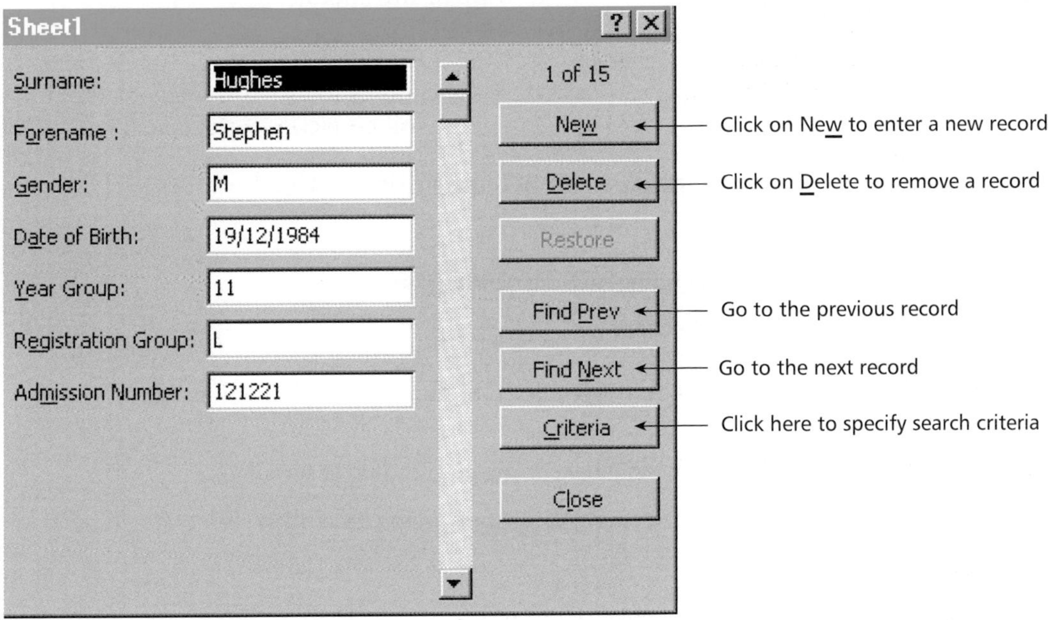

The screen below shows what you see when you click on Criteria in the menu of the screen above.

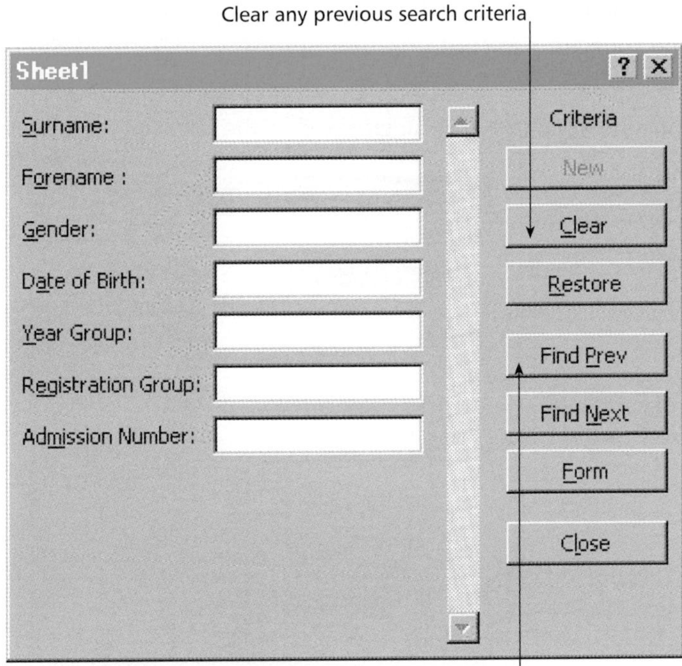

Sorting the data in the database

You can sort on as many as three fields and this is particularly useful if the database is very large and a search on just one field would retrieve lots of records. When the data is sorted all the records are kept together.

There are several orders you can sort on, which are:

Ascending order (A to Z for letters and 0 to 9 for numbers)
Descending order (Z to A for letters and 9 to 0 form numbers)

Exercise 8.2

Sorting the database created in Exercise 8.1 into different orders

In this spreadsheet you will learn to:

- **place the fields into different ascending and descending orders**
- **sort into more than one order at a time.**

1 Open the database created in Exercise 8.1. Notice that the data is not in any particular order, only the order in which it was entered.

It would be useful if the data were in alphabetical order according to surname.

Click on any surname in the surname column or the field name itself, then click on the ascending order (A to Z) icon in the standard toolbar.

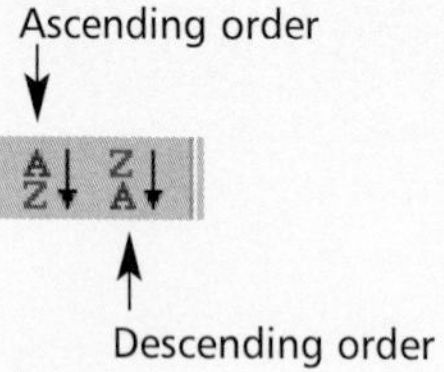

Your database will now be in order of surname. Print out a copy of your worksheet.

2 Click on any item in the Date of Birth column and then sort in descending date of birth. This will put the data in order, with the youngest pupil first.

3 You can sort into several orders at once. We might want to sort in order of year group and then have the pupils in alphabetical order within each year group. Take the following steps to do this.

Click on Data in the menu toolbar and then on Sort.

The following menu will appear:

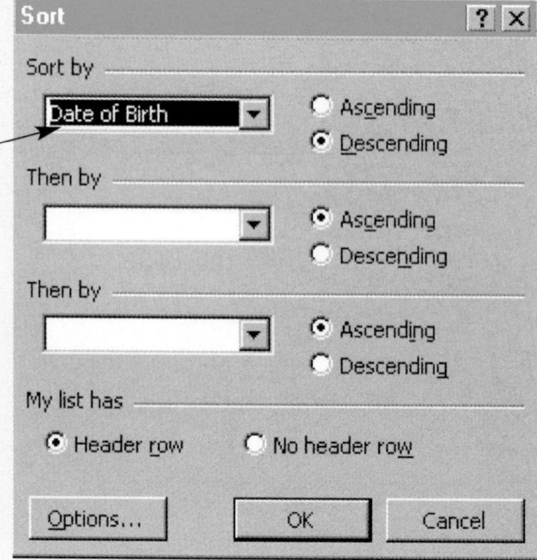

Click to get the pull down menu as shown and pick Year Group.

Fill out this menu as shown below. We want to sort on year group and then in alphabetical order according to surname within the year group.

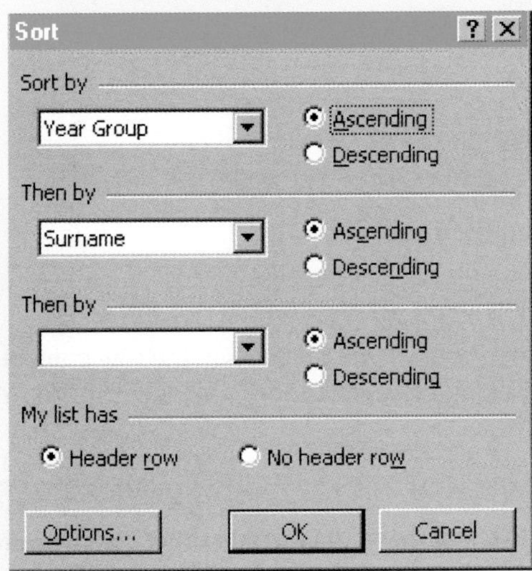

Click on OK. Your sorted worksheet will now look like this:

	A	B	C	D	E	F	G
1	**Surname**	**Forename**	**Gender**	**Date of Birth**	**Year Group**	**Registration Group**	**Admission Number**
2	Adams	Victoria	F	03/04/89	6	B	140075
3	Ferris	Jack	M	09/07/89	6	B	140091
4	Mason	Veronica	F	03/08/89	6	B	140090
5	Scott	Susan	F	04/06/89	6	A	140087
6	Wilson	Pamela	F	01/02/88	7	C	149999
7	Chaudrey	Saleha	F	17/12/87	8	F	110900
8	Green	Amy	F	11/06/86	9	H	150078
9	Robinson	Peter	M	18/09/87	9	G	110899
10	Harman	Paul	M	11/05/85	10	I	138988
11	King	Jason	M	11/07/85	10	I	138971
12	Corkhill	Kylie	F	01/02/89	11	L	121223
13	Furlong	John	M	01/05/89	11	K	121200
14	Hughes	Stephen	M	19/12/84	11	L	121221
15	Roberts	Darren	M	18/11/84	11	L	121897
16	Wiliams	Paul	M	01/02/84	11	L	121223

4 Save your sorted worksheet under the filename Exercise 8.1 and then print out a copy.

Using filters

Filters are features in Excel that allow you to search for data that meets certain criteria. Basically they filter out the unwanted data leaving the required data to be displayed.

Exercise 8.3

Using filters

In this spreadsheet you will learn to:

- **use the Autofilter to display only the required records.**

1 Load the database called 'Exercise 8.1' created in the last exercise.

2 Click on Data then Filter and then Autofilter. You will see that cells in the row containing the field names now have drop-down arrows. Clicking on any of these, produces a drop down menu from which a selection can be made.

	A	B	C	D	E	F	G
1	Surnar	Forenar	Gend	Date of Bi	Year Gro	Registration Gro	Admission Numbe
2	Adams	Victoria	F	03/04/89	6	B	140075
3	Ferris	Jack	M	09/07/89	6	B	140091

3 Click on the drop down arrow for Surname and the following drop down menu appears:

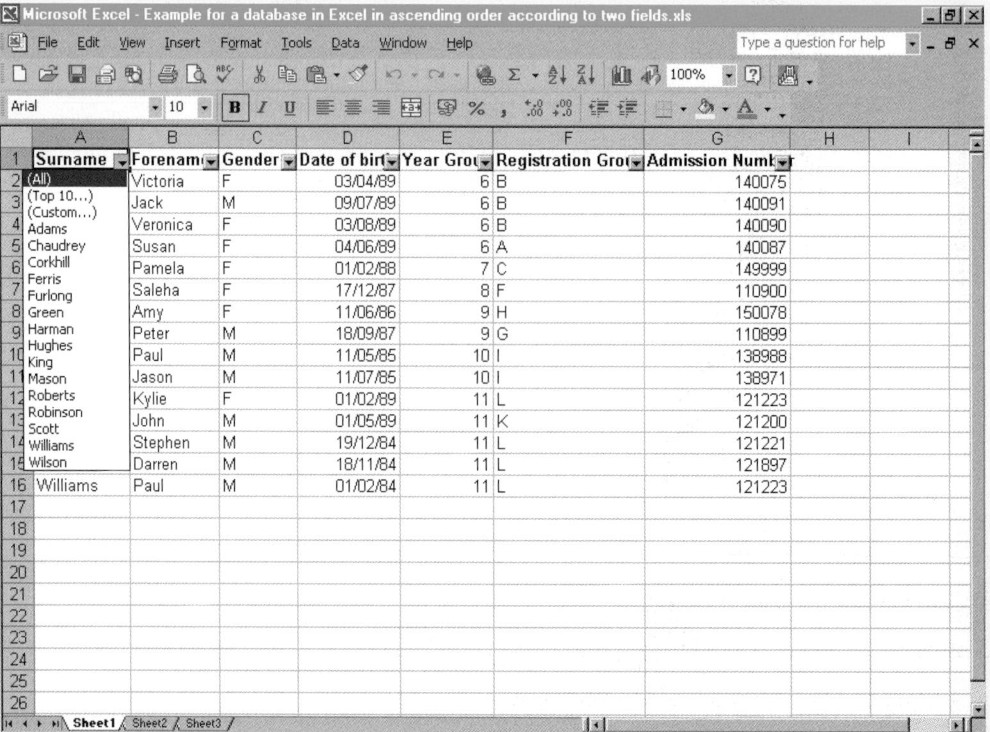

	A	B	C	D	E	F	G
1	Surname	Forenam	Gender	Date of birt	Year Grou	Registration Grou	Admission Numb
2		Victoria	F	03/04/89	6	B	140075
3		Jack	M	09/07/89	6	B	140091
4		Veronica	F	03/08/89	6	B	140090
5		Susan	F	04/06/89	6	A	140087
6		Pamela	F	01/02/88	7	C	149999
7		Saleha	F	17/12/87	8	F	110900
8		Amy	F	11/06/86	9	H	150078
9		Peter	M	18/09/87	9	G	110899
10		Paul	M	11/05/85	10	I	138988
11		Jason	M	11/07/85	10	I	138971
12		Kylie	F	01/02/89	11	L	121223
13		John	M	01/05/89	11	K	121200
14		Stephen	M	19/12/84	11	L	121221
15		Darren	M	18/11/84	11	L	121897
16	Williams	Paul	M	01/02/84	11	L	121223

4 Select Harman from this list and notice that only this record is displayed.

Exercise 8.3

5 To get back to the whole list of records just click on (All) in the drop down list for Surname.

6 You can also use more than one search criterion. To search for pupils in registration groups K or L click on the drop down arrow for Registration Group and select (Custom...) from the menu. The following menu will appear. We want to show the rows where the Registration Group equals L or equals K. Fill in the appropriate boxes as shown, making use of the drop down menus.

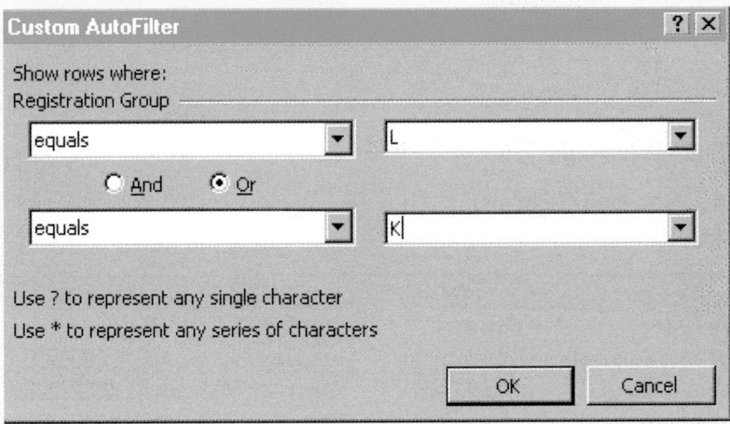

You will now see the following records:

	A	B	C	D	E	F	G
1	Surnar	Forenar	Gend	Date of Bi	Year Gro	Registration Gro	Admission Numbe
12	Corkhill	Kylie	F	01/02/89	11	L	121223
13	Furlong	John	M	01/05/89	11	K	121200
14	Hughes	Stephen	M	19/12/84	11	L	121221
15	Roberts	Darren	M	18/11/84	11	L	121897
16	Wiliams	Paul	M	01/02/84	11	L	121223

IT TASKS

Using filters produce the following:

- a printout of the record for the pupil with surname Williams
- a printout of all the pupil details in year group 11
- a printout of all the pupil details in registration group L
- a list of all the female pupils in registration group B.

QUESTIONS

1 Explain the following terms in relation to databases:
(a) database
(b) record
(c) field.

2 (a) When creating a database it is always advisable to have one field that is unique. Explain why.
(b) In the database in Exercise 8.1, why might surname not be unique?
(c) One of the fields is unique. Which one is it?

3 Explain briefly the difference between a flat file database and a relational database.

4 The screen below shows a simple database for a job agency. It has been created in the spreadsheet package Microsoft Excel.
(a) One of these fields is unique. Which one is it?
(b) Write down the job numbers of the record selected using the following search conditions:
(i) pay < £20000
(ii) pay >= £28000 AND Area = 'London'
(iii) job = 'Sales Clerk' OR Job = 'Shipping Clerk'.

	A	B	C	D	E	F
1	**Job Number**	**Job Type**	**Area**	**Employer**	**Pay**	
2	1010	Systems Analyst	London	Am Bank	£35,000	
3	1023	Programmer	Blackburn	Minstral Finance	£28,000	
4	1012	Accountant	Liverpool	Mutual Insurance	£42,000	
5	1034	Sales Clerk	Liverpool	Mututal Insuranc	£18,000	
6	1011	Sales Manager	Birmingham	DC Switches Ltd	£28,000	
7	1045	Sales Manager	Lancaster	Air Products LTd	£31,500	
8	1024	Electrical Engineer	Bristol	Manners Ltd	£27,800	
9	1021	Network Manger	Warrington	D&Q Ltd	£19,800	
10	1000	Trainee Programmer	Cardiff	PCSoft	£7,500	
11	1002	Systems Analyst	Liverpool	AmSoft	£24,000	
12	1013	Junior Accountant	Liverpool	AmSoft	£17,000	
13	1018	Accountant	Manchester	DC Switches Ltd	£45,000	
14	1035	Sales Clerk	Preston	FR Venn & Co	£16,900	
15	1078	Shipping Clerk	London	P&R	£21,800	
16	1080	Trainee Programmer	London	Arc Systems	£19,300	
17	1079	Programmer	London	Arc Systems	£35,600	

IT TASKS

Have you ever come home, gone to the telephone and dialled 1471 to find the phone number of the last call? You often get a number that you slightly recognise, but whose is it? You could, of course, dial the number, but it might be someone who you are trying to avoid.

A way around this problem is to set up a database of your friends' names, addresses and telephone numbers. Also, it might be useful to have their dates of birth, so you know when their birthdays are.

Create a simple database in Excel to store these details. Enter details for around ten of your friends. Produce printouts of the sorts and searches you would be able to do using your database.

Modelling

What is a model?

Modelling basically means mimicking reality. One way of doing this is by producing a series of mathematical equations that parallel the real situation. For example, we could look at a ball being dropped though a certain height and try to describe its motion using a model. We could look at the distance it travels with time and also its velocity at certain times. In order to check our model we compare it with the real situation. So we could look at the actual distances and velocities measured during an experiment and compare these with those predicted by the model we have produced.

What is the difference between a model and a simulation?

When values are put into the model and the model is exercised in some way, then we are said to be performing a simulation. For example, the government has a model for the economy, so if interests rates may change, they can see the effect it might have on inflation. Models are also used in weather forecasting, where the future weather is predicted on the basis of what has happened in the past.

Specialist modelling software is available and your teacher may be able to show you some. In this chapter we will just look at those models that may be created using the spreadsheet Microsoft Excel.

Managing your money

When you start work and perhaps live away from home, you will have to be able to manage your money. It can be very stressful if you do not manage your money properly. You will have to consider questions such as 'can I afford a car?' or 'how do I cope with the odd unexpected bill such as a television repair bill?'

A prudent person would sit down and look at the money coming in (called income) and the money going out (called expenditure). They could try to model their income and expenditure using spreadsheet software. Using the spreadsheet they could alter the figures and see what happens.

Exercising the model!

Exercise 9.1

Managing your money

In this exercise you will learn how to:

- **create a simple model using Excel.**

1 Load Excel and start a new worksheet.

2 Enter the data into the worksheet exactly as shown.

	A	B	C	D
1	**Monthly income and expenditure for Amy**			
2				
3	**Income**			
4	Wages	£840.87		
5				
6	**Expenditure**			
7	Food			
8	Rent			
9	Electricity			
10	Gas			
11	Telephone			
12	TV licence			
13	Insurance			
14	Entertainment			
15	Clothes			
16	Travel			
17	Holiday savings			

3 By looking at her bank statements and bills for the previous month, Amy has come up with the following figures:

food £150;
rent £180;
electricity £23.57;
gas £34.65;
TV licence fee £8.20;
insurance £23.59;
entertainment £160;
travel £112;
holiday savings £80;
telephone £24;
clothes £80.

Enter these figures into the worksheet in the correct positions. After doing this verify the data in your worksheet by proof reading it against the original figures.

4 Enter the text into cells D8, D9 and D10 and embolden it.

Your worksheet should now look like this:

	A	B	C	D
1	**Monthly income and expenditure for Amy**			
2				
3	**Income**			
4	Wages	£840.87		
5				
6	**Expenditure**			
7	Food	£150.00		
8	Rent	£180.00		**Total Income**
9	Electricity	£23.57		**Total Expenditure**
10	Gas	£34.65		**Balance at end of month**
11	Telephone	£24.00		
12	TV licence	£8.20		
13	Insurance	£23.59		
14	Entertainment	£160.00		
15	Clothes	£80.00		
16	Travel	£112.00		
17	Holiday savings	£80.00		

5 Enter formulae in cells E8, E9 and E10 to calculate the total income, total expenditure and balance at end of month respectively.

6 Check that your formulae produce the following results:

Total Income	£840.87
Total Expenditure	£876.01
Balance at end of month	-£35.14

7 Save this model of Amy's finances using the filename 'Income & Expenditure model'.

8 Produce a printout of the model.

Exercise 9.2

Using the model

In this exercise you will learn how to:

- **change the figures in the model created in Exercise 9.1 to help Amy see how changes in her income and expenditure affect her finances.**

The whole purpose of creating a model is to use it. Amy can use her model to see the effect of changes in her finances.

1 Load the 'Income & Expenditure model' created in Exercise 9.1.

2 Amy needs to review her finances since she is spending £35.14 more than she is earning. Notice that this negative amount appears in red on your worksheet.

She decides that there are two areas where she can lower her expenditure.

Change the entertainment spend to £140.00 and the amount spent on food to £130.00. She now looks at her worksheet and is satisfied.

3 The boss is very impressed with Amy's work and to encourage her, Amy has been given a pay rise of £60 per month after deductions (tax, national insurance, etc.)

Add this extra amount to Amy's income.

4 Amy looks at her spreadsheet and feels a lot better about her finances.

Amy would like to buy a car and wants to use some money she has saved to do so, taking a loan for the rest. The loan repayments will be £80 per month.

Add the loan repayment to the expenditure. She will also need to spend £50 per month on road tax, petrol, insurance and maintenance. She will enter these as Car Expenses. Add these two amounts and make sure that you now take account of these extra amounts in any formulae.

5 Because she will now be travelling by car Amy's travelling expenses will fall. Change the figure for travelling expenses to £21.50.

6 Check your final results for the model are the same as those at the top of the next page.

7 Save the final model under the file name 'Income & Expenditure final model'.

8 Print a copy of this final model.

Exercise 9.2

	A	B	C	D	E
1	**Monthly income and expenditure for Amy**				
2					
3	**Income**				
4	Wages	£900.87			
5					
6	**Expenditure**				
7	Food	£130.00			
8	Rent	£180.00		**Total Income**	£900.87
9	Electricity	£23.57		**Total Expenditure**	£875.51
10	Gas	£34.65		**Balance at end of month**	£25.36
11	Telephone	£24.00			
12	TV licence	£8.20			
13	Insurance	£23.59			
14	Entertainment	£140.00			
15	Clothes	£80.00			
16	Travel	£21.50			
17	Holiday savings	£80.00			
18	Car loan repayment	£80.00			
19	Car expenses	£50.00			

IT TASKS

Can you produce a similar model for your (or another member of your family's) expenses? How will you find out the inputs to the system (i.e. where does the information come from)? How will you arrange the worksheet? What formulae will you need to use?

Produce a model, accompanied by documentation, outlining the above. Produce printouts showing how you can use your model to help budget.

Exercise 9.3

Book Sales; another simple model

In this exercise you will learn how to:

- **design a simple model.**

A book publisher keeps records of the sales of a book over a number of years. The purpose of the spreadsheet is for the publisher to be able to predict future sales of the book more accurately, since he has to know how many books to print. If too few are printed a reprint will be needed, which is more expensive than printing the right number in the first place. The more that are printed in one go, the cheaper they will be. However, if too many are printed there will be a lot of money tied up in books sitting in the warehouse. To get as near as possible to the ideal number a model can be produced of the situation, using a spreadsheet. Table 9.1 shows sales details for two books.

1 Set up a worksheet and enter the above information into it. (You decide where everything goes and the titles for columns and rows).

Exercise 9.3

2 The sales manager has asked for a column to show the percentage error in actual sales based on the predicted sales. He has written down a formula to help you with this:

$$\% \text{ error} = \frac{(\text{actual sales} - \text{predicted sales})}{\text{actual sales}} \times 100$$

Put this extra column in for both books and calculate the percentages.

3 Save your work using a suitable filename and produce a printout of the model.

Answer the following questions on this model:

(a) What is meant by the term 'computer model'?
(b) What four features of spreadsheets make them particularly suited to modelling?
(c) Why might it be important to publishers to be able to
  (i) predict the sales
  (ii) predict the profit?

Table 9.1 *Sales details for two books*

	HTML for You		C++ for You	
	Predicted	Actual	Predicted	Actual
Number of books sold	72,000	51,800	127,000	143,782
Money from the sales of books	£291,200	£234,876	£689,789	£745,902
Profit from the sales of books	£43,680	£34,800	£72,612	£98,090

Modelling electricity usage

Suppose we wish to investigate electricity usage in our homes to see how we might reduce our bills; we could utilise a spreadsheet. Once the spreadsheet has been created we can simulate the use of electricity in the home.

Things to find out first

First we need to write a list of all the devices we have which use electricity. Devices that produce heat, use up much more electricity, so we must make sure we have included all of these. There are some electrical devices which are only used now and again. You may wish to disregard these in your simple model.

On each of your devices you will find a label or marking that tells you how much power it consumes. This power is in watts (W) or kilowatts (kW). You need to record this next to the name of the device. Here is an example of a data capture form you could use.

Device Name	Number of kilowatts	Number of hours use/day	Number of devices	Total hours use/day	Number of units of electricity/day
Electric fire	2	4	1	4	8
Light bulbs	0.1	6	4	24	2.4

Essential facts

- One kilowatt = 1000 watts.
- To convert watts to kilowatts you divide by 1000.
- Electricity is measured in Units.
- A Unit of electricity is 1 kWh (one kilowatt hour).
- Number of units = number of kilowatts × number of hours.
- To convert minutes to hours, you divide the time in minutes by 60.

Electricity bills are produced quarterly (i.e. every three months). You will need to work out how many units of electricity your house will use per quarter. You should get a copy of one of your electricity bills and use the same quarter for your estimates.

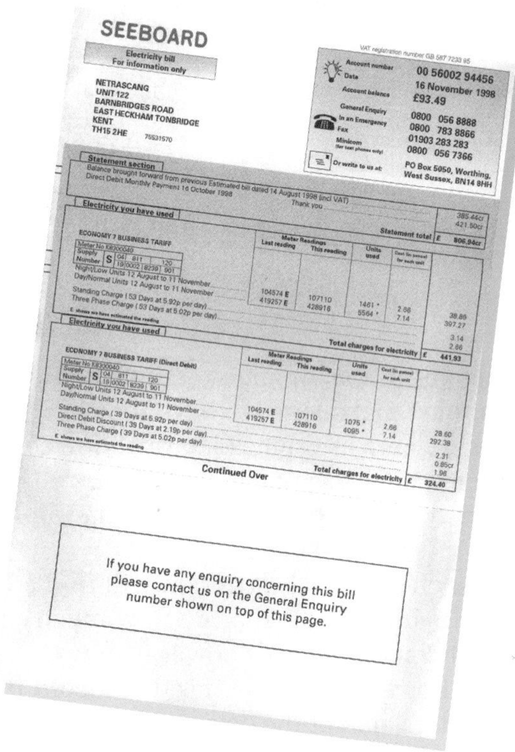

SEEBOARD

Electricity bill
For information only

NETRASCANG
UNIT 122
BARNBRIDGES ROAD
EAST HECKHAM TONBRIDGE
KENT
TH15 2HE 75531570

VAT registration number GB 587 7233 95

Account number 00 56002 94456
Date 16 November 1998
Account balance £93.49
General Enquiry 0800 056 8888
In an Emergency 0800 783 8866
Fax 01903 283 283
Minicom (for text phones only) 0800 056 7366
Or write to us at: PO Box 5050, Worthing, West Sussex, BN14 8HH

Statement section

Balance brought forward from previous Estimated bill dated 14 August 1998 (incl VAT) 385.44cr
Direct Debit Monthly Payment 16 October 1998 421.50cr
Thank you
Statement total £ 806.94cr

Electricity you have used

ECONOMY 7 BUSINESS TARIFF

	Last reading	This reading	Units used	Cost (in pence) for each unit	
Night/Low Units 12 August to 11 November	104574 E	107110	1461 *	2.66	38.86
Day/Normal Units 12 August to 11 November	419257 E	428916	5564 *	7.14	397.27
Standing Charge (53 Days at 5.92p per day)					3.14
Three Phase Charge (53 Days at 5.02p per day)					2.66
Total charges for electricity					£ 441.93

E shows we have estimated the reading

Electricity you have used

ECONOMY 7 BUSINESS TARIFF (Direct Debit)

	Last reading	This reading	Units used	Cost (in pence) for each unit	
Night/Low Units 12 August to 11 November	104574 E	107110	1075 *	2.66	28.60
Day/Normal Units 12 August to 11 November	419257 E	428916	4095 *	7.14	292.38
Standing Charge (39 Days at 5.92p per day)					2.31
Direct Debit Discount (39 Days at 2.19p per day)					0.85cr
Three Phase Charge (39 Days at 5.02p per day)					1.96
Total charges for electricity					£ 324.40

E shows we have estimated the reading

Continued Over

If you have any enquiry concerning this bill please contact us on the General Enquiry number shown on top of this page.

Figure 9.1 *A typical electricity bill*

Things to think about

Can you build the following into your model?

- Electricity usage depends on the time of year. Is it possible to adjust your model to cope with this?
- Some devices (such as hedge trimmers, drills, foot spas) are used very occasionally. Is it possible to take these kinds of devices into account?

Evaluating your model

You will need to compare the total electricity predicted by your model with the actual usage as printed on the electricity bill. How near was it? Obviously the weather will be an important factor. Are there any changes you would now want to make to your model to make it more realistic? Try these changes and see if they work.

The cost of the electricity is 6.68 pence per Unit. Adapt your model so that an electricity bill can be worked out.

VAT is payable on fuel and there is also a service charge that is paid no matter how much or little electricity is used. The service charge is currently £10.50 per quarter. VAT is calculated after the electricity charges and the standard charges have been added together, and is currently 17.5% of this total.

Modelling your water usage

In a similar way to the above, you can model your usage of water. Older houses have a fixed charge for their water so the resident can use as much or little water as they want and still pay the same amount. Newer properties have a water meter that records in cubic metres the volume of water used. Having a water meter usually makes people a little more careful about the amount they use. It is also fairer, because otherwise two similar houses, one with a single person in it and another containing a large family, would pay the same without the meter. With the meter the family, using lots more water, would pay a lot more.

Produce a water consumption model for your household.

If you have a water meter compare your volume with the figures on your bills.

Modelling the throwing of two dice using a spreadsheet

In this exercise you will learn how to:

- **use the random number function of the spreadsheet**
- **simulate the random throwing of a pair of dice**
- **evaluate the model by comparing the results with those obtained from probability theory and also with those obtained by experiment.**

In this exercise we model the throwing of two dice using the random number function of the spreadsheet. The two dice have their numbers added together and the results are compared with those obtained when two real dice are thrown. We can also vary the number of throws using the spreadsheet and in reality see what effect this has.

Here are some instructions to start you off on this exercise.

1 Type in the heading as shown below. Embolden this heading.

2 Type in the column headings and embolden them.

3 A formula is needed that will select a random whole number between one and six. The formula is:

=RANDBETWEEN(1,6)

Enter this formula into cells A4 and B4.

	A	B	C	D	E
1	**A worksheet simulating the throwing of two dice**				
2					
3	**1st die score**	**2nd die score**	**Total score**		
4	2	4	6		
5	5	5	10		
6	5	6	11		
7	4	5	9		
8	6	5	11		
9	5	1	6		
10	6	1	7		
11	3	3	6		
12	3	1	4		
13	2	2	4		

4 Enter a formula into cell C4 to add cells A4 and B4 together.

5 Copy each formula down the column until twenty throws have been simulated.

You now have the system with which to conduct further investigation. There are 36 ways in which two dice can be thrown, but the probability of getting a particular total varies depending on the number of ways the total can be obtained. For example, a total of 12 can only be obtained with a six on one dice and a six on the other. A total of seven can be obtained in the following ways: (1 + 6), (6 + 1), (5 + 2), (2 + 5), (4 + 3) and (3 + 4).

The theoretical probability is therefore 1/36 for a total of 12 and 6/36 (or 1/6) for a total of seven. Ask your maths teacher for help if you need it.

IT TASKS

Look at Exercise 9.4 on the previous page. Here are some things you may consider doing. Feel free though to explore and develop the model on your own.

- Work out the theoretical probability of obtaining all the possible scores as worked out above, for seven and 12.
- Simulate the throwing of 20 dice and compare the totals obtained with reality (i.e. actually throwing dice yourself) and the theoretical probability as worked out in the way shown above.
- Increase the number of throws and compare your answers again. This process can be extended further. Do you notice anything? If so, what?

Spreadsheet project example: boats in the park

John has the opportunity to run a business. It has become possible for him to hire out rowing boats and small motor boats on a lake in a park. He has to borrow some money in order to get the business going. To borrow the money, he has to convince Mr Miser, the bank manager, that the business is going to be a success and that he will be able to pay the money back.

His business is seasonal since a lot more people hire boats in the summer than in the winter. He therefore needs to make sure that he makes enough money in the summer to last through the winter.

To be able to assess whether the bank should lend John the money, the bank manager has asked him to produce a business plan or cash projection. This outlines the expected money coming into the business though the hire of the boats and the money going out of the business (i.e. the costs). This is produced on a month-by-month basis for a whole year.

Monthly costs

The following fixed costs are incurred on a monthly basis and are the same from one month to another. They need to be paid even if no boats are hired that month. The other type of costs, (called variable costs) increase according to how many times the boats are hired. For example, fuel costs for the motor boats depend on how much they are used. Also, the more the boats are used, the higher will be the cost of maintenance.

Fixed costs

Repayment of bank loan	= £467.00
Wages	= £890.00
Hire of premises	= £200.00
Hire of lake	= £368.00
Insurance	= £43.50

Variable costs

Fuel and oil costs for each motor boat	= £1.10 per hour
Maintenance costs for each rowing boat	= £0.13 per hour
Maintenance costs for each motor boat	= £0.30 per hour

Income

In this business, there is only one source of income; the money paid to hire the boats. John could estimate these figures for each month but it would be better to show the number of hours and the price separately. John estimates that the total number of hours that the boats will be hired each month is as shown in Table 9.2.

Motorboats are hired out at £6.00 per hour.

Rowing boats are hired out at £4.00 per hour.

Using the figures above, how will you work out the variable costs for fuel and oil?

Table 9.2 *Estimate of boat hiring for each month of the year*

	Jan	Feb	Mar	Apr	May	Jun	Jul	Aug	Sep	Oct	Nov	Dec
Motorboat hire (hours/month)	100	100	200	400	900	1000	1500	1700	850	600	200	250
Rowing boat hire (hours/month)	50	60	130	300	700	1000	1300	1400	700	300	100	100

John wants to work out how much money he will get from the hire of each type of boat and also his total income each month from the business.

He also needs to show the total costs (i.e. fixed and variable costs added together) for each month.

Planning your worksheet

Plan your worksheet out on paper first. Use a pencil and have a rubber handy. Decide where you are going to put each part. Keep all the copies of your drafts and include these in your documentation for the project. Once you have arrived at a version with which you (or John in this case) are satisfied you should justify the choice in your documentation. You can also mention, with reasons, why the drafts were rejected.

Here is a draft design for the worksheet.

Cash projection for boats in the park

Monthly fixed costs	
Repayment of bank loan	*£467.00*
"	"
"	"
etc.	*etc.*

Hourly charge for rowing boats £4.00

Monthly variable costs	
Fuel and oil for motor boats	*£1.10 per hr*
"	"
"	"
etc.	*etc.*

Hourly charge for motor boats £6.00

	Jan	*Feb*	*Mar*	*etc.*
Hrs motorboat hire per month	*100*	*etc.*		
Hrs rowing boat hire per month	*50*	*etc.*		
Fixed costs	"	*etc.*	*Formulae needed to calculate these*	
Variable costs	"	*etc.*		
Total costs	"	*etc.*		
Total income	"	*etc.*		
Monthly profit/loss	"	*etc.*		
Cumulative profit/loss	"	*etc.*		

Figure 9.2 *Draft design for a worksheet*

To make sure you have understood the problem correctly you arrange a meeting with John to show him your design and get his comments. John says the bank manager will probably give him the loan, but he will have to start the business in January, which he reckons will be one of the quietest months. Starting in January could mean making an initial loss. John suggests that another row should be inserted on the worksheet to show the profit/loss for each month.

He would also like another row to show the cumulative profit/loss. This is the profit/loss carried from one month to the next. From this, John will be able to see in which month he will start to make an overall profit.

Implementing the model

Once you have created the model it needs to be tested. Do not just assume that all the formulae are correct; you may have made a mistake. Check the worksheet thoroughly by comparing the results with those obtained using a calculator. It is best to present the results of testing in the form of a table.

You should show how the model can be used. For example, some costs, such as wages, may rise, and John will have to decide whether to absorb the pay rise out of his profits or increase the hourly rate for his boats.

Think of things John could use the model for then explain how they would be done and produce a printout of the results.

Evaluating the model

You could show John the model and simply ask him his opinion of it. A better way of getting him to evaluate it would be to ask him to fill in a questionnaire.

Exercise 9.5

Cartons

In this exercise you will learn how to:

- **produce a model that may be described by a mathematical equation**
- **use 'trial and improvement' to solve this equation.**

A supermarket sells cartons of milk. Each carton is formed from a cube and a triangular prism as shown here.

If the side of the cube is x cm and the height h of the prism is 2 cm, you can prove that the volume of the carton, V is given by the formula:

$$V = x^3 + \frac{x^2h}{2}$$

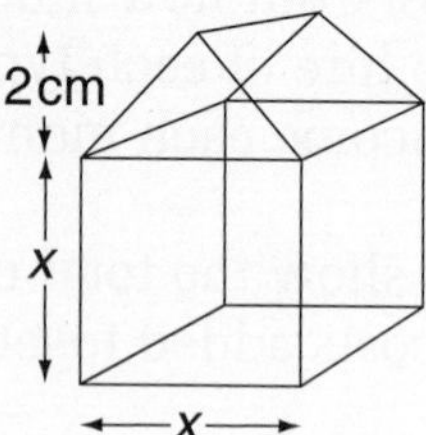

(If your maths is up to it, you may like to see if you can prove this!)

These cartons need to hold 500 cm^3 of milk.

Use a spreadsheet and the process of trial and improvement to work out to two decimal places the value of x that will give you a volume of 500 cm^3.

Once you have determined the value of x, what is the total height of the carton?

First you have to understand the problem. Here we must substitute values of x into the formula until we get near to 500. We then find that our value is either greater than 500 or less than 500 as we would be very lucky to hit 500 exactly on our first attempt. Next we look at values of x to one decimal place between the closest two whole numbers. We can repeat this process until we get a value of x to as many decimal places as we require that gives us 500 or very nearly 500. You should have come across this technique as part of your GCSE mathematics course; it is called 'trial and improvement'.

Although you can do this exercise with just a pen, paper and calculator it is much quicker to use a spreadsheet.

Our first task is to organise the worksheet.

We need to have a series of x values, but where do we start from and where do we finish.

Without thinking too much about it we will start at one and go up to 20 in steps of one. If we are wrong it is so easy to change things on our worksheet that it is not worth thinking too long about it. Three other columns are used, one for x^3, one for $x^2h/2$ and another for the answer when we add these two values together. This will be the value of V in the formula; that is, the number we are trying to make equal 500.

Follow these instructions to build the model.

1 Load the spreadsheet software.

2 Type the heading **'Spreadsheet to determine the side *x* of a container to give a volume of 500 cm^3'** across row 2. Embolden this title.

3 Type the headings ***x*, *x* cubed, $x^2h/2$** and ***V*** in cells A4, B4, C4 and D4 respectively. Embolden and centre these column headings.

4 Enter the values of x from one to 20 into cells A5 to A24. A quick way to do this is to use Autofil. Type in the first three numbers into cells A5, A6 and A7 then highlight them. After highlighting, move the cursor to the bottom right hand corner of cell A7. It will change to a small cross when in the right place. Now keep your finger on the left mouse button and drag it down until you reach 20.

	A	B	C	D	E	F	G
2	Spreadsheet to determine the side x of a container to give a volume of 500						
3							
4	**x**	**x cubed**	**x^2h/2**	**V**			
5	1	1	1	2			
6	2	8	4	12			
7	3	27	9	36			
8	4	64	16	80			
9	5	125	25	150			
10	6	216	36	252			
11	7	343	49	392			
12	8	512	64	576			
13	9	729	81	810			
14	10	1000	100	1100			
15	11	1331	121	1452			
16	12	1728	144	1872			
17	13	2197	169	2366			
18	14	2744	196	2940			

5 We need to find the value of x that will give us a value of 500 when put it into the formula for *V*. Enter the following formulae:

into cell B5 enter the formula **=A5*A5*A5**

into cell C5 enter the formula = **A5*A5*2/2** (since $h = 2$ cm)

into cell D5 enter the formula **=B5+C5**.

Now copy each of these formulae down the column.

6 You can see that there is no value of x that gives an exact value for *V* of 500.

When $x = 7$ the value of *V* is 392 and when $x = 8$ the value of *V* is 576.

The value of x that will make *V* equal to 500 lies between seven and eight.

On the same worksheet, but in a different place, show values of x between seven and eight in steps of 0.1 and set up the spreadsheet similar to the one in steps 1 to 5.

7 From the spreadsheet created in step 6, find the two values (to one decimal place) between which x must lie so that *V* is as near to 500 as possible.

8 Now use the two values found in step 7 and create another set of data, this time using two decimal places to determine the value of x that makes *V* nearest to 500.

9 The value found for x to two decimal places will need to be added to 2 cm to give the total height of the carton.

10 Save your worksheet under the filename 'Trial and improvement using a spreadsheet'.

11 Print out a copy of your worksheet, trying to get it on a single page if you can.

Exercise 9.6

Using the goal seek function: a really quick way to find the value of *x* which makes *V* near to 500

In this exercise you will learn how to:

- **use the Goal Seek function to solve an equation.**

This exercise shows one of the most powerful functions of Excel and saves all the work in the previous exercise. Here's what you do.

1 Set up the spreadsheet in a similar way to the previous exercise. All you need is the data and the formulae for the data as shown in the diagram. You could use the worksheet from the previous example; if so highlight and then clear all the cells except the ones shown. If instead you decide to type in the data, make sure that you enter the formulae in cells B5, C5 and D5.

	A	B	C	D	E	F	G
1							
2	Spreadsheet to determine the side x of a container to give a volume of 500						
3							
4	**x**	**x cubed**	**x^2h/2**	**V**			
5	1	1	1	2			
6							
7							

2 Move the cursor to cell D5, which is the cell we want to set at a certain value (i.e. as near to 500 as possible in this case).

Click on Tools in the menu toolbar and then on Goal Seek...

We want to set D5 at 500 by varying the value of *x* which is in cell A5.

Fill in the pull-down menu shown here:

Check the box is correct and click on OK.

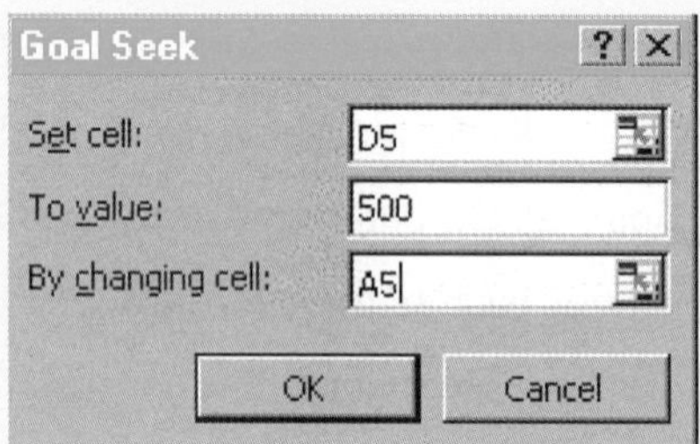

3 The following box appears saying that a solution has been found:

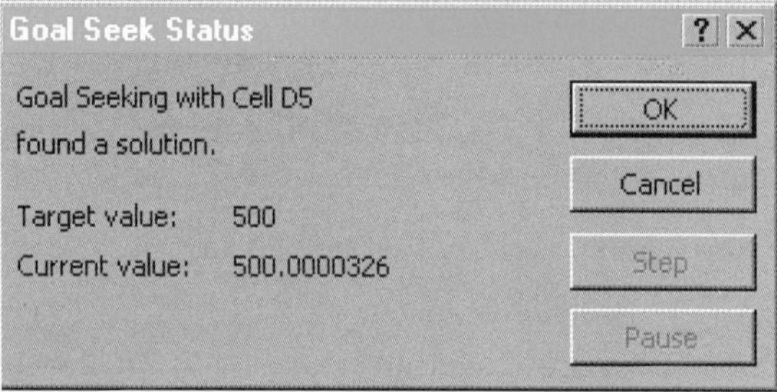

It has not found 500 exactly, but it is near enough!

Click on OK to show the worksheet with the value of x shown.

Exercise 9.6

	A	B	C	D	E	F	G
1							
2	Spreadsheet to determine the side x of a container to give a volume of 500						
3							
4	x	x cubed	$x^2h/2$	V			
5	7.61728	441.97708	58.02295	500.00003			

We need the value of x to two decimal places, so we can format all the numbers in the spreadsheet to two decimal places. This is done by highlighting the cells A5 to D5 and then clicking on Format and then cells. Click on Number and then check that two decimal places have been shown on the menu.

Check that your screen looks like this:

	A	B	C	D	E	F	G
1							
2	Spreadsheet to determine the side x of a container to give a volume of 500						
3							
4	x	x cubed	$x^2h/2$	V			
5	7.62	441.98	58.02	500.00			
6							

The height of the carton will be $2 + 7.62 = 9.62$ cm.

Break-even analysis

Rachel, a whiz computer programmer, has written a really good games program. Everyone who has tried the game reckons it will be a winner. A few magazines have reviewed it and have told her that she must market it. Rachel decides rather than let one of the large games companies market it for her (and take most of the profits), she will try to sell it direct to customers through advertisements in games magazines.

Before starting the business Rachel needs to be sure that she will make some money out of it. One way of doing this is to determine the break-even point. The break-even point is the number of games she must sell to cover her costs. Once Rachel sells more than this number she will start to make a profit.

Costs in the business can be divided into two types, called fixed costs and variable costs.

Fixed costs are those that need to be paid even if none of the games were sold. Rental for the premises, computer hardware and software, wages, loan repayments and interest, etc. are all fixed costs.

Variable costs are those that depend on the number of games sold. Variable costs such as packaging, CDs, etc., all go up as the number of games sold rises.

Rachel has sat down and worked out the following:

Fixed costs = £18,000
Variable cost per game = £7.68
Selling price per game = £21.99

Variable costs are the costs of making a certain number of games and sales revenue is the money received when the same number of games is sold.

Total costs of producing games = variable costs + fixed costs

Variable costs = variable costs per game × number of games

Sales revenue = selling price per game × number of games

Exercise 9.7

Determining the break-even point for Gamesmaster

In this exercise you will learn how to:

- **set up a worksheet to simulate the revenue and expenditure for a product**
- **determine the break-even point**

1 Load the Excel program and start a new worksheet.

2 Enter the title **Gamesmaster** into cell A1. Increase the font size to 12 point and embolden the title.

3 Enter the subheading **Finding the break-even point Try One** into cell A2 and embolden it.

4 In cells A4, A5 and A6 respectively enter the following **Fixed costs**, **Variable costs per game** and **Selling price per game**.

5 Enter the following amounts, including the pound sign into the following cells:

£18,000 into cell B4, **£7.68** into cell B5 and **£21.99** into cell B6.

6 Check that your part of the spreadsheet is the same as this one.

	A	B	C
1	**Gamesmaster**		
2	**Finding the break-even point Try One**		
3			
4	Fixed costs	£18,000	
5	Variable costs per game	£7.68	
6	Selling price per game	£21.99	
7			

7 Enter the column headings across row 8 as shown below and embolden them.

	A	B	C	D	E
1	**Gamesmaster**				
2	**Finding the break-even point Try One**				
3					
4	Fixed costs	£18,000			
5	Variable costs per game	£7.68			
6	Selling price per game	£21.99			
7					
8	**Number of games sold**	**Variable costs**	**Fixed Costs**	**Total Costs**	**Sales Revenue**

8 Now fill in the numbers in the Number of games sold column. We want to go from 100 to 1500 in steps of 100. There is a quick way to do this. In cell A9 enter the starting number of 100. Now click on Edit and then Fill and then Series. The Series box appears. Change the settings in this box to those shown here.

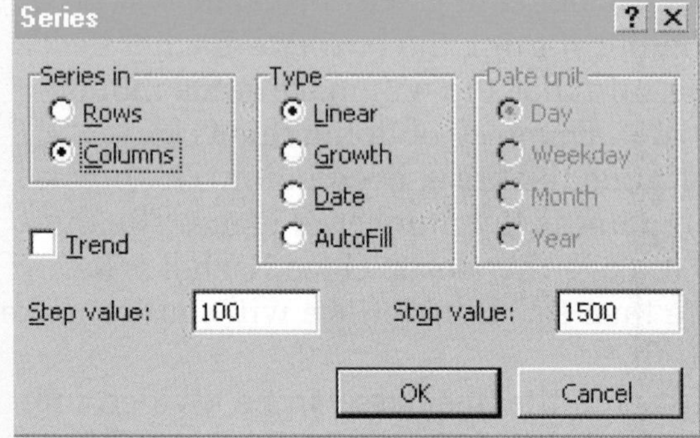

Now click on OK.

Notice that the series of numbers has been automatically entered.

9 Enter the following formula into cell B9:

=$B$5*A9

Notice that this formula contains an absolute cell address for cell B5. This is because when we copy this formula down the column we need to keep it referring to cell B5.

10 Copy the formula in cell B9 down the column as far as cell B23.

11 Enter the formula **=$B$4** into cell C9. The value is copied from cell B4 and placed in cell C9.

12 Copy the formula in C9 down column C.

13 To work out the total costs in column D, the variable costs and fixed costs are added together. Enter the following formula to do this into cell D9:

=B9+C9

Copy this formula relatively down the column.

14 Enter the following formula into cell E9:

=A9*$B$6

Copy this formula relatively down the column.

15 Your worksheet will now look like this:

	A	B	C	D	E	F
1	**Gamesmaster**					
2	**Finding the break-even point Try One**					
3						
4	Fixed costs	£18,000				
5	Variable costs per game	£7.68				
6	Selling price per game	£21.99				
7						
8	**Number of games sold**	**Variable costs**	**Fixed Costs**	**Total Costs**	**Sales Revenue**	
9	100	£768.00	£18,000	£18,768.00	£2,199.00	
10	200	£1,536.00	£18,000	£19,536.00	£4,398.00	
11	300	£2,304.00	£18,000	£20,304.00	£6,597.00	
12	400	£3,072.00	£18,000	£21,072.00	£8,796.00	
13	500	£3,840.00	£18,000	£21,840.00	£10,995.00	
14	600	£4,608.00	£18,000	£22,608.00	£13,194.00	
15	700	£5,376.00	£18,000	£23,376.00	£15,393.00	
16	800	£6,144.00	£18,000	£24,144.00	£17,592.00	
17	900	£6,912.00	£18,000	£24,912.00	£19,791.00	
18	1000	£7,680.00	£18,000	£25,680.00	£21,990.00	
19	1100	£8,448.00	£18,000	£26,448.00	£24,189.00	
20	1200	£9,216.00	£18,000	£27,216.00	£26,388.00	
21	1300	£9,984.00	£18,000	£27,984.00	£28,587.00	
22	1400	£10,752.00	£18,000	£28,752.00	£30,786.00	
23	1500	£11,520.00	£18,000	£29,520.00	£32,985.00	

16 Save this worksheet using the filename 'Break-even point Try One'.

17 Print a copy of the worksheet.

How is the break-even point found?

We have built a model of the business, showing the sales revenue and total costs for selling different numbers of games. We can now play around with the figures.

For example, we might find that by changing our supplier of blank CDs that we can reduce the variable costs from £7.68 to £7.00 a CD and see the effect on the other figures in the worksheet.

Altering the figures in this way is called 'performing a simulation'.

The break-even point is the number of games that Rachel needs to sell when the total costs equals the sales revenue.

If you look at your worksheet you will see that this point occurs somewhere between 1200 and 1300 games sold.

We therefore need to produce another worksheet this time starting with 1200 games sold and going up to 1300 games sold in steps of 10. Rather than create a new worksheet you can alter the one you have already created.

Exercise 9.8

Getting nearer to the break-even point

In this exercise you will learn how to:

- **use another spreadsheet to move closer towards determining the break-even point.**

1 Load the worksheet you have created in the previous exercise.

2 Alter the number of games sold in column A so that it goes from 1200 to 1300 in steps of 10.

3 The bottom section of the old spreadsheet will still be shown, so highlight it and then click on Edit then Clear and then All. This will remove the unwanted section.

4 Alter the sub-heading to **Finding the break-even point Try Two**. Embolden this.

5 After all this, your worksheet will now look like this:

	A	B	C	D	E
1	**Gamesmaster**				
2	**Finding the break-even point Try Two**				
3					
4	Fixed costs	£18,000			
5	Variable costs per game	£7.68			
6	Selling price per game	£21.99			
7					
8	**Number of games sold**	**Variable costs**	**Fixed Costs**	**Total Costs**	**Sales Revenue**
9	1200	£9,216.00	£18,000	£27,216.00	£26,388.00
10	1210	£9,292.80	£18,000	£27,292.80	£26,607.90
11	1220	£9,369.60	£18,000	£27,369.60	£26,827.80
12	1230	£9,446.40	£18,000	£27,446.40	£27,047.70
13	1240	£9,523.20	£18,000	£27,523.20	£27,267.60
14	1250	£9,600.00	£18,000	£27,600.00	£27,487.50
15	1260	£9,676.80	£18,000	£27,676.80	£27,707.40
16	1270	£9,753.60	£18,000	£27,753.60	£27,927.30
17	1280	£9,830.40	£18,000	£27,830.40	£28,147.20
18	1290	£9,907.20	£18,000	£27,907.20	£28,367.10
19	1300	£9,984.00	£18,000	£27,984.00	£28,587.00

6 Save this worksheet using the filename 'Break-even point Try Two'.

7 Print a copy of the worksheet.

When you look carefully at the figures in the Total Costs and Sales Revenue columns you can see that the two figures are equal when between 1250 and 1260 games are sold. To get nearer to the break-even point we must look in detail at between 1250 and 1260 games being sold, now going up in steps of one.

Exercise 9.9

The final worksheet to find the break-even point

In this exercise you will learn how to:

- **determine the break-even point exactly.**

1 You now need to repeat the process described in Exercise 9.8, this time starting with the number of games sold at 1250 and then going up in steps of one to 1260. Use the previous worksheet rather than starting from scratch.

2 Get rid of any unwanted part of the previous worksheet.

3 Save this worksheet using the filename 'Break-even point Try Three'.

4 Print a copy of the worksheet.

5 Check that your worksheet looks like this:

	A	B	C	D	E
1	**Gamesmaster**				
2	**Finding the break-even point Try Three**				
3					
4	Fixed costs	£18,000			
5	Variable costs per game	£7.68			
6	Selling price per game	£21.99			
7					
8	**Number of games sold**	**Variable costs**	**Fixed Costs**	**Total Costs**	**Sales Revenue**
9	1250	£9,600.00	£18,000	£27,600.00	£27,487.50
10	1251	£9,607.68	£18,000	£27,607.68	£27,509.49
11	1252	£9,615.36	£18,000	£27,615.36	£27,531.48
12	1253	£9,623.04	£18,000	£27,623.04	£27,553.47
13	1254	£9,630.72	£18,000	£27,630.72	£27,575.46
14	1255	£9,638.40	£18,000	£27,638.40	£27,597.45
15	1256	£9,646.08	£18,000	£27,646.08	£27,619.44
16	1257	£9,653.76	£18,000	£27,653.76	£27,641.43
17	1258	£9,661.44	£18,000	£27,661.44	£27,663.42
18	1259	£9,669.12	£18,000	£27,669.12	£27,685.41
19	1260	£9,676.80	£18,000	£27,676.80	£27,707.40

Finding the final break-even point

If you look at the Total Costs and Sales Revenue figures again you can see that they are almost the same when 1258 games are sold. The break-even point is therefore 1258. If Rachel sells only 1257 games Total Costs are greater than the Sales Revenue and a small loss will be made. If 1259 games are sold, then a small profit will be made.

Project work on modelling

Modelling is one of the five strands for coursework and you may consider producing a piece of coursework based on this important area of computing.

Things to look at:

- Pick a suitable title.
- Write clearly what the problem is that you are trying to solve.
- Say which software you are going to use and state the reasons why this software is

the most suitable. You could either use specialist modelling software or use spreadsheet software such as Excel.

- Explain how you arrived at the rules of the model. Explain how these may be expressed in terms of mathematical equations.
- Your first attempt at the model will usually be a simplification and you may need to add further equations to make it more complex to better mimic the real situation.
  Sometimes it may be necessary to change some of the formulae you initially thought were correct. Again, these changes need to be documented.
- Change the variables in the model and produce printouts of the results obtained. Try to explain what the results show.

Models need to be thoroughly tested. In many cases they can be used to compare the results with the results obtained in the real situation. Sometimes the model will predict results that can be compared against experimental values.

You should explain how your model can be used to help someone make predictions and decisions. If appropriate you can also explain how the model can be used to explore patterns and relationships.

A model should be designed so that it is easy to use. Remember in many cases in IT you will be developing the model for other people to use. You need to evaluate its ease of use. One way to do this is to give it to someone else to use. You could obtain feedback by getting them to complete a questionnaire. You can also mention how the software made the task easier.

Include printouts of things that work and also things that don't. This shows the teacher/moderator how you have worked through the problem. Even if the work is fairly rough, it is still important to include it. Produce printouts at every stage, showing the results; also have printouts showing the formulae used.

As with all GCSE coursework particularly remember to produce ...

Evidence All The Way!

In the next section there are some models for you to try.

Models for you to try

Here are some models you can try developing for practice. As well as solving the problem, provide the documentation for your solution as if you were doing these for your GCSE project work.

1 Model the population of goldfish in a garden pond

In this example you have to model the population of goldfish in a pond.
If conditions were ideal, the goldfish would breed, the population would soon rise and the pond would be overrun by fish. This does not happen because there are factors constantly at work which remove some of the goldfish from the system. These factors include the following:

- bad winters causing some of the goldfish to die
- herons eating goldfish
- diseases causing the death of goldfish when their resistance is low
- goldfish dying due to poor water conditions/overcrowding
- goldfish dying of old age.

For the model you will need to start off with a certain number of goldfish and then try to assess what the breeding rates and death rates are in each month of the year. You will also need to display the population of the fish in the pond for each month, taking into account the breeding and death rates.

The more you can find out about goldfish (i.e. will all the fish breed? How many eggs do they lay? What percentage of these eggs hatch? How many of the baby fish eventually mature to become adults? How old does a female fish need to be before it can breed? How long do goldfish live?) the more accurate the model will become.

2 Counting the calories

Look at the following labels. They show certain nutritional properties of food. This information is particularly important if you want to make sure you have a balanced diet or are 'watching calories' as part of a diet.

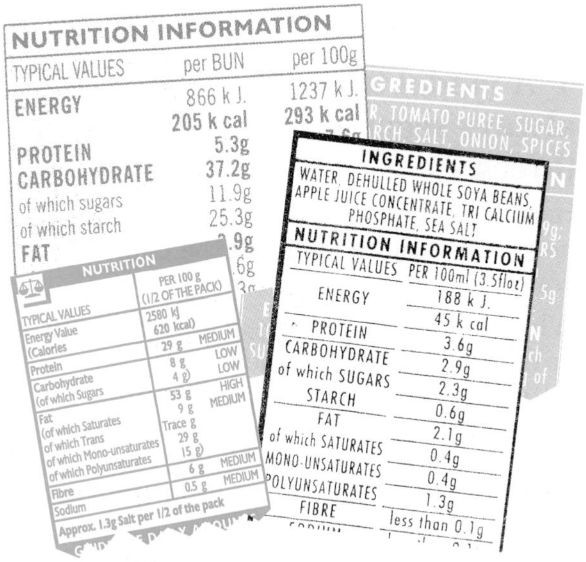

Fig 9.3 *A variety of different food labels*

Produce a spreadsheet to model the number of calories you eat and burn up in one day.

Suggested approach
Find out the calories used in various activities and assess the amount of time (on average) you spend each day doing these activities. Sitting down, watching TV or even sleeping, burns up some calories so you need to take these into account.

For the same day you also need to work out what food you have eaten and how many calories per 100 g it contains. The amount and type of food you eat will vary from day to day, so you should choose a fairly typical day. If you divide the calories per 100 g by 100 you will get the calories in each gram. You can then multiply this by the number of grams of this particular food you have eaten, to get the total calories for this food. Putting this into the spreadsheet, you can add up to find your total calorie intake for the day. Subtracting the total calories used up from the total calories taken in you can find whether you have gained or lost calories.

Counting the calories!

- If your calorie intake is greater than the calories you use up you will gain weight.
- If your calorie intake is less than the calories you use up you will lose weight.
- If your calorie intake and use are the same, your weight will stay constant.

3 Modelling a traffic queue caused by roadworks

One lane of a half-mile section of busy road has had to be dug up to repair a collapsed sewer pipe. This has resulted in temporary traffic lights having to be installed at either end of the half-mile section. Only one lane of traffic can pass at a time, and this has resulted in serious delays. A diagram of part of this section of the road is shown below.

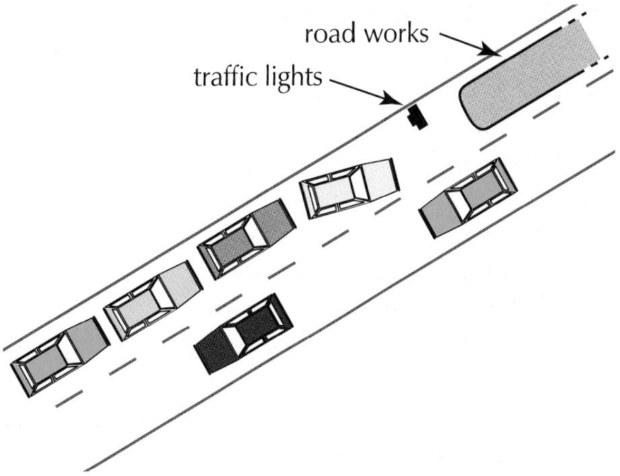

Fig 9.4 *Diagram of part of the section of the road*

The idea is to produce a model to explain and investigate the factors causing the queue.

A few hints to get you started
You need to think about what a queue is and try to describe it as an equation.

Basically there are three things to consider:

- traffic arriving
- traffic already in the queue
- traffic leaving the queue.

The length of queue (i.e. the number of vehicles in the queue) can be described using this equation:

Length of queue = traffic arriving + traffic already in the queue – traffic leaving the queue

You can see from this equation that if the traffic arriving and the traffic leaving the queue are the same, the queue will not change in length.

To make the situation easier to start with, assume that the traffic flow is the same on both sides of the roadworks. Also assume that the lights are on green for the same amount of time each way.

You will have to consider the time it takes each block of traffic to travel the half-mile section. Remember that this traffic at peak time will probably start from rest since much of the traffic will already have joined the queue.

As you can see, the problem has many factors. The key to doing a model like this is to simplify the situation by making assumptions, then develop something that works. You can then start to build-in more of the factors seen in the real situation until you have a model that behaves in a way that is very close to the real thing.

4 A model to explain why buses always seem to arrive in twos or threes

Here is a problem statement (you should have one of these in any of the coursework you do):

Why do buses always seem to come in twos or threes? I intend to model two buses setting off ten minutes apart from the depot and picking up passengers along the way. Once I have a model that works I will extend the project to looking at three buses, also setting off ten minutes apart from the bus station.

I will investigate:

- the dependence on the amount of traffic
- the dependence on the number of passengers picked up at each stop.

By using my model I will be able to suggest reasons why buses seem to come in groups.

Your task is to continue with the development and documentation of this model.

10 Wordprocessing: the Basics

Introduction

Wordprocessing is by far the most popular computer application and its popularity is due to the ease by which professional-looking documents can be produced by anyone. Years ago you would have had to attend a long course in typing just to type a simple letter.

The basics of wordprocessing are looked at in this chapter. You will already be familiar with the use of wordprocessing in your work for KS3 and I have assumed that you already have this knowledge.

Word XP (provided as part of the package Office XP) will be looked at here. Most of the features and instructions also work if you have previous versions of Word, such as Word 2000 or Word 97.

Loading the software

Your teacher will show you how to load the wordprocessing program, Microsoft Word. If you need to keep your work on a floppy disk then your teacher will show you how to do this too. If you are working on a network your teacher will advise you where to store files.

> **QUESTIONS**
>
> It is important that you are able to load Word.
>
> Write down a brief set of instructions to remind you how to do this.

Toolbars and menus

How Word looks when you first load it depends on how it has been set up. If the settings have not been altered, it will look like the figure below. The top bar (containing File, Edit, View, etc.) is called the menu bar because when you click on a word a menu with options appears. The next toolbar is the formatting toolbar where you can alter the font, font size, change the way the text appears on the page, etc. The bottom toolbar is called the standard toolbar and contains buttons to print, save, open, spellcheck, etc.

The screen to the right of the page is called the task pane and this is used to select the type of document you want to work on.

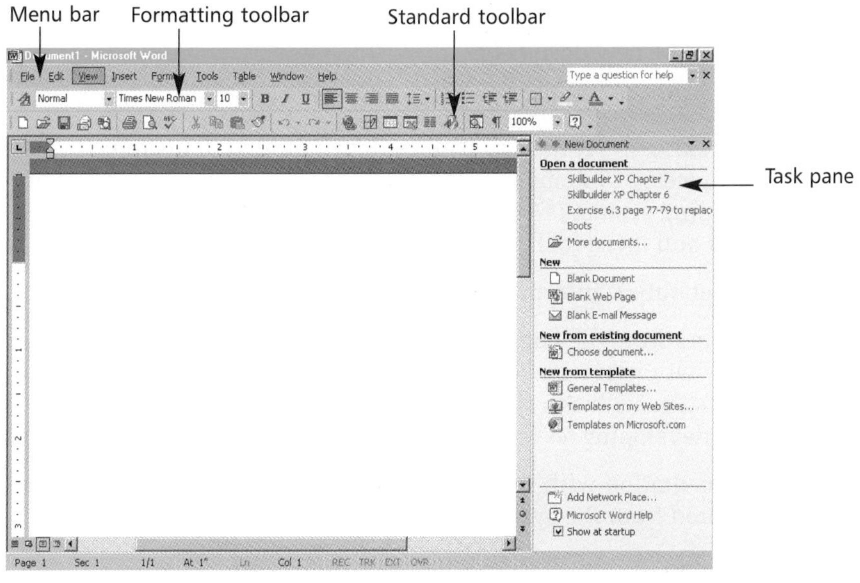

Advice when wordprocessing your work

Here are some tips that should save you time when wordprocessing your work.

- As with all work done on computers, always keep backup copies. Get into the habit of saving regularly onto two disks (one could be the hard disk) and keep these disks apart (i.e. not in the same disk box).
- Get into the habit of typing your work straight into the wordprocessor rather than writing it down first. You can still change things round later (you can still plan work on paper though.) Sometimes it is a good idea to first type in the main titles, headings and sub-headings at the top of the page, then you can see where you are going.
- Do not bother too much about the layout at the start. This can be done later when you have typed in your work. It is probably best to concentrate on the content first.
- Do not edit as you go along. Get all the typing done first and then make your corrections.
- Proofread your document carefully.
- Use the spellchecker to correct any words misspelled (underlined by a red wavy line).
- Always save your work before printing.
- Use Print preview to see the layout of each page on the screen before printing. This will save you time and paper.
- Print out your work only when completely satisfied it is what you want.

Exercise 10.1

Getting the hang of editing

In this exercise you will practise:

- **loading the wordprocessing software**
- **proofreading the document**
- **making alterations to the document**
- **saving and printing the document.**

1 Load Word and start a new document.

2 Here is a piece of text concerning spreadsheet design. Type it in carefully.

If you are working in IT, then as well as developing systems to use yourself you will also have to develop systems for other people to use. In fact, most of your time will be spent developing systems for others. There are various complications in developing such systems and these include:

Knowing what output information is wanted.

We always work from the end result (the output from the system) because this in turn determines what input is needed and the type of processing needed. The person who develops a system such as a spreadsheet should be clear about what the user requires. It is no good developing a system that fails to give the users what they really want.

Constant consultation with the user is necessary at all stages so that everyone knows what is required from the system.

How the information is currently obtained (if at all)

In some cases the information may already be available. For example, a college may need information about the results, percentage attendance and percentage of the students who completed the course out of those who started. This information may have come from a variety of sources such as registers, mark books, student registration details and so on. It may have been prepared manually, the output written down on a form.

A college has many different courses and they might need to produce a summary for all their courses in different subject areas. They may need to produce a blank spreadsheet to be sent to course tutors on which they can enter the data about their own students. This makes it easy for someone to merge the data together to produce the large spreadsheet with the data for all the courses.

3 Proofread your document by comparing it with the original document. Make any alterations so that they are identical.

4 Change the first sentence to;

   If you work in IT you will develop systems for others to use as well as develop systems for yourself.

5 In the second sentence delete the words 'In fact', and change 'most' to 'Most'.

6 In the second paragraph change the second sentence from 'The person who develops a system such as a spreadsheet should...' to 'The person who develops a system for someone else should...'.

7 In paragraph 4, after the sentence 'In some cases the information may already be available.' insert a new sentence 'In others it might be necessary to develop a system to produce the information'.

8 In the last paragraph, first sentence, delete the word 'they'.

9 In the last paragraph, first sentence change 'might need to produce a summary for all their courses' to 'might need to produce a summary of statistics for all their courses'.

10 In the final sentence, delete the first occurrence of the word 'the'.

11 Proofread the document to check that all the changes have been made correctly.

12 Save the document using the filename 'Editing exercise'.

13 Print out a copy of the document.

QUESTIONS

How much do you already know about wordprocessing?

1 You are talking to a writer who always uses a typewriter. They have explained some of the reasons why they like the typewriter. In particular they say:

(a) they know how to use the typewriter and would have to learn how to use the wordprocessor, which would take time
(b) they can take their typewriter anywhere with them since it needs no power supply
(c) computers and their software are expensive.

Write a couple of brief paragraphs explaining how useful wordprocessing would be to the writer.

2 Find out (by experiment or by using the help menu), one way to:

(a) delete a single letter
(b) insert an extra word into the middle of a sentence
(c) delete a single word
(d) delete an entire sentence
(e) delete a paragraph
(f) delete a couple of pages.

3 A screenshot from Word is shown below. The arrows point to various parts of the screen. Either by using Help or experimentation, find out what each of the items does.

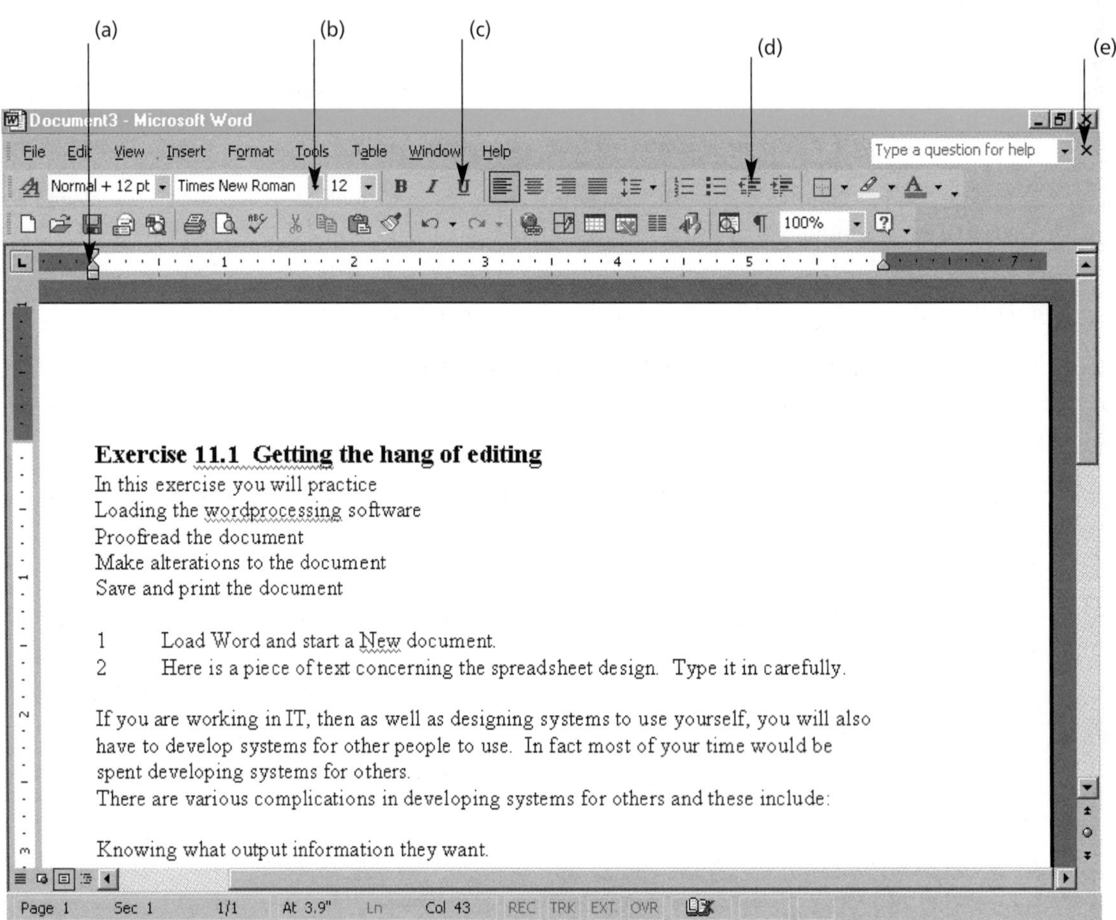

Selecting text

With Word you can select one or more characters, a word, a sentence, a paragraph or a huge block of text. There are several reasons why you might want to select text. You might want to:

- move it to a new position
- copy it
- delete it.

To mark a block of text, position the mouse pointer to the left of the start of the text and then press the left mouse button down. Keep the button down and drag the mouse so that the cursor highlights the text to be selected then release the button.

Exercise 10.2

Moving text around

In this exercise you will learn to:

- **select text**
- **move blocks of text into a different order.**

It is sometimes necessary to move text around. To do this, you need to first select the text you want to move by highlighting it. Moving text is useful when on proofreading you feel that the order of sentences should be changed.

1 Load Word, open a new document and type in the following terms that are used in computing.

> Desktop publishing: software that can be used to combine text and pictures on a screen to produce neat looking posters, newsletters, brochures, etc.
>
> Bitmap graphics: graphics formed by a pattern of pixels. The whole picture is stored as a series of dots.
>
> Character: any symbol that you can type from the keyboard.
>
> Backup file: a copy of a file that is used in the event of the original file being corrupted (damaged).
>
> Edit: change something stored on a computer.
>
> Ink-jet printer: a printer that works by spraying ink through nozzles onto the paper.

2 Select the paragraph on desktop publishing by highlighting it.

3 Click on Edit and then Cut. This piece of text disappears from the screen and is put in a temporary storage place called the clipboard.

4 Move the cursor to the end of the paragraph on character and press Enter to start a new line. Make sure that a blank line is left between the definition for character and the position of the cursor.

5 Click on Edit and then Paste. This inserts the text stored on the clipboard, starting at the point where the cursor is situated.

6 Proofread this glossary and make sure that there is a blank line left between one term and the next.

7 Using these steps put all these terms into alphabetical order.

8 Save your work using the filename 'Sorted DTP glossary'.

9 Print out a copy of your document.

Exercise 10.3

Copying blocks of text

If the same piece of text needs to be repeated you do not need to type it again; you can copy it instead.

In this exercise you will learn how to:

- **copy a selected piece of text to the clipboard**
- **insert a copy of the text into another part of the document.**

Here is an advertisement for private tuition to be placed on a school noticeboard:

> Are you having difficulty with your maths?
>
> Would you like some help?
>
> A teacher with ten years experience will help you.
>
> Reasonable rates starting at £14 per hour.
>
> Ring Jayne on 0123-232-3828

The idea is that this advertisement appears many times on an A4 page and cuts are made in the paper so that the details can be torn off by anyone interested in tuition.

1. Load the wordprocessing software and type in the above text.
2. Select the entire block of text by highlighting it.
3. Click on Edit and then Copy.
4. Move the cursor down about four lines using the Enter key.
5. Click on Edit and then Paste. A copy of the advert will appear.
6. Repeat steps 4 and 5 as many times until you get to the end of the page.
7. Save your work using the filename 'Advertisement for private tuition'.
8. Print out your page.

Formatting text to make it stand out

You can with any particular font and size use the following styles:

Bold	**B**
<u>Underline</u>	U
Italics	*I*

To format text, select it and click on the relevant button.

Fonts

Changing the font alters the appearance of the characters. Fonts are given names and you can change the font by selecting the text and then clicking on the part of the formatting toolbar shown below. Notice also that there is a section for altering the font size.

Click here to alter the font size

Click here to alter the font (each font is given a name; in this case the font is called Times New Roman)

When the arrow pointing down (correctly called the downscroll arrow) is clicked, a list of fonts appears from which you can choose (see the screen below). Click on any one to make your choice.

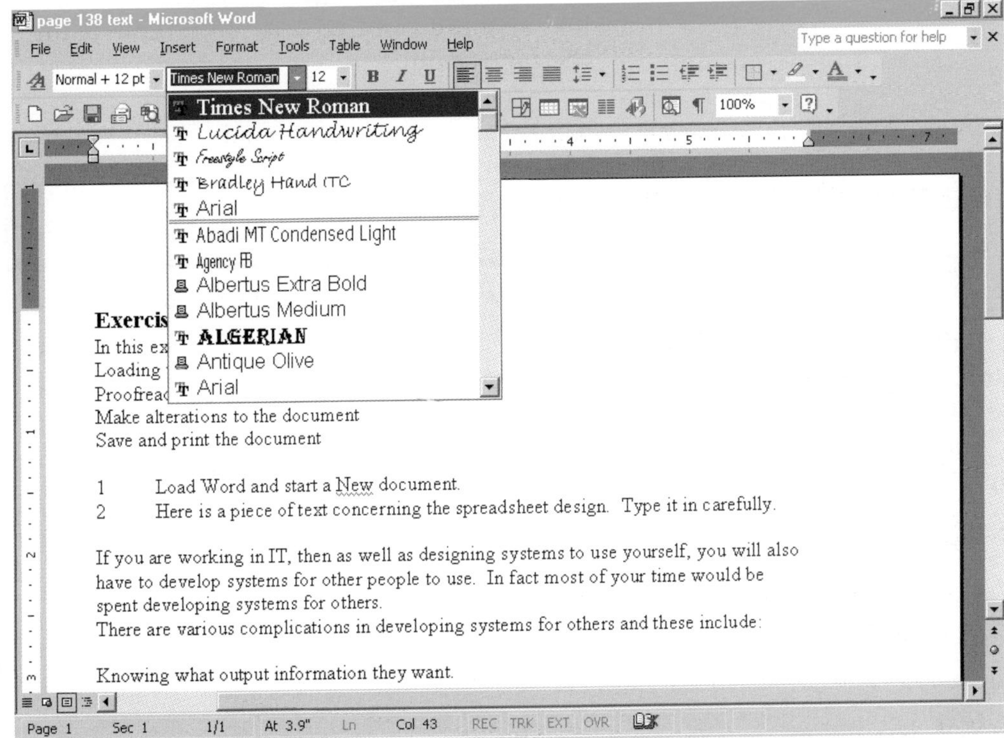

Choosing a font

The two most popular fonts for normal typing are Arial and Times New Roman.

Font size

Once again, select the text to be altered and click on the downscroll arrow next to the font size.

A series of numbers appears. Most text is typed with a font size of 10 or 12 points.

Font colour

To change font colour, select the text, click on Format and then select Font...

The font menu appears as shown in the screen to the right.

Click on the downscroll arrow in the font colour box. This opens up a palette where you can click on a font colour to select it. The selected text now changes colour.

Notice that you can get many text effects and other things using this menu.

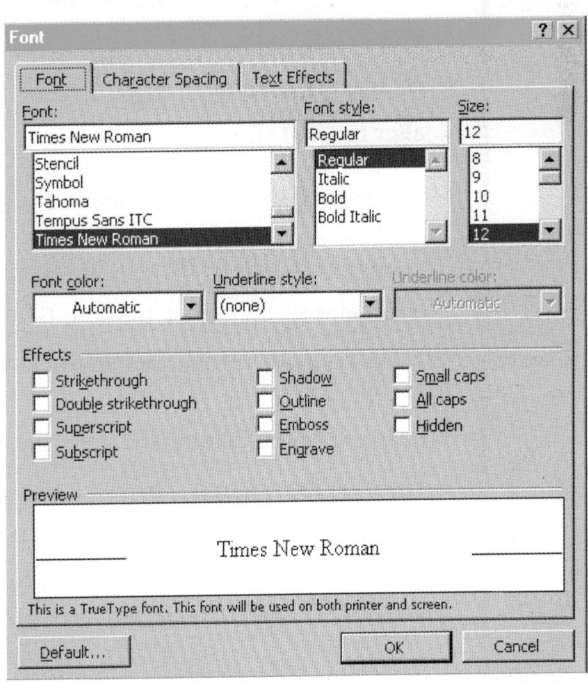

The font menu offers many options

IT TASKS

Type in a short piece of text and experiment with items on the font menu.

To align text you first select the relevant text and then click on one of the alignment buttons.

There are a few other ways of aligning text and you can find out about them using the help menu.

Aligning text

There are four buttons for aligning text:

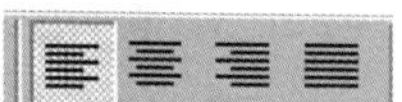

Working from left to right, the first button is the 'align left' button. This is followed by the 'centre' button, the 'align right' button and finally the 'justify' button. The justify button produces text which is straight down both margins.

QUESTIONS

Explain by reference to both the right and left margins, what each of the following mean:

(a) align right

(b) align left

(c) justify.

Exercise 10.4

Aligning text

In this exercise you will learn how to:

- **format text**
- **change the alignment of text**
- **alter the font size.**

Mrs Jones is off sick today and the following notice is to be placed on her classroom door.

> Mrs Jones will be off sick today.
>
> All classes should go to room B23.
>
> Wait outside until a member of staff arrives.

1 Load the wordprocessor and enter the above text.

2 Highlight the text and change the font size to 18 point and also make the text bold.

3 With the text still highlighted, click on the centre text button.

4 Click the left mouse button to de-select the highlighted text and then highlight just the word 'All'. Click on the underline button.

Exercise 10.5

Practice exercise

In this exercise you will gain practice at:

- **changing fonts**
- **changing font styles (bold, underline and italics)**
- **changing font sizes**
- **changing font colours.**

The restaurant manager has given you a copy of the day's menu. You tell her that the appearance of the menu could be improved.

The Riverbank Hotel
Starters
Prawn Cocktail
Soup of the Day
Garlic Mushrooms
Sliced Melon
Main Course
Beef Wellington
Lemon Sole
Vegetarian Lasagna
Half Roast Chicken
Dessert
Black Forest Gateau
Sticky Toffee Pudding
Strawberries and Cream
Cheese and Biscuits
Coffee and Mints

Improve the appearance of this menu by using some, or all, of the following:

- font
- font style (bold, underline and italics)
- font size
- font colour.

Some advice about keying in text

Do not press enter at the end of each line. Any partially completed words will be moved to the next line automatically. This is called wordwrap.

So that wordprocessed work looks consistent (i.e. looks the same no matter who types it) you should obey the following rules when keying in text.

Paragraphs – there should be a blank line between paragraphs.

Commas – there should be a single blank space after a comma.

Full stops – two blank spaces should be left after a full stop.

Colons – one blank space should be left after a colon.

Question marks – one blank space should be left after a question mark.

Print and print preview

Word provides something called print preview where you can see a smaller copy of your document and what it looks like on the page.

To see the print preview of a document you must have the document on the screen. Click on File and then move the pointer onto the two arrows pointing down, so that the further drop down menu is displayed. On this menu select Print Preview and a screen like the one below will appear.

Once the layout has been checked and is OK you click on Close.

Printing

Always make sure that you save your work before printing: the program could freeze if there is a problem with the printer. If this happens, you will have to turn off your computer and will lose any work in progress. Also, make sure that the printer is switched on and that it has paper.

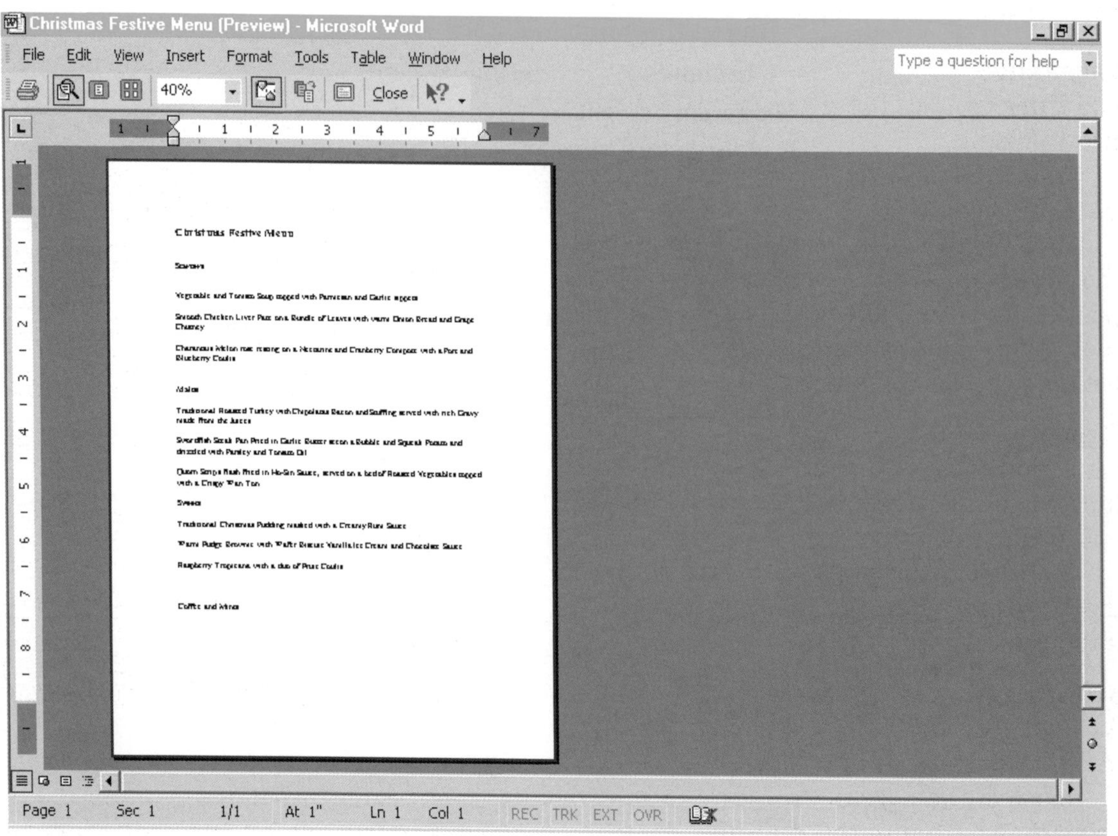

Print preview *shows on the screen what your document will look like when it is printed*

To print a document, just click on the print button on the standard toolbar. The whole document will now be printed.

This method is fine if you just want to print one copy of the entire document. If you don't want this you will need to use the Print menu. To display the Print menu select File and then Print... The following menu appears:

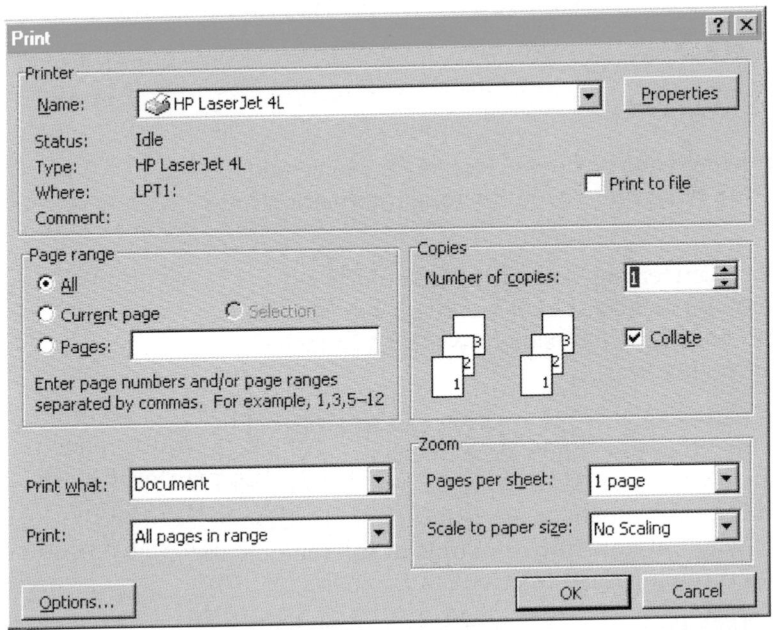

This menu has the following parts:

Page range
Click on All if all the pages in the document need printing.

Click on Current page if you want to print only the page where the cursor is positioned.

Click on Pages and then type in the box the page numbers or ranges that need to be printed. (e.g. '2–5' means pages 2 to 5 inclusive; '3' means just page 3; and '2, 5, 6' means pages 2, 5 and 6 will be printed).

Copies
Click on the arrows pointing up or down to increase or decrease the number of copies you need to print.

There are other parts to this menu, but those covered here are by far the most important ones.

Selecting the paper orientation
As with spreadsheets, printing can be done in either portrait or landscape orientation.

To select the page orientation click on the Properties button in the Print menu. The following menu appears:

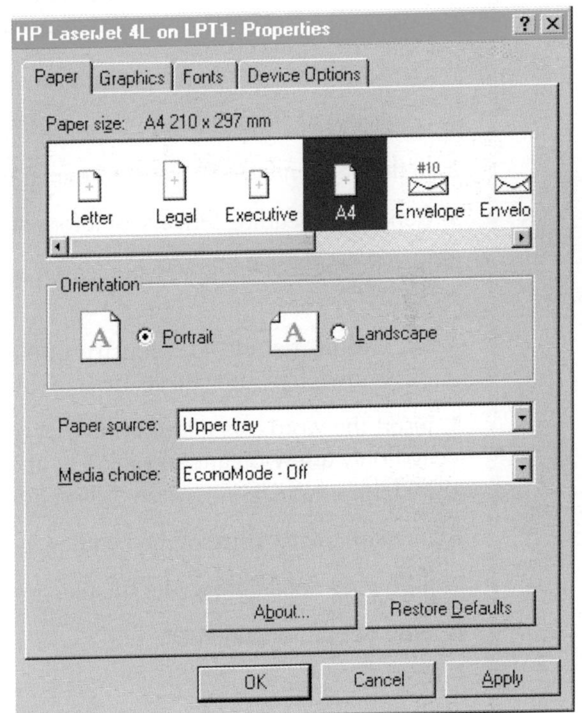

Click on the orientation you need and then click on OK. Notice that using this menu you can also select the paper size.

Exercise 10.6

Revision of skills

In this exercise you will practise most of the skills learnt in Chapter 10.

1 Open a document and type in the text shown below, making sure that you obey all the rules mentioned earlier in the chapter when keying in text.

> Privacy of information
>
> Do you like everyone knowing your business? Has anyone ever said anything untrue about you? What effect would wrong information have on your life?
>
> All the above are questions concerning something called privacy. Although private information (such as school records, medical records, criminal records, etc.) has been kept for years, it was kept in locked filing cabinets away from prying eyes.
>
> With the introduction of networks, this information can be accessed by many more people, provided that they know how to use the system and have a password. It is much harder to be anonymous now because so many organisations hold information about us. Years ago only a few organisations knew about you but now huge amounts of information are held and this information is often passed from one to another.
>
> There is a law called the Data Protection Act 1998 which seeks to restrict what can and cannot be done with personal information.

2 In the first sentence of the third paragraph, delete the word 'this'.

3 Centre the heading 'Privacy of information' and embolden and underline it.

4 Include the following new paragraph between the first and second sentences in the third paragraph.

> Unfortunately lax security often means that these passwords can become common knowledge and the security of any personal data held is compromised.

5 Insert the word 'organisation' so that the last sentence in the third paragraph now reads 'Years ago only a few organisations knew about you but now huge amounts of information are held and this information is often passed from one organisation to another'.

6 Increase the font size of the heading to 16 point.

7 Save your document under the filename 'Privacy'.

8 Print out this document.

Saving a document

There are several ways to save a document.

Using Save As...

This method is useful because you can see where (i.e. on which drive) the document is being saved. To use this method click on File and then Save As... and the following menu appears:

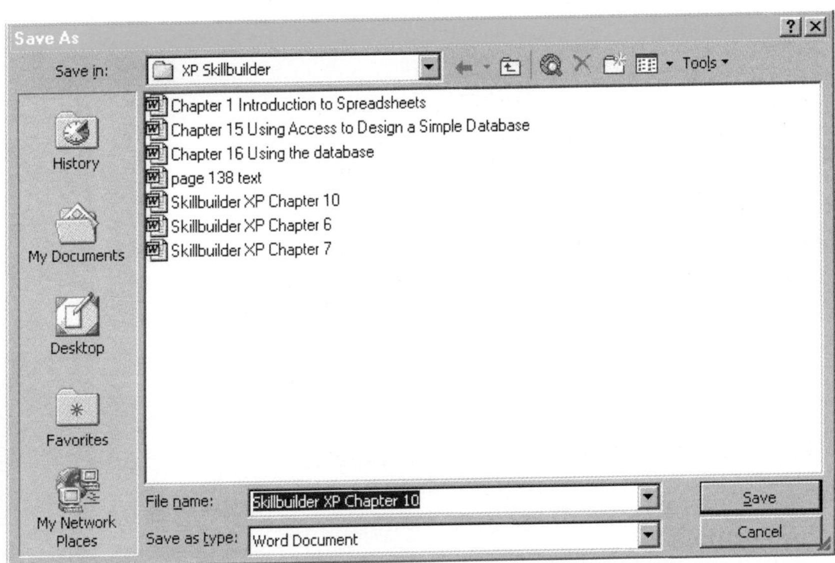

In the Save in box you can alter the drive where the work is to be saved. You can also alter the folder where it is to be saved. If you have not saved the document before, a file name will be given which is the name of the first few words in the document. If you do not want this, just type in a new name.

Save As also allows you to give an existing document a different name when you next save it. It can also be useful for making sure that you have a backup copy on a different drive to the original.

Save

To save you can go to File and then Save or use the save button which has a picture of a floppy disk on it: .

When you save for the first time using save you can tell the computer where document is to go (i.e. floppy or hard-drive) and into which folder it is to be put; you can also give the document a name. If you save the document again it will automatically assume that you are using the same place to store the document and that name remains as before.

Improving the Appearance of your Work

In this chapter, the many ways of improving the appearance of a wordprocessed document will be examined.

Laying out documents

The content of a document is important, but the way the text looks on the page is also important. It is a good idea to look at the print preview of the document and ask yourself if the layout of the text on the page looks good. Another way to do this is to print the document and hold it at arm's length to see how the layout looks.

Margins

Margins are the blank spaces around the edges of the page. Page margins are set by the program but you can change them in several ways one of which is to use the horizontal ruler. Look at the diagram below. The margin is shown as a shaded area at the end of the ruler. If you point to the line between the working area (i.e. where the marked ruler is) and the margin, the pointer changes to a double-headed arrow. You can now drag this (move it keeping the left mouse button down) to increase or decrease the margin. To keep both margins the same, you need to do this with the right margin too.

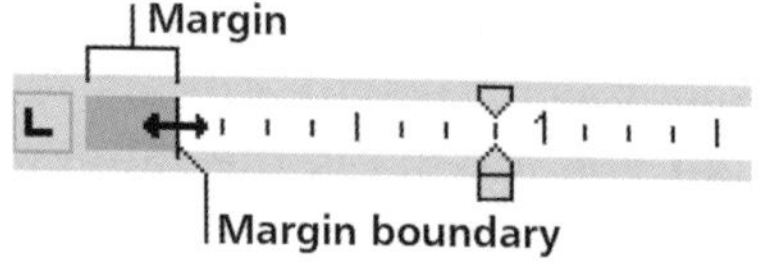

Another way to change margins is to use the page setup menu. To get to this menu click on File (wait a few seconds and the further menu will appear) and then Page Setup... The following menu appears:

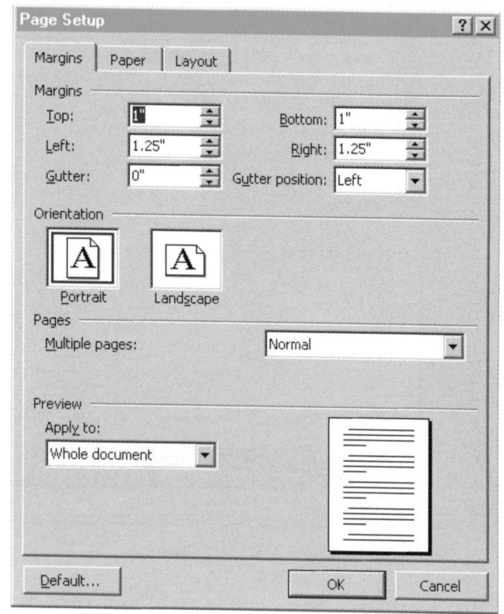

The page setup menu

You can alter the original settings, called the default settings. Notice the preview screen where you can see the immediate results of your alterations.

Indenting text

It is possible to indent the text from the margins and the easiest way to do this is to use the markers on the ruler.

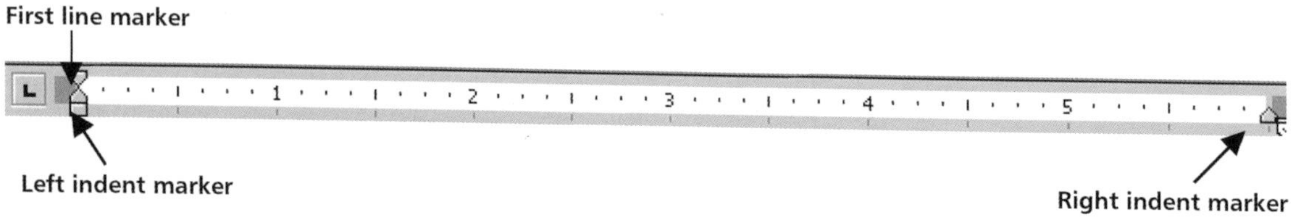

Exercise 11.1

In this exercise you will learn how to:

- **position the markers.**

1 Open a document and type in the following text.

> Whenever you want to indent your work you should always use the correct way and not simply insert spaces by pressing the space bar. If you insert spaces by pressing the space bar, you will find it difficult to alter your text subsequently.

2 Click on any part of the paragraph you have just typed. Click on the square part of the marker on the left of the ruler and then drag it. You will notice that as well as the left indent marker moving, the hanging indent and the first line indent marker move as well. Move this group of markers to the position shown below.

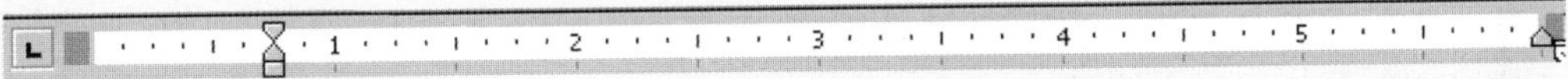

3 Now move the right indent marker to the position shown below.

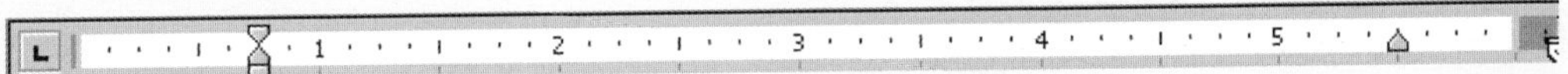

4 Check that your text now looks like that below, indented from the two margins.

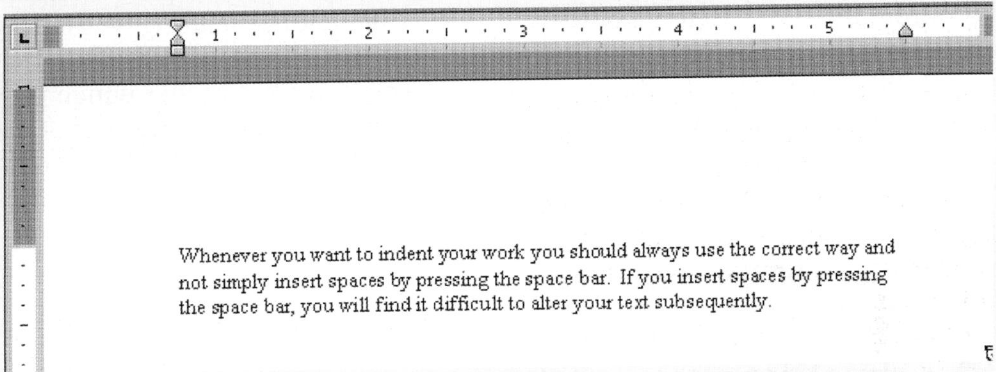
Whenever you want to indent your work you should always use the correct way and
not simply insert spaces by pressing the space bar. If you insert spaces by pressing
the space bar, you will find it difficult to alter your text subsequently.

5 Save this piece of text using the filename 'paragraph'.

6 Check how this text looks on the page using the print preview. To use this click on File and then Print Preview.

7 Print out a copy of the document.

Exercise 11.2

In this exercise you will learn how to:

- **indent the first line of a paragraph.**

1 Open the document 'paragraph', saved in the last exercise.

2 Indent the first line by moving the markers to the positions shown below.

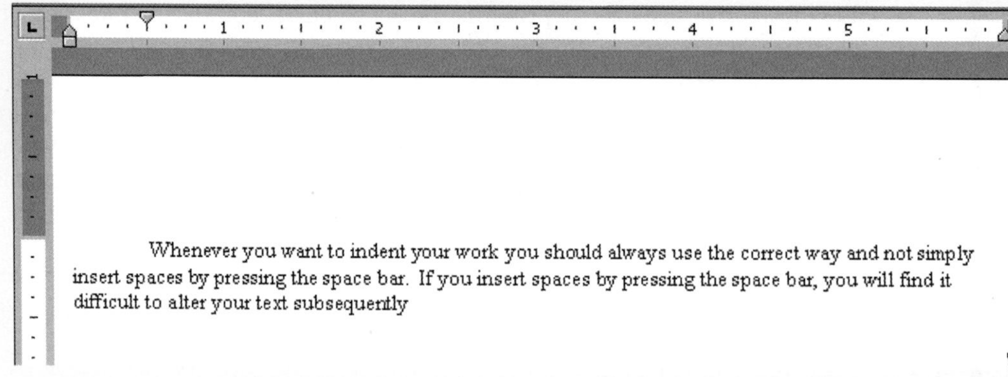
Whenever you want to indent your work you should always use the correct way and not simply insert spaces by pressing the space bar. If you insert spaces by pressing the space bar, you will find it difficult to alter your text subsequently

Adding borders

One way to make a particular piece of text stand out from the rest is to use a border. The border is a box around the text. There are several different borders to choose from. Once a border has been added you can add shading to the background inside the border. When adding shading be careful that it does not make any text difficult to read. There is a second type of border which produces a border around the edge of the page.

Exercise 11.3

Placing a border around text

In this exercise you will learn how to:

- **place a border around some text**
- **shade the area inside the border.**

1 Start a new document and type in the following text.

Borders are very useful if you want some text to stand out. If you want certain text to be really noticed then put a border around it. As well as adding a border you can also highlight the text by applying shading.

2 Click anywhere inside the paragraph if you want to put the border around the whole paragraph. Otherwise just select the text.

3 Click on Format then on the two arrows pointing down to show more menu items. Next click Borders and Shading... and the following menu appears:

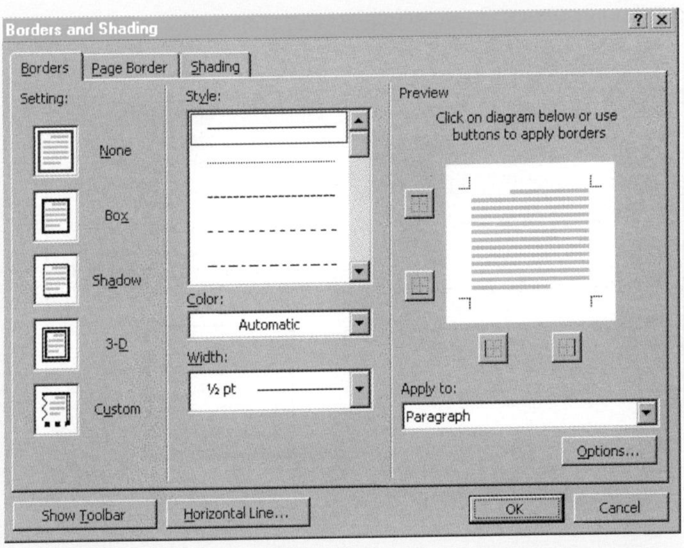

Using the above menu alter the settings to those shown below.

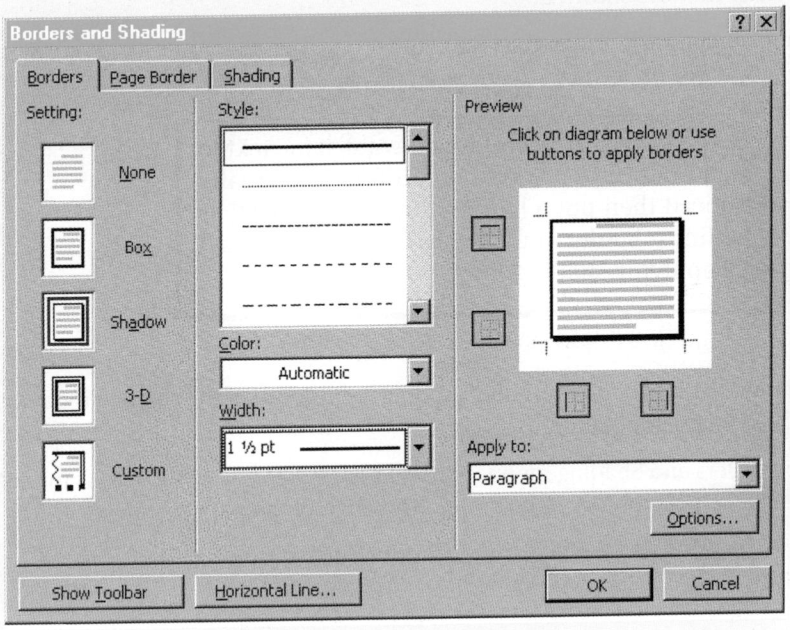

4 Notice that there are three parts to the Borders and Shading menu; Borders, Page Border and Shading. Click on Shading.

Exercise 11.3

5 The following shading menu appears:

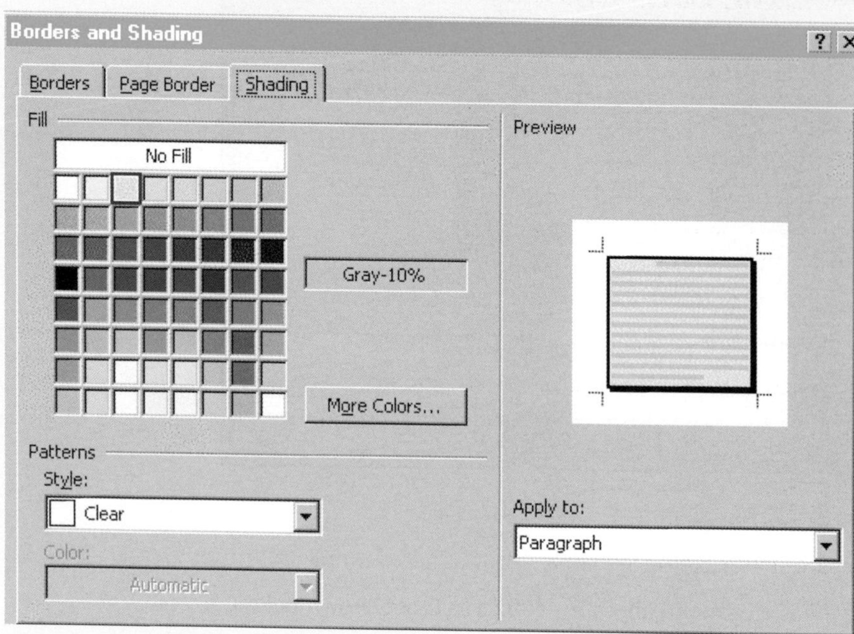

Alter the settings to those shown above.

6 Your paragraph will now look like this.

> Borders are very useful if you want some text to stand out. If you want certain text to be really noticed then put a border around it. As well as adding a border you can also highlight the text by applying shading.

7 Try experimenting using the Borders and Shading menu. Also, if the shading is dark, try changing the text to bold to make it stand out more.

8 Look at the Borders and Shading menu. You will notice that one of the tabs is for a Page Border. Produce a suitable page border to go around the edge of the page.

9 Give your document a suitable filename and print out a copy.

Bullet points

Bullet points are used to emphasise a list of items. There is usually a dot before each item, although squares or other symbols can be used.

Producing a bulleted list: rules of the computer room

In this exercise you will learn how to:

- **produce a bulleted list.**

Shown below is a piece of text that covers the rules of a school computer room. This will now be turned into a bulleted list.

1 Open a new document and key in the following text.

> **Rules of the computer room**
>
> No pupil is allowed in the room unless they are accompanied by a member of staff or have the permission of the Head of IT.
>
> You must neither drink nor eat in this room.
>
> The use of personal headsets is prohibited.
>
> The unauthorised copying of software is prohibited by the school as well as being against the law.
>
> There must be no tampering with the equipment (disconnecting cables, swapping monitors, etc.).
>
> All floppy disks must be scanned for viruses before use in the computers. A designated computer is left free for this purpose.
>
> Pupils must keep the room tidy at all times.
>
> Use of the Internet must be logged in the book provided.

2 Select the list of items (but not the bold heading) and click on Format and then on Bullets and Numbering … . A menu as shown below appears, from which you can choose the type of bullets.

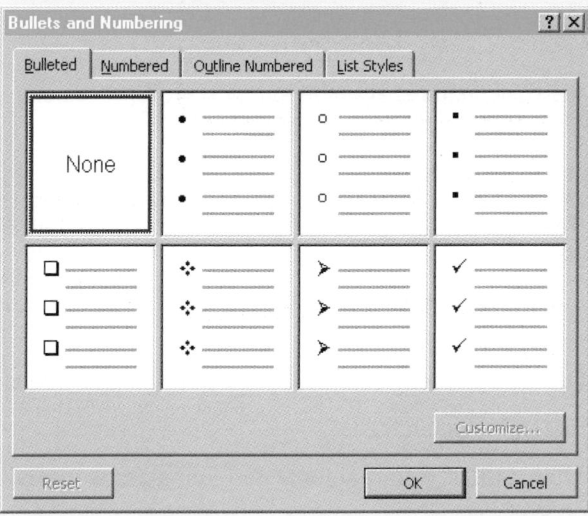

3 Select the bullet list with the arrows pointing to the right then click on OK to confirm your choice. Notice that in each place where a new line was forced by pressing Enter, a new bullet point is made.

4 An extra rule needs to be added: 'Waste paper must be placed in the bin provided'. Move the cursor onto the end of the last bulleted point (i.e. after the full-stop) and press Enter. Notice that the bulleted list is extended. Now type in the text.

5 If you press Enter after some text in a bulleted list, a new bullet appears. To get rid of it so that normal text can be entered, press Enter again. Try this to see how it works.

6 Save this document under the filename 'Rules of the computer room' and then print a copy.

7 See if you can improve this document even further. Bear in mind that it is to be hung on the wall of the computer room. Save your result under a different filename to the original and produce a printout.

Numbered lists

Numbered lists are produced in a similar way to bulleted lists. The list to be numbered is selected by highlighting it. Click on Format and then on Bullets and Numbering.... The menu shown here appears, from which you can choose the type of numbering.

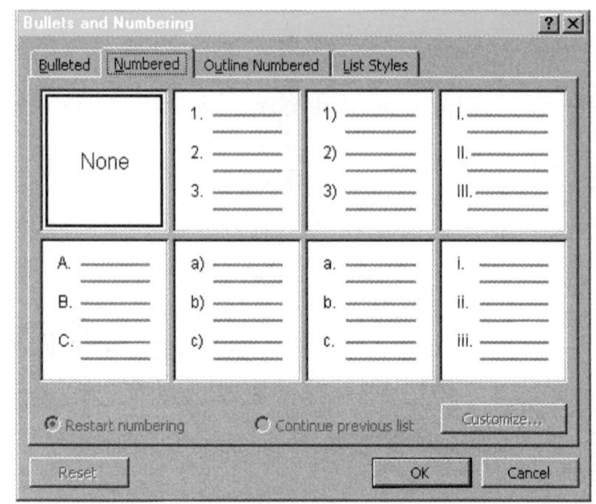

IT TASKS

Producing a numbered list

Type in the following heading and list of the basic features available on most wordprocessors. Turn the text you have typed into a numbered list.

Basic features available on most wordprocessors

Text can be entered using automatic wordwrap. This means that partly completed words at the end of a line are automatically carried to the next line so that they are not split between lines.

Text can be amended by correcting, amending, inserting and deleting characters, words, lines and paragraphs.

A document can be formatted (i.e. set out) by setting margins, page lengths and line spacing.

Text can be tabulated so it fits into neat columns.

Text can be formatted (i.e. bold, underline, italics, different fonts and font sizes to make it stand out).

The cursor can be moved to any part of the document ready for editing.

You can search for a word and replace it with another.

You can perform a check on the spelling of all the words in a document.

The grammar can be checked in a document.

Creating tables

Putting data, especially numerical data, into a table makes it look neat and professional. It also makes it easy to read. Tables may also be used to summarise information. There are many different tables in Word that may be inserted into a document.

Exercise 11.5

Using a table to provide a summary

In this exercise you will learn how to:

- insert a table into a document
- adjust the column width and row heights
- input data to a table.

We are going to produce a table to show two of the main differences between a wide area network (WAN) and a local area network (LAN).

1 Load Word and start a new document.

2 Click on Table on the menu toolbar and select Insert and then Table. The following menu appears, where you can specify the number of columns and rows. Change the number of columns to three and the number of rows to three and click on OK.

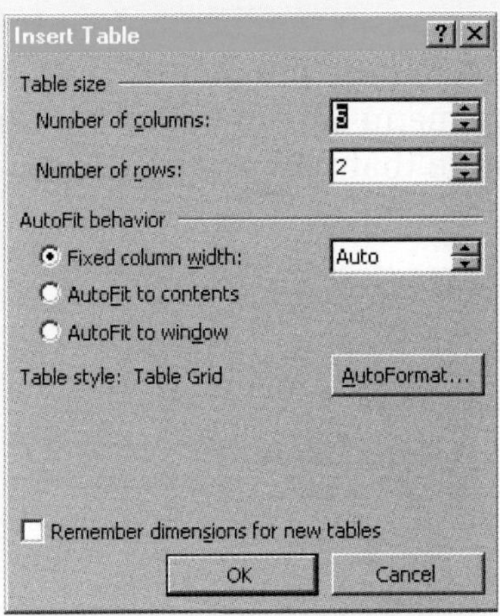

3 The following table will appear at the cursor position. Notice that it spans from one margin to the other.

Exercise 11.5

Adjust the width of the columns and the height of the rows in the following way. Move the pointer onto the lines and you will notice that the cursor changes to two parallel lines (either vertical or horizontal). Press the left mouse button and drag until the widths are similar to those shown below.

	LAN	**WAN**
Difference 1	Confined to a small area, usually a single site.	Cover a wide geographical area spanning towns, countries or even continents.
Difference 2	Usually uses simple cable links owned by the company	Uses expensive telecommunications links not owned by the company.

4 Type in the data shown above. You can centre the headings LAN and WAN by typing them in, highlighting them and then clicking on the centre button on the toolbar. Also, embolden the words 'LAN', 'WAN', 'Difference 1' and 'Difference 2'.

5 See how neat this now looks. Save your document using the filename 'The differences between a LAN and a WAN'. Print out a copy of your document.

Selecting a table

The table created in Exercise 11.5 is the simplest table you can produce in Word. There are some pre-stored tables you can use. Once you have selected the number of rows and columns in the Insert Table menu click on Autoformat... and the menu shown below appears. By flicking through the sample formats you can select a style that will suit your data.

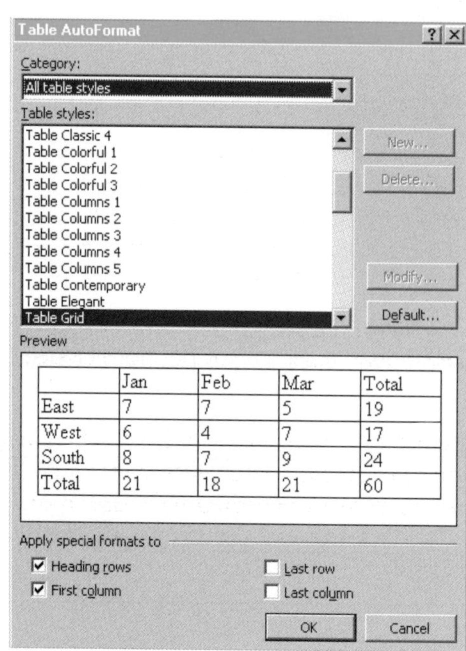

IT TASKS

Here are some data concerning the stopping distances for cars on dry roads. The data is presented as a very simple table. Your task is to use the Autoformat to find a more appealing design for the table and to use different fonts, formatting techniques (bold, underline, italics) to improve the presentation of this important data. You could also centre some of the data in the columns.

Speed (km/h)	**Thinking distance (m)**	**Braking distance (m)**	**Overall stopping distance (m)**
32	6	6	12
48	9	14	23
64	12	24	36
80	15	38	53
96	18	55	73
112	21	75	96

Save your work using the filename 'Table showing stopping distances' and then print out a copy.

Exercise 11.6

In this exercise you will:

- **practise typing**
- **practise formatting**
- **practise creating a table.**

1 Type in the following text.

Flying supersonically on Concorde

Breaking the sound barrier is only done over sea to avoid any disturbance on the ground. For this reason, the flight plan may call for a levelling off at the subsonic speed of Mach 0.93 and at an altitude of 29,500 feet over the land after takeoff until water can be reached. Once Concorde is over water, it proceeds to climb rapidly to reach its cruising speed and altitude.

Since there is a change in the aerodynamic centre of the aircraft when going from subsonic to supersonic speed, fuel is pumped to the rear of the aircraft to compensate for this shift.

As Concorde accelerates, the resistance due to the surrounding air increases and the thrust from the engines needs to be increased considerably. You then feel two slight impulses a second apart as Concorde breaks the sound barrier. The machmeter in the cabin now reads Mach 1. After this the aircraft rapidly reaches Mach 2 (1,350 mph) which is the aircraft's cruising speed.

Exercise 11.6

Concorde's cruising altitude ranges between 52,000 feet and 59,000 feet. Because this is too high for normal aircraft, the ideal cruising altitude is chosen by the captain. At this height you are travelling in the stratosphere where the atmospheric pressure is only one tenth of that on the earth. Here the sky is an intense blue, almost purple. Flying is very smooth at this height since no weather disturbances occur here.

Comparison of flying times and speeds from Paris to New York (or the reverse journey in the case of the Ryan Nyp).

2 Embolden the heading 'Flying supersonically on Concorde' and centre it.

3 Produce a table at the bottom of your document and input the following data.

Year	Aircraft	Flying time	Speed (km/h)
1927	Ryan Nyp	33h 30mins	188
1946	Douglas DC4	23h 45mins	350
1957	Superstaliner	14h 40mins	530
1959	Boeing 707	8h	900
1977	Concorde	3h 45mins	2200

4 Proofread the entire document and make any corrections.

5 Use the page preview to make sure that the table is in a suitable place in the document.

6 Save the document using the filename 'Concorde'.

7 Print a copy of this document.

Spell and grammar checking your work

The spellchecker is one of the most useful features provided and this means that you can produce text without any embarrassing spelling mistakes. The grammar checker is also useful but you need to be a bit careful using it. The system offers several approaches to spell and grammar checking.

Using AutoCorrect

By default (i.e. provided no one has changed the original settings) Word 2000 will check both spelling and grammar as you type the text in and any spelling mistakes are automatically corrected. For example, if you type 'recieve' the AutoCorrect will automatically change it to 'receive'. The spellchecker does this without asking you.

Check the spelling as you type

Here both the spelling and grammar are checked, but spelling mistakes are not automatically corrected. Any spelling mistakes are underlined with a wavy red line. Grammatical errors are marked with a wavy green line.

Check the spelling and grammar all at once

Another method is to type in the entire document and not worry about any grammatical or spelling errors until the end. You can then click on Tools and then Spelling and Grammar. You must make sure that the cursor is at the beginning of the document you want to check.
As soon as the checker reaches a wrongly spelt word the following menu appears:

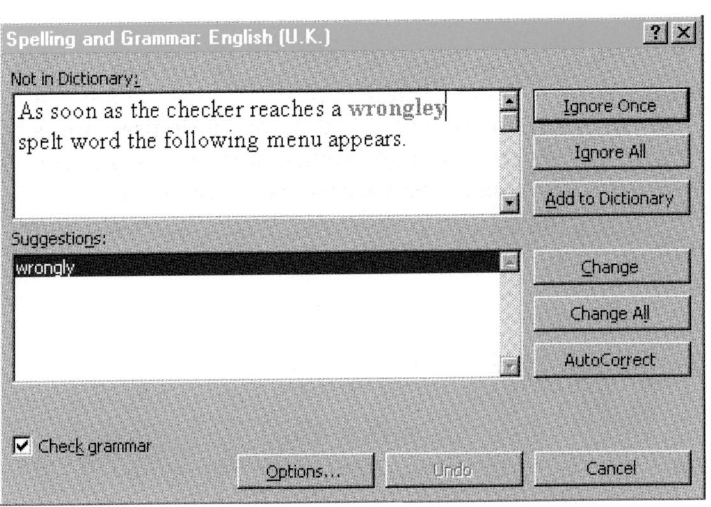

Checking spelling and grammar

Click on Change to correct the wrong spelling

Using the thesaurus

A thesaurus is used when you want to find an alternative word to the one you have originally thought of. Words with similar meanings are called synonyms.

Exercise 11.7

Using the thesaurus

In this exercise you will learn how to:

- **use the thesaurus.**

1 Start a new document and type in the following text:

> The students were sitting down, contemplating their futures, on the grass outside the building where the examination results had been posted. Some had got better results than expected and were surprised, others were disappointed and almost in tears.

2 We want to find an alternative word to 'surprised' in the second sentence. Select the word 'surprised' by highlighting it.

3 Click on the Tools menu, click on Language and then on Thesaurus. The menu shown to the right appears:

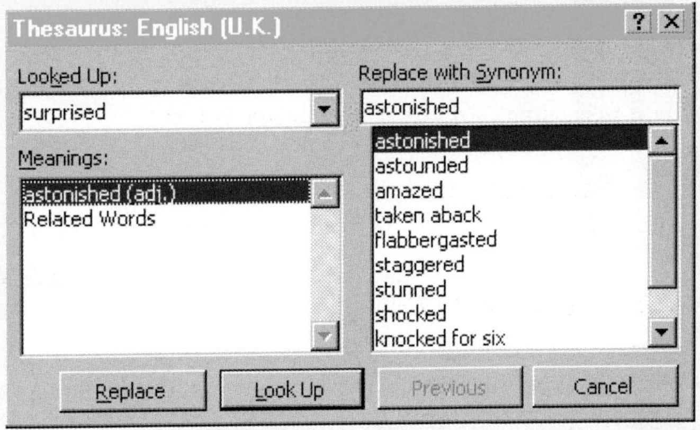

Synonyms are listed in a box on the right-hand side. Click on the one you want and it will appear in the Replace with Synonym box. In this case 'amazed' is probably the best word. To replace the word 'surprised' with 'amazed' click the Replace button.

4 Experiment with the thesaurus, using other words in the paragraph.

Headers and footers

Headers are small bits of text at the top of the page that tell the reader what is in the document. A typical header might include the title of the document, the author's name and the page number.

Footers are the same as headers except the small piece of text is placed at the bottom of the document.

Advice: Use headers and footers in the documentation for your coursework

The documentation for the coursework should always have page numbers and you can use headers and footers to hold other important information such as your name, candidate number, date and so on

Exercise 11.8

Producing headers and footers

In this exercise you will learn how to:

- **create headers and footers.**

1 Open a new document. Select View and then Header and Footer. The header and footer toolbar appears along with a dotted rectangle with the word Header above it.

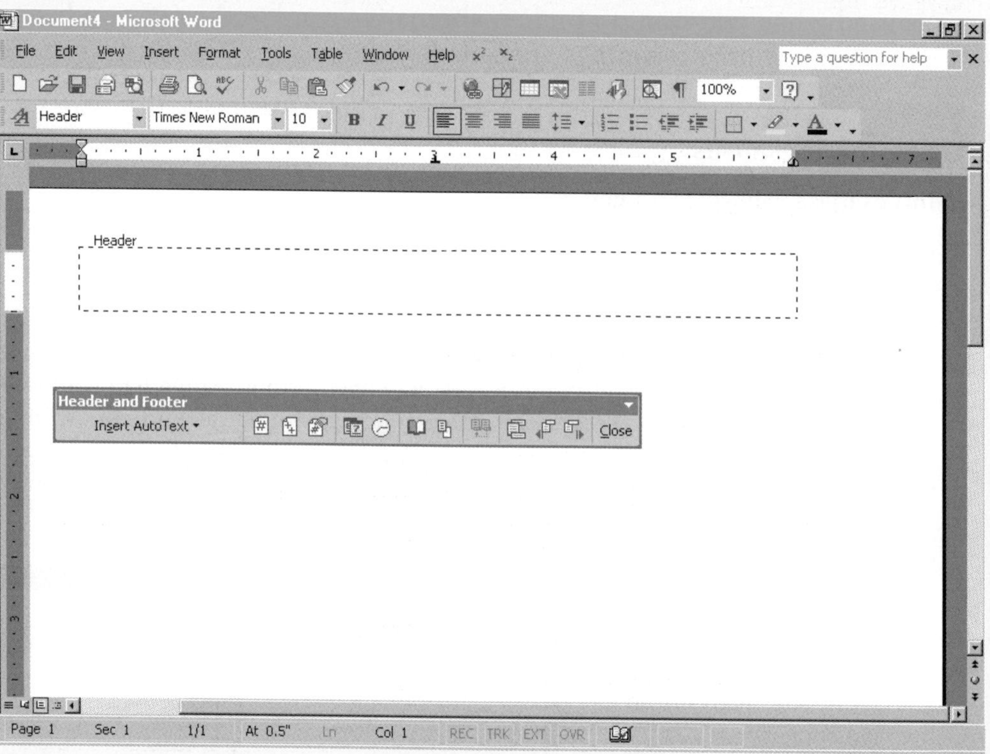

2 Type the following text into the header box (put your own name where 'Your Name' appears):

Insert: **Your Name** **GCSE IT Coursework** **Communicating Information**

3 Select this text and reduce the size of the font to 8 point to make it different from the rest of the text.

4 You can use most formatting commands with text in the header.

5 Click on the Switch Between Header and Footer button on the header and footer toolbar. This takes you to a footer box at the bottom of the page.

6 Put the following in the footer box:

Your Name

The page number

Today's date

7 Select the text in the footer and reduce the font size to 8 point.

8 Save your document under the filename 'An example of using headers and footers'.

9 Print a copy in portrait orientation.

QUESTIONS

Wordprocessing packages provide the user with ways to improve the appearance of their documents. One such way is to alter the following:

- text alignment (e.g. left-justified, right-justified, fully-justified and centred)
- page orientation (e.g. portrait or landscape)
- text styles (e.g. bold, underline and italic).

(a) (i) Label the document to show the three types of text alignment.

(ii) Name two text styles used in this document.

(b) Give two facilities which wordprocessors have which help the user to produce error free documents.

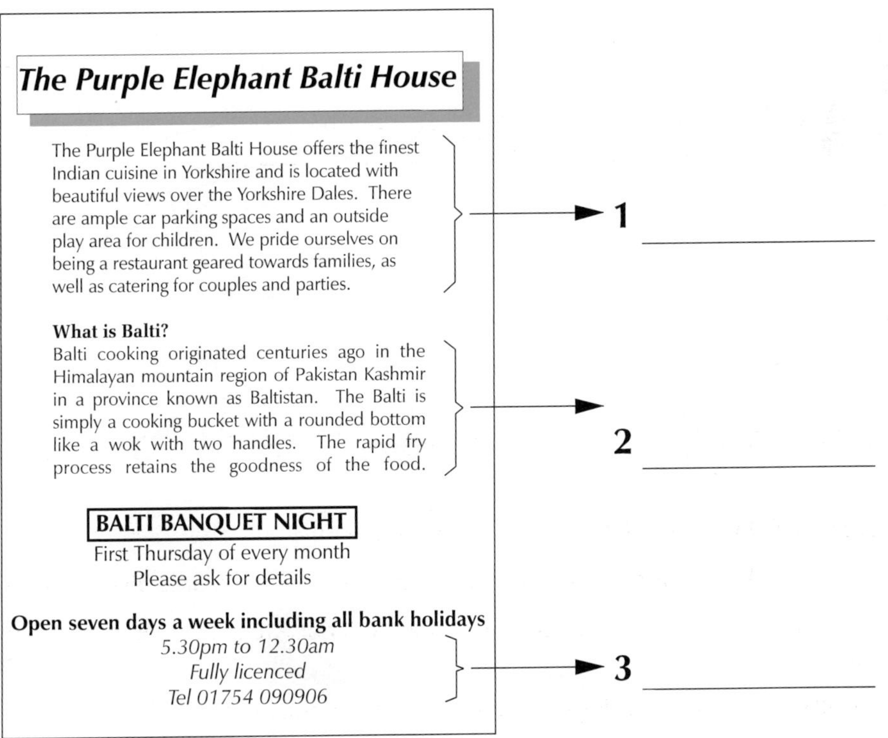

The Purple Elephant Balti House
The Purple Elephant Balti House offers the finest Indian cuisine in Yorkshire and is located with beautiful views over the Yorkshire Dales. There are ample car parking spaces and an outside play area for children. We pride ourselves on being a restaurant geared towards families, as well as catering for couples and parties.
What is Balti?
Balti cooking originated centuries ago in the Himalayan mountain region of Pakistan Kashmir in a province known as Baltistan. The Balti is simply a cooking bucket with a rounded bottom like a wok with two handles. The rapid fry process retains the goodness of the food.
BALTI BANQUET NIGHT
First Thursday of every month
Please ask for details
Open seven days a week including all bank holidays
5.30pm to 12.30am
Fully licenced
Tel 01754 090906
1
2
3

Using Word for Desktop Publishing

Why use Word?

There are many specialist desktop publishing packages such as Microsoft Publisher, so why use a wordprocessing package?

You may decide to use Word for desktop publishing (DTP for short) for these reasons:

- you may not have a specialist DTP program
- you may feel you can already use Word and it would be easier to understand the DTP parts of Word than learn a specialist package
- your DTP requirements are simple and Word satisfies your limited needs.

When considering DTP coursework you will need to explore the possibilities of using different software. Make sure you justify the reasons for your choice in your project documentation.

Limitations of Word as a DTP package

Word is primarily a wordprocessor with some DTP facilities. If you have used a specialist DTP package (such as Publisher) you will know that Word's facilities are limited. The main problem is that Word is not a page layout program like Publisher. This means that everything is attached to everything else and if you move or delete any part, it affects everything else. This can be frustrating, because one false move can lead to disaster as the whole page is wrecked.

The main advice when playing around with DTP using Word is to **save frequently** under **different files names** so that you can always go back to a previous version. Also, don't forget Edit and then Undo to remove an unwanted action; it can be very useful indeed.

Publisher versus Word!

Putting text into columns

In this exercise you will learn how to:

- **put text into two columns**
- **insert clip art**
- **use the zoom feature to see the layout of the whole page.**

1 Open a new document and type in the following text:

> Computer control in Formula One
>
> Formula One (F1) car racing attracts a huge amount of money each year so it is not surprising that much of this is spent on information technology. Digital sensors are placed around each car and these continuously relay data about engine revolutions, oil temperature, gearbox performance, suspension characteristics, etc. Radio signals are used to transmit this data to computers in the pits. The computer system in many F1 cars is so advanced that it could, in theory, drive a car at high speed around the track; the driver is needed only to keep the car clear of other competitors.
>
> Features on some Formula One racing cars include:
>
> Active suspension
>
> Active suspension uses sensors to measure the position of a car on its suspension when on the straight or cornering. It can use the speed of the car and information about the corner being taken to adjust the hydraulics in the suspension unit. In simple terms, this determines the height of the car above the ground. On a straight the suspension alters so that the car is low, thus reducing air drag. When the car is going around corners the suspension is raised to increase the grip on the track.
>
> Computer-controlled gear boxes
>
> Computers are used to tell the driver the optimum time to change gear, based on the data received from sensors which detect the engine speed, the speed of the car and its position on the track.
>
> Traction control
>
> Traction control is used to make sure that cars do not skid because the power from the wheels is too great for the grip of the tyres on the road. Sensors are used to detect the power and the grip and if there is a risk of skidding the power is reduced until grip is established.
>
> Launch control
>
> Launch control uses data on the grip of the tyres and the power transmitted to the wheels from the engine to ensure a car gets away quickly from the starting grid.

2 Proofread the text in your document against the text shown and correct any mistakes.

3 Save the text using the filename 'Computer control in Formula One'.

4 Select all the text in the document and then click on Format and then Columns...

The columns menu appears as shown below.

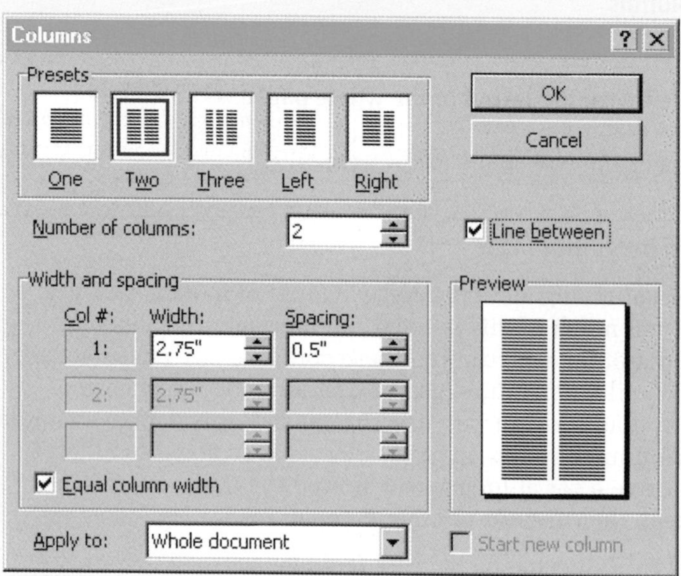

5 Click on Two and also click Line between. The text is automatically put into two columns with a vertical line separating them.

Your screen should now look similar to the next one. Notice the way the text snakes from one column to the next.

Computer control in Formula One

Formula One (F1) car racing attracts a huge amount of money each year so it is not surprising that much of this is spent on information technology. Digital sensors are placed around each car and these continuously relay data about engine revolutions, oil temperature, gearbox information, suspension characteristics, etc. Radio signals are used to transmit this data to computers in

Sensors are used to detect the power and the grip and if there is a risk of skidding the power is reduced until grip is established.

Launch control
Launch control uses data on the grip of the tyres and the power transmitted to the wheels from the engine to ensure a car gets away quickly from the starting grid.

6 Highlight the heading 'Computer Control in Formula One', increase the font size to 24 point and embolden this heading.

7 Centre both lines of this heading.

8 Increase the font size of the sub-headings to 16 point and embolden them.

9 Position the cursor at the end of the last sentence in the second column and press Enter twice to leave a couple of blank lines.

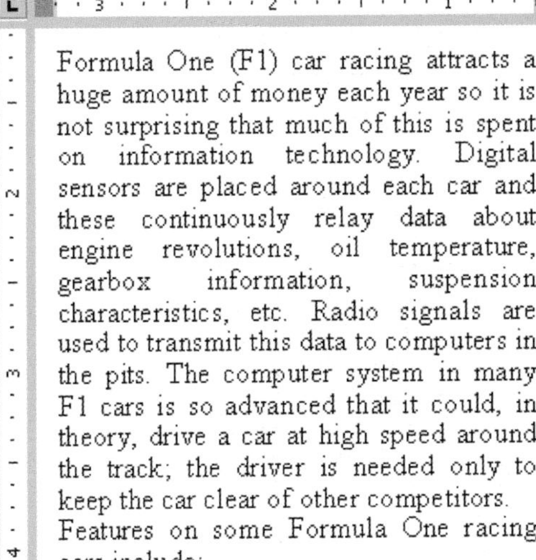

Formula One (F1) car racing attracts a huge amount of money each year so it is not surprising that much of this is spent on information technology. Digital sensors are placed around each car and these continuously relay data about engine revolutions, oil temperature, gearbox information, suspension characteristics, etc. Radio signals are used to transmit this data to computers in the pits. The computer system in many F1 cars is so advanced that it could, in theory, drive a car at high speed around the track; the driver is needed only to keep the car clear of other competitors.
Features on some Formula One racing cars include:
Launch control
Launch control uses data on the grip of the tyres and the power transmitted to the wheels from the engine to ensure a car gets away quickly from the starting grid.

10 Click on Insert then on Picture and finally on Clip Art... The following clip art screen appears.

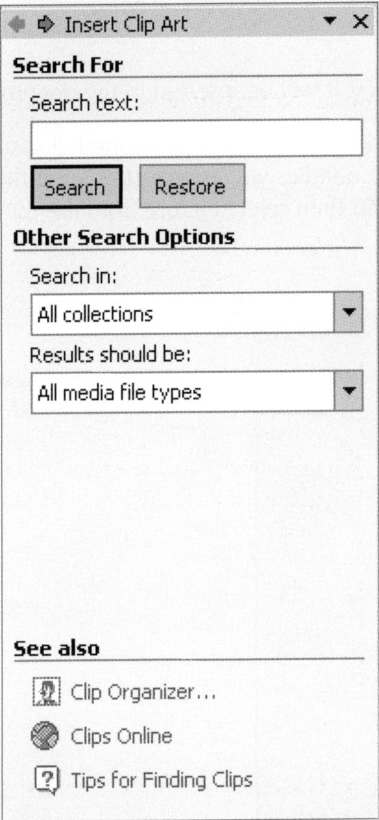

Insert Clip Art
Search For
Search text:
Search
Restore
Other Search Options
Search in:
All collections
Results should be:
All media file types
See also
Clip Organizer...
Clips Online
Tips for Finding Clips

11 Type in racing car in the Search for clips box. This finds the clip art quickly.

Here are some choices that might appear. Do not worry if your clip art does not look like this, it depends what has been loaded into the system.

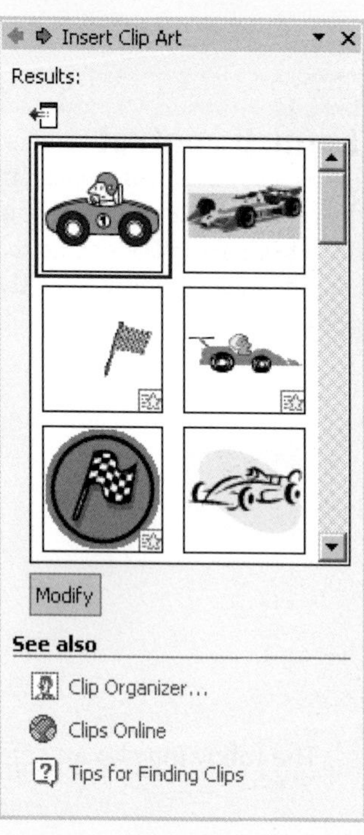

Click on one of the pictures that takes your fancy. It will be inserted in the document.

12 The chosen piece of clip art will now appear where the cursor is positioned. If you can only see part of the picture, click on the picture and the handles will appear (these are the small black squares). Now click on Format in the toolbar and then select Picture from the menu.

The following screen appears.

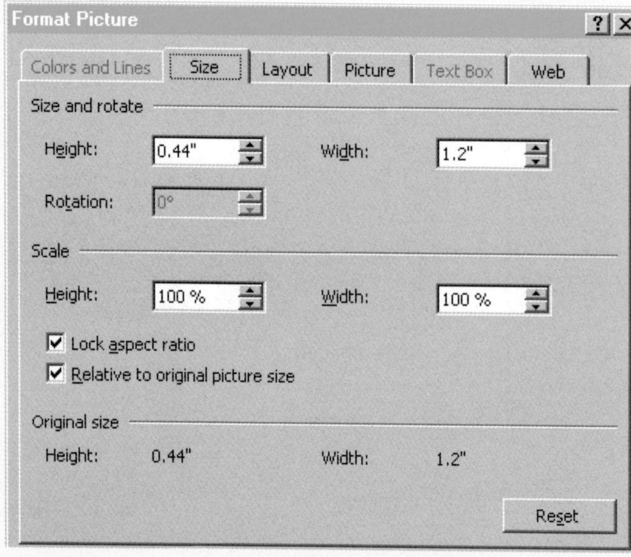

Click on the Layout tab and the following screen appears. Select the Wrapping style In front of text by clicking on it.

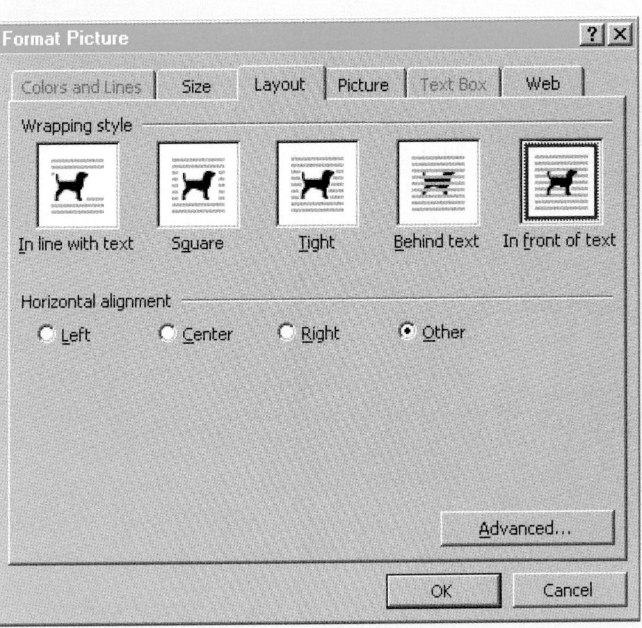
Format Picture
Colors and Lines
Size
Layout
Picture
Text Box
Web
Wrapping style
In line with text
Square
Tight
Behind text
In front of text
Horizontal alignment
Left
Center
Right
Other
Advanced...
OK
Cancel

The picture is now in position. You may have to move it or size it by clicking on it and using the handles.

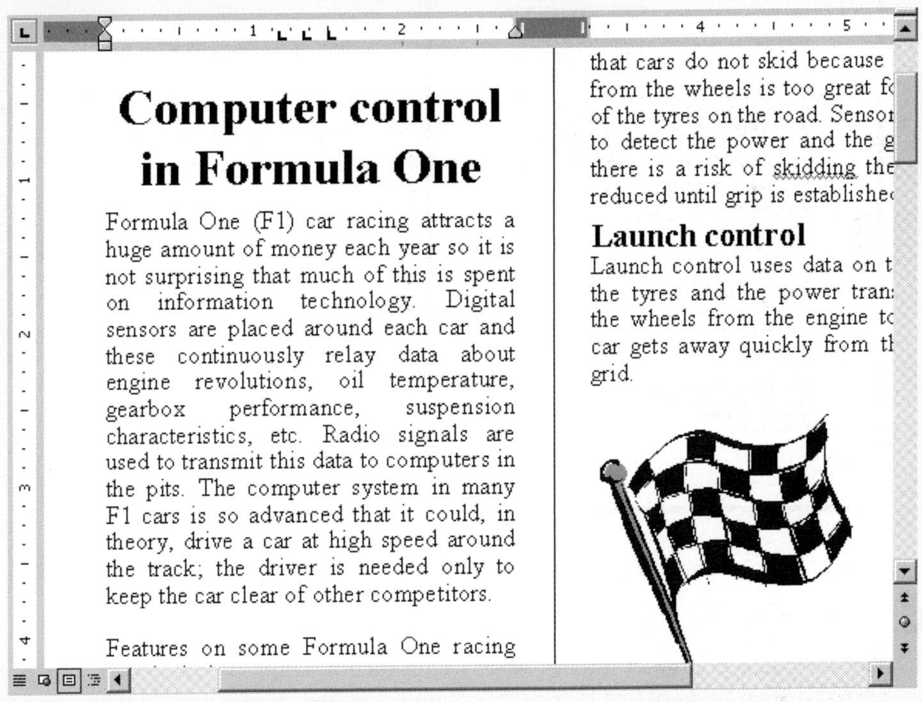
Computer control in Formula One
Formula One (F1) car racing attracts a huge amount of money each year so it is not surprising that much of this is spent on information technology. Digital sensors are placed around each car and these continuously relay data about engine revolutions, oil temperature, gearbox performance, suspension characteristics, etc. Radio signals are used to transmit this data to computers in the pits. The computer system in many F1 cars is so advanced that it could, in theory, drive a car at high speed around the track; the driver is needed only to keep the car clear of other competitors.
Features on some Formula One racing
that cars do not skid because
from the wheels is too great fo
of the tyres on the road. Sensor
to detect the power and the g
there is a risk of skidding the
reduced until grip is establishe
Launch control
Launch control uses data on t
the tyres and the power tran
the wheels from the engine to
car gets away quickly from th
grid.

13 Notice in the print preview screen on the next page that the computer makes the clip art fit between the margins. You can alter the size and position by clicking on the picture and using the handles.

14 At the moment you cannot see all the document on the screen. Click on View and then Zoom... The zoom menu appears as shown here.

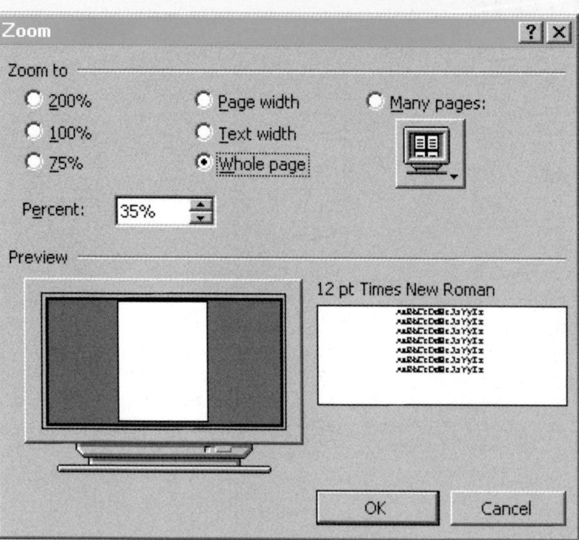

In the Zoom to section, click on Whole page and then OK. The page looks like the one below.

To get the page back to normal again click on View and Zoom and then on 100%.

15 There is quite a lot of white space in this design.

Put the cursor in front of the first word in the second column. Press enter until the text is level with the main body of text in the first column; the text should now look like the screen on the next page.

Computer control in Formula One

Formula One (F1) car racing attracts a huge amount of money each year so it is not surprising that much of this is spent on information technology. Digital sensors are placed around each car and these continuously relay data about engine revolutions, oil temperature, gearbox performance, suspension characteristics, etc. Radio signals are used to transmit this data to computers in the pits. The computer system in many F1 cars is so advanced that it could, in theory, drive a car at high speed around

Traction control is used to make sure that cars do not skid because the power from the wheels is too great for the grip of the tyres on the road. Sensors are used to detect the power and the grip and if there is a risk of skidding the power is reduced until grip is established.

Launch control

Launch control uses data on the grip of the tyres and the power transmitted to the wheels from the engine to ensure a car gets away quickly from the starting

The text and the clip art are pushed further down the page.

16 Look at the Page view to see how it looks (see the screen below).

17 There is still some white space at the bottom of the page. You have to fill the page completely. You could add more clip art or text. You could even have an advertisement in a box or maybe a photograph. It is now up to you to produce a full page.

18 Save your final document. You should also have saved your document at intervals along the way.

19 Produce a printout.

Some tips when doing your DTP coursework

Think before you start.
Always plan your work on paper first. It is much harder to think onto a blank screen than sketch ideas onto a blank sheet of paper.
Think about the following:

- Who is the document aimed at?
- What is its purpose?
- Are there any language considerations (e.g. are the readers mainly adults or children)?
- From how far away will the document be read (e.g. it could be a poster or a leaflet). This affects the font, font size and paper size.
- Is it to be printed in colour? Is a colour printer available? What are the cost implications of using colour?

Always plan your work out on a blank piece of paper the same size as the paper used for the final printout. Work in pencil and have a rubber handy. Don't be afraid to experiment. Try several designs and pick the best one. Enrol other people to comment on your ideas, most obviously the person for whom you are doing the design (if there is one). Feedback from other people is extremely important.

Brightening up your work

In DTP you are often presented with some brief text (usually wordprocessed) and asked to brighten it up.

IT TASKS

Task 1

Your parents are holding a cocktail party and have asked you to produce a menu of drinks. Not everyone knows how certain cocktails are made, so they plan to produce a menu with names and ingredients.

Here are the details that need to be included.

Margarita
lemon juice and coarse salt for frosting
1.5 msrs tequila
1 msr lemon juice
0.5 msr Cointreau
cracked ice
1 slice of lemon
1 wedge of lime

Strawberry Daiquiri
1.5 msrs light rum
0.5 msr strawberry liqueur
juice of half a lime
5 strawberries
crushed ice
1 maraschino cherry

Cocktail Menu
Black Russian
3 msrs vodka
1 msr Kahlua
ice cubes

Rusty Nail
1.5 msrs whisky
1.5 msrs Drambuie
ice cubes
strip of lemon peel

Pink Lady
2 msrs gin
4 dashes grenadine
1 dash egg white

Pina Colada
Bacardi
cracked ice
1.5 msrs pineapple juice
1 msr coconut milk
0.5 msr cream
1 maraschino cherry
piece of pineapple

Tequila Sunrise
1 msr tequila
ice cubes
4 msrs orange juice
2 dashes grenadine
1 slice of orange
1 maraschino cherry

Produce a series of designs for this menu. Consider importing clip art, borders, using WordArt, etc. to improve the appearance. Produce the designs as part of your solution.

Now produce a suitable menu using Word and print it out (preferably in colour).

QUESTIONS

Your grandmother has just bought a computer (she has never shown any interest in them before now) and has enrolled on an evening course in DTP at her local college. In order to impress her grandchildren, she decides to produce an invitation to a party she is having. She needs to design a card which will be suitable for all ages. She will print them using her colour ink-jet printer.

Answer the following questions:

1 Who is the intended readership for the card?

2 What is the purpose of the card?

3 Are there any limitations in the production of this card?

Now see if you can produce a couple of designs, on paper, for her to choose from.

Screendumps

When you come to do your GCSE coursework you will have to provide documentation to show how you have solved a particular problem. One way to do this is to produce screendumps. A screendump, as the name suggests, simply copies whatever appears on the screen.

Exercise 12.2

Producing a screendump

1 Open a new document and type in the following information:

A screendump is a picture of the screen that is useful when giving the user instructions on how to use the system or software. Although you may think that a screendump just shows what is on the screen, this is not always the case. If there is a menu on top of the screen, when the screendump is done, you may find that only the top menu is shown and not what is underneath.

2 Position the cursor two lines below the last line of the above text.

Press the Alt key down, keep it pressed down and then press the Print Screen key.

This pastes the picture of the screen in the clipboard which is a temporary storage area.

Check that the cursor is in the position where the picture of the screen is to go and press the Paste button on the toolbar.

Your screen should look like that at the top of the next page.

3 To size the diagram, click anywhere on the picture. You will see the handles (the small squares). By placing the cursor on any one of these handles and keeping the left mouse button down, you can adjust the size of the picture.

4 See if you can:
(a) position the picture so that it is in the centre of the page
(b) use the drawing tools to mark five features on the screen (e.g. any buttons, toolbars etc.) with arrows and then suitable labels.

Screendumps are very useful if you need to explain to someone else how to use a system. You should always provide a user guide when producing an IT system for someone else. Using screendumps in a user guide enables the user to see exactly what should be appearing on their screen. Screendumps have been used throughout this book to help explain things.

Exercise 12.2

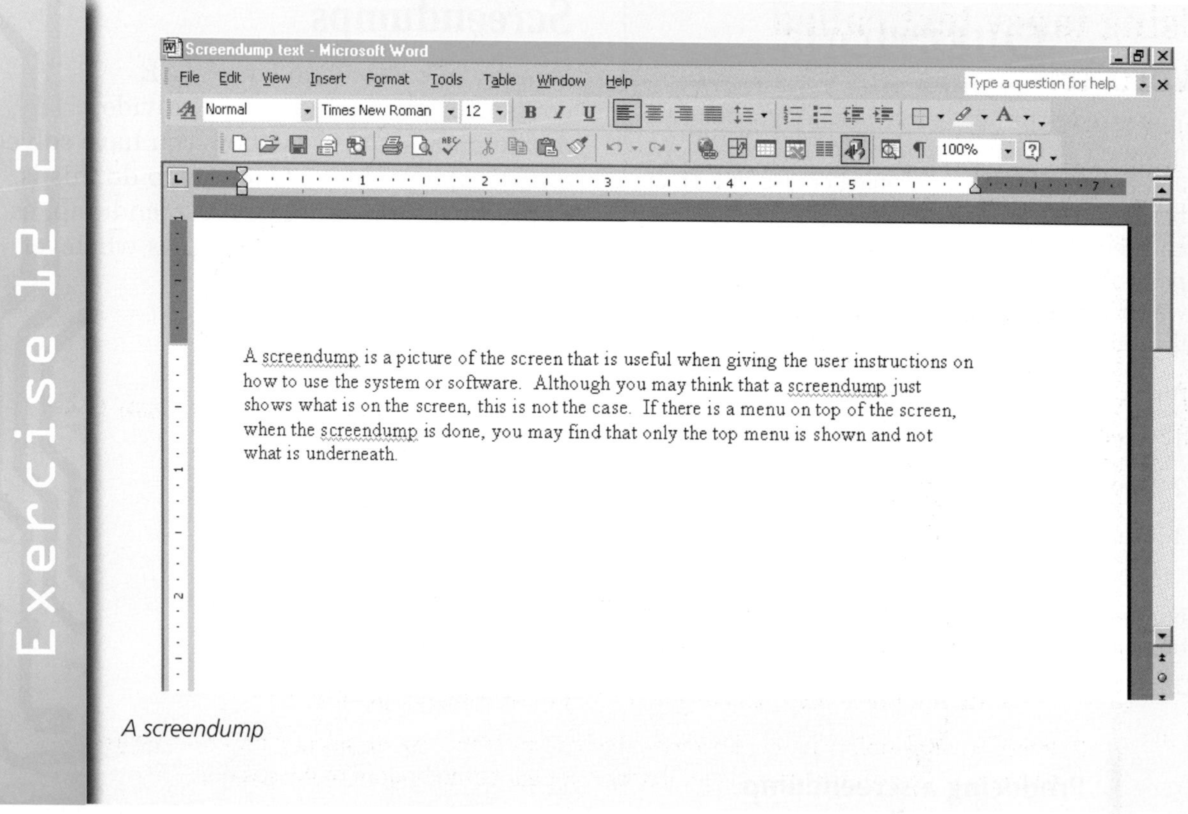
Screendump text - Microsoft Word
File Edit View Insert Format Tools Table Window Help
Type a question for help
Normal
Times New Roman
12
100%
A screendump is a picture of the screen that is useful when giving the user instructions on how to use the system or software. Although you may think that a screendump just shows what is on the screen, this is not the case. If there is a menu on top of the screen, when the screendump is done, you may find that only the top menu is shown and not what is underneath.

A screendump

IT TASKS

Here is an advertisement that is to appear as a special holiday offer in a local newspaper.

> Lapland Fantasy
>
> Begin the Christmas celebrations with a Fantasy-filled Day Break in Lapland to visit Father Christmas.
>
> Fly from Manchester Airport on December 16th.
>
> LAPLAND ENCOUNTER, from £349
>
> The magical Lapland Encounter is an all-inclusive fun-packed day where you will enjoy a ride on a snowmobile, take sleigh rides pulled by reindeer and husky dogs, and sample the food, customs and ceremonies of traditional Lappish culture, all on an adventurous search for the real Father Christmas! Santa will even have in his possession the letters written to him by children up to 12 years of age in your party and will normally be happy to chat to them about their Christmas list.
>
> Find out more by requesting a full colour brochure.
>
> Telephone 0111–221–3029, 9 a.m. to 5 p.m. Monday to Friday (Answerphone service in operation outside these hours).

You have to liven up this advert by using any techniques with which you are familiar. You do not need to add any text. Plan your design on paper first and only use colour in your design if you have a colour printer to print it on. Remember to regularly save your work, using different filenames.

Print a copy of your advert.

Using fancy text called WordArt

WordArt allows you to do all sorts of fancy graphics effects with text. Basically WordArt changes the text you type in into graphics pictures.

Exercise 12.3

In this exercise you will learn how to:

- **change a piece of text into WordArt.**

1 Open a new document and key in the following text entitled 'Looking after your floppy disks'.

Looking after your floppy disks:

- always label them properly with your name and form
- check them regularly for viruses
- make sure you do not leave them in the drives when leaving the room
- do not place them near magnetic or electric fields
- do not place them anywhere there are extreme temperatures.

2 If the drawing toolbar is not already on the bottom of the screen, select View and then Toolbars. Click on Drawing. The drawing toolbar will appear at the bottom of the screen.

3 Highlight the title 'Looking after your floppy disks' and click on the WordArt button in the drawing toolbar at the bottom of the page.

4 The following screen will appear.

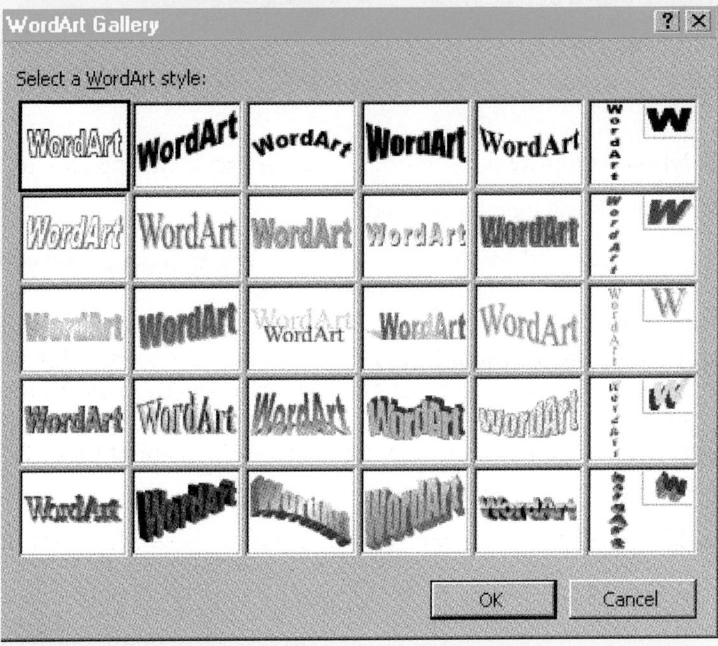

5 Click on a suitable graphic for this title and then on OK. You will see a screen called Edit WordArt Text. At this screen click on OK.

6 Click anywhere on the WordArt title. Handles will appear, and using these you can adjust size and position.

You will notice that a WordArt toolbar appears and you can use this to add new WordArt, change the shape of the title, change the font etc.

7 Insert a picture of a floppy disk next to the text. You first have to put the cursor in the position where you want the image to appear. To do this click on Insert, then Picture and then ClipArt... You now have to tell the computer where the clip art is situated. It could be on the hard drive or a CD-ROM. Your teacher will tell you how to do this.

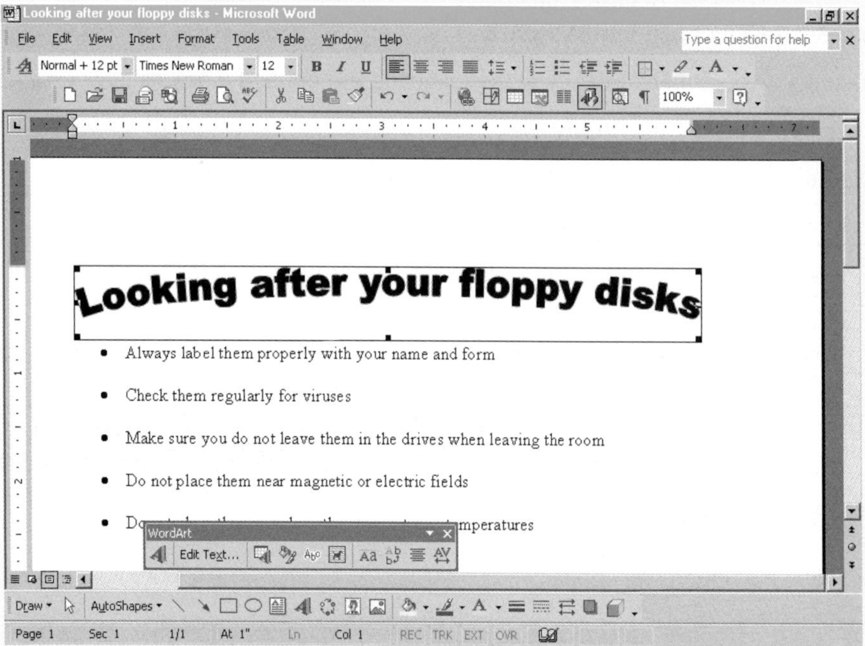

8 Rather than flick through thousands of clip art images it is easier to do a search and just look over the results.

In the search box, type in Floppy Disk.

Click on a suitable image. It will then be inserted.

9 Click on the clip art and size it and position it using the handles. Your design will now include the WordArt and a piece of clip art like the design shown below.

Looking after your floppy disks

- Always label them properly with your name and form
- Check them regularly for viruses
- Make sure you do not leave them in the drives when leaving the room
- Do not place them near magnetic or electric fields

Exercise 12.3

Tips on document design

Here are some useful tips when designing your own documents.

- It is not necessary to fill all the page with text and graphics. The best effects are produced when there is quite a bit of blank space (called white space) on the page. Make sure that this space is spread over the page and not just in one place.
- Always keep the design consistent right the way through the document.
- Always plan the document on paper first. Think about fonts and font sizes for headings and subheadings.
- Use the special templates provided by Word if you can. When you select a new document you can select one of these templates.
- Keep the design simple. Fussy designs that use too many features don't often appeal to the reader.

IT TASKS

Designing an invoice

You have been asked by a local garden centre to design an invoice (another name for a bill) for them. This invoice is given to those customers who are having goods delivered.

After a meeting with the owner of the garden centre you look back at the information you collected. The owner and you decided that the information contained in the following notes should be included.

Forrest View Garden Centre
Forrest Road
Cheltenham
GL45 7UY

01242 454545

Customer name

Customer address

Special instructions (e.g. leave in front garden)

Customer telephone number

Invoice number (all invoices are given a unique number)

Sold by (this is the person who made the sale)

Date sold

Delivery date and approximate time

Qty

Description

Amount

Delivery charge

Total cost

Payment method used (either cash, cheque or card)

Note that the information about the goods will need to be repeated if several items appear on the invoice.

Produce your designs (you should have at least three) on paper first.

Choose the best design.

IT TASKS

Business cards

Business cards are quite small (typically 2 × 3.5 inches). How can a person or a business describe themselves or what they do in such a small space? Your task is to produce a card to describe another person (not yourself). The subject could be a footballer, fashion model, singer, actor or actress or a prominent political figure.

Now it is your chance to produce a card for yourself. You can make it humorous or serious. The main thing is that people to whom you give the card should remember you. You should describe aspects of your life, your school and your activities.

Produce a business card for a historical character. Focus on their achievements and what they are best known for.

Produce as evidence of your efforts your rough designs, details of how you went about the task and also printouts of your designs.

IT TASKS

Anti-smoking posters

Produce two anti-smoking posters, one for each of these targets:

(a) Junior school pupils (aged up to 11) to put them off ever starting to smoke.

(b) Senior school pupils (aged up to 16) to put them off starting to smoke or to make them give up.

Points to bear in mind:

- consider the readership carefully
- use language appropriate to the reading level
- be harder-hitting with the older pupils
- use a more complex design for the older pupils.

Plan out your designs on paper first.

Produce several drafts for each of these posters.

Get some feedback from people of the age group the posters are aimed at.

Use this feedback to modify your design and then show the same people your improved version.

Save and print each version carefully, marking on it whether it is a draft (i.e. a rough) or a final version.

QUESTIONS

1 There is an anti-smoking campaign at your school. During your ICT lessons, you will be producing anti-smoking leaflets aimed at the students in your school.

You will start off by planning your design, using the following questions:

(a) Name four factors you would need to consider when planning your design.

(b) For each factor, you should give a feature of the desktop publishing package that would help you deal with the factor.

For example:

Factor – There should be no grammatical errors in the leaflet.

Feature of the DTP package – the grammar checker can be used.

Advanced Features of Word

In this chapter some of the more advanced features of Word will be looked at. Although they are advanced features they are still quite easy to use, since a Wizard (a step-by-step guide provided by Word) takes you through the process.

Mail merge

Mail merge can be used to send the same basic letter, with just slight differences, to a large number of people. A mailing list is often used to supply the names, addresses and other details of the people to whom the letter is to be sent. Sometimes this list is created in Word but it could be obtained from another package such as the spreadsheet package Excel or the specialist database package Access.

Before performing a mail merge, ask yourself if the number of letters you are sending warrants the effort. If you have ten letters it may not be worth the trouble. You could simply create the letter with one lot of details and then change these for the next letter and so on. If you need more than ten or may need to send a similar letter to the same people in the future, then you should consider using mail merge.

If you need to send letters out to the same people over and over again, it is worth setting up a mailing list or a special database in another package.

Planning a mail merge

Click on Tools and then click on Letters and Mailings. Click on Mail Merge Wizard…

The following screen appears, to help you through the steps.

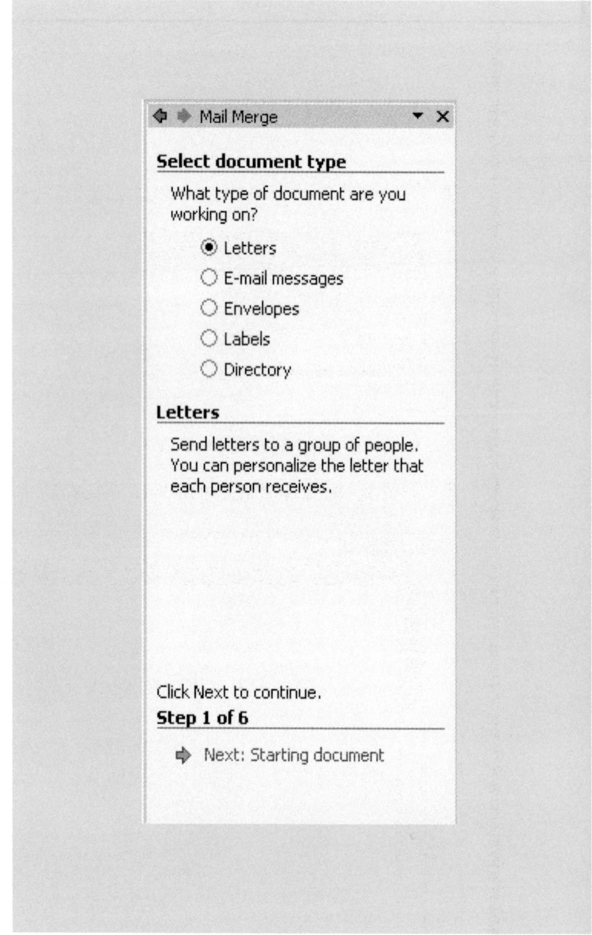

Exercise 13.1

Performing a mail merge

In this exercise you will learn how to:

- **create a letter to be sent to different people**
- **create a name and address list for the recipients of the letter**
- **insert the variable fields into the letter**
- **merge the names and address details with the letter to produce the personalised letters.**

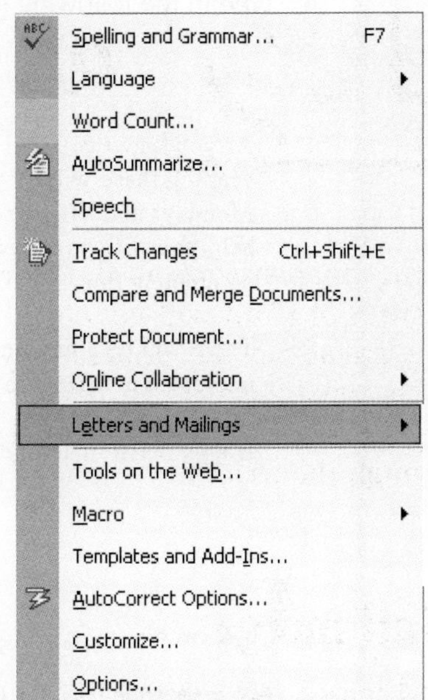

1 Load Word and create a new document. Click on Tools and the following menu drops down. Move down to Letters and Mailings.

2 The following menu appears. You need to select Mail Merge Wizard...

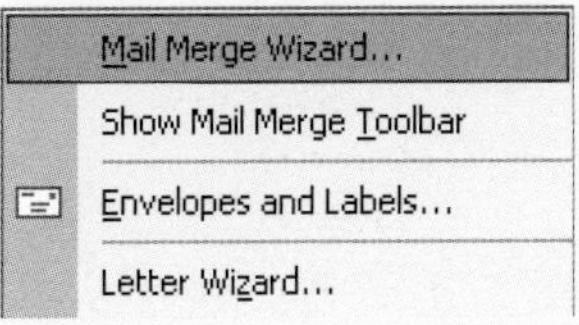

Click on Mail Merge Wizard.

3 The screen divides into two with the right-hand side containing instructions for you to follow.

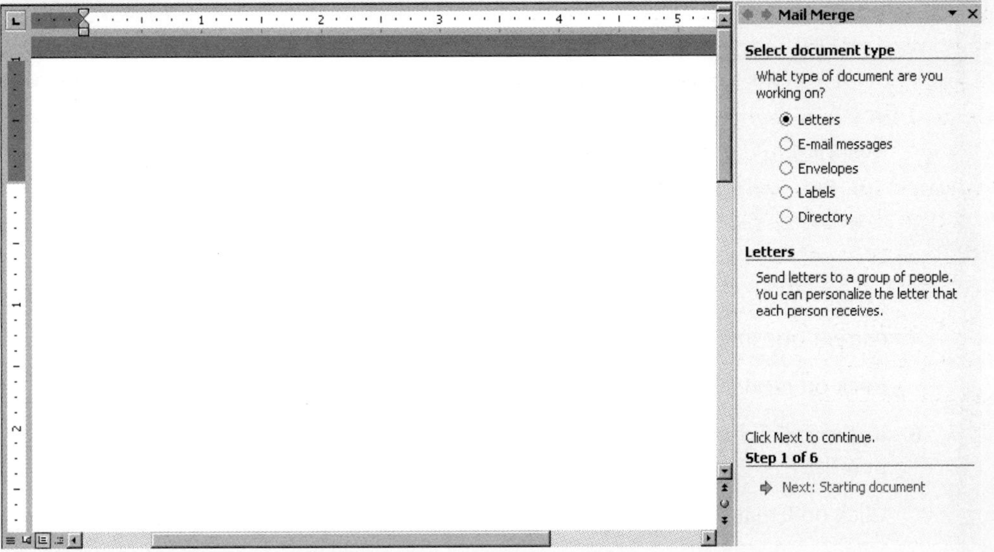

Make sure that Letters is selected. You can then start typing.

Exercise 13.1

4 Type in the following letter.

Dear

As you know you will soon be taking your end of year examinations. For those of you in year 11, these will be your GCSE exams. We will be holding a revision club on Mondays and Wednesdays from 4 p.m. to 6 p.m. A variety of staff will be on hand to help you with your revision questions. You should take advantage of this as it is completely free.

There will be a meeting on Wednesday 3rd May at 4 p.m. in the hall for any of you interested in taking up the offer.

Happy revision and good luck.

5 Click on Next: Starting document.

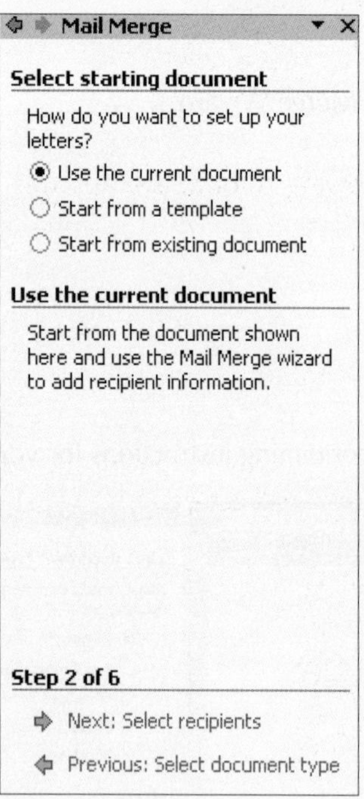

Make sure that the option 'Use the current document' has been selected.

Click on Next: Select recipients.

6 In the following screen, select 'Type a new list'.

Click on Create…

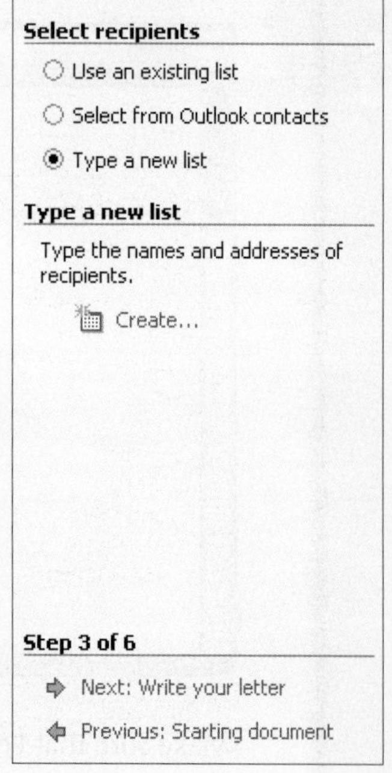

7 The following screen appears. Here you can select the name and address details.

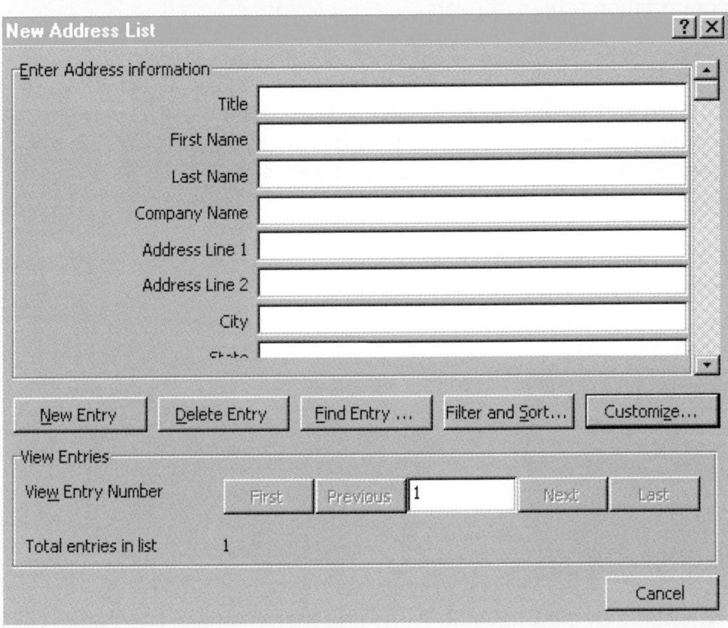

To send the letters out we need to have the following information for the names and addresses:

- surname
- forename
- street
- town
- postcode.

8 Click on the Customize... button and the following screen will appear.

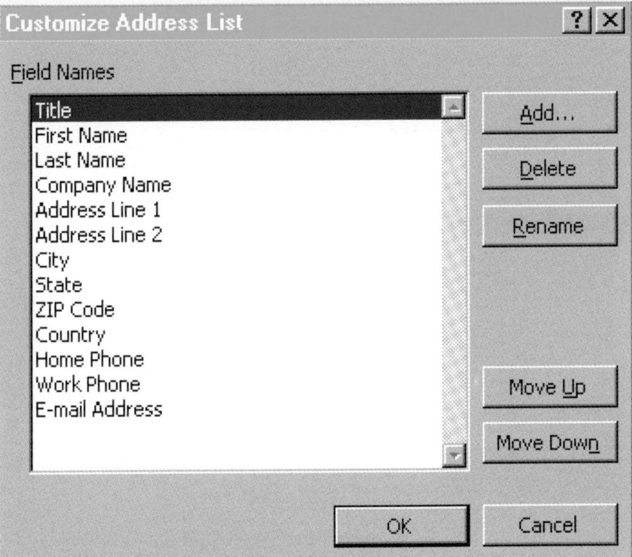

Make sure that Title is highlighted. Click on the Delete button to remove it from the list.

The following confirmation screen appears.

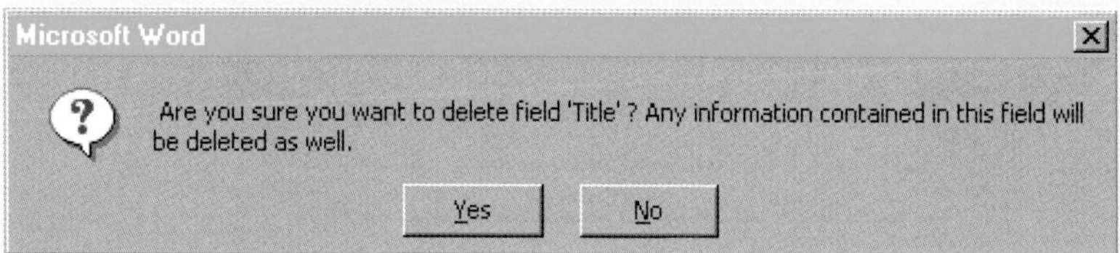

Click on the Yes button to confirm that you want it deleted.

9 Move the cursor to First Name.

Change this to Forename by clicking on Rename and then typing in Forename. Click on the OK button.

In a similar way change Last Name to Surname.

Now make the following changes, using the steps outlined in 7 and 8.

- Delete Company Name
- Rename Address Line 1 to Street
- Rename Address Line 2 to Town
- Rename City to Postcode
- Delete the rest of the fields.

Your list will now look like this after you have made the changes.

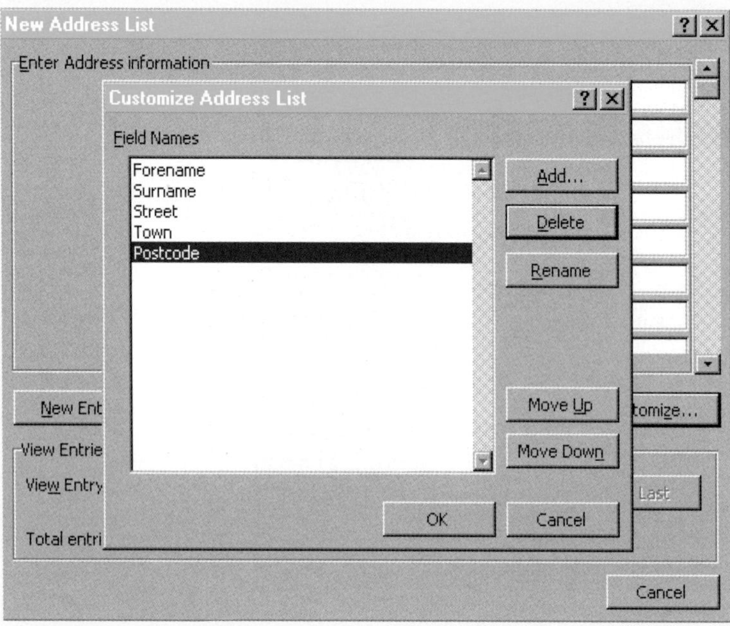

10 Click on the OK button. The following screen appears where you can type in your list of names and addresses.

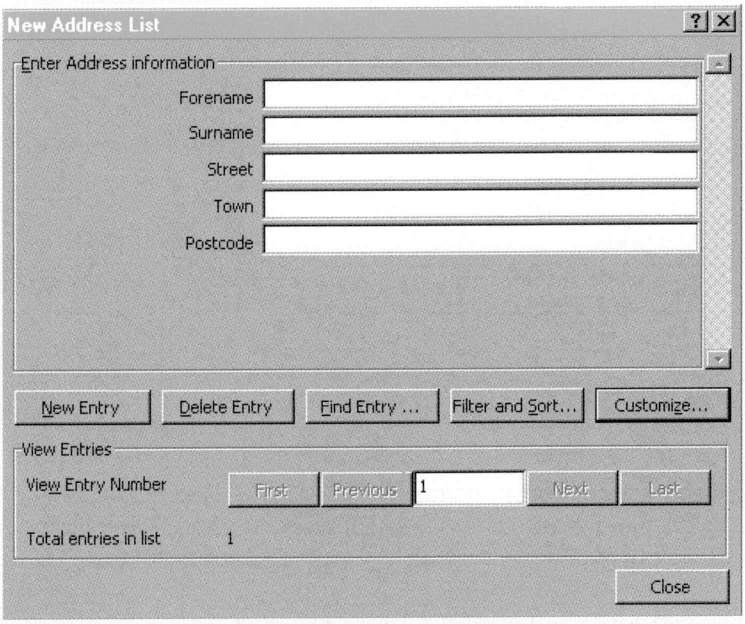

New Address List

Enter Address information

Forename
Surname
Street
Town
Postcode

New Entry | Delete Entry | Find Entry ... | Filter and Sort... | Customize...

View Entries

View Entry Number | First | Previous | 1 | Next | Last

Total entries in list 1

Close

11 Now enter the pupil data (i.e. their names and addresses) into your list.

Enter the details as shown in the following screen.

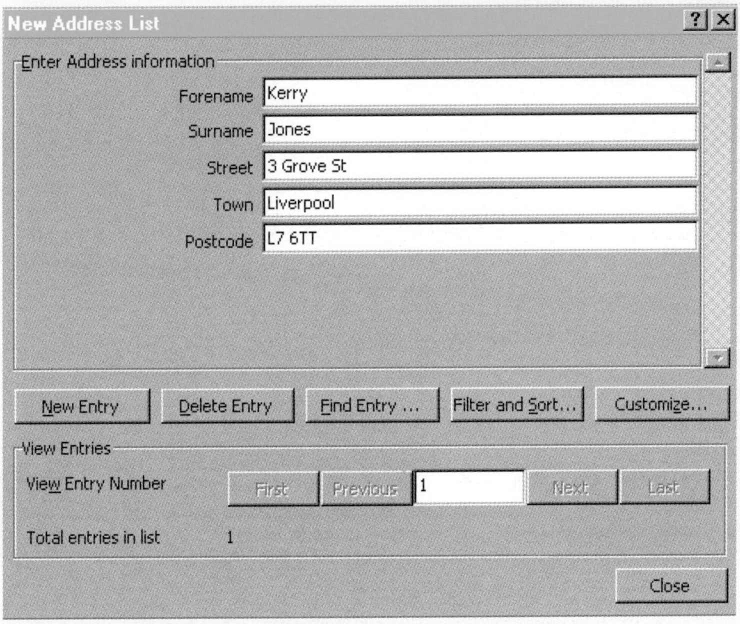

New Address List

Enter Address information

Forename Kerry
Surname Jones
Street 3 Grove St
Town Liverpool
Postcode L7 6TT

New Entry | Delete Entry | Find Entry ... | Filter and Sort... | Customize...

View Entries

View Entry Number | First | Previous | 1 | Next | Last

Total entries in list 1

Close

When you have typed in the details, click on New Entry.

Now repeat this by typing in the details for these two pupils.

Forename	Adam	Robin
Surname	Keel	Jackson
Street	12 Moor Grove	34 Fell St
Town	Liverpool	Warrington
Postcode	L13 7YH	WA 4ER

Now click on the Close button.

12 You will see a screen where you can name the file of names and addresses and also specify where they are to be stored. If you are storing your work on a floppy disk make sure that Save in is altered to the Floppy A drive.

Type in the filename Pupil list and then click on the Save button.

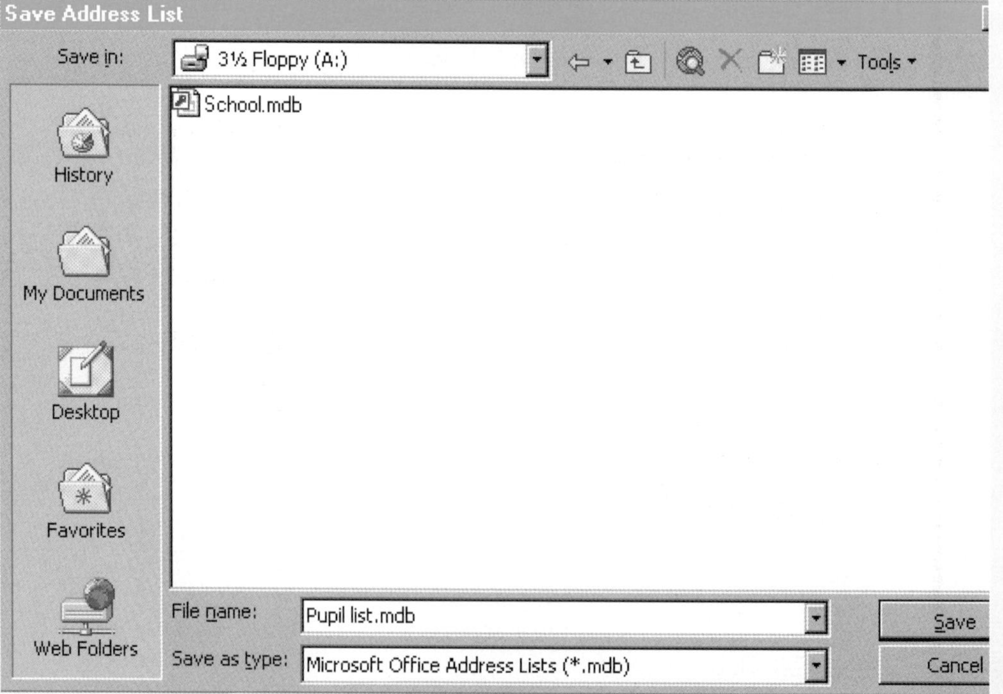

13 The following screen appears.

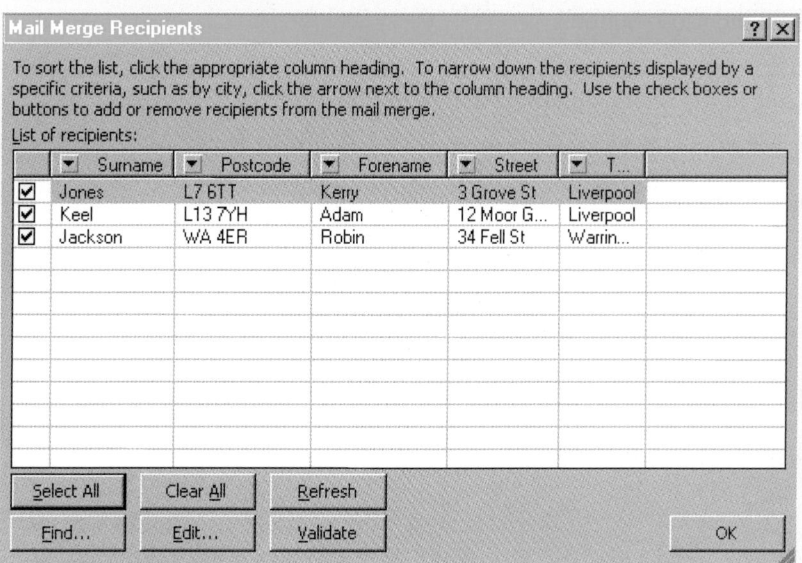

Make sure that there are ticks by the three records. This means that we have selected them for the mail merge.

Now click on the OK button.

14 Near the bottom right of the screen click on Next: Write your letter. Look at the right section of the screen. It should look like this.

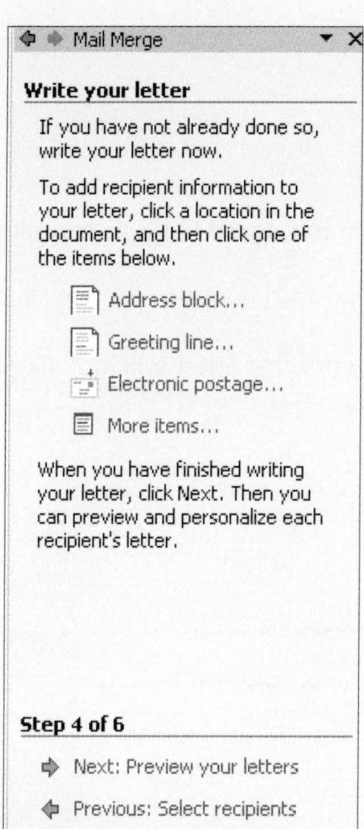

15 Click on More items...

The following window will be opened.

16 Move the cursor to a position in the original document above the word Dear and then click on the Insert button on the screen shown in 15. This will insert the Forename details here. Now click on the Close button.

Leave two spaces by pressing the spacebar twice. Click on More items… again and then highlight Surname in the screen and press the Insert button.

Your letter will now look like this:

«Forename» «Surname»

Dear

As you know you will soon be taking your end of year examinations. For

17 Now add the following fields in a similar way until your letter looks like this.

«Forename» «Surname»
«Street»
«Town»
«Postcode»

Dear

As you know you will soon be taking your end of year examinations.

18 Add the Forename field next to 'Dear' like this:

«Forename» «Surname»
«Street»
«Town»
«Postcode»

Dear «Forename»

As you know you will soon be taking your end of year examinations.

19 We can now get the computer to insert the variable data into these fields to complete the mail merge.

Click on Next: Preview your letters.

The first name and address details will be inserted and your first letter will look like this.

Kerry Jones
3 Grove St
Liverpool
L7 6TT

Dear Kerry

As you know you will soon be taking your end of year examinations. For those of you in year 11, these will be your GCSE exams. We will be holding a revision club on Mondays and Wednesdays from 4 p.m. to 6 p.m. A variety of staff will be on hand to help you with your revision questions. You should take advantage of this as it is completely free.

There will be a meeting on Wednesday 3rd May at 4 p.m. in the hall for any of you interested in taking up the offer.

Happy revision and good luck.

Exercise 13.1

20 Click on Next: Complete the merge.

21 Click on Print… to print the three letters out.

22 On closing the windows you will come to this screen. Here you can save the letter.

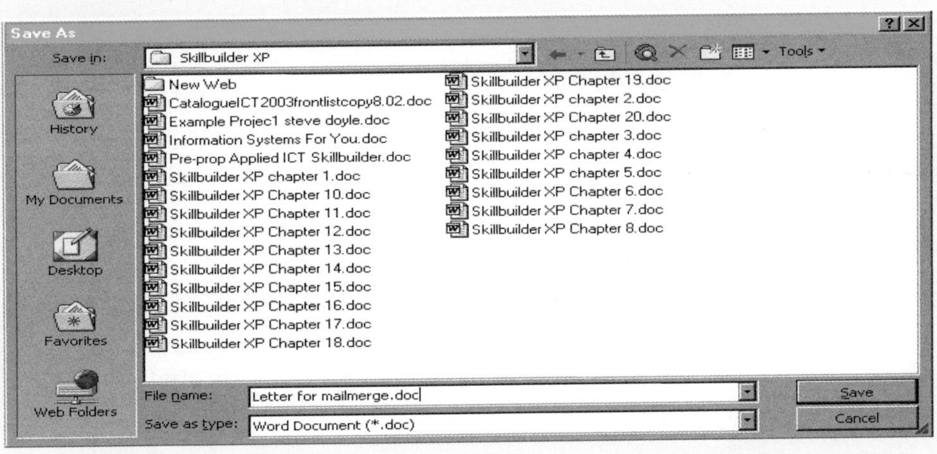

Data sources

In Exercise 13.1 you created the data source in Word. You can also create the data source in Excel or Access. You can even use data from a table in Word. You may like to explore for yourselves some of the possibilities of using data sources from other packages when doing your coursework. Remember to use the Help facility to find out how to do this.

Customising a mail merge

In the dentist's surgery example we created the data source specially for the mail merge. What would normally happen is that all the patient details would be recorded and a search performed to identify those patients who needed a check-up.

Here are some examples of customised mail merges:

- Sending a letter inviting customers to a sale preview if they have spent over £500 in the last year using their account.
- Sending letters to the parents of year 11 pupils in a school, inviting them to a parents' evening.
- Sending a letter to all the customers of a bank who have gone overdrawn by more than £100 without first arranging an overdraft with the manager.
- Producing a letter to be sent to customers who live in a certain postal area.

Printing envelopes and mailing labels

There is not much point in getting the computer to write hundreds of letters for a mail merge and then having to sit down and write all the envelopes by hand. We can also use the data source file to get the computer to either type the addresses onto self-adhesive mailing labels or print directly onto the envelopes.

Printing directly onto an envelope

The method for printing envelopes differs depending on whether you are going to print just a couple or are going to use a data source for the addresses on the envelopes.

Printing one envelope at a time

Click on Tools, then Letters and Mailings, then on Envelopes and Labels… If the Labels menu appears on top, click the Envelopes tab. The following menu now appears.

If you have just one envelope to type, you can simply type in the name and address in the Delivery Address box.

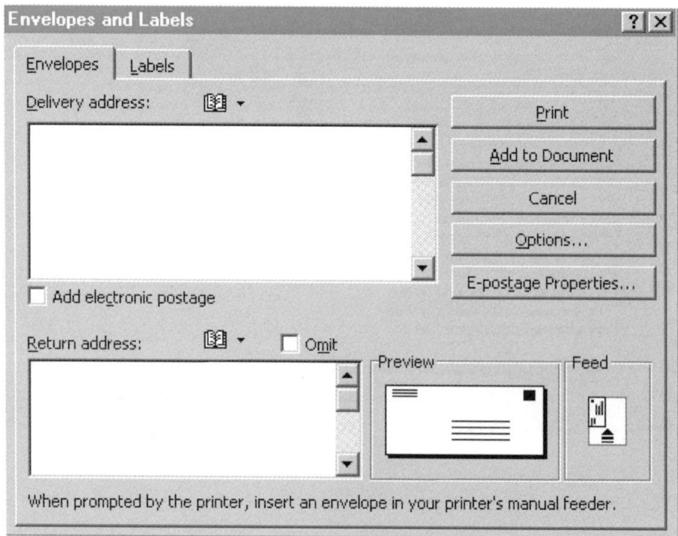

Printing an envelope

Click on options. This menu appears.

Here you can tell the printer about the size of the envelope you are using. Find out from your teacher, look at the box or packet of envelopes, or actually measure them, then click on Envelope size and make your selection.

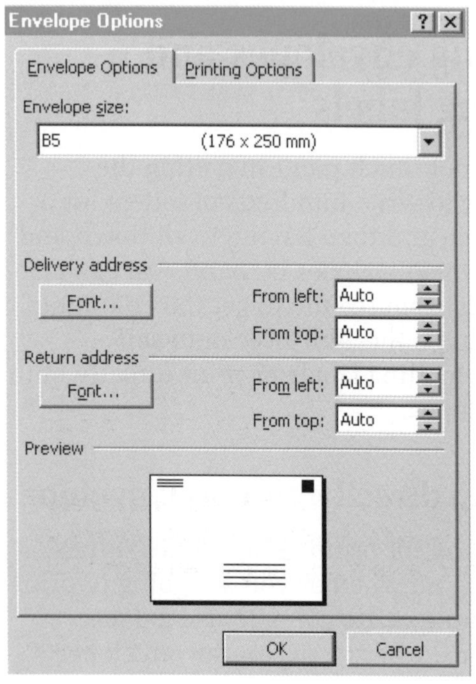

Printing labels

Click on Tools, then Letters and Mailings, then on Envelopes and Labels… If the Envelopes menu appears on top click on the Labels tab. The menu below now appears.

Using this menu, you can type in the address in the Address box and then print it on a label. Experiment with labels (you can print them on ordinary paper).

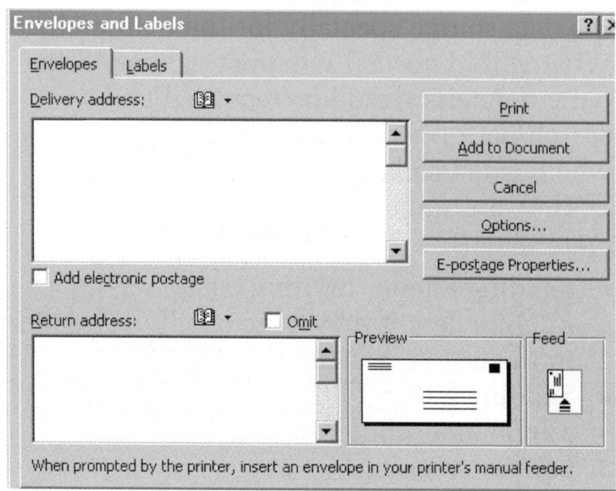

QUESTIONS

Obtain a brown envelope and use the computer and printer to print the following address on it:

Mr C Hawton
12 Old Mill Lane
Crosby
Liverpool
L23 4RI

Find and replace

The find facility in Word can be very useful for finding:

- where a particular sentence or phrase occurs in a document
- if a particular word has been used too many times
- where a person's name, which has been misspelled, appears in a letter.

Once the piece of text has been found, you can change it. This is useful if you have misspelled someone's name. Instead of looking through the document, hoping that you have found all the misspellings, you can get the computer to replace them all automatically.

Exercise 13.2

Using find and replace

In this exercise you will learn how to:

- **find all the occurrences of a word (a surname in this case) in a document**
- **replace all the occurrences with a different surname.**

1 Load Word, create a new document and type in the following letter:

Whizzo Cleaners Ltd
121 The High Street
Liverpool
L34 6TY

0800 901201

Dear Mrs Hughes

The Hughes family have been specially selected to go into our prize draw to win a fortnight's Caribbean cruise.

Just imagine, Mrs Hughes, you and your family waking up in the morning to a new destination each day.

All you have to do to enter this prize draw is to allow us to come and demonstrate our wonderful vacuum cleaner. This vacuum cleaner has been developed to make cleaning a pleasure rather than a chore. The Whizzo Vacuum Cleaner has the greatest amount of suction of any cleaner on the market.

All you have to do now Mrs Hughes is to ring the freephone number at the top of the page to arrange a visit by one of our demonstrators. No sales tactics are used and you are under no obligation at all to purchase one. All we ask Mrs Hughes is that you give up a few minutes of your time. If you are the lucky winner of the cruise, the Hughes family will all agree that these were a few minutes well spent.

We look forward to hearing from you.

Yours sincerely

Joe Murray

(Regional Marketing Manager)

2 Click on Edit, then on Find. The Find and Replace menu below is displayed.

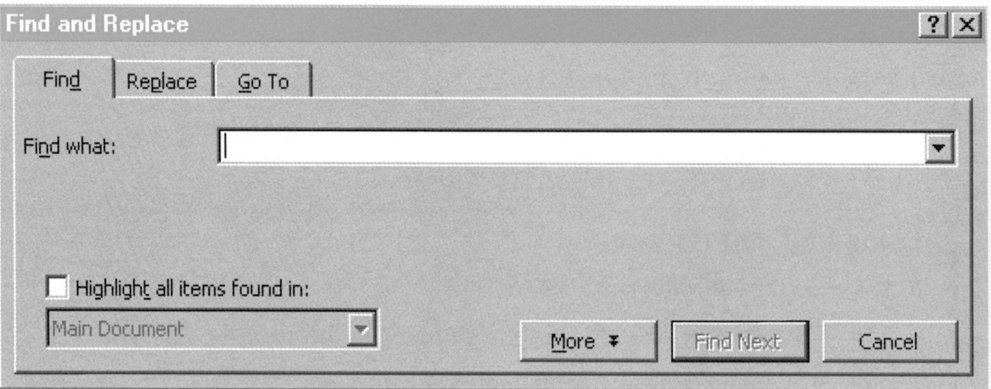

3 Enter the word **Hughes** into the box. This surname needs replacing with Smith so that the same letter can be used for another person.

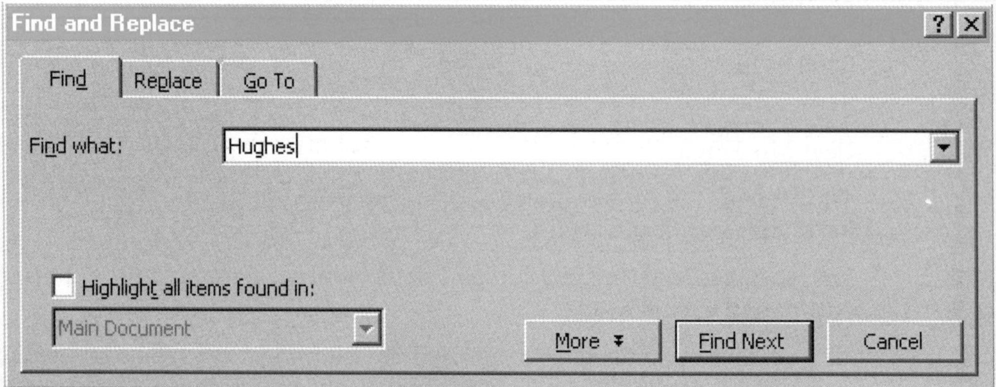

4 Now click on the Replace tab on the screen above. The screen below now appears.

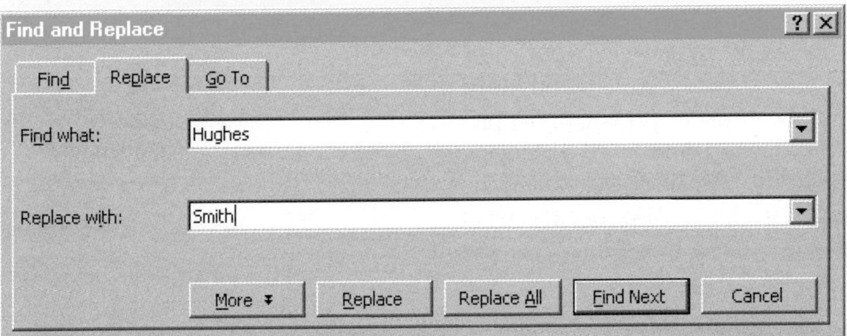

Enter the new name **Smith** in the Replace with box and click the Replace All button.

5 Word now replaces all the occurrences of 'Hughes' with 'Smith'.

The following box appears to let you know how many replacements it has made.

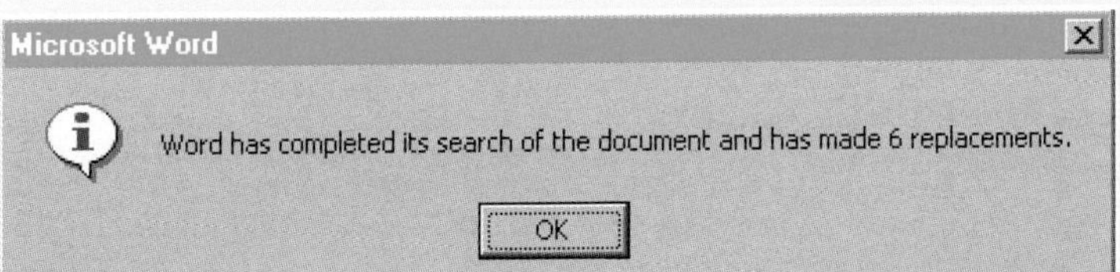

6 Click on OK and you will be able to see the document to check it.

7 Save the document and print a copy.

Creating web pages

Word is fine for producing simple web pages. Provided you just want to use text, graphics and hyperlinks (these provide a method to move from one item to another) Word is suitable.

As usual, to make things easy for you, Word XP has a few templates you can use and also a Wizard to guide you through the steps involved in creating a web page.

How to design your own web pages

As with all documents, you should make your pages appeal to the intended readership. Since there are no real rules regarding the design of web pages you can use your artistic talents.

Some things you might consider are:

- Make sure that any text used contrasts with the background. Dark text on a light background is best.
- Use subheadings to break up large amounts of text.
- It is better if the text in a web page does not stretch right across the screen.
- Make sure that the design is consistent from one page to another.
- Do not use too many graphics on one page. Remember that big graphics take time to load and can therefore be annoying to users of your page who will have to wait and incur phone charges during that wait.

Exercise 13.3

Designing a web page

Step 1

Design your web page on paper first. Decide on the graphics you intend using (e.g. clip art, scanned-in photographs, pictures from a digital camera, etc.). Decide how you want the very first page, called the default page, to look. Also decide what other pages you need to be linked to the default page.

Decide how the text is to look. Remember that you are free to use all the text enhancements that you have if you were designing a normal document.

Step 2

1 Load Word.

2 Click on File and then New..., this screen will appear. Now click on General Templates... in the **New from template** section.

Click on the Web Pages tab. The following screen appears.

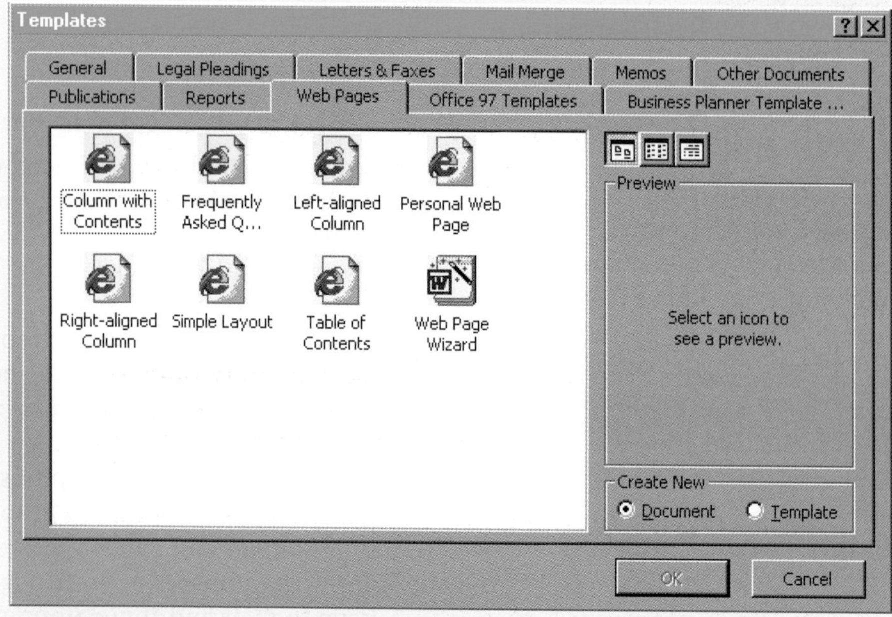

3 Double click on the Web Page Wizard icon on the above screen. The screen on the next page will now appear.

Exercise 13.3

4 Look at the left-hand side of the screen above. It shows stages in creating the web pages. Click on the Next> button to go onto the next step.

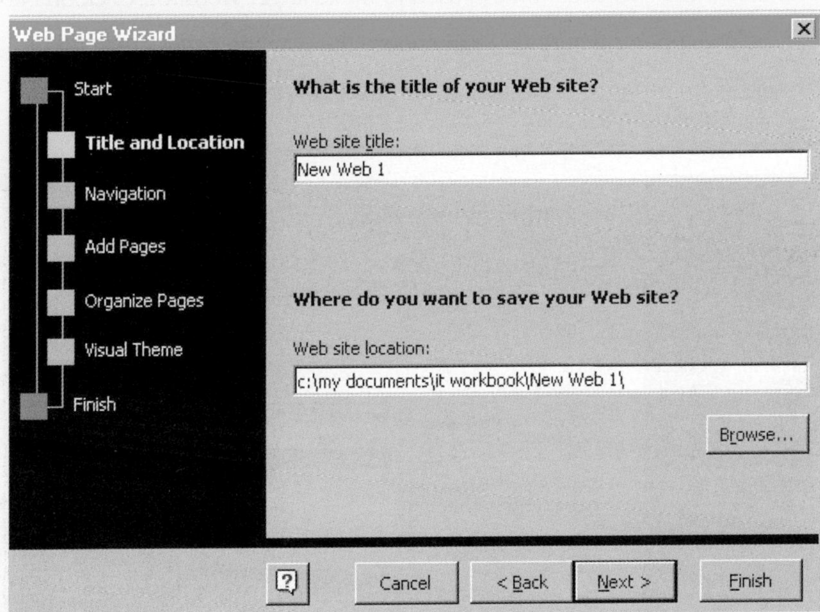

Type in the website title (**New Web 1** in this case); your teacher will tell you what you should type here.

You also have to specify where the website is to be saved. Again, you will need advice from your teacher.

Click on the Next> button to move to the next step.

5 This screen appears, in which you can choose the navigation style:

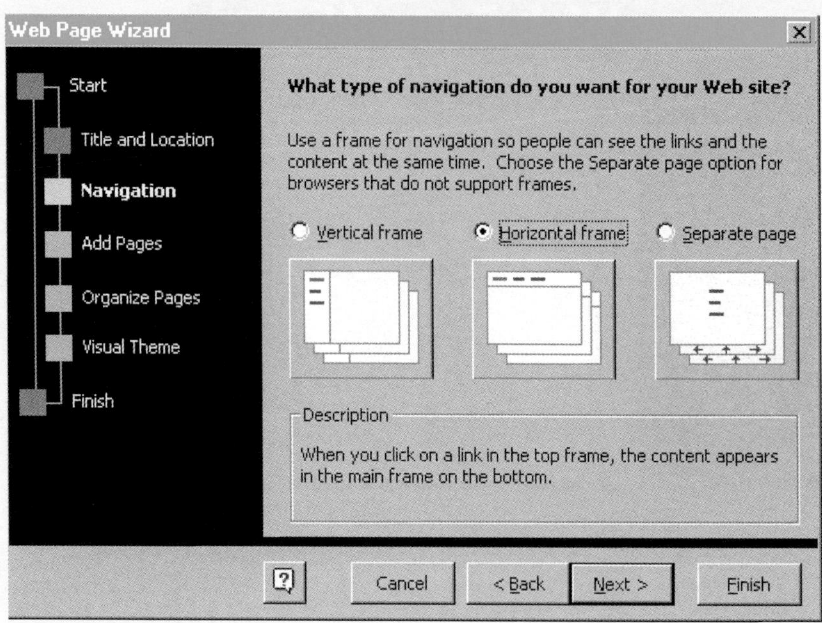

Choose the Horizontal frame option. This is the best option for a small website with no more than four linked pages. Vertical frame is used to make larger websites. Click on Next>.

6 The screen below appears where you can choose the way the pages are lined up.

This is where the importance of designing the pages on paper becomes clear.

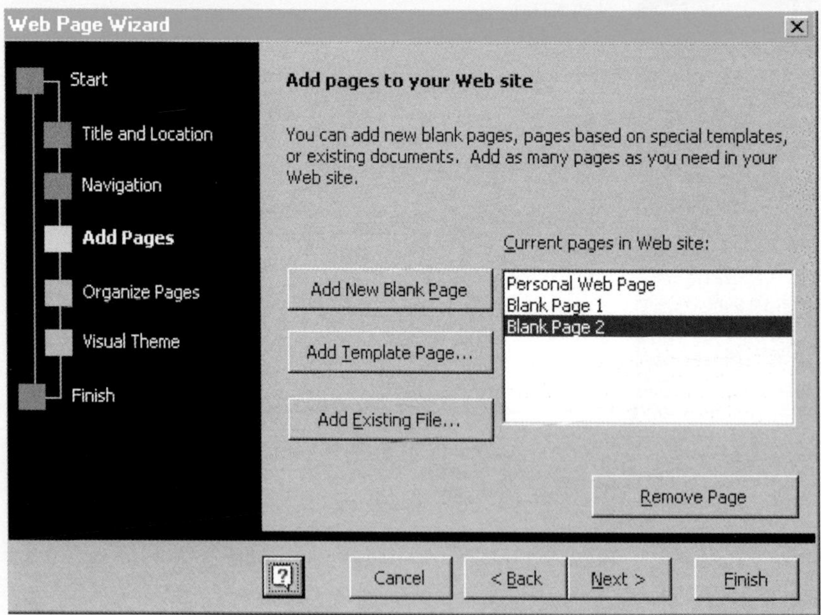

By default (i.e. unless you tell the computer otherwise) there is first a Personal Web Page and then two blank pages. Using this screen you can add and delete pages. Keep these default settings and click on Next>.

7 The following screen appears with which you can organise the order of the pages and give each page a name.

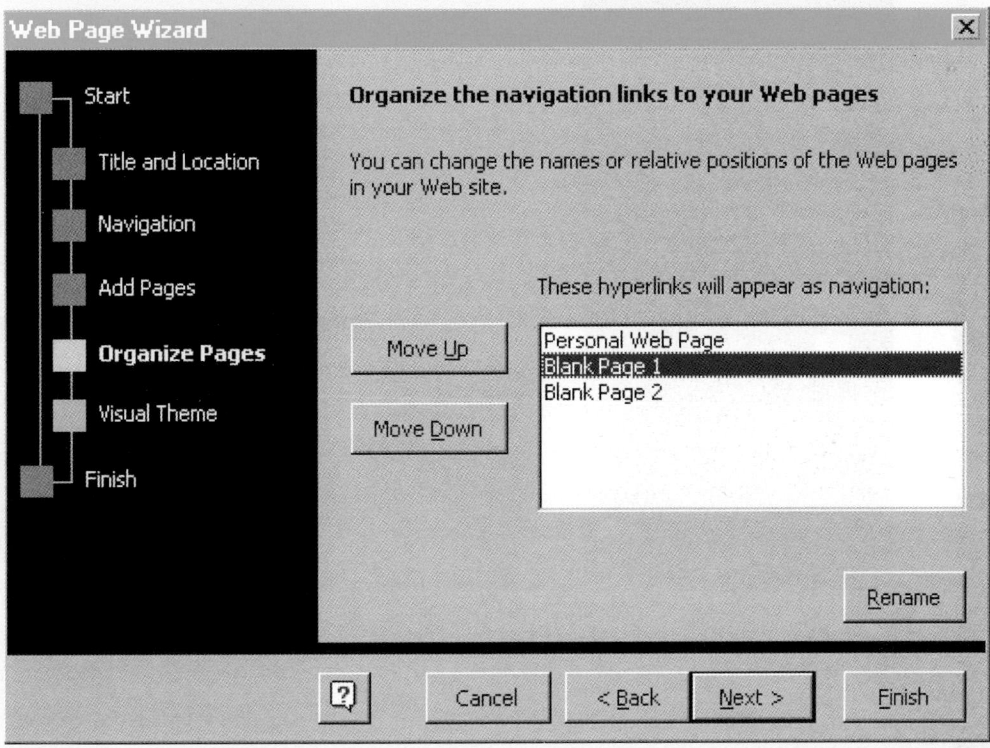

The order is OK but Blank Page 1 and Blank Page 2 need better names.

Double click on Blank Page 1 and then on the Rename button.

In the box shown here replace 'Blank Page 1' by **Hobbies and Interests**.

Click on the OK button.

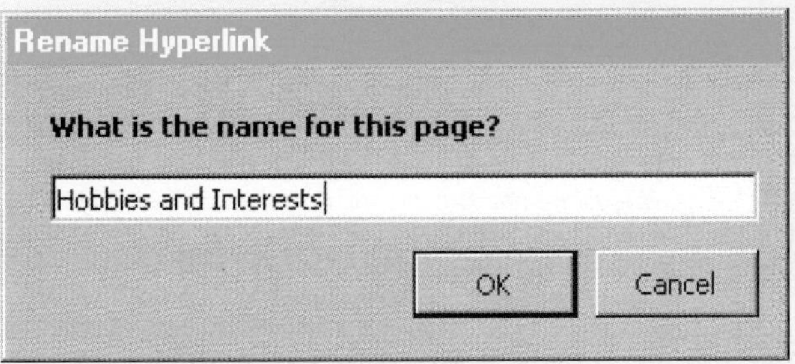

In a similar way replace the name 'Blank Page 2' with **About my family and where I live**. Click on OK after you have entered the new name.

8 The screen below now appears.

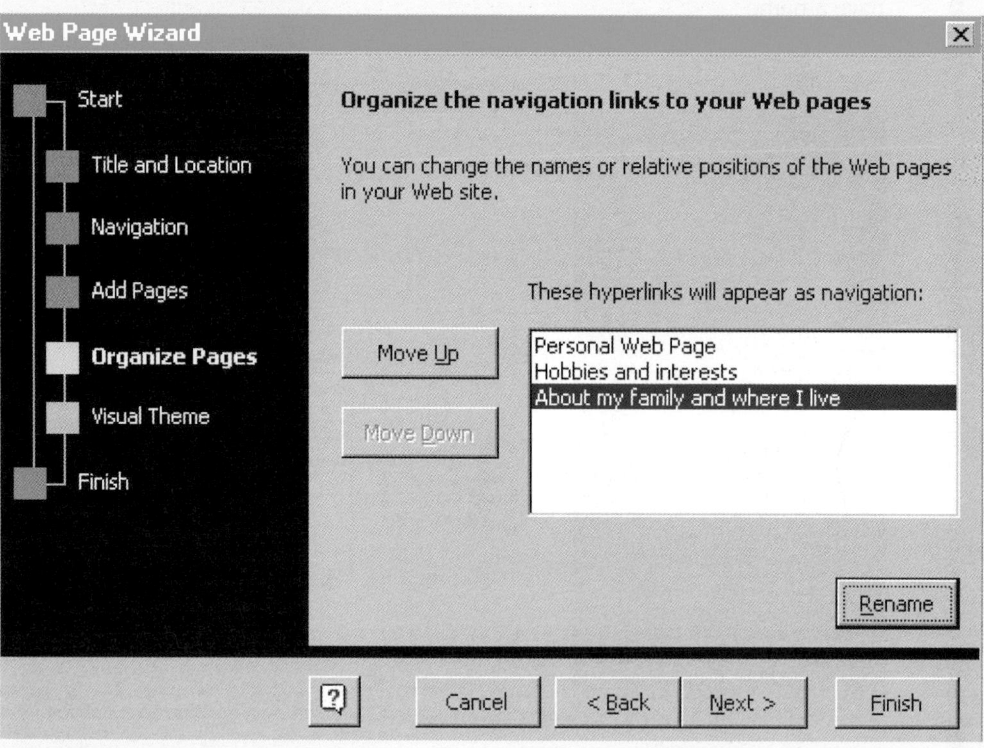

Click on Next>.

9 You can now choose a theme which gives your website a consistent look.

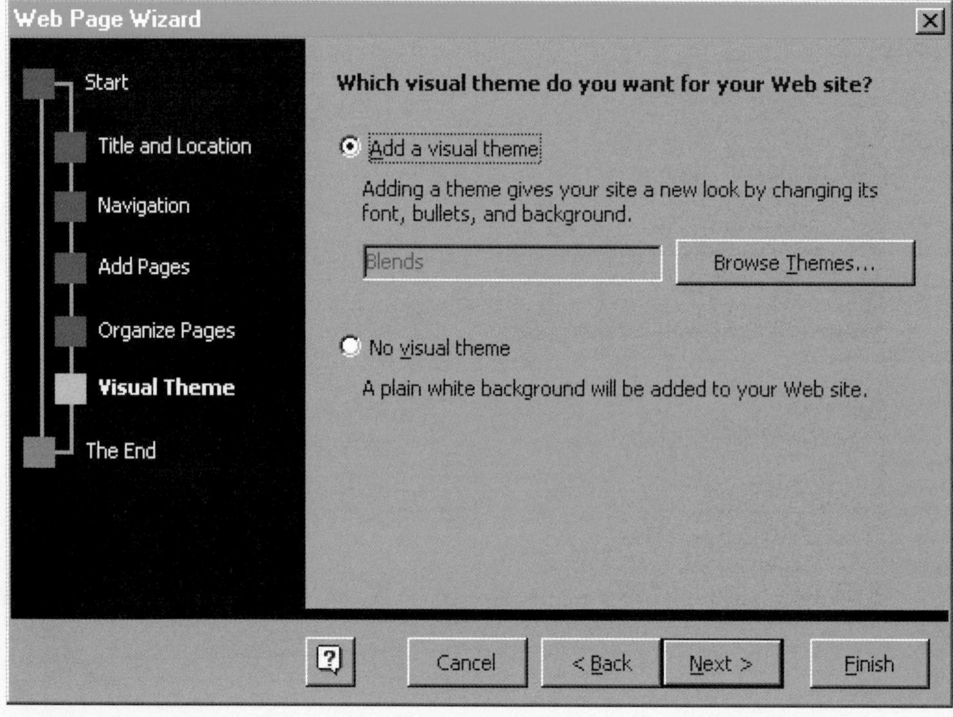

10 Click on the Browse Themes… button shown on the screen on page 196. A screen showing all the possible combinations of fonts, bullets, backgrounds and colour schemes is displayed below.

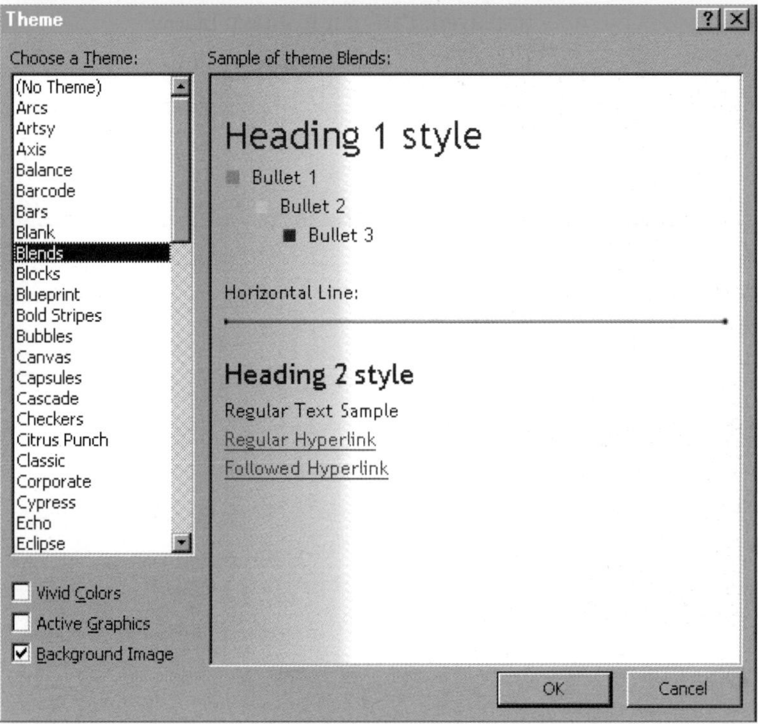

You can look at the different themes by clicking in turn on their names on the left of the screen. Select the theme 'Blends' and click on the OK button. Then click on Next>.

11 The final screen of the Wizard appears as shown below. Click on the Finish button.

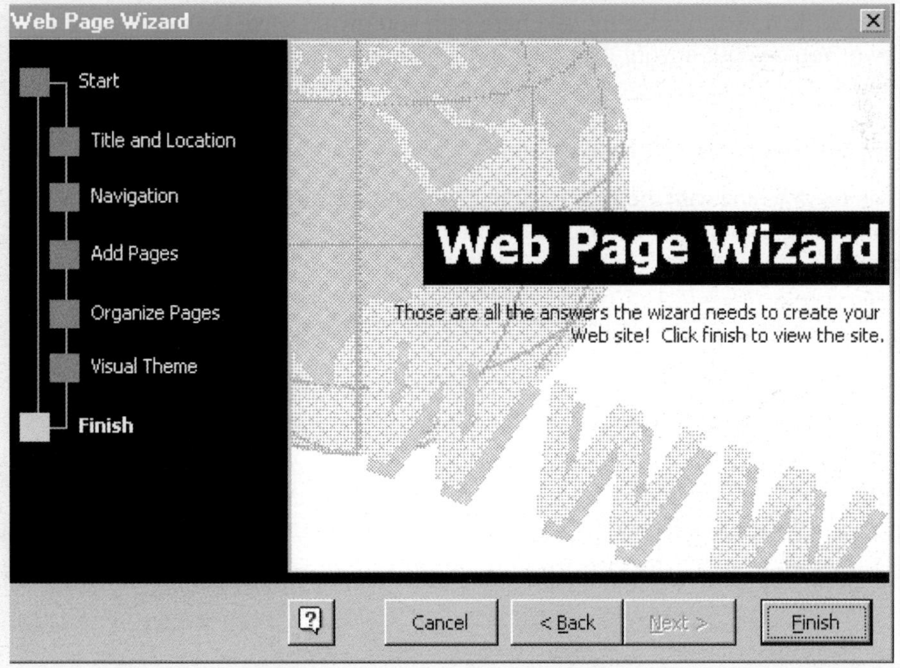

Exercise 13.3

As soon as you click on Finish, your web pages are saved in the location you specified earlier. The new default page is now loaded ready for editing.

12 The default screen is now displayed. Part of it is shown below.

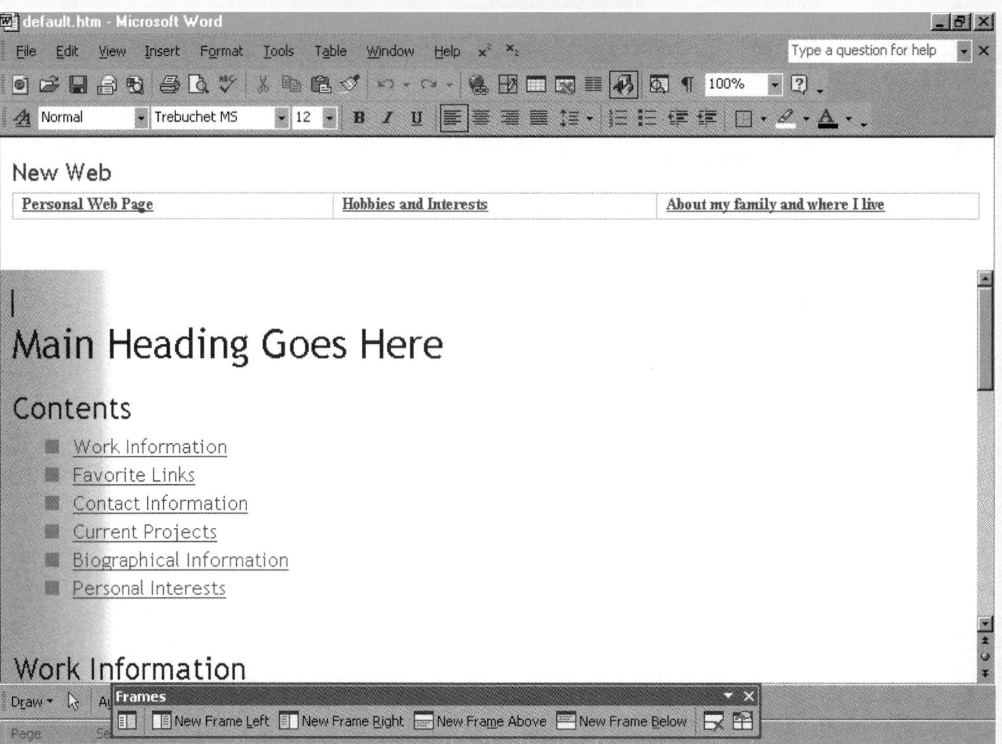

All you do now is replace the text here with you own. Delete the existing text and type in your own. You can put in your own titles in the contents list but make sure that you do not include information that you intend putting on any of the other web pages that are linked to this one.

Editing the web pages you have created

You can do anything with the web page that you can do otherwise with Word. This means you can use formatting techniques, change the fonts and font sizes, you can add pictures and change the colours.

Building a Database

All organisations need to hold a store of data. In a school, the data is about pupils and staff. In a company it could be about customers or stock. These data need to be organised in some way so that information can be found easily. When stores of data are computerised, the result is called a database.

This chapter explains what a database is and how to create one. First we need an application to computerise. You will all be familiar with a video hire store. In this chapter we look at the information needs of a video library and in the following chapters we will start to design and build a video tape database.

Moviereel Video Hire Store

Suppose you have been asked to set up a video hire store from scratch. Once you have the premises, the next thing you will need are the videos to hire. Once the videos arrive from the supplier, you will have to record certain details about them.

What details do you store? Think carefully about these details. You might first write a list then put details onto cards in a card box. An example of what might be contained on these cards is shown here.

The data must be written by hand onto each card as indicated by the dotted lines.

Recording data onto cards in this way presents some problems:

- Each Video_ID needs to be unique otherwise it is impossible to keep track of what has been hired out. Remember also that there are often several copies of the same video title.
- As the videos will be given different numbers, if we store them in order of Video_ID, it will not be easy to locate all the copies of a particular video title (e.g. Titanic).
- Altering details means crossing out data and adding the amended data. This is untidy and confusing, especially if the data has been altered several times.
- If all rental prices of £2.50 need to be increased to £3.00, many cards will need to be altered.
- The cards have to be placed in a certain order so that it is easy to locate a particular card. Ordering them according to the title would be best. Once placed in this order, putting them into any other order becomes very time consuming. Imagine there are 1000 cards in title order and you were asked to put them into Video_ID order. How would you do it and how long would it take?

Once all the stock data has been entered, we can use the collection of data (called a database) to supply the manager of the shop with information such as:

- How many copies are there of a certain video?
- How many category PG films are there?
- Who supplied the film *Titanic*?

Moviereel Video **Stock List**

Video_ID ....

Title ....

Supplier ....

Category ....

Rating ....

Copies_in_Stock ....

Rental_Price ....

Storing data on cards

Some processing of the data needs to be performed to produce this information. Processing in these cases would be rearranging the cards and searching for the data. Processing data in some way produces information.

Why use a computerised database?

Using a computerised database to hold the data has many advantages, which include:

- It is easy to alter the structure of the database in case you miss a field out and need to add it later. For example, suppose you left out borrowers' telephone numbers from your database design. As soon as you realise, you can add it to the structure.
- Keeping the database up-to-date is much easier. You can modify, delete or add details.
- You can process the data in many different ways. You can summarise, calculate, select or sort the data quickly.
- Reports (another name for printouts) of the results can be produced, such as a list of videos with a rental price of £3.50.

Fields, records and files: what do they all mean?

Here are some database terms you will need to familiarise yourselves with.

Data

These are facts about a specific person, place or thing.

Information

Information is data that has been rearranged into a form that is useful to the user.

Field

A field is an item of data on the form. A video title would be an example of a field.

Record

Information about a particular person or thing is called a record. A record consists of several fields containing data about the same subject. All the information about a particular video (e.g. Video_ID, Title, Supplier, etc.) is contained in a record.

Files

A collection of related records is called a file. The group of records for all the videos in the library could be the video file. The collection of membership details for each member of the video hire store could be called the members file.

Tables

In one type of database, called a relational database, we do not store all the data in a single file or table. Instead the data is stored in several tables although the data in the separate tables can be combined if needed.

In the video hire shop we have only considered the videos themselves. As well as holding these details, we also need data about the members and the rentals (i.e. we need to know which member has borrowed a certain video). These will need to be held in separate tables.

Three tables are needed which will be called:

- videos
- members
- rentals.

Tables consist of columns and rows organised in the following way:

- The rows (apart from the first row) represent records in the database.
- The columns contain the database fields.
- The first row contains the field names.

Questions

Look at the table below and, using the words **field**, **field names**, **column**, **row**, **table** and **record**, copy and complete the following sentences.

1 Video_ID and Title are examples of ....

2 '5 Go HG Scene Thriller 18 2' is an example of a ....

3 'ABC Ltd ' is an example of a ....

4 An arrangement of data in columns and rows is called a ....

5 Records are represented by the .... in a table whereas fields are represented by the .... in the table.

Field names

Video_ID	Title	Supplier	Category	Rating	Copies_in_Stock
1	South Park	Videotrak Ltd	Family	15	6
2	Ravenous	Videotrak Ltd	Thriller	18	3
3	The General's Daughter	HG Scene	Thriller	18	3
4	The Trench	Videotrak Ltd	Action	15	4
5	Go	HG Scene	Thriller	18	2
6	Never Been Kissed	ABC Ltd	Family	12	3
7	Star Wars Episode 1	ABC Ltd	Sci-Fi	U	3
8	Eyes Wide Shut	Videotrak Ltd	Drama	18	3
9	Italian Job	Videotrak Ltd	Family	PG	4
10	A Simple Plan	ABC Ltd	Thriller	15	1
11	Drop Dead Gorgeous	Videotrak Ltd	Drama	15	3
12	The Thomas Crown Affair	ABC Ltd	Thriller	15	2
13	Varsity Blues	Videotrak Ltd	Family	15	3
14	Notting Hill	HG Scene	Romance	15	2
15	Mickey Blue Eyes	Videotrak Ltd	Family	15	1
16	Night Of The Hunter	Videotrak Ltd	Family	15	2
17	A Midsummer Nights Dream	Videotrak Ltd	Family	PG	3

Creating the video table

Data in a database created using the database package Microsoft Access is stored in tables. The first step in building a database is to create the tables. The videos table will store data about all the videos in the store. Before this table is created, we have to think about the answers to the following questions.

What is the purpose of the database?

The manageress of the shop needs to know what videos they have in stock. He needs to answer questions such as 'Do you have a copy of *Titanic*?' 'What videos do you have priced at £1.50'? Such questions will be asked both by customers and staff, so the system needs to provide answers quickly. At present a card box with the video details is used.

The manageress has asked us to develop a simple database to enable her to answer such questions.

What information would the manageress need to get out of the system?

You need to establish what is expected of the system. You could ask the manageress the following questions:

- What information do you need to get out of the database? Can you give me some examples?
- What lists or reports (another name for printouts) do you need?

- What questions need to be asked of the database, because you can only search for information that has been previously stored or can be calculated from what is already there?

How does the existing system work?

If the video hire shop is a new one you could find out about the system other similar shops use. If there is an existing system, you will need to perform a fact-find by questioning the users of the system and recording the answers.

Is there a user to ask?

You must not develop a system that you **think** the user wants. To do so is a bit like someone going out to buy clothes for you; they are unlikely to pick what you like. The user will understand the system (i.e. the way of doing things) much better than you, although they may have little IT knowledge. The user has to use your system on a day-to-day basis so you need to make sure that it is as near perfect as possible. The only way you can make sure that you are developing a system the user wants, is to involve them in all the parts of the analysis and design of the new system. Keep showing the user what you have done and ask them if it is OK. Get them to give you regular feedback.

The problems in using a single card to store all the data

Using a single card means that the details on videos, members and rentals are all kept together. We could, therefore, only hold video details if they were being borrowed by a member. Also, there would be no record of a member unless they had borrowed a video.

Clearly more than one set of cards is needed. Three sets is the minimum to enable video, member and rental details to be stored.

The differences between flat file databases and relational databases

If you think about it, you need three tables for a video library database.

A database that uses a single table is called a flat file database and its use is fairly limited, although such databases can be useful for simple uses, such as just names, addresses and telephone numbers.

IT TASKS

Designing a manual system for running a video library

Imagine you were actually trying to run a video library.

You need to store data about videos, members and rentals.

1 Design a card that could be used to store the essential details about videos, members and rentals. You can do this either on a card or on paper. You are only allowed **one** card to store all the information.

  Compare your card with your friends' cards. Discuss your findings with the rest of the class and your teacher.

2 Add some sample data to three such cards. Make up the data yourself.

3 What would be the problems with your card system in answering questions such as:
  - What order should the cards be sorted into?
  - How would you search for a certain video?
  - How would you search for a certain member?
  - How can you find out if a particular video is overdue?

IT TASKS

Using three card boxes (i.e. three files) for the video hire database

You are now allowed to use three card boxes; one each for members, videos and rentals.

1 What fields need to be on each of these cards? Produce suitable designs for each of these cards (you can do this on card or paper).

2 To make it easy to find a particular card in each of these card boxes the cards need to be sorted into a certain order. What order would be best for the cards in each of the three boxes?

3 Explain how the card box system could be used for the following:
(a) finding out how many copies of a particular video are held
(b) recording the details when a video is borrowed
(c) finding out the names, addresses, etc. of members who have not returned their videos
(d) deleting video details when videos become too old for borrowing
(e) recording the details of a new member who has just joined the library
(f) working out the fines payable by members who have not returned their videos on time.

Databases consisting of more than one table with links between the tables, are called relational databases. Almost all the databases used by companies and other organisations are relational databases.

Why use more than one table?

If you do use a single table you could experience some of the following problems:

- You may find there is a lot of duplicate data. Time is wasted re-typing the same data.
- When a record is deleted a lot of data which is still useful, may also be deleted.

Single tables are useful only for very simple databases.

Planning a table

Planning should always be done first on paper. This allows you to think just about the problem rather than worrying how the database software works. It is much quicker to plan first and then use the software, rather than trying to correct mistakes once the database has been constructed. Here are some things that you will need to think about:

1 Decide on a name for the whole database and where you will store it (e.g. hard drive, floppy drive).

2 Decide on a name for the table (you can use the same name for a database and a related table as the program will be able to distinguish between them). Most databases have many tables and each needs a different name.

3 Plan the structure of the table bearing in mind the following points:
(a) Decide, after consulting the user (if there is one), what fields should be stored. You can also agree a name for each field. Try to use names that are obvious.
(b) Decide on the order that these fields appear in the table. It is best that the most important one (usually a unique property such as Membership_Number) should come first. Give appropriate field names to each of these fields.
(c) Decide on the data type for these fields (e.g. character, numeric, date etc.)

Data types

Once you have given a field a name you have to specify the type of data that is allowed in the field. This allows you to restrict the type of data which can be entered into a certain field.

In Access (and most other databases) the possible data types are as shown in the table below.

Data types possible in Access

Data type	Description
Text	Used for storing names, words and numbers not used in calculations (e.g. telephone numbers, code numbers, bank account numbers.)
Number	Used for storing numbers that can be used in calculations.
Date/time	Used for storing dates and times.
Currency	Used for storing monetary values to two decimal places.
AutoNumber	These are numbers in sequence, allocated by the computer. Each record is given a different number. If you use AutoNumber the number given will always be unique.
Yes/No	Used for storing data such as yes/no, true/false etc.
OLE object	Used for storing data from other programs. You could put a picture in under this data type.
Memo	Used for storing long notes which are not suitable for putting in a field.

Choosing a primary key

When you create a table you need to choose a primary key. The primary key is one or more fields that may be used by Access to identify a particular record.

Let's look at an example. Suppose we were designing a table to hold membership details for a sports club and we decide on these fields:

Title; Surname; Forename; Street; Town; Postcode; Telephone number.

In this list there are no unique fields. People living at the same address can have the same surname and forename so these cannot be used. Postcodes are not unique since several houses down the same road have the same postcode.

When there are no unique fields we can create one. We can arrange Membership_Number so that no two members have the same number. Here the data type AutoNumber can be used. AutoNumbers are useful since the computer allocates them making sure no two numbers are ever the same. The computer remembers the last number it has given, so if we have 100 members and a new member joins they will be given the Membership_Number 101.

If you do not want to create a new field you can look for two or more fields that will together, uniquely define a row in a table. We will see how this is done in Chapter 17.

Validation checks

When data is being entered into a database it is important that any errors are spotted by the program so that it can alert the user to check and if necessary re-enter the data.

When the structure of the database is being designed, a series of validation rules can be devised to govern what can and cannot be entered into each field. It is impossible to trap every type of error; if someone's address is 4 Bankfield Drive and the user incorrectly types in 40 Bankfield Drive, no simple validation check could detect this.

Questions

1 Picking data types

Here are some examples of data. Using the data types in the table on the previous page, fill in the last column in this table with the best data type for the field.

Field name	Example of data	Data type
Surname	Hughes	
Membership_Number	00901	
Date of birth	12/12/83	
Sex	M or F	
Driver	Y or N	
Street	12 Blackwood Drive	
Account balance	£256.98	
Postcode	L23 5TR	
Price	£34.56	
Age	15	

2 Text or numbers?

Here are some items of data that are to be stored in the tables of a database. Your task is to identify whether they should be stored as text or numbers. Examples of the data to be entered are shown in brackets.

(a) the number of units in stock (234)
(b) an invoice number (0001 to 9999)
(c) a telephone number (0161 876 2302)
(d) a tax code (488H)
(e) an employee number (00234442)
(f) the rate of VAT (17.5%)
(g) the rate of pay (£10 per hour)
(h) a National Insurance Number (TT232965A).

Data type checks

Databases automatically check to see if the data being entered into a field fits what is allowed by the data type for that field, so text cannot be entered into a field that has a numeric data type.

If a field is given a data type of text, you can enter any characters from the keyboard into this field. You can, therefore, enter numbers into a text field but you cannot perform any calculations on them. This type of check is called a data type check. Always try to specify the most appropriate data type when setting up the structure of the database.

Range checks

As well as the checks on the data type, you can devise other checks.

Range checks are performed on numbers to make sure that they lie within a specified range. Range checks will only detect absurd values. For example, if you typed in the number of children in a household as '50', instead of '5', then a range check will spot the error; if you typed in '7' then the range check would not pick up the error.

Presence checks

You can specify that some fields must always have data entered into them. For example, when a video is borrowed from the library you should always have to enter the Video_ID and the Membership_Number. However, some fields such as Telephone_Number can be left blank since not everyone has a telephone. Checks such as this are called presence checks.

In Microsoft Access we have to decide on two things when we want to validate data: the validation rule and the validation text.

Validation rule

The easiest validation checks are on numbers and dates.

For example, the database can check that a number being entered is above a certain value, below a certain value or within a range of values.

Validation text

The validation text is a message that appears if the data breaks the validation rule. An example is shown below right.

The screen at the bottom of the page shows the table structure being set up. The cursor is on the field Rental_Price. Because there are only three rental prices (£1.50, £2.50 and £3.50) we do not want the user to be able to put in any other value.

Notice that the validation rule line is in the Field Properties box. The validation rule is =1.5 Or =2.5 Or =3.5

We also need to enter a message that will appear should the user enter any value other than these. Rather than just tell the user that they are wrong it is better to tell them what values they can enter. A suitable message for the validation text would be 'Enter £1.50, £2.50 or £3.50'. The validation rule should be tested by entering data into a table. You should attempt to enter some data that should pass and some that should fail validation. This is the message that appears when a rental price of £4.50 is entered:

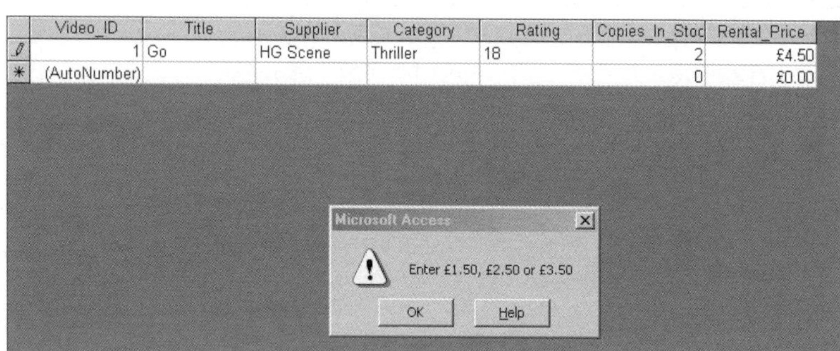

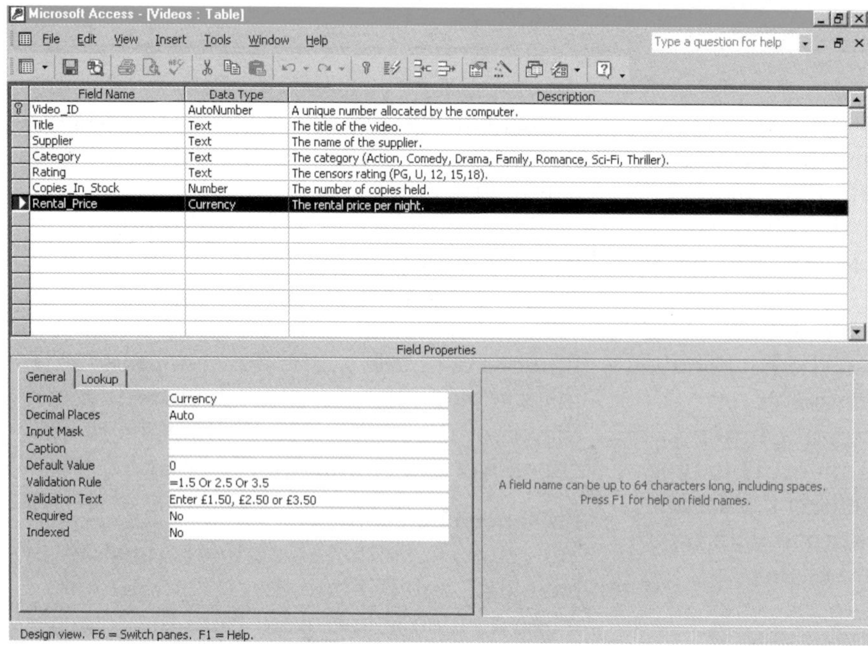

Some validation rules are shown in the table at the top of the next page.

Examples of validation rules

Validation rule	Validation text (message that appears if the rule is not obeyed)
<>0	A value other than zero has to be entered
>100	A number greater than 100 has to be entered
<=16	A number less than or equal to 16 has to be entered
'Male' or 'Female'	Only the text Male or Female can be entered
Like 'A???'	You have to enter four characters starting with the letter A
=£100 or =£200	Only £100 or £200 can be entered
>12/12/00	The date entered must be after 12/12/00 (note that it does not include this date)
Is null	The field can be left blank
>=#1/1/2000 and <#1/1/2001#	The date entered must be in the year 2000

QUESTIONS

1 A doctors' surgery keeps information on all the patients and their treatments. Part of this file is shown below.

(a) How many records are shown?

(b) How many fields does each record have?

(c) In all databases there should be a unique field.

(i) Which is the unique field in this section of the file?

(ii) Why is it important to have a unique field?

(d) Give an example of a field name in the section of the file shown below.

(e) Data in a database is often coded, for example, the doctors' names are coded using their initials. What is the main advantage in doing this?

Patient number	Surname	Forename	Date of birth	Doctor's initials
2001	Symonds	Carl	17/03/49	KP
2903	Hollis	William	09/12/78	JH
2109	Freeman	Debbie	01/05/91	KP
2009	Doyle	Jayne	03/04/87	JH
2187	Jackson	Joanne	30/09/70	JH
2177	Smith	Julie	11/09/76	KP

2 A tennis club committee is thinking of using a computerised database to store details about members. At present they use a cardbox system. There are currently 300 members.

(a) What advantages are there in storing the members' details on a computer rather than on cards?

(b) The club secretary is convinced that a computerised system would be better. He suggests the following fields for the database:

- name
- address
- age
- date joined
- membership category (Junior or Senior).

(i) Rather than use Name as a field you suggest that it should be broken down further into: Title; Surname; Forename. Why is this much better?

(ii) Address is also broken down into several fields.
Suggest suitable field names for each of these.

(iii) Why is it inadvisable to store age in a database?
What should be stored instead?

(iv) The club secretary has been told by one of the members that databases should always have a unique field, called a primary key. Explain why this is.

(v) Membership_Number is to be added to the list of fields as the primary key. This will be a number allocated automatically by the computer. What is the main advantage of letting the computer allocate this number rather than just typing it in?

3 (a) When setting up the structure of a database you have to specify the data type for each field. Text and numbers are two data types. Name two other data types that you might find in a database.

(b) Why is it so important to specify the type of data that can be entered into a field?

(c) What is meant by validation and why is it so important?

4 There are many different validation checks. Explain how each one of the following validation checks works:

(a) data type check

(b) presence check

(c) range check.

Using Access to Design a Simple Database

A word about Microsoft Access

Microsoft Access is the database package that comes with the full version of Microsoft Office XP. It is a powerful relational database package but you can also use it for building simple flat file databases. The main problem in using Access is that you need to know quite a lot about system design before you start. In the previous chapter we looked at setting up the structure of a table to store the video details for the video hire store. In this chapter the software is used to create a table.

If you are still using Office 97 or 2000, then some of the screens in Access XP will look quite different to those you are familiar with.

Loading Access

Your teacher will show you how to load the spreadsheet program, Microsoft Access. If you need to keep your work on a floppy disk your teacher will show you how to do this. You may be working on a network in which case your teacher will advise you where your files will be stored.

QUESTIONS

It is important that you are able to load Access.

Write down a brief set of instructions to remind yourself how to do this.

Exercise 15.1

Creating a flat file database in Microsoft Access

A flat file database is a database consisting of just one table. In this exercise you will create the video table. The video table is used to store all the video details for the video hire store.

In this exercise you will learn how to:

- **create a blank Access database**
- **give the database a name**
- **create a table in Design view**
- **set field names, data types and descriptions**
- **set a primary key field**
- **move between Data Design and Datasheet views**
- **enter data into the table**
- **give a name to the table**
- **exit the database.**

Exercise 15.1

1 Load the Access software.

The screen below appears.

On the right hand part of the screen, click on Blank Database.

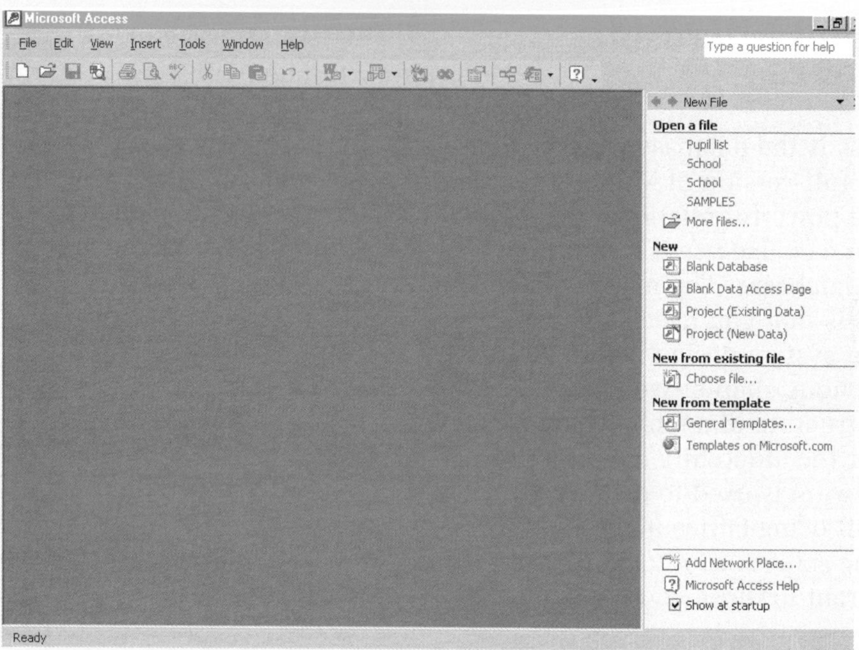

2 The menu below appears. There are two things you need to specify.
(a) A name for the database; we will call the database file 'Video Hire Store'.
(b) A place to store the database file; in this case we will use the floppy disk drive. Your teacher will inform you where to save your files.

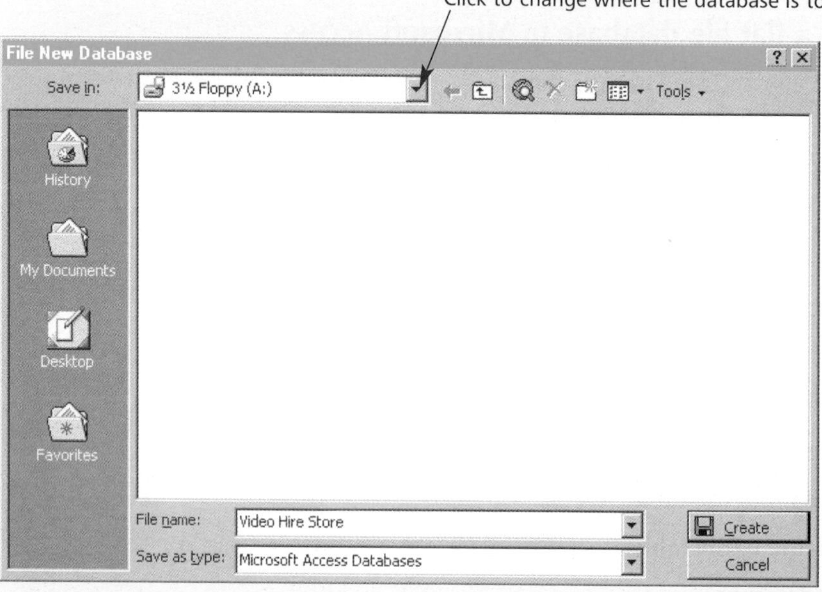

Enter the file name **Video Hire Store**.

Click on the Create button.

3 The screen below now appears. Notice that the name of the database, Video Hire Store, is shown.

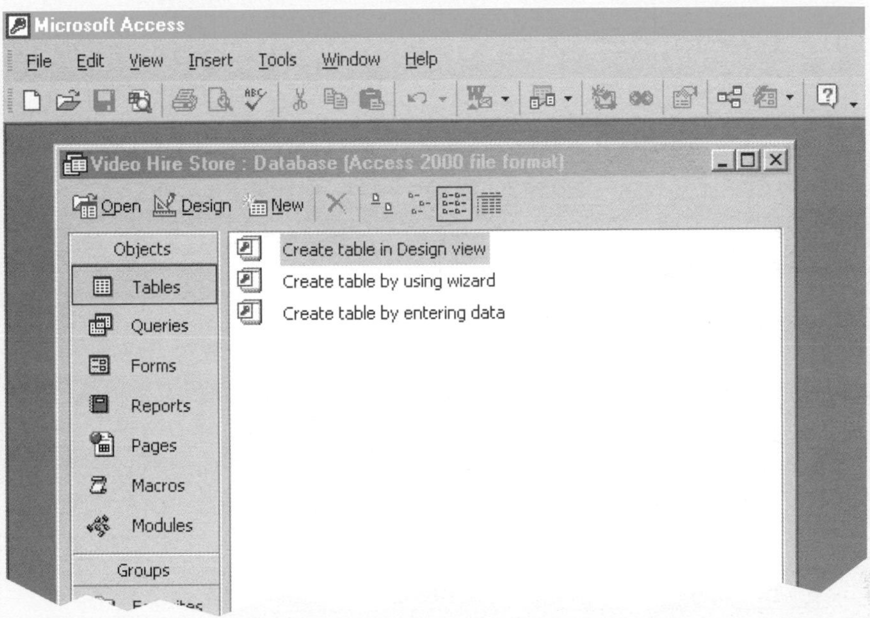

Double click on Create table in Design view.

4 The following screen appears, where you can specify the Field Name, Data Type and Description. This is the design screen where you can specify the design/structure of the database/table.

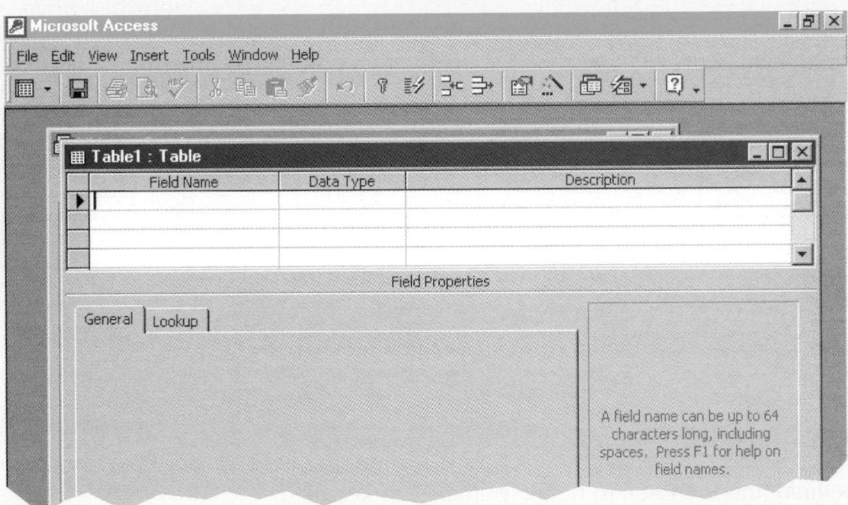

Where the cursor is positioned (i.e. on the first line of the table and in the column below Field Name) enter the field name **Video_ID**. Press Enter.

The cursor now moves onto the Data Type column. Click on this and a list of data types will appear (see the top of page 212). Select AutoNumber from this list. This gets the computer to

Exercise 15.1

allocate a unique number to each video. When the first video details are entered, it will be given the Video_ID of 1; when the second video's details are entered, they will be given the Video_ID of 2 and so on. By getting the computer to allocate this number automatically we do not need to remember what the next number is when a new video is added.

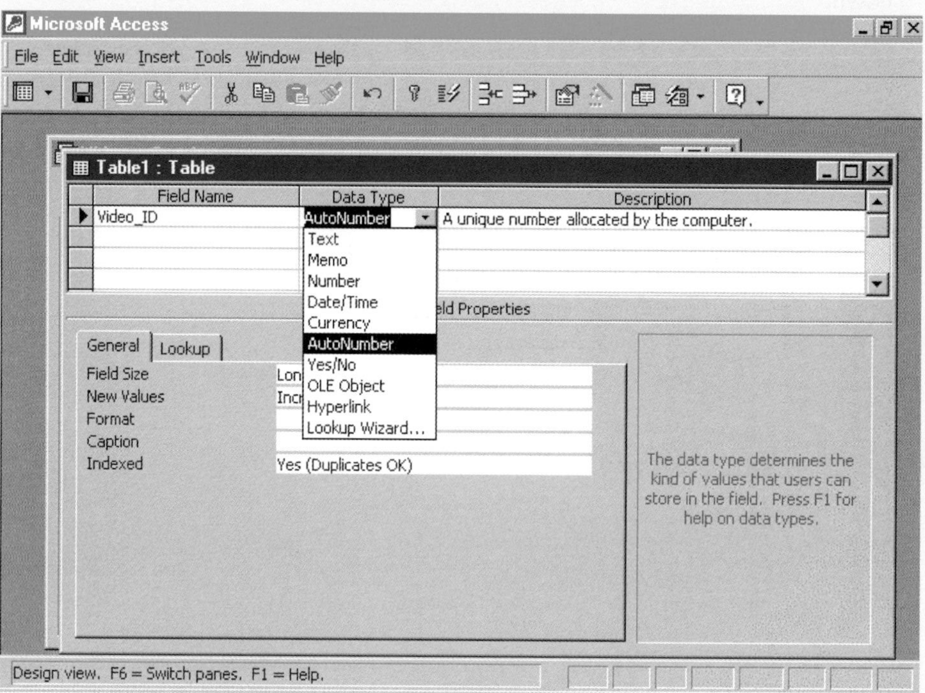

In the Description column, type in the description for the field, **A unique number allocated by the computer**. Press Enter and the cursor moves to the next line.

The description here allows someone who did not develop the database to understand what each field name represents. Most of the field names used in the structure of this table are easy to understand.

In a similar way complete the structure as shown below.

Field Name	Data Type	Description
Video_ID	AutoNumber	A unique number allocated by the computer.
Title	Text	The title of the video.
Supplier	Text	The name of the supplier.
Category	Text	The category (Action, Comedy, Drama, Family, Romance, Sci-Fi, Thriller).
Rating	Text	The censors rating (PG, U, 12, 15, 18).
Copies_in_Stock	Number	The number of copies held.
Rental_Price	Currency	The rental price per night.

5 A primary key/key field has to be set. This is a unique field for this data. Since Video_ID is a unique field, this is chosen to be the primary key/key field.

Move the cursor to anywhere on Video_ID and then click on the button with the key (see below) on the toolbar to set this as the primary key/key field.

Set primary key/key field

Exercise 15.1

6 Make sure that a picture of a key shows next to the Video_ID field like this:

Field Name	Data Type	Description
Video_ID	AutoNumber	A unique number allocated by the computer.

7 Click on the save button on the toolbar. The following screen appears, allowing you to name the table you have just created. Change the Table Name to **Videos**.

8 Click on the Datasheet button on the toolbar.

A blank datasheet appears into which you can enter data.

9 Enter the following data into this datasheet:

Video_ID	Title	Supplier	Category	Rating	Copies_in_Stock	Rental_Price
1	South Park	Videotrak Ltd	Family	15	6	£3.50
2	Ravenous	Videotrak Ltd	Thriller	18	3	£2.50
3	The General's Daughter	HG Scene	Thriller	18	3	£2.50
4	The Trench	Videotrak Ltd	Action	15	4	£3.50
5	Go	HG Scene	Thriller	18	2	£3.50
6	Never Been Kissed	ABC Ltd	Family	12	3	£2.50
7	Star Wars Episode 1	ABC Ltd	Sci-Fi	U	3	£3.50
8	Eyes Wide Shut	Videotrak Ltd	Drama	18	3	£3.50
9	Italian Job	Videotrak Ltd	Family	PG	4	£1.50
10	A Simple Plan	ABC Ltd	Thriller	15	1	£1.50
11	Drop Dead Gorgeous	Videotrak Ltd	Drama	15	3	£2.50
12	The Thomas Crown Affair	ABC Ltd	Thriller	15	2	£2.50
13	Varsity Blues	Videotrak Ltd	Family	15	3	£3.50
14	Notting Hill	HG Scene	Romance	15	2	£2.50
15	Mickey Blue Eyes	Videotrak Ltd	Family	15	1	£1.50
16	Night Of The Hunter	Videotrak Ltd	Family	15	2	£2.50
17	A Midsummer Nights Dream	Videotrak Ltd	Family	PG	3	£3.50

Now click on the OK button.

10 You have now created a simple database called Video Hire Store consisting of a single table called Videos.

To leave the program click on File and then Exit.

Saving your work

The program Microsoft Access is more complex than many other programs you will have used. When you use Access there are often many files open at once which means that it is easy to lose data if you do not exit the program properly. Files need to be closed down one by one and if any file has not been named you will be asked to supply a name for it. By using the cross at the top of each screen you can exit properly. If you just remove the disk or switch the computer off to save time, you will almost certainly lose work.

Ways of viewing a table

Access has two ways of viewing a table: using Design view or using Datasheet view.

The Design view is used when you want to look at or alter the structure/design of the database. It is therefore used for designing the database. The Datasheet view is used when you want to enter data into a table. The two screens below show how easy it is to flick from one view to the other.

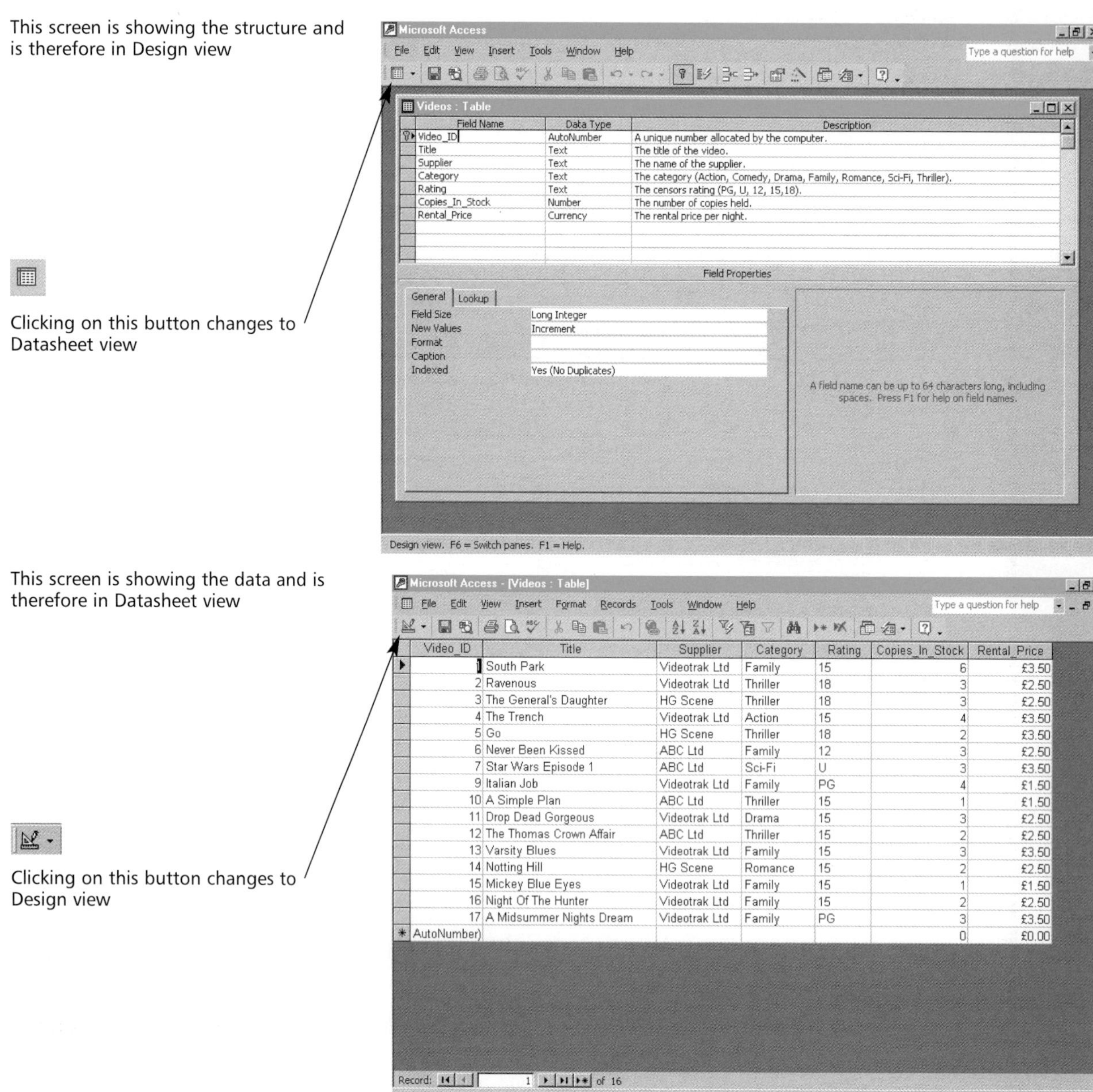

Field Name	Data Type	Description
Video_ID	AutoNumber	A unique number allocated by the computer.
Title	Text	The title of the video.
Supplier	Text	The name of the supplier.
Category	Text	The category (Action, Comedy, Drama, Family, Romance, Sci-Fi, Thriller).
Rating	Text	The censors rating (PG, U, 12, 15,18).
Copies_In_Stock	Number	The number of copies held.
Rental_Price	Currency	The rental price per night.

Video_ID	Title	Supplier	Category	Rating	Copies_In_Stock	Rental_Price
1	South Park	Videotrak Ltd	Family	15	6	£3.50
2	Ravenous	Videotrak Ltd	Thriller	18	3	£2.50
3	The General's Daughter	HG Scene	Thriller	18	3	£2.50
4	The Trench	Videotrak Ltd	Action	15	4	£3.50
5	Go	HG Scene	Thriller	18	2	£3.50
6	Never Been Kissed	ABC Ltd	Family	12	3	£2.50
7	Star Wars Episode 1	ABC Ltd	Sci-Fi	U	3	£3.50
9	Italian Job	Videotrak Ltd	Family	PG	4	£1.50
10	A Simple Plan	ABC Ltd	Thriller	15	1	£1.50
11	Drop Dead Gorgeous	Videotrak Ltd	Drama	15	3	£2.50
12	The Thomas Crown Affair	ABC Ltd	Thriller	15	2	£2.50
13	Varsity Blues	Videotrak Ltd	Family	15	3	£3.50
14	Notting Hill	HG Scene	Romance	15	2	£2.50
15	Mickey Blue Eyes	Videotrak Ltd	Family	15	1	£1.50
16	Night Of The Hunter	Videotrak Ltd	Family	15	2	£2.50
17	A Midsummer Nights Dream	Videotrak Ltd	Family	PG	3	£3.50
(AutoNumber)					0	£0.00

This screen is showing the structure and is therefore in Design view

Clicking on this button changes to Datasheet view

This screen is showing the data and is therefore in Datasheet view

Clicking on this button changes to Design view

Using the Database

In Chapters 14 and 15 the database was planned and then created. In this chapter you will learn how to open the database and use it to search for specific information. You will also learn how to make a more user friendly input screen for inputting data into the database.

Exercise 16.1

Opening the video database

In this exercise you will learn how to:

- **open a previously saved database**
- **open a table**
- **sort the records into different orders**
- **filter the data so that only certain records are shown**
- **print out filtered records.**

1 Load Access. The following section will appear on the right hand side of the screen.

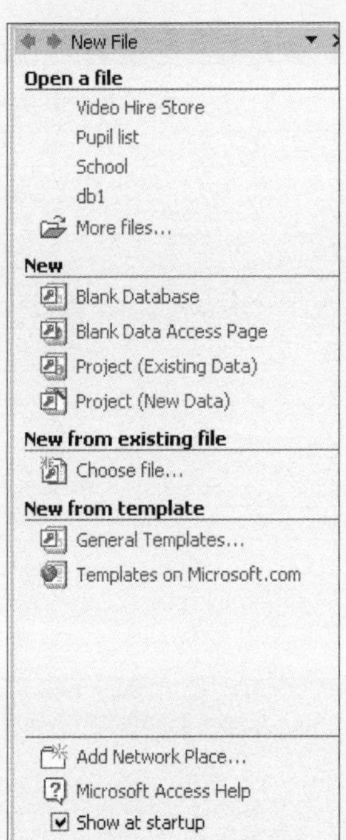

You should see the Videos file listed in the **Open a file** section. If you see it, click on it and it will be opened.

If you do not see it, click on More files... in the Open a file section. This will allow you to look for your file on different drives.

2 The following screen now appears.

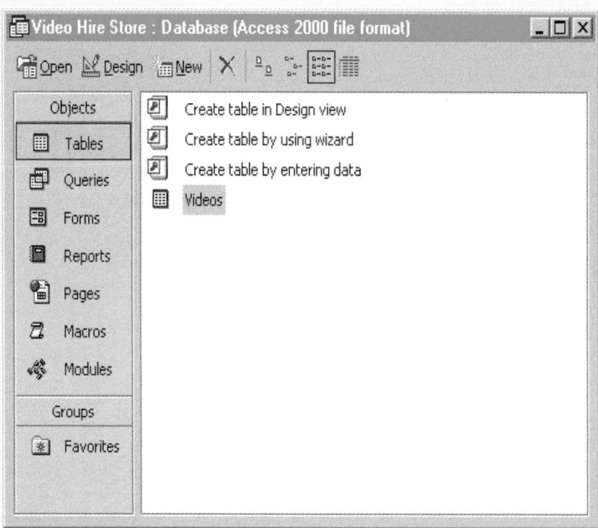

You can now see an icon for the video table. Double click on this and the table is opened in datasheet view as shown below.

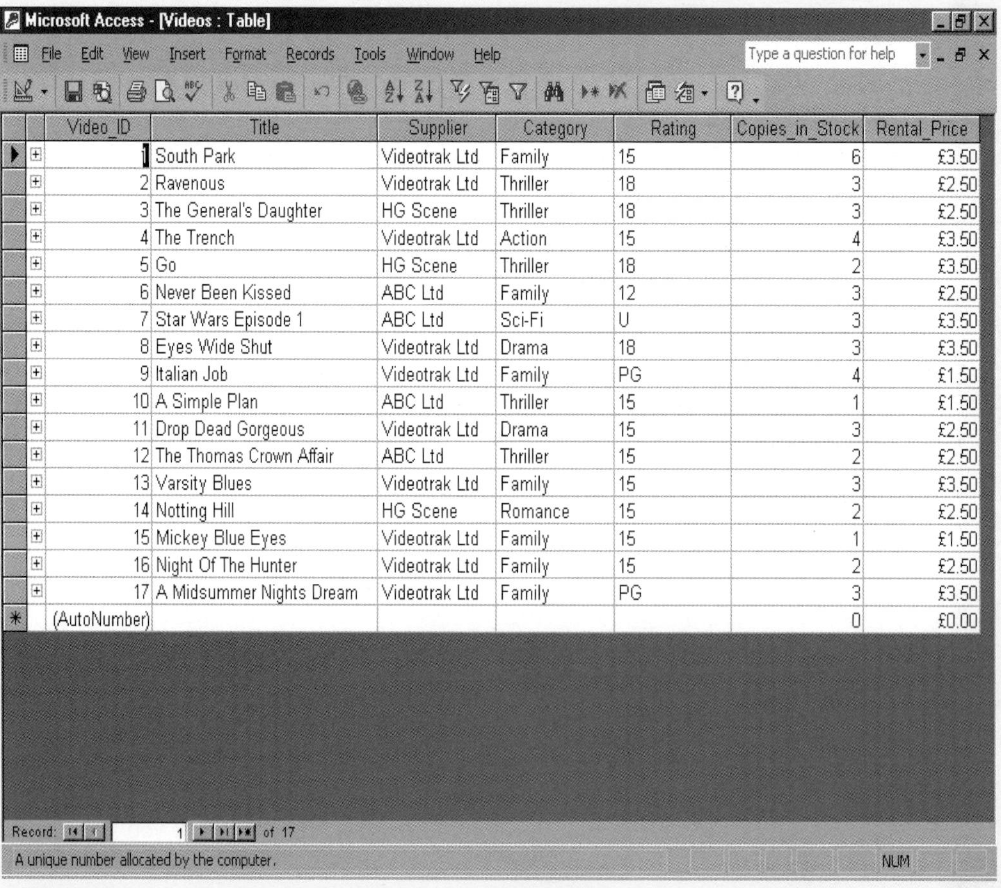

Video_ID	Title	Supplier	Category	Rating	Copies_in_Stock	Rental_Price
1	South Park	Videotrak Ltd	Family	15	6	£3.50
2	Ravenous	Videotrak Ltd	Thriller	18	3	£2.50
3	The General's Daughter	HG Scene	Thriller	18	3	£2.50
4	The Trench	Videotrak Ltd	Action	15	4	£3.50
5	Go	HG Scene	Thriller	18	2	£3.50
6	Never Been Kissed	ABC Ltd	Family	12	3	£2.50
7	Star Wars Episode 1	ABC Ltd	Sci-Fi	U	3	£3.50
8	Eyes Wide Shut	Videotrak Ltd	Drama	18	3	£3.50
9	Italian Job	Videotrak Ltd	Family	PG	4	£1.50
10	A Simple Plan	ABC Ltd	Thriller	15	1	£1.50
11	Drop Dead Gorgeous	Videotrak Ltd	Drama	15	3	£2.50
12	The Thomas Crown Affair	ABC Ltd	Thriller	15	2	£2.50
13	Varsity Blues	Videotrak Ltd	Family	15	3	£3.50
14	Notting Hill	HG Scene	Romance	15	2	£2.50
15	Mickey Blue Eyes	Videotrak Ltd	Family	15	1	£1.50
16	Night Of The Hunter	Videotrak Ltd	Family	15	2	£2.50
17	A Midsummer Nights Dream	Videotrak Ltd	Family	PG	3	£3.50
(AutoNumber)					0	£0.00

This table contains all the data you input in Exercise 15.1.

3 The data is in Video_ID order. It is easy to change this.

Click anywhere on a video title and then on the sort ascending (A to Z) button in the toolbar  .

The records are ordered into alphabetical order according to video title. Your sorted films should now look like this:

Video_ID	Title	Supplier	Category	Rating	Copies_in_Stock
17	A Midsummer Nights Dream	Videotrak Ltd	Family	PG	3
10	A Simple Plan	ABC Ltd	Thriller	15	1
11	Drop Dead Gorgeous	Videotrak Ltd	Drama	15	3
8	Eyes Wide Shut	Videotrak Ltd	Drama	18	3
5	Go	HG Scene	Thriller	18	2
9	Italian Job	Videotrak Ltd	Family	PG	4
15	Mickey Blue Eyes	Videotrak Ltd	Family	15	1
6	Never Been Kissed	ABC Ltd	Family	12	3
16	Night Of The Hunter	Videotrak Ltd	Family	15	2
14	Notting Hill	HG Scene	Romance	15	2
2	Ravenous	Videotrak Ltd	Thriller	18	3
1	South Park	Videotrak Ltd	Family	15	6
7	Star Wars Episode 1	ABC Ltd	Sci-Fi	U	3
3	The General's Daughter	HG Scene	Thriller	18	3
12	The Thomas Crown Affair	ABC Ltd	Thriller	15	2
4	The Trench	Videotrak Ltd	Action	15	4
13	Varsity Blues	Videotrak Ltd	Family	15	3

Now put the data into the following orders:

- ascending order according to supplier
- ascending order according to category
- descending order according to rental price
- ascending order according to copies in stock.

4 Put the data back into the original order (ascending order according to Video_Number).

5 We will now show only the data which fit a certain criterion. Let's show only those videos supplied by ABC Ltd. Move the cursor to any of the fields where ABC Ltd occurs. This shows the computer that we only want these details.

Click on the filter by selection button in the toolbar.

Only those records having the supplier ABC Ltd are displayed as shown below.

Video_ID	Title	Supplier	Category	Rating	Copies_in_Stock
6	Never Been Kissed	ABC Ltd	Family	12	3
7	Star Wars Episode 1	ABC Ltd	Sci-Fi	U	3
10	A Simple Plan	ABC Ltd	Thriller	15	1
12	The Thomas Crown Affair	ABC Ltd	Thriller	15	2
AutoNumber)					0

To print these records out, click on File and the Page Setup...

Exercise 16.1

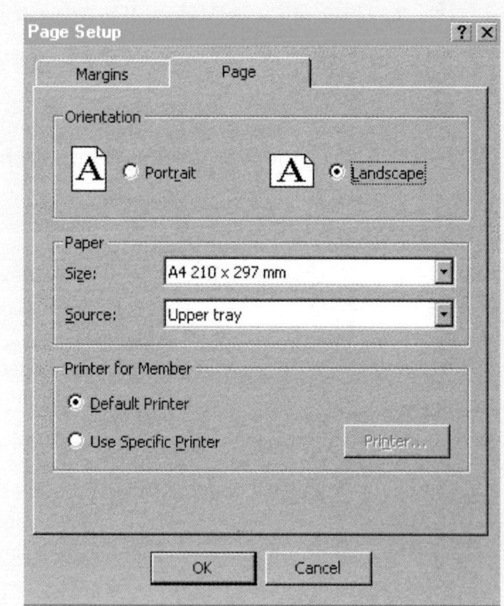

The Page Setup menu appears.

Click on the page tab. Change the orientation to landscape since this data is wider than it is long. Click on OK.

Check that the printer has paper and is on-line.

Now click on the printer button in the toolbar and the printer will print these records.

6 To remove the filter and see all the data in the table, press the remove filter button.

7 In a similar way use the filter to produce the following:
(a) a list of all the films with a 15 rating
(b) a list of all sci-fi films
(c) a list of those films having a rental price of £1.50.

As evidence that you have done each correctly, print out a copy of the list in landscape orientation.

8 Close the table and the database.

Querying a database for information

Querying a database means searching for specific information. You ask the database a question and it comes up with the answers.

Exercise 16.2

Creating a query

We will now start to extract information from the video tables by constructing a query.

In this exercise you will learn how to:

- **design a query**
- **show the results from a query**
- **save a query**
- **print out the results of a query.**

1 Load the program Microsoft Access.

2 Open the database Video Hire Store by clicking on this name in the Open a File list.

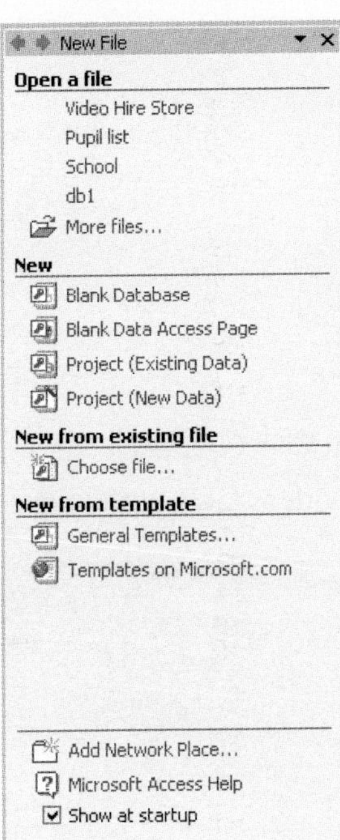

3 The following screen appears.

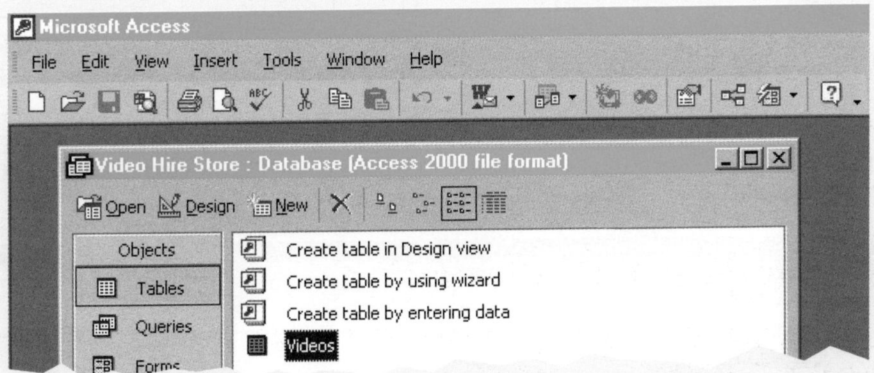

Click on Queries in the Objects column.

4 In the following screen you can now select the method you want to use to create the query.

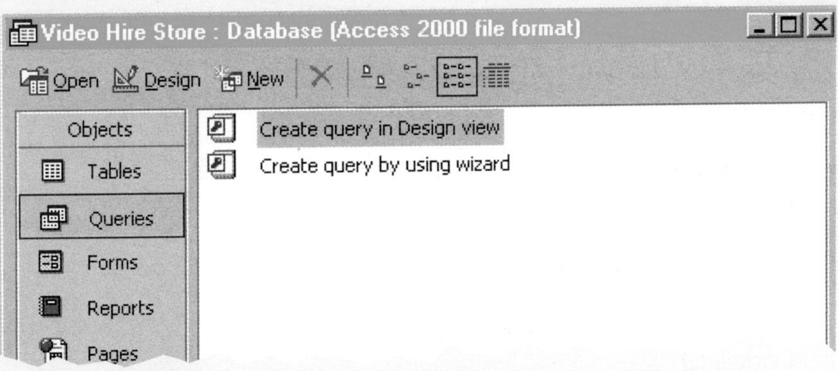

Double click on Create query in Design view.

5 The menu below appears where you can select the table or tables that contains the data for the query. Notice that the only table is Videos in this case.

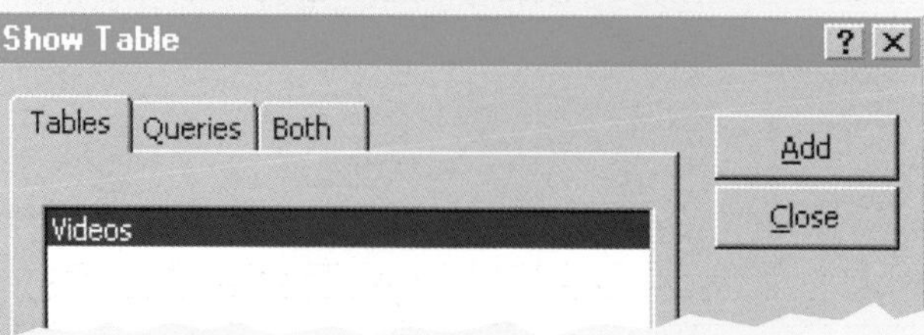

Click on the Add button to add the table Videos and then click on Close.

6 You will now be looking at the screen below. Notice the Videos table at the top of the screen.

Move to the first column and first row and specify the first field you want to show. Click on the arrow pointing down in this box. This pulls down a menu containing a list of the field names as shown below.

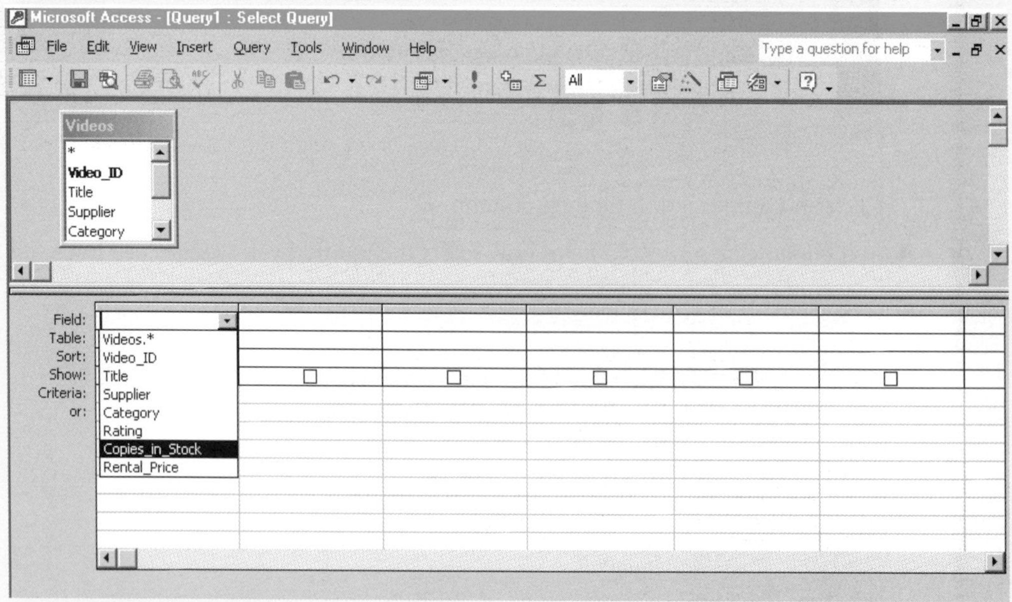

Click on Video_ID

7 Move the cursor to the other columns in turn and select the fields as shown below.

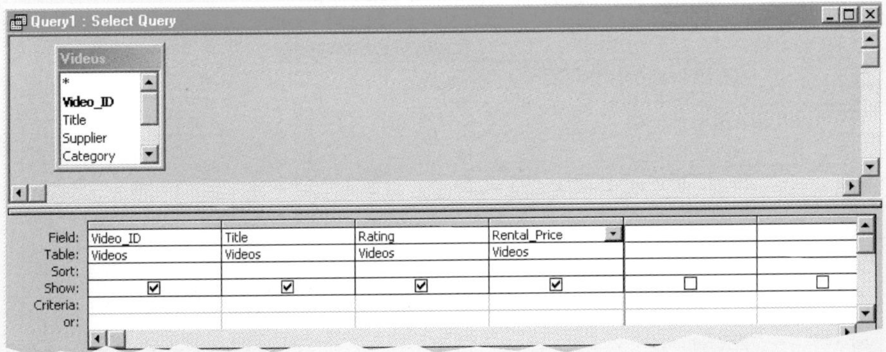

8 This query will list the Video_ID, Title, Rating and Rental_Price.

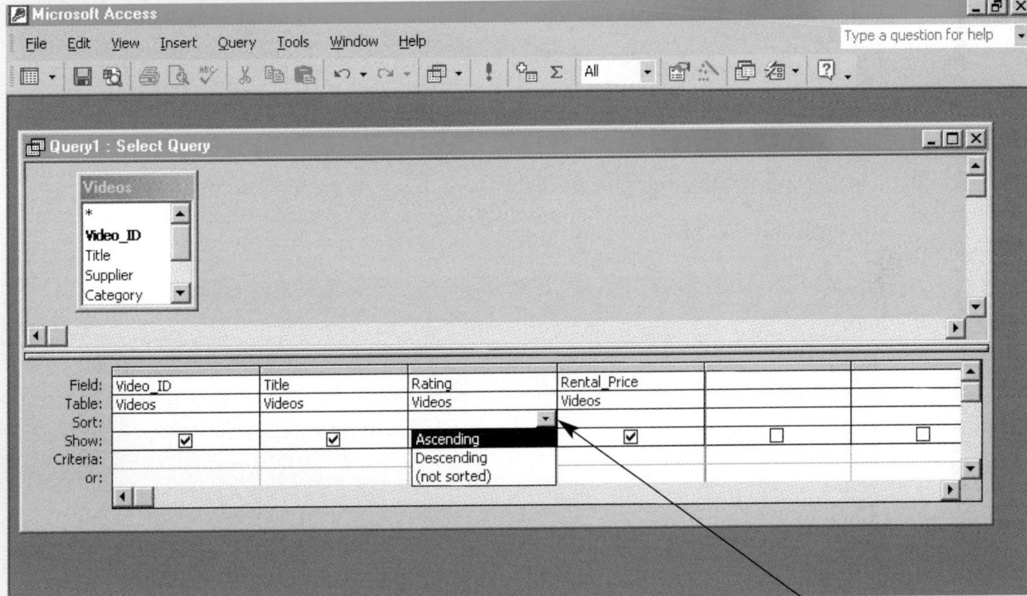

To put the fields in ascending alphabetical order according to title click here. A pull down menu appears. Select Ascending.

9 Your screen will now look like the one below.

To see the results when you run the query, click on the Datasheet view button on the toolbar.

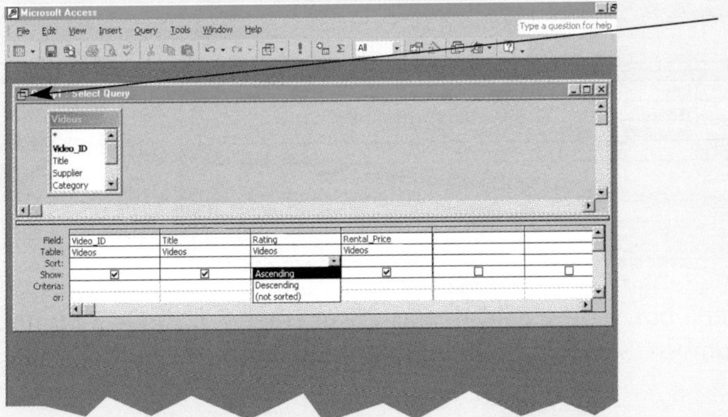

10 The query results are now displayed. Check your results are the same as those below.

Query1 : Select Query

Video_ID	Title	Rating	Rental_Price
17	A Midsummer Nights Dream	PG	£3.50
10	A Simple Plan	15	£1.50
11	Drop Dead Gorgeous	15	£2.50
8	Eyes Wide Shut	18	£3.50
5	Go	18	£3.50
9	Italian Job	PG	£1.50
15	Mickey Blue Eyes	15	£1.50
6	Never Been Kissed	12	£2.50
16	Night Of The Hunter	15	£2.50
14	Notting Hill	15	£2.50
2	Ravenous	18	£2.50
1	South Park	15	£3.50
7	Star Wars Episode 1	U	£3.50
3	The General's Daughter	18	£2.50
12	The Thomas Crown Affair	15	£2.50
4	The Trench	15	£3.50
13	Varsity Blues	15	£3.50
AutoNumber)			£0.00

Record: 1 of 17

11 If you want to alter the design slightly you have to go back to the Design view.

Click on the Design view button.

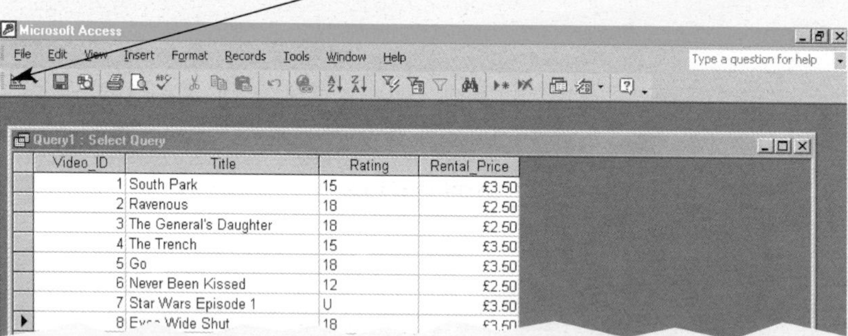

12 The Design view appears:

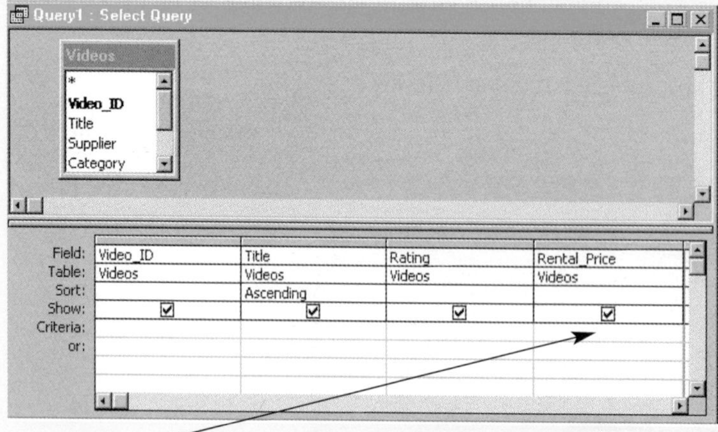

In this box (the criteria box for the field Rental_Price) enter **=1.50 Or 2.50**. (N.B. you only need to enter the numbers, so do not put the pounds signs in.)

This expression means that we only want the fields listed where the rental price is either £1.50 or £2.50. (A customer may have come into the shop and could only afford to rent a video at either of these prices.)

13 Run the query by clicking the Datasheet view button on the toolbar.

You will get the following:

Query1 : Select Query

	Video_ID	Title	Rating	Rental_Price
▶	10	A Simple Plan	15	£1.50
	11	Drop Dead Gorgeous	15	£2.50
	9	Italian Job	PG	£1.50
	15	Mickey Blue Eyes	15	£1.50
	6	Never Been Kissed	12	£2.50
	16	Night Of The Hunter	15	£2.50
	14	Notting Hill	15	£2.50
	2	Ravenous	18	£2.50
	3	The General's Daughter	18	£2.50
	12	The Thomas Crown Affair	15	£2.50
*	AutoNumber)			£0.00

Record: 1 of 10

14 Close the screen. You will be asked if you want to save the query.

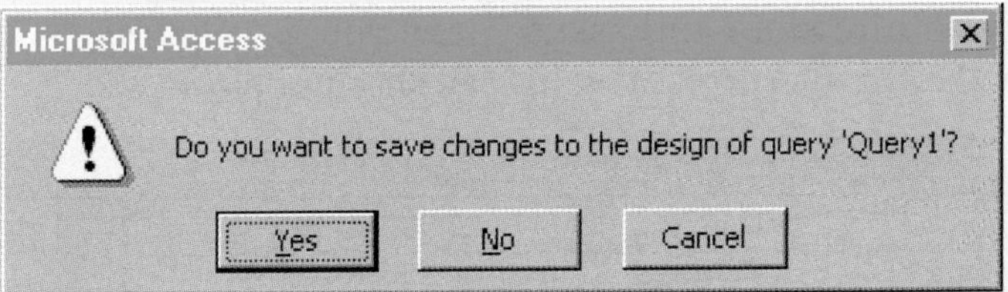

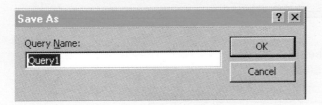

Click on the Yes button. You have the option to give the query another name.

Keep the query name the same (i.e. Query1) and click on the OK button.

Query criteria

If you want to find only those records that satisfy certain conditions (called criteria) then enter the criteria into the criteria box when designing the query.

For example, you could just look for the details of a particular video title, say *Notting Hill*. To do this enter the name *Notting Hill* in the criteria box under Title.

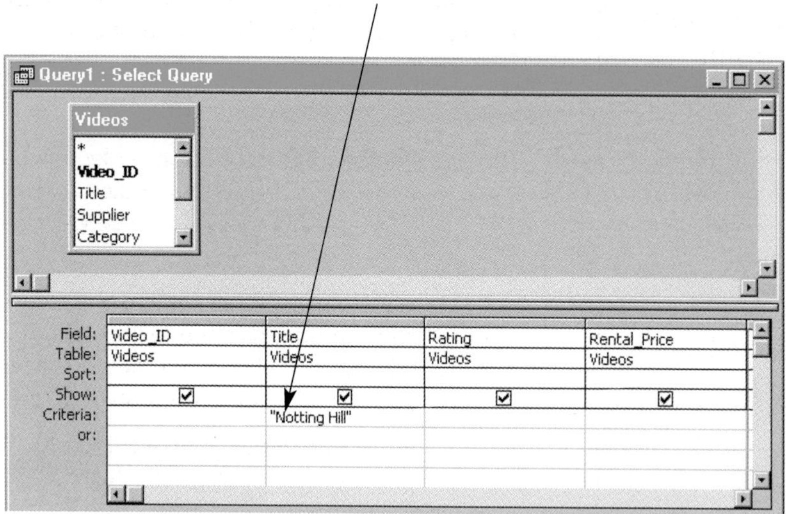

You can put quotes around the text, otherwise Access will put them in for you.

The results of this query are shown below.

	Video_ID	Title	Rating	Rental_Price
▶	14	Notting Hill	15	£2.50
*	AutoNumber)			£0.00

If a customer came into the video hire store and asked 'Have you got *Notting Hill* or *The Trench* or *Go*' you could enter the three criteria as a list, as shown below.

Field:	Video_ID	Title	Rating	Rental_Price
Table:	Videos	Videos	Videos	Videos
Sort:				
Show:	☑	☑	☑	☑
Criteria:		"Notting Hill"		
or:		"The Trench"		
		"Go"		

The result of this query is shown below.

	Video_ID	Title	Rating	Rental_Price
▶	4	The Trench	15	£3.50
	5	Go	18	£3.50
	14	Notting Hill	15	£2.50
*	AutoNumber)			£0.00

The table below shows some criteria that can be placed in a criteria box and their meaning.

Criteria	Meaning
"Word"	Selects exact matches of the text Word
=18	Number has to equal 18
>=18	Number has to equal or be greater than 18
<=18	Number has to equal or be less than 18
<15	Number has to be less than 15
>20	Number has to be greater than 20
Between 300 And 400	A number between 300 and 400
=12/12/00	Has to be the date 12/12/00
>=01/12/98	On or after the data 01/12/08
Between 04/12/99 And 11/12/99	Between the dates 04/12/99 and 11/12/99

QUESTIONS

Making up your own queries

You have to design a query to come up with answers to each of the following questions.

1 Do you have all the details on the video *South Park*?

2 A representative has called from Videotrak Ltd. He wants a list of the Titles and Copies_In_Stock supplied by his company. Can we produce this for him?

3 The manager needs a list containing Video_ID, Title, Rating and Rental Price to be ordered by Rental Price in ascending order (i.e. the cheapest rental prices first). Can you supply this list?

4 Can you list the Video_ID and Title for all videos with a Rental_Price greater than £2.00?

5 Can you list the Video_ID and Title for all videos of which there are more than three copies?

For each of these queries you should first produce a design on paper, then design the query on the computer and save each query using a suitable name. Produce a printout of your results for each query.

Deciding on the input interface

So far, whenever data has been entered into a table it has been entered straight into the table using the datasheet view. The datasheet looks a little bit like a spreadsheet and may be a bit intimidating for an inexperienced user. To make things easier we can use a form. A form on the computer is just like a form on paper. You have the title of each field next to a box, into which the user can type the data in for that field.

As well as being used to enter data into tables, forms can be used to view the data one record at a time. While the record is on the screen you can make alterations to the data. You can also delete the record.

The main advantage in using a form to enter data rather than the datasheet view, is that with the form you can see all of the fields.

Exercise 16.3

Creating an input form for the Videos table

In this exercise you will learn how to:

- **create a form to be used to input data into a table using the Form Wizard**
- **use the form to view records one at a time.**

1 Load Access and select the Video Hire Store Database. The Video Hire Store: Database window appears. Click on Forms and the screen to the right will appear.

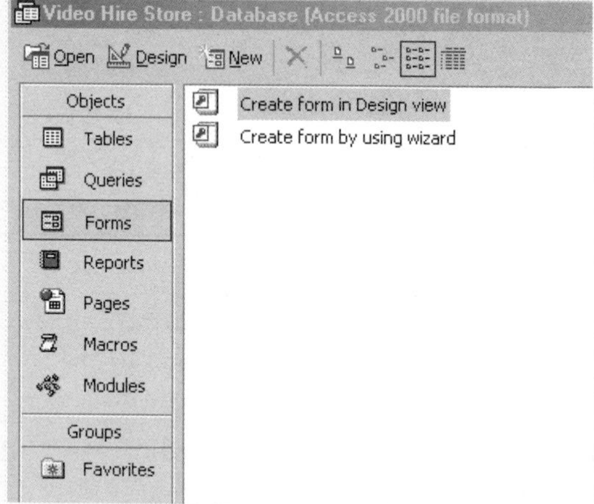

2 Click on Create form by using wizard in the menu above and the following screen will appear.

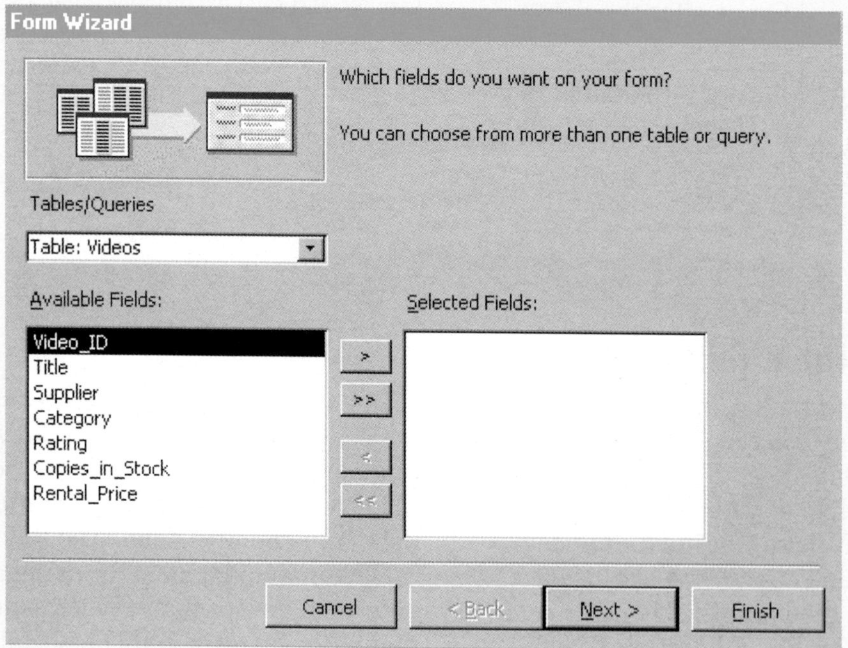

You can see the name of the table in the top left box, and a list of all the fields that are available in this table in the box underneath. You can add these fields to the form one by one, by clicking on the button with the single arrow on it. If you want to add all the fields in one go, just click on the button with the double arrows.

3 Add all the fields by clicking on the button with the double arrows.

Your screen will now look like this:

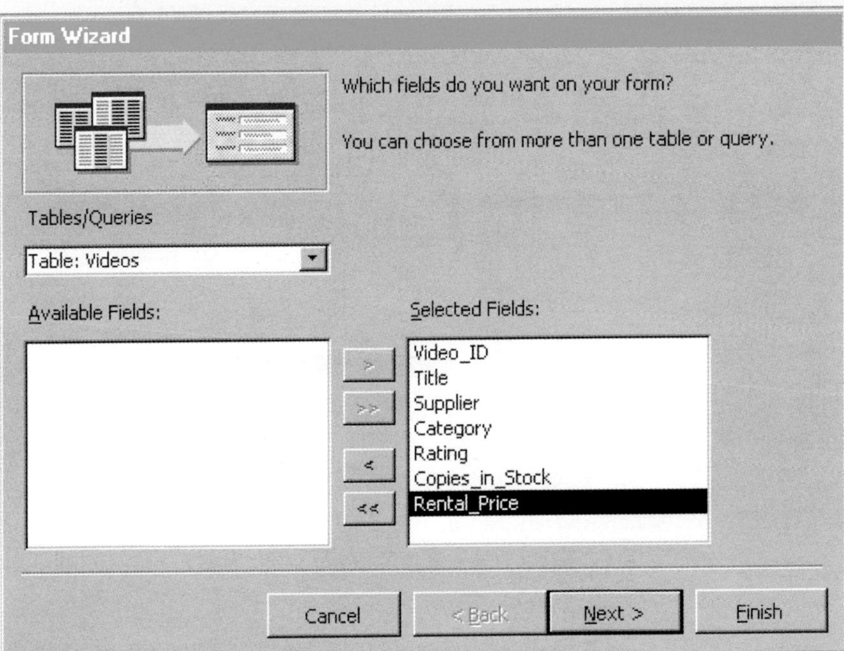

4 Click on the Next > button. The Form Wizard screen appears:

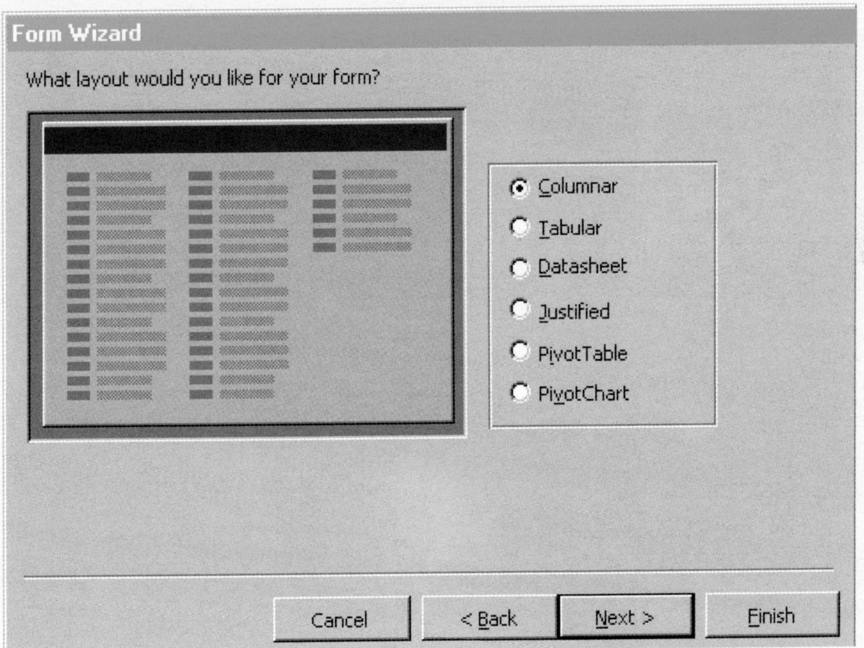

Select Columnar as the layout and then click on Next >. This will arrange the field names and boxes for the data in columns on the form.

5 The screen below appears, in which you select the style of the form you want to use.

Notice that when you move through the list of styles on the right a picture of the style appears on the left.

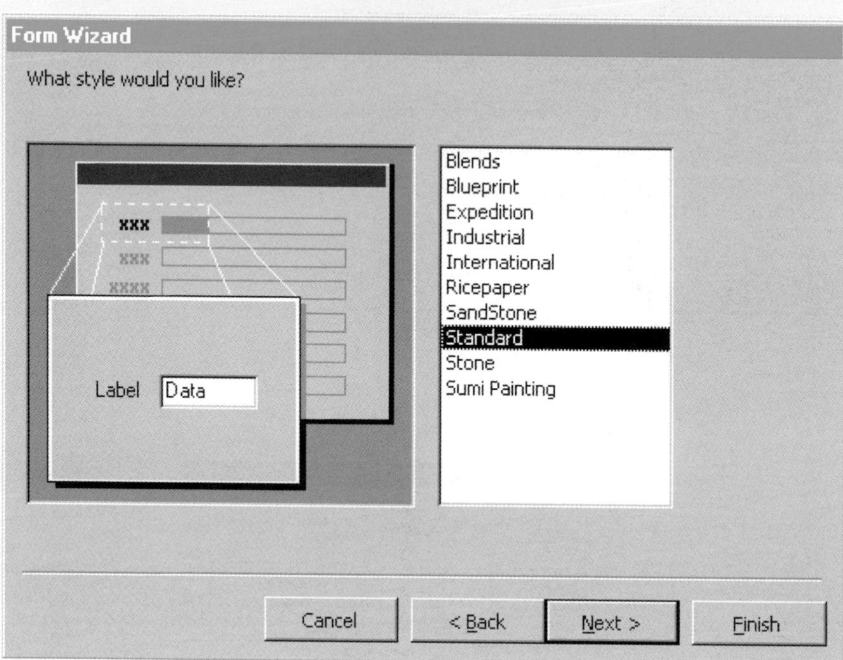

Select Standard as the style and then click on Next >.

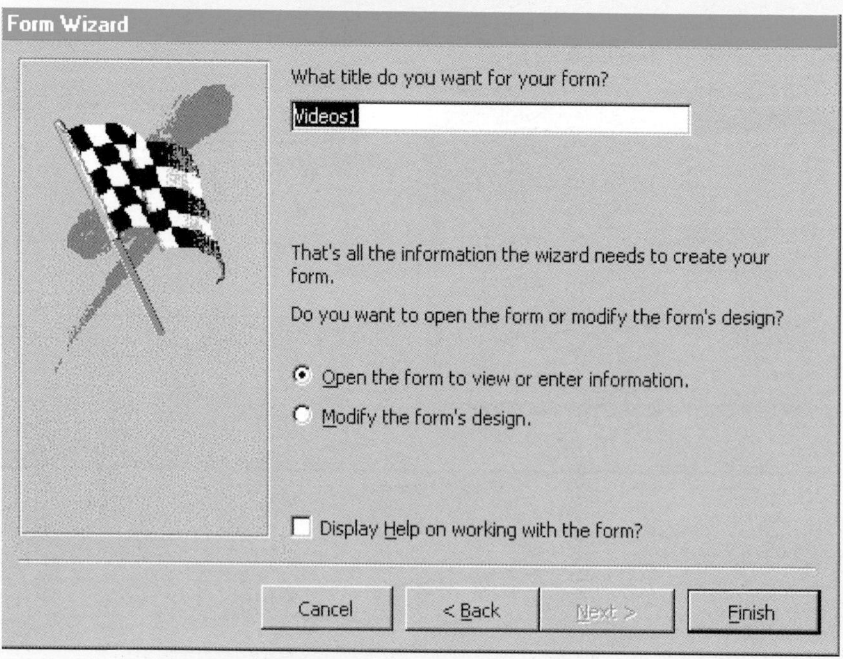

The form has been given the name Videos1. We will keep this as the name.

Exercise 16.3

Click on the Finish button.

After a brief wait the form shown below appears.

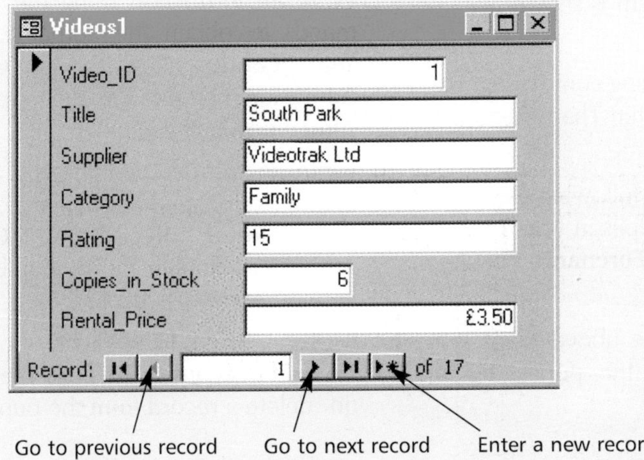

You can use the toolbar at the bottom of the screen to move from one record to another.

QUESTIONS

1 A secondhand car dealer imports high performance sports cars from Japan. The information about the cars held in stock is kept on a database. Part of the information held is shown below.

(a) How many records are shown in the table below?

(b) How many fields does each record have?

(c) Give the field names of those fields which are numeric.

(d) Explain why it is so important to carefully proof read any data being put into a database.

(e) Look carefully at the data. There is an obvious error. Write down the error.

(f) If the price field was sorted into descending order, what is the make and model of the car that would come first.

(g) Why is it important that each record has a primary key field (its reference number in this case)?

Make	Model	Engine	Year	Mileage	Price	Reference number
Honda	Prelude	2200 VTEC	99	12000	£8995	1020
Honda	Integra	1797	99	8000	£17000	1023
Honda	S2000	1997	98	15000	£22000	1024
Mitsubishi	GTO	2972	19	12000	£19995	1034
Mitsubishi	FTO	1999	00	3000	£16000	1035
Mitsubishi	Lancer Evo VI	1997	00	2000	£28000	1040
Nissan	Skyline	2498	00	5000	£23000	1036
Subaru	Imprezza	1894	00	7000	£20000	1043

2 Hollyoaks High School have installed a computer system to help run the school. Part of the system is a database to hold pupil details.

Some of the data held in the system is shown in the table below.

To search this database, the following commands are used: List; For; Equals; Greater Than; Less Than; And; Or.

These commands are used in the following way. To obtain a list of the names of pupils in year 11 you would type: **List Surname, Forename For Year Group Equals 11**

(a) Write an instruction using the above commands to list the names of the pupils in registration group P.

(b) Write an instruction using the above commands to list the names of pupils who are in year group 11 and registration group P.

(c) Write an instruction using the above commands to obtain the Surname, Forename, Year Group, Registration Group and Admission Number for the pupils with the surname Hughes.

(d) Write an instruction using the above commands to obtain the Surname, Forename, Year Group, Registration Group and Admission Number for the pupils born on or before the date 04/05/83.

(e) Explain why the headteacher should need to:
(i) add a record to the pupil file
(ii) delete a record from the pupil file.

Surname	Forename	Sex	Date of birth	Year Group	Registration Group	Admission Number
Hughes	Kirsty	Female	12/04/84	11	R	15670
Jenkins	Amy	Female	12/05/84	11	P	16003
Adams	Victoria	Female	04/05/83	10	S	18030
Hughes	James	Male	12/04/84	11	P	16045
Greenbank	Vicky	Female	09/04/83	10	T	15090

IT TASKS

Database activity

Using a single table, create a database to store data about your friends and relatives.

It is important to think about the way the database will be used before setting it up. On thinking about it you would like to use the database in the following circumstances.

- You need to list the names of friends and relatives who have their birthdays in a certain month so that you can send them cards, presents, etc.
- The last telephone number has been recorded by the telephone exchange and you dial 1471 to see whose number it is. Before ringing them back you want to see if it is anyone you know.
- You want to produce a list of names and addresses to send Christmas cards.

Before you start using the computer you should plan out your design on paper. Include in your design the name of the database and the name of the table.

Write a list of the fields you think should be included. Think carefully about the names of these fields. It is best if you can immediately see from the field name what data should be inserted for that field.

Order these fields. The most important field (usually the primary key) should be the first in the list. One of the fields should be a primary key. If there is no obvious one, then perhaps one should be created.

Think about the data type for each field.

Fill in a table like this one:

Field name	Data Type	Description
Title	Text	Title of the person (Mr, Miss, Mrs, etc.)

Show the table design to your teacher. If they give you the OK then you can start using the computer to build the table.

Once you have designed the table produce a printout of the structure of the table.

Enter at least 15 people's details into your table using the Datasheet view (this is the view that looks like a spreadsheet).

Use the following to produce examples of how you can make use of the table you have just created:

- filters
- queries.

17 Creating a Relational Database

Using more than one table

In the previous chapters, we have only looked at creating a single table. Single tables are not, strictly speaking, databases and only have limited uses. If you put more than one table together and link the tables, you have a really useful database called a relational database.

To develop the video hire system we will need to use a relational database. We have already seen that with the manual system it is impossible to use a single box of cards. What we need are three boxes of cards; one each for videos, members and rentals. We therefore need three tables for the database and these tables we will call videos, members and rentals.

The members table

The members table will contain all the members' details. On joining the video library each member will be given a unique membership number. This prevents confusion between members with the same name who live at the same address. The members table will include details such as membership number, title, surname, etc.

The videos table

We have already created the video table in the previous chapter. Each video is given a unique number called the Video_ID and this prevents confusion with videos having the same title.

The rentals table

The rentals table contains the details generated when a video is hired out. To know who has which video, the membership number and the Video_ID would be recorded. We do not need to store the name of the members or the title of the video being borrowed. Both of these can be obtained using links to other tables. We also need to know the date the video is borrowed (so that a fine can be calculated if applicable). Some videos are hired out for more than one day so a Days_Hired field is also needed.

Deciding on the fields to go into each table

If there is a user, then they will know better than you what fields should be included in each table. In this case we are creating the video hire store from scratch, so we need to work this out for ourselves. You could find all these details by looking at the way existing video libraries operate.
We have already created the videos table. Let's now consider the fields we need to have in the other two tables. Here are the lists of the fields we would need.

Members table

Membership_Number
Title
Surname
Forename
Street
Town
Postcode
Phone_Number

Rental table

Membership_Number
Video_ID
Date_Rented
Days_Hired

Notice that in the rental table we only need these four fields. If we want to know any further details they can be obtained from the other tables. For example, there will be a link between the Membership_Number in the rental table and the Membership_Number in the member table. So if a certain member had not returned their video we could use the Membership_Number to find their name and address.

There will also be a link between the Video_ID in the rental and videos tables.

The links between the tables are called relationships, and these make relational databases very powerful tools.

Determining the types of relationships

After fields have been placed in each table we need to think about the relationships between tables.

Relationships between tables will be one-to-one, one-to-many or many-to-many. Many-to-many relationships cause problems, but we need not concern ourselves with these here.

One-to-many relationships

If we look at the relationship between the members and the rentals tables we can see that one Membership_Number in the members table can appear many times in the rentals table. Each time a member borrows a video, the Membership_Number is recorded in the rentals table.

We also need to look at the relationship from the other end (i.e. from the rental table to the members table). Each Membership_Number in the rentals table corresponds to a single occurrence of the Membership_Number in the members table.

The relationship between the members and rentals tables is a one-to-many relationship.

One-to-one relationships

With a one-to-one relationship, one record in one table has only one matching record in one of the other tables.

Many-to-many relationships

Here one record in a table matches many records in another table. When the tables are looked at from the other end, then one record also matches many.

This type of relationship is called a many-to-many relationship. If you think you have a many-to-many relationship, then you will need to see your teacher since you cannot link tables with this kind of relationship.

Forming relationships between tables in Access

In order to form a link (called a relationship) between two tables you must have the same field in both tables. They do not need both to be primary key fields.

It is important that you make sure that these common fields have exactly the same name and also that the data type is the same. If AutoNumber has been used as a field in one table you can use a number field in another table and still be able to link them because they are both numbers. You cannot link a text field in one table with a number field in another. Make sure that the name of the field is spelt the same in both fields and check that the use of upper and lower case letters is the same. You can create a link between two fields that have identical field names.

Creating the members table

Having created the videos table for all the video details, we will create the members table to hold all the details about the members. We will also set the primary key/key field and enter data into the table. Only brief instructions will be given to do this. The technique to create the table is the same as that used when the videos table was created in Exercise 15.1. Look back if you need to.

In this exercise you will practise:

- **creating the structure of a table**
- **entering data accurately into a table**
- **switching between datasheet and design view**
- **saving a table.**

1 Open the Video Hire Store database and create a new table to contain the details about members.

2 Enter the following field names, data types and descriptions into the positions shown in the first screen below.

Make the Membership_Number field in the table, a primary key/key field. When this is done you will notice a small key appear next to the field name.

Field Name	Data Type	Description
Membership_Number	AutoNumber	A unique number allocated by the computer
Title	Text	The title of the member (e.g. Mr, Miss, Mrs, Ms, Dr etc.)
Surname	Text	The surname of the member
Forename	Text	The forename of the member
Street	Text	The first line of the member's address
Town	Text	The town where the member lives
Postcode	Text	The postcode where the member lives
Phone_Number	Text	The main contact telephone number for the member

3 Save the table using the filename Members.

4 Enter the following data into the members table you have just created.

Membership number	Title	Surname	Forename	Street	Town	Postcode	Phone number
1	Mr	Hughes	John	13 Brook Street	Liverpool	L24 4RT	0151-230-2929
2	Ms	Harrington	Hayley	121 Moor Close	Liverpool	L23 5TY	0151-420-0913
3	Miss	Prenton	Cheryl	34 Earle Road	Liverpool	L25 6EF	0151-210-9824
4	Mr	Johnstone	Christopher	12 West Way	Liverpool	L32 7YU	0151-342-2232
5	Miss	Doyle	Amy	132 Hart Street	Warrington	WA2 6GH	01925-23220
6	Ms	Corkhill	Tracy	12 Fir Street	Liverpool	L2 6TY	0151-292-0329
7	Mrs	Prescott	Julie	34 Forrest Drive	Liverpool	L3 5FR	0151-672-9292
8	Mr	Thomas	Charles	76 Grove Street	Liverpool	L54 9YU	0151-672-2492

5 After entering the above table close the DataSheet view by clicking on the cross at the top right hand corner of the screen (not the very top cross which will take you out of the whole program!) and go back to the Database menu ready for creating the rentals table in the next exercise.

Creating the rentals table

In this exercise you will create the rentals table and select the fields to make up the primary key/key field.

1 Create a new table to contain the details about rentals.

2 Enter the following field names, data types and descriptions into the positions shown below.

Field Name	Data Type	Description
Video_ID	Number	The unique number of the video borrowed
Membership_Number	Number	The unique number of the members who is borrowing the vid
Date_Rented	Date/Time	The date when the video was hired
Days_Hired	Number	The number of days the video is hired for

If you look at the Video_ID field you will see that the Data Type for this field is a Number and not an AutoNumber like it was in the videos table. We cannot use AutoNumber here because the computer would give the Video_ID automatically. We need to be able to type in the number of the video being borrowed so we must use a Number data type. We can still use these fields to link the tables because AutoNumber is a number.

3 The next step is to determine the primary key/key field for this table. Imagine this table full of data, collected over a period. The same Video_ID will appear many times as different members take the same video out. Also, the Membership_Number will appear many times in this table since the same member can hire many videos over a period of time.

Neither of these on their own would be unique in a row.

It is, however, possible to have several fields which can be used together as a primary key/key field.

We can now think about using two or even three fields together.

Suppose we consider using Membership_Number and Video_ID together as the primary key/key field. Would this be unique? The answer is no, because the same member could watch a video and then hire the same one again.

What about Membership_Number and Date_Rented? This would not be suitable because the same member could rent more than one video on the same date.

What about using three fields together as the primary key/key field? Suppose we used Membership_Number, Video_ID and Date_Rented. This would be unique since a member would not hire the same video out twice on the same date.

Hence Membership_Number, Video_ID and Date_Rented can be used together as a primary key/key field.

To make more than one field a primary key/key field click on the right pointing arrow on the left of the Video_ID field in the position shown below and keep your finger on the left mouse button.

Field Name	Data Type	Description
Video_ID	Number	The unique number of the video borrowed
Membership_Number	Number	The unique number of the members who is borrowing the vid
Date_Rented	Date/Time	The date when the video was hired
Days_Hired	Number	The number of days the video is hired for

Exercise 17.2

Notice that a right-pointing arrow appears and the entire row is highlighted. Keeping your finger on the mouse button, drag down until Video_ID, Membership_Number and Date_Rented, along with all their details, have been highlighted. Your screen will now look like this:

Field Name	Data Type	Description
Video_ID	Number	The unique number of the video borrowed
Membership_Number	Number	The unique number of the members who is borrowing the vid
Date_Rented	Date/Time	The date when the video was hired
Days_Hired	Number	The number of days the video is hired for

Now click on the primary key/key field button on the toolbar.

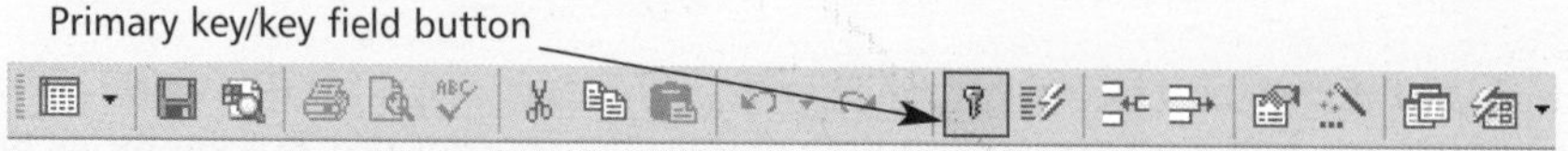

4 You will see three keys at the side of the three fields as shown below.

Field Name	Data Type	Description
Video_ID	Number	The unique number of the video borrowed
Membership_Number	Number	The unique number of the members who is borrowing t
Date_Rented	Date/Time	The date when the video was hired
Days_Hired	Number	The number of days the video is hired for

5 Close the table design and save the table using the filename 'Rentals'.

Creating the relationships between the tables

The three tables now need to be linked together. Without these links it would be impossible to combine data from more than one table.

Only those tables with a common field (i.e. the same field in each table) can be linked directly. Even if the field names are only slightly different, you will be unable to link tables using them.

Looking at the fields in the three tables you can see that only two tables can be linked directly: Members and Rentals and Videos and Rentals.

We cannot link Members and Videos directly since there is no common field. However, since they both have links to the rentals table there is an indirect link between them.

Putting data into the rentals table

Be careful when you put data into the rentals table. Suppose you decide to enter 20 into the Video_ID field. We do not have a video with Video_ID of 20 in the Videos table. As soon as you try to enter 20 the computer will check that such a number exists in the video table and if it doesn't, you will not be allowed to enter it.

Hence when data is entered in the rentals table you need to make sure that it does not conflict in any way with the data in any of the other tables.

QUESTIONS

Why is it better to enter the data into the tables after you have created the relationships than before?

Creating relationships between the tables

To combine the data in the three tables it is necessary to link them.

In this exercise you will learn how to:

- **add tables so that relationships can be established**
- **form the relationships between the tables**
- **enforce referential integrity.**

1 Load Access and open the Video Hire Store database. You will see a screen like this. Notice the names of the three tables are listed.

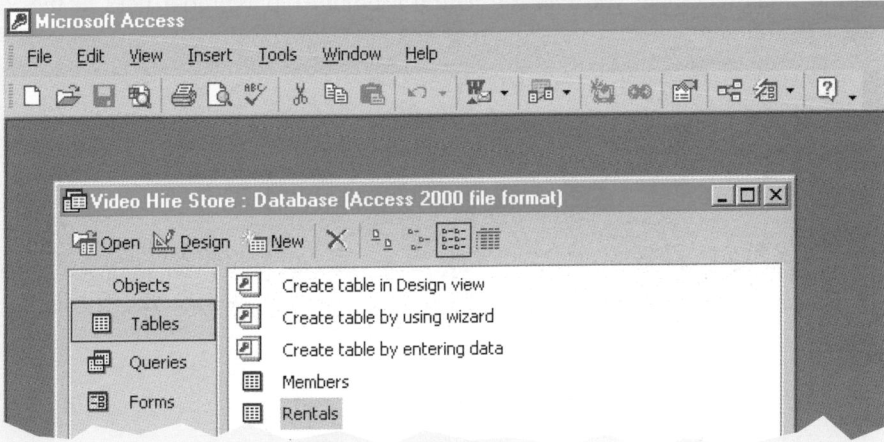

2 Click on the relationships button on the toolbar.

3 The following screen appears. This enables us to tell the computer which tables are going to be used.

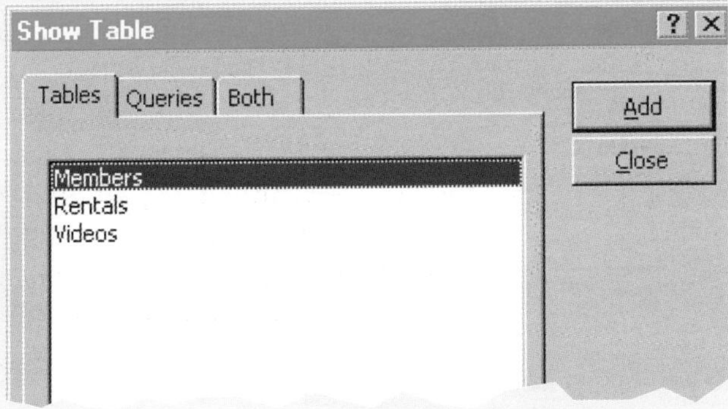

Make sure that Members is highlighted and then press the Add button.

Click on Rentals and then press Add.

Click on Videos and then press Add.

Then click on the Close button.

Exercise 17.3

4 The three tables are shown below. Notice the names of the tables at the top and also the highlighted primary keys.

Click on Membership_Number in the members table and hold down the mouse button. Now drag the small rectangle you will see to the Membership_Number field in the Rentals table. Release the mouse button.

The following screen will now appear.

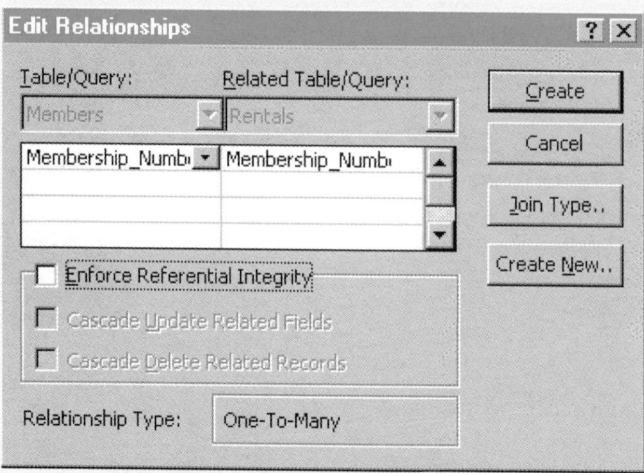

Notice that the Relationship Type is One-To-Many.

Click on the box marked Enforce Referential Integrity.

Click on the Create button.

A line is drawn between the two tables (see above). Notice the way the one-to-many relationship is indicated on this line.

5 Let's now make a similar relationship between the videos and rentals tables.

Click on the field Video_ID in the videos table and then drag across to the Video_ID in the rentals table. When the Edit Relationships box appears, check that the relationship is one-to-many and also that referential integrity has been enforced. Do not worry about what this means for the moment; it will be explained later.

Your screen showing the relationships will now look like this:

Exercise 17.4

Entering data into the rentals table

In this exercise you will learn how to:

- **ensure that only valid data is entered into a table**
- **make sure that the referential integrity rules are not breached by the data you enter.**

Before entering data into the rentals table we have to make sure of two things:

- We must not try to rent out a video we do not have. Since referential integrity has been enforced, the computer checks to make sure that any Video_ID we enter appears in the video table.
- We must not allow anyone who is not a member to borrow a video. Again, by enforcing referential integrity the computer checks any Membership_Number with the members table to make sure that it exists.

We have only eight members, so the only valid numbers that can be entered into the Membership_Number field are from one to eight. There are only 17 videos to hire so only numbers from one to 17 can be entered for the Video_ID.

1 Load the database software and open the rentals table.

2 Enter the following data into the rental table.

	Video_ID	Membership_Number	Date_rented	Days_Hired
	1	7	01/12/00	1
	3	5	01/12/00	1
	3	5	02/12/00	1
	2	1	03/12/00	2
	7	6	03/12/00	1
	14	7	03/12/00	1
	10	6	03/12/00	1
	17	1	04/12/00	1
	9	3	04/12/00	3
	8	4	04/12/00	1
	1	6	04/12/00	1
	1	7	04/12/00	1
	3	4	05/12/00	1
	15	2	05/12/00	1
	12	8	05/12/00	1
	1	7	06/12/00	1
▶	0	0		0

3 Close the datasheet view and save the data.

Documenting a relational database

You may wish to produce a relational database to solve a problem for your GCSE IT project work. As with all project work, you will be required to thoroughly document your solution. As part of this documentation you should include:

- a section explaining how you have arrived at the number of tables you are going to use
- an explanation of your choice of the primary key or keys for each table
- a section explaining how you decided on the type of relationship you are going to use between the tables (e.g. one-to-one, one-to-many).

The development of a relational database makes a good choice for a project. It is not an easy choice but in many ways it is easier to document than projects using other software.

QUESTIONS

1 A patient database used by a hospital contains two data files. The structure of these two files is shown below.

Patients
Patient number
Title
Surname
Forename
Date of birth
Street
Town
Postcode
Contact phone number
Home phone number
Consultant number

Consultants
Consultant number
Consultant name

(a) How many fields are there in:

(i) the Patients file?

(ii) the Consultants file?

(b) Why is it better to store the data in two separate files, rather than keeping it all in one file?

(c) Why is Date of birth stored in the Patients file rather than age?

(d) Which field would be the primary key:

(i) in the Patients file?

(ii) in the Consultants file?

2 Your school is planning to use a relational database to help the headteacher and the other staff run the school.

The head of IT suggests that the following tables should be used. The fields in each table are listed below the table's name.

Pupil table	**Form table**	**Teacher table**
Pupil_number	Form	Teacher_ID
Surname	Teacher_ID	Teacher_name
Forename		
Street		
Town		
Postcode		
Form		

(a) Why is it more efficient to store the data in three tables rather than one?

(b) What is the best primary key for each table?

(c) What kind of relationship would there be between:

(i) the Pupil and Form tables?

(ii) the Form and Teacher tables?

IT TASKS

Relational database task

In question 2 on page 240, you were asked about a relational database being used by a school. Your task now is to set up this database. Imagine you are setting it up for your own school.

1 Produce a simple questionnaire for your teacher to find out anything that might help you to set up the database. Here are three questions to start you off:
   - What are the names of all the forms in the school?
   - How many teachers are there in the school and what are their names?
   - How is the Pupil_number allocated to a pupil?

2 Design the tables as shown in the lists in question 2 (N.B. do not add any extra fields of your own.)

3 Enter data for at least ten records into each table. Make sure that data in one table does not conflict with the data in another.

4 Produce three queries which the headteacher might like to run. Say what each query is designed to do and produce a printout showing the results.

18 Using More than One Table

Extracting data from more than one table

Once there are relationships between tables you can extract and combine the data from more than one table. This is done using a query. Queries are used to ask questions of databases.

Extracting data from a computer!

Exercise 18.1

Making up queries that use more than one table

Suppose someone leaves a bag in the video hire store and a member of staff spots it at the end of the day. You noticed that someone who rented a video put the bag down but can't remember who.

The manager suggests that, since it was a very quiet day, we could ring up everyone who hired a video that day to find out whose it is.

The date was 04/12/00 and the manager needs a list of the following for members who hired out videos on that date:

Title
Surname
Forename
Phone_Number
Date (Just to check that the right data has been extracted)

In this exercise you will learn how to:

- **select the tables to be used for the query**
- **select the fields in each table**
- **give a name to a query**
- **use search criteria with a query**
- **produce the results**
- **produce a printout.**

1 Load Access and then select the Video Hire Store database. The following screen appears.

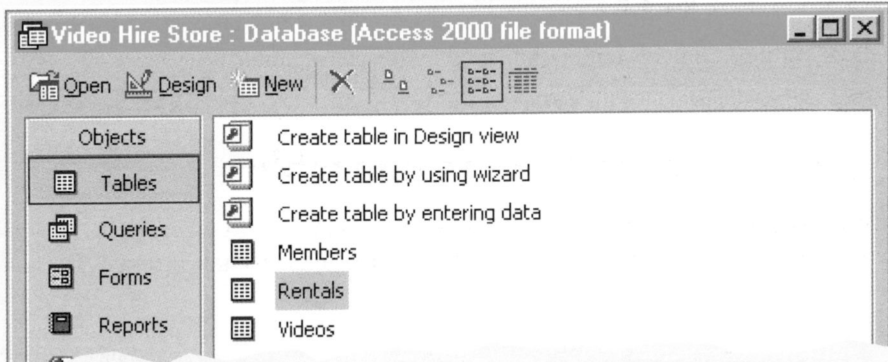

2 Click on the Queries button on the screen above. The queries screen now appears:

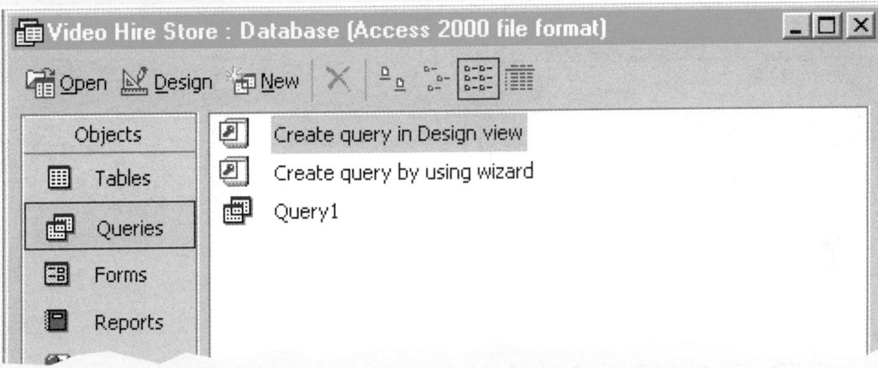

Click on Create query by using wizard.

3 The following screen appears to guide you through the process of producing a query.

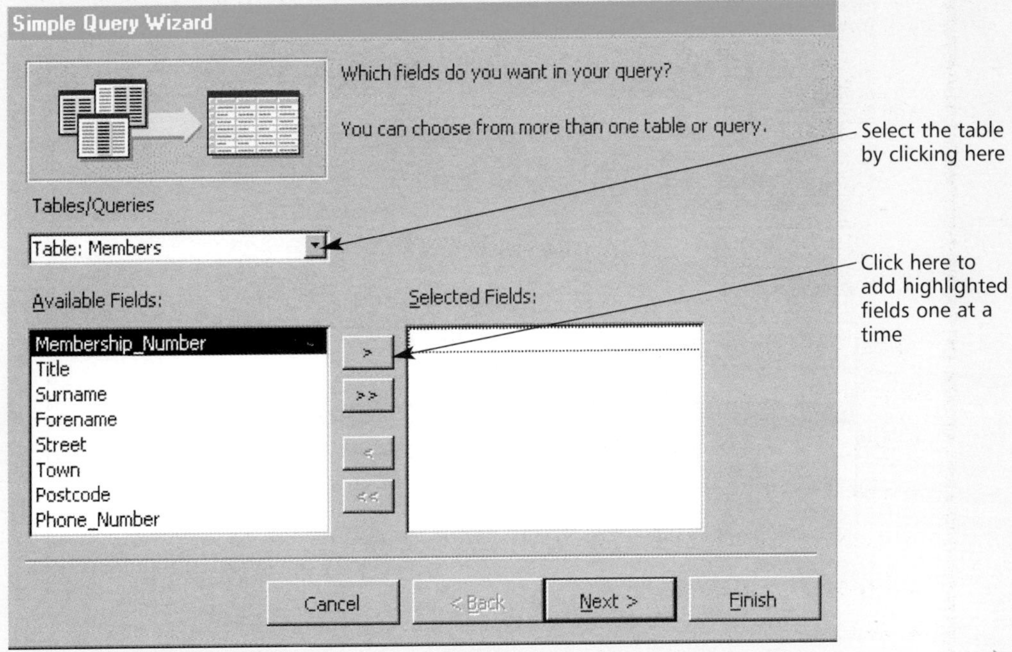

Make sure that the Table:Members appears in the Tables/Queries box.

Click on Title so that it is highlighted in the Available Fields box.

Click on the Add fields button indicated by the single arrow.

Title will now appear in the Selected Fields box. Your screen will look like this:

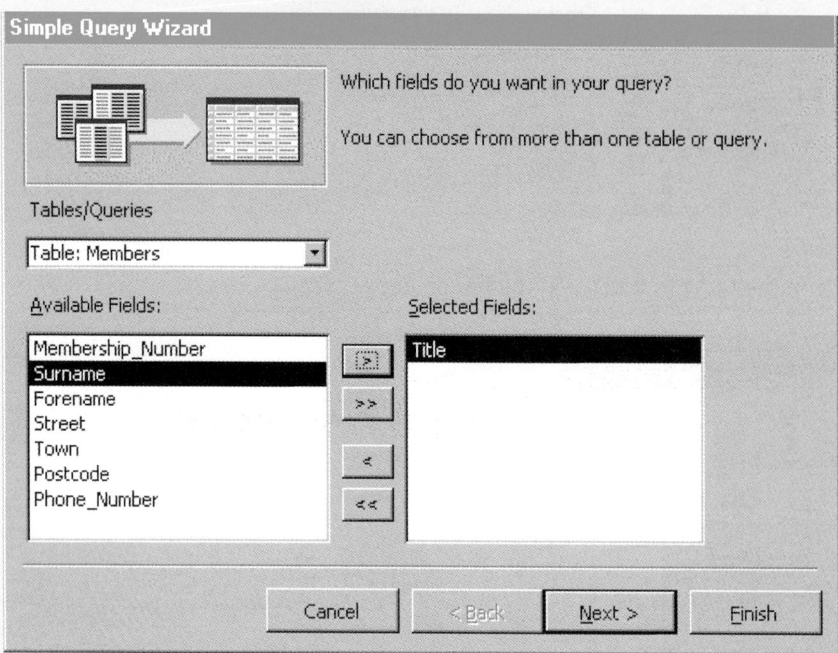

4 In a similar way add these fields to the Selected Fields box:

Title; Surname; Forename; Phone_Number

Your screen will now look like this:

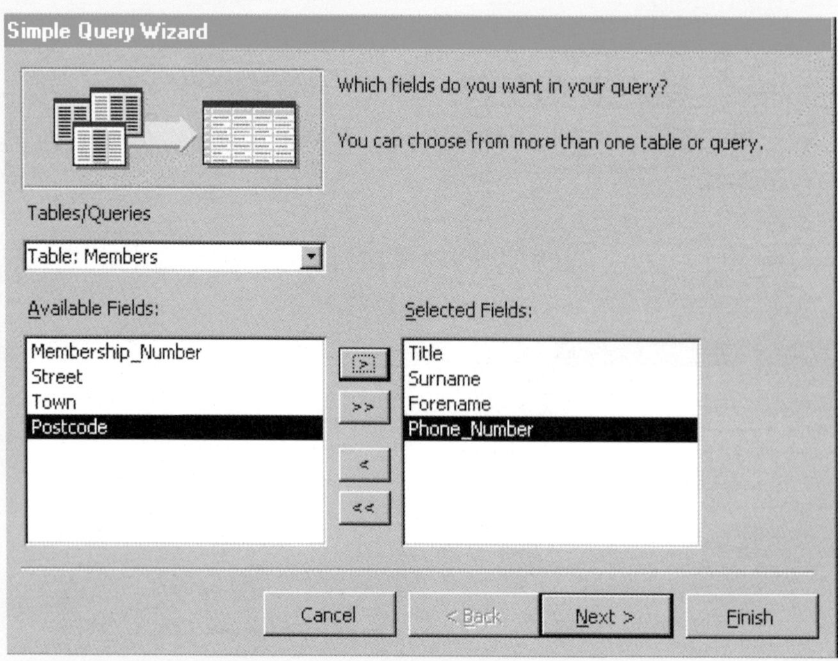

5 Click on the drop down arrow in the Tables/Queries box and select Table:Rentals.

Add Date_rented to the selected fields.

After doing this you will see the following screen.

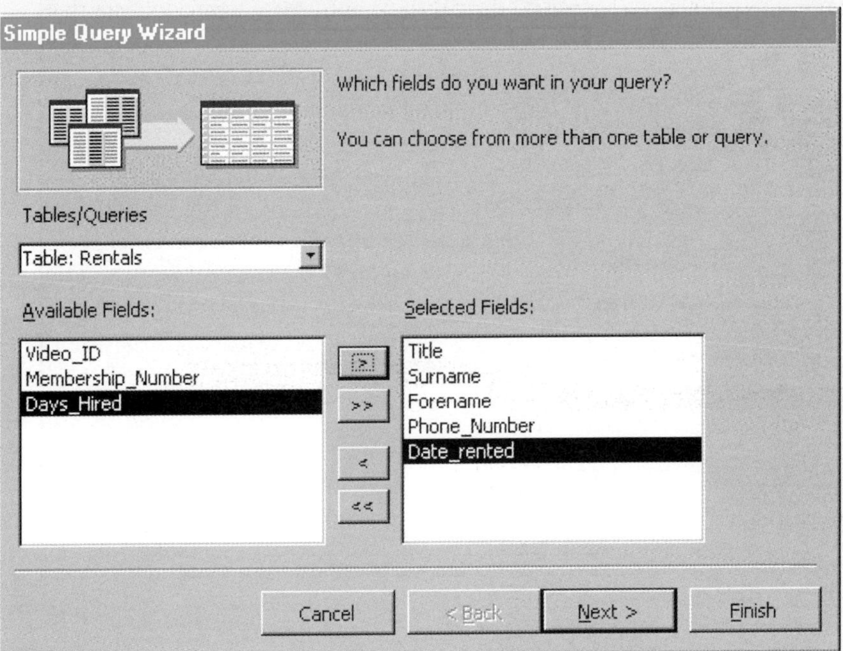

Click on the Next> button.

6 The screen below now appears. Make sure Detail has been selected and then click on the Next> button.

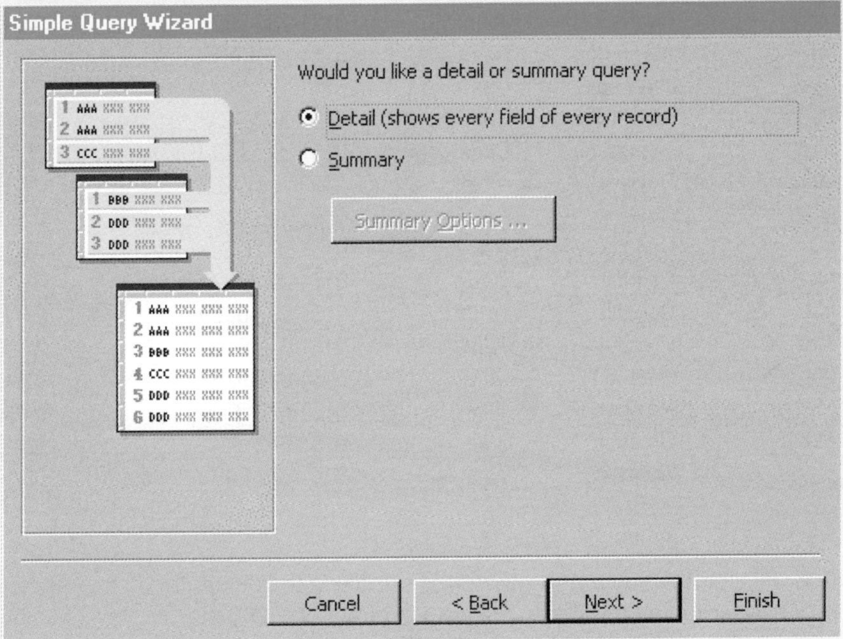

Exercise 18.1

7 Change the name of the query to **Lost bag**.

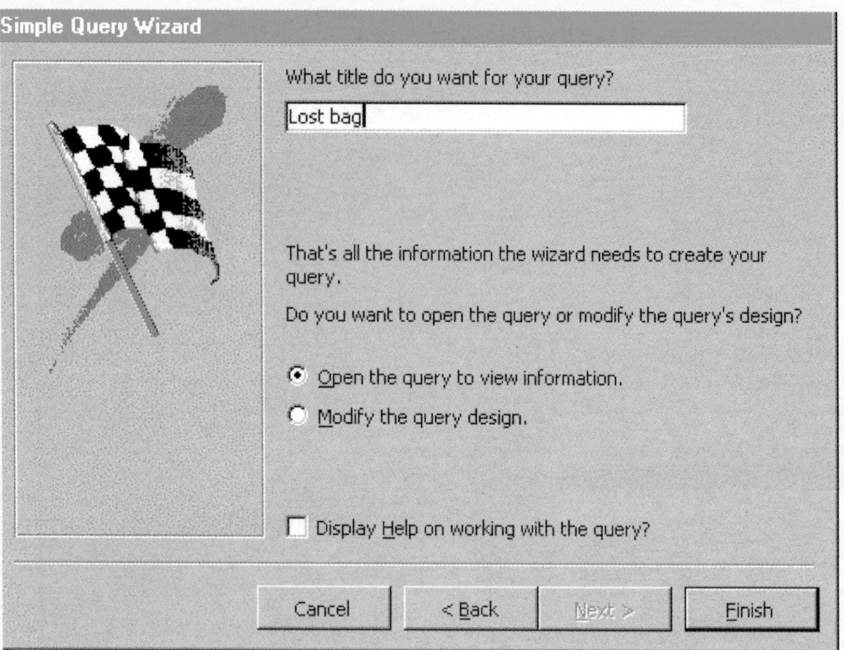

Click on Finish.

The query will now run and the results are shown below.

Title	Surname	Forename	Phone_Number	Date_rented
Mr	Hughes	John	0151-230-2929	03/12/00
Mr	Hughes	John	0151-230-2929	04/12/00
Ms	Harrington	Hayley	0151-420-0913	05/12/00
Miss	Prenton	Cheryl	0151-210-9824	04/12/00
Mr	Johnstone	Christopher	0151-342-2232	04/12/00
Mr	Johnstone	Christopher	0151-342-2232	05/12/00
Miss	Doyle	Amy	01925-23220	01/12/00
Miss	Doyle	Amy	01925-23220	02/12/00
Ms	Corkhill	Tracy	0151-292-0329	03/12/00
Ms	Corkhill	Tracy	0151-292-0329	03/12/00
Ms	Corkhill	Tracy	0151-292-0329	04/12/00
Mrs	Prescott	Julie	0151-672-9292	01/12/00
Mrs	Prescott	Julie	0151-672-9292	03/12/00
Mrs	Prescott	Julie	0151-672-9292	04/12/00
Mrs	Prescott	Julie	0151-672-9292	06/12/00
Mr	Thomas	Charles	0151-672-2492	05/12/00

There is still a problem with this query. It is extracting the details for all the dates. We just need those details for the date when the bag was found (04/12/00).

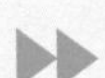

8 Click on Design view

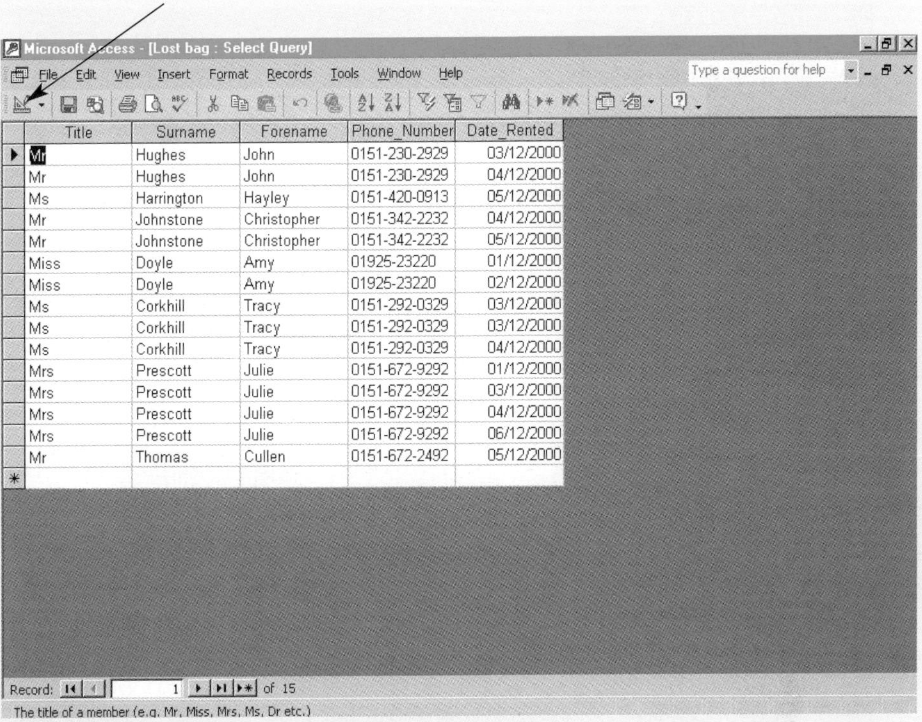

Title	Surname	Forename	Phone_Number	Date_Rented
Mr	Hughes	John	0151-230-2929	03/12/2000
Mr	Hughes	John	0151-230-2929	04/12/2000
Ms	Harrington	Hayley	0151-420-0913	05/12/2000
Mr	Johnstone	Christopher	0151-342-2232	04/12/2000
Mr	Johnstone	Christopher	0151-342-2232	05/12/2000
Miss	Doyle	Amy	01925-23220	01/12/2000
Miss	Doyle	Amy	01925-23220	02/12/2000
Ms	Corkhill	Tracy	0151-292-0329	03/12/2000
Ms	Corkhill	Tracy	0151-292-0329	03/12/2000
Ms	Corkhill	Tracy	0151-292-0329	04/12/2000
Mrs	Prescott	Julie	0151-672-9292	01/12/2000
Mrs	Prescott	Julie	0151-672-9292	03/12/2000
Mrs	Prescott	Julie	0151-672-9292	04/12/2000
Mrs	Prescott	Julie	0151-672-9292	06/12/2000
Mr	Thomas	Cullen	0151-672-2492	05/12/2000

The following screen now appears:

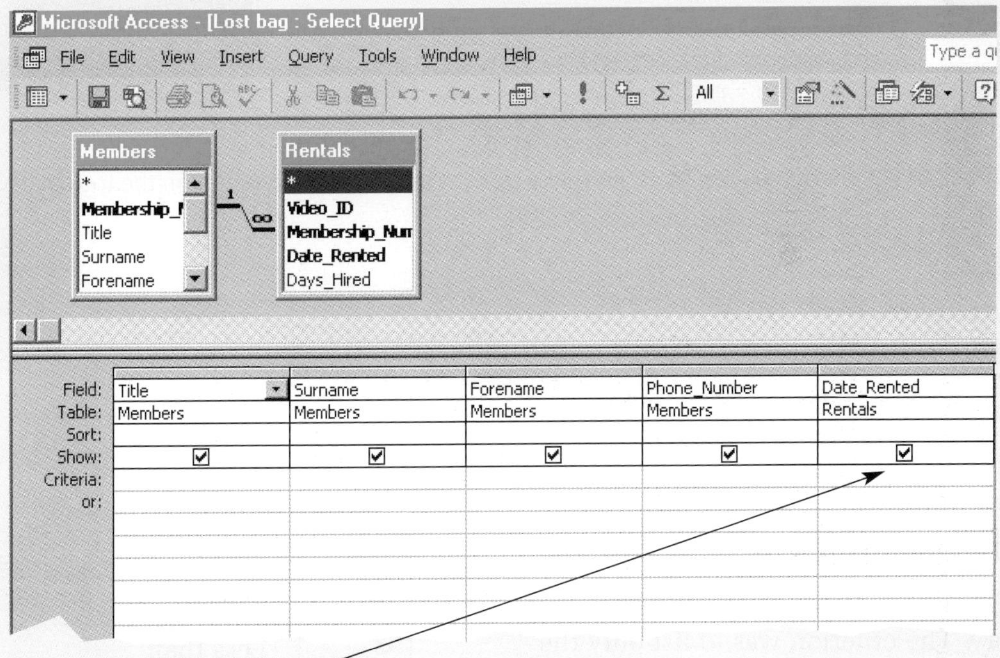

Enter **=04/12/00** here.

This is the date for which we want the details. Press Enter.

Exercise 18.1

9 Change the view to Datasheet view by clicking here.

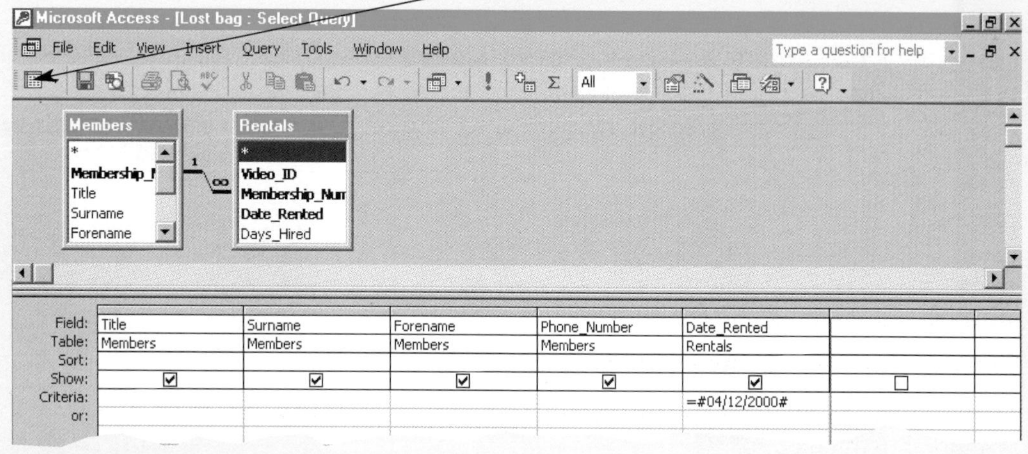

10 The following screen appears.

Click on the Save button and the amended query will be saved under the original name.

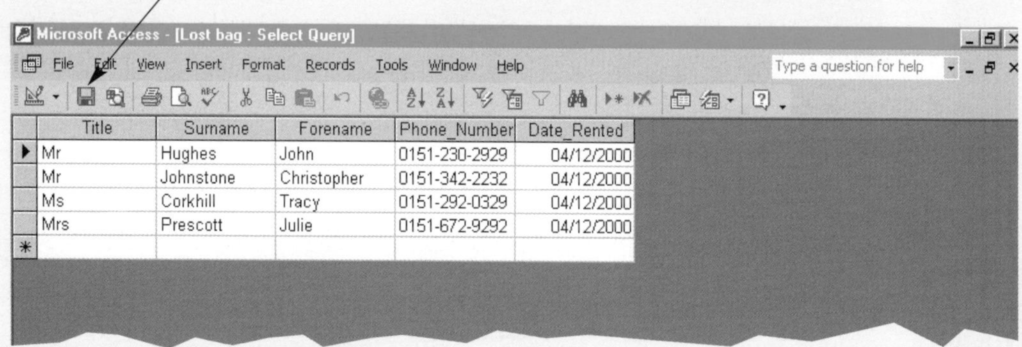

Title	Surname	Forename	Phone_Number	Date_Rented
Mr	Hughes	John	0151-230-2929	04/12/2000
Mr	Johnstone	Christopher	0151-342-2232	04/12/2000
Ms	Corkhill	Tracy	0151-292-0329	04/12/2000
Mrs	Prescott	Julie	0151-672-9292	04/12/2000

11 Print out the results of this query by clicking on the print button on the toolbar.

Adding criteria to a query

In Exercise 18.1 we used a criterion in the query. The criterion was to list only the details for a certain date. The operators listed in this table can be used for the search criteria in a query.

Operator	Meaning
=	Equal to
>	Greater than
<	Less than
>=	Greater than or equal to
<=	Less than or equal to
<>	Is not equal to

Constructing and using queries

In the last exercise you saw how queries can extract data from more than one table. Here, you will practise the use of queries.

Using the video hire database you have already created, produce queries to extract the relevant data for each of the following.

For each one, explain how you constructed the query, and also produce a printout showing the results.

IT TASKS

Constructing and using simple queries

1 A customer comes in and asks for a list of titles for all those videos with a rating of 15. Produce a suitable list for the customer.

2 A video has been returned. Since the shop was closed, the borrower posted it through the letter box. When the video case is opened there is no video in it. The case is labelled with the Video_ID 12.

Produce a list of the members' names, addresses and phone numbers who have borrowed this video.

3 It is also known that the video was hired out on 04/12/00. Construct another query to determine the person who hired out the video.

4 Produce a list of video details (Video_ID, Title, Category, Rating) for all those videos having a rental price of £1.50.

5 Produce a list of the titles of videos and surnames of members who borrowed videos on 01/12/00.

6 Produce a list of five fields (Title, Rating, Surname, Date_Rented, Days_Hired) for all the members who have borrowed videos for more than one day.

IT TASKS

Constructing and using harder queries

1 The manager of the video hire store would like to know the titles of videos that each member has borrowed and also the date that they borrowed them. Produce a list.

2 Produce a list showing the Video_ID, Title and Copies_In_Stock for all the videos where the Copies_in_Stock is three or over.

3 Produce a list of the members' names along with the titles of the videos they have borrowed for all the members who have hired videos for more than one day.

4 A video has come back to the store damaged. The Video_ID was 13. Produce a list showing the surname, forename, telephone number and the date borrowed for all the members who have borrowed this video.

5 Alter query 1 so that the list is ordered according to descending date borrowed.

(Hint: to sort a field you need to click on the sort box under the field heading you want to sort. You will then be offered a choice between ascending, descending or not sorted. Click on the one you require.)

Using calculations in queries

We do not store in tables any data that can be calculated from other items of data already stored in a table. For example, we would not have a field called Rental_Fee in a table because this can be calculated by multiplying the Rental_Price by the Days_Hired. These fields are in different tables, so by using a query they can be used in a calculation. Make sure that the fields are spelt exactly the same in the formula as they are spelt in the tables.

In this exercise you will learn how to:

- **set up a query containing a calculated field.**

1 Load the Video Hire Store database.

2 From the Database screen select Create query by using wizard. When asked, give the name **An example of a calculation in a query** to the query.

3 Select the fields from the tables as shown in below.

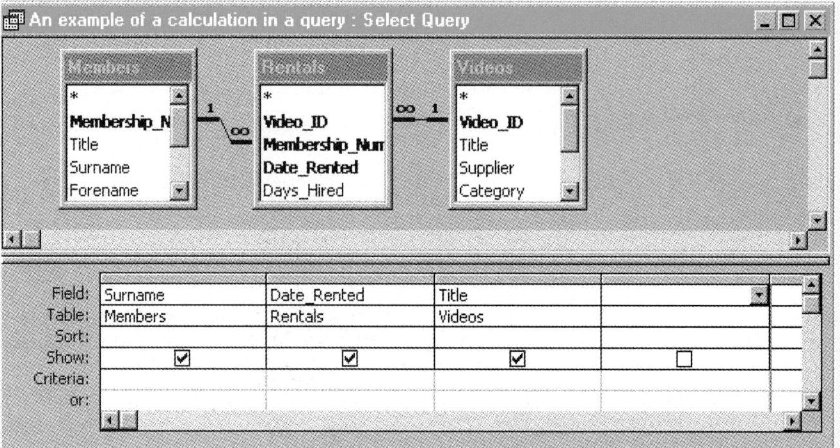

4 In the next blank column, and in the Field: row, enter the following:

Rental_Fee:[Rental_Price]*[Days_Hired]

Rental_Fee is the name of the new field in which the amount will be calculated and stored. Notice that the two fields to be multiplied together are enclosed between square brackets.

Your screen will now look like this:

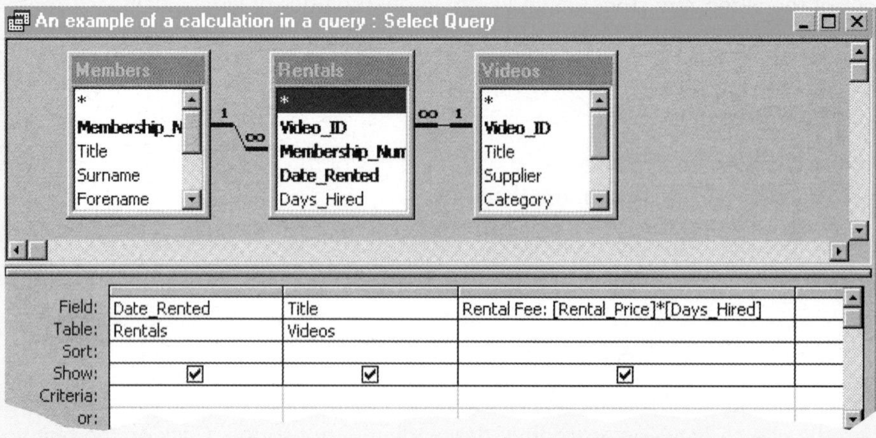

In the previous screen, the column with the formula in it has been widened so that all the formula can be seen. This is done by clicking on the grey area at the boundary of the two columns and dragging to adjust the width of the column.

5 Click on the datasheet button to see the results of the query.

Your results should look like this:

Surname	Date_Rented	Title	Rental Fee
Prescott	01/12/00	South Park	£3.50
Doyle	01/12/00	The General's Daughter	£2.50
Doyle	13/12/00	The General's Daughter	£2.50
Hughes	03/12/00	Ravenous	£5.00
Corkhill	03/12/00	Star Wars Episode 1	£3.50
Prescott	03/12/00	Notting Hill	£2.50
Corkhill	03/12/00	A Simple Plan	£1.50
Hughes	04/12/00	A Midsummer Nights Dream	£3.50
Prenton	04/12/00	Italian Job	£4.50
Johnstone	04/12/00	Eyes Wide Shut	£3.50
Corkhill	04/12/00	South Park	£3.50
Prescott	04/12/00	South Park	£3.50
Johnstone	05/12/00	The General's Daughter	£2.50
Harrington	05/12/00	Mickey Blue Eyes	£1.50
Thomas	05/12/00	The Thomas Crown Affair	£2.50
Prescott	06/12/00	South Park	£3.50
*			

Notice that the name of the new calculated field has been placed above all the calculated values.

Click to close the screen and the query will be saved under the filename 'An example of a calculation in a query'. This name will now appear in the list of queries as shown.

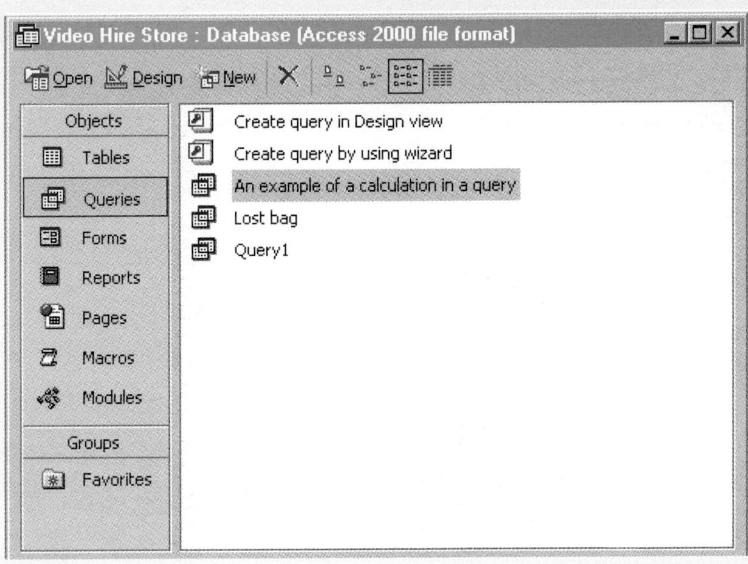

6 Produce a printout of the results for this query.

QUESTIONS

1 Explain each of the following terms used in this chapter:
(a) query
(b) criteria
(c) wizard.

2 The table below contains field names (in the first row) and data.

For each search criterion below, write down the record or records that will be displayed when the following search criteria are applied to the data in the table.

(a) Dept = "Production"
(b) Date_Joined ="04/08/99"
(c) Hols_Total <= 41
(d) Date_Joined < 01/01/90
(e) Date_Joined >= 04/08/99
(f) Hols_Taken = 0

Explain how another field could be created called Holidays_Due, calculated by subtracting Hols_Taken from Hols_Total.

Employee_No	Dept	Date_Joined	Hols_Total	Hols_Taken
0001	Sales	12/12/97	42	30
0002	Production	09/01/79	42	12
0003	Sales	03/07/90	40	24
0004	Admin	08/07/98	42	20
0005	Sales	05/06/96	40	18
0006	Admin	01/12/00	45	0
0007	Admin	04/08/99	40	10

19 Producing Reports

Reports are used to present the output from a database. Although you can print out the results of queries or print the contents of tables or forms, it is easier and looks more professional to use reports. Using reports gives you more control over the look of the printed output. Other forms of output are more suited to presenting data on the screen than on paper.

Exercise 19.1

Producing reports

In this exercise you will learn how to:

- **add fields from different tables to a report**
- **select a field to sort the data on**
- **choose the layout of a report**
- **select the style of a report**
- **select a filename and save a report**
- **preview a report before printing.**

1 Load Access and then open the Video Hire Store database.

The Database screen appears as shown below.

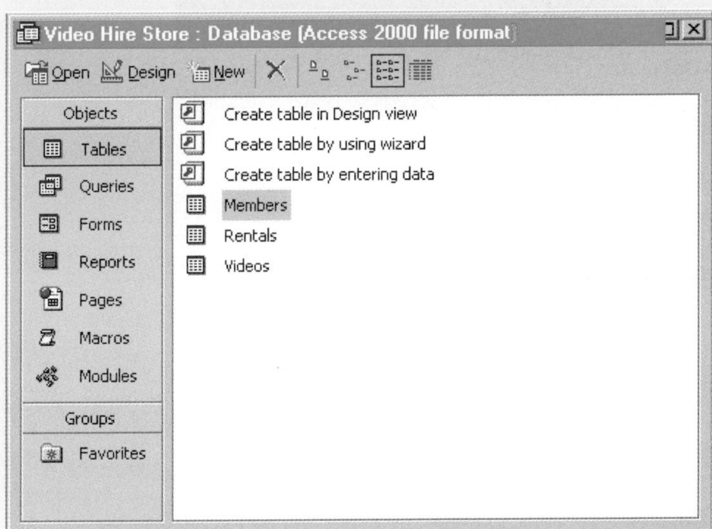

2 Click on Reports (if it is not already selected) and then on Create report by using wizard. You will remember that a wizard in Office guides you step-by-step through the process of doing something.

The first screen of the Report Wizard appears (see the first screen on page 254).

Notice the name of the Tables/Queries in the box. The members table is shown but this may be changed to any previously stored table or query by clicking on the drop-down arrow and selecting.

In the Available Fields box, all the fields in the selected table or query are displayed. In this case all the fields shown are the fields in the members table.

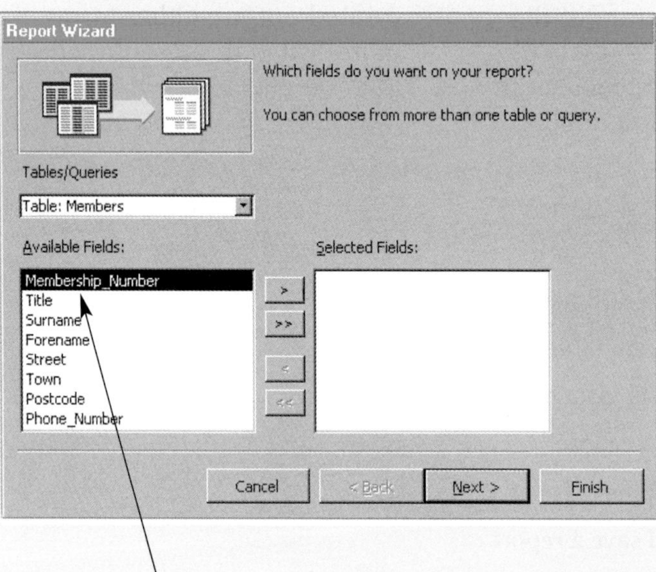

3 Membership_Number is highlighted (if not click on it to select it) then press the add field button (single arrow). This adds another field to the Selected Fields box.

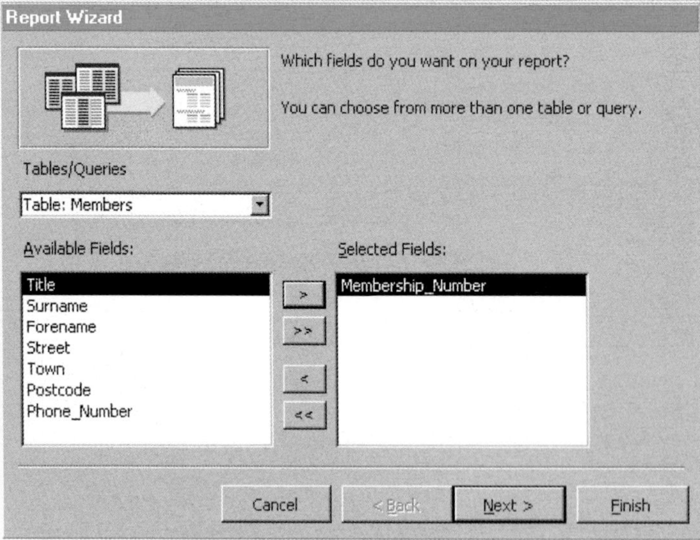

4 Highlight the field Surname and then press the add field button again.

The screen will now look like the screen at the top of the next page.

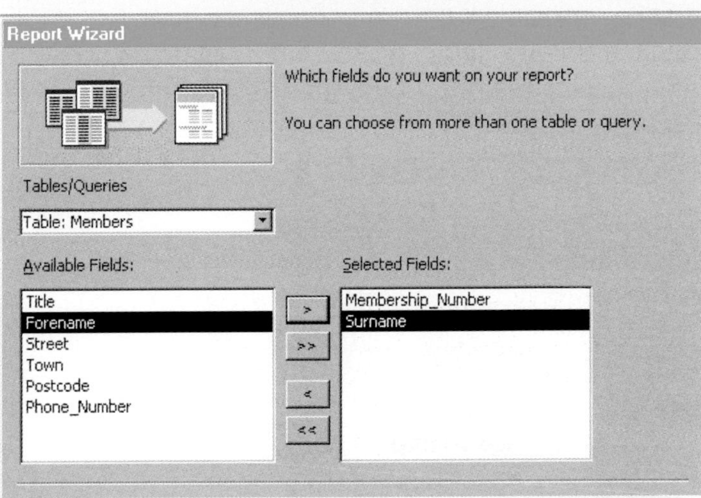

5 Now change to the rentals table by clicking here and selecting from the pull-down menu that appears.

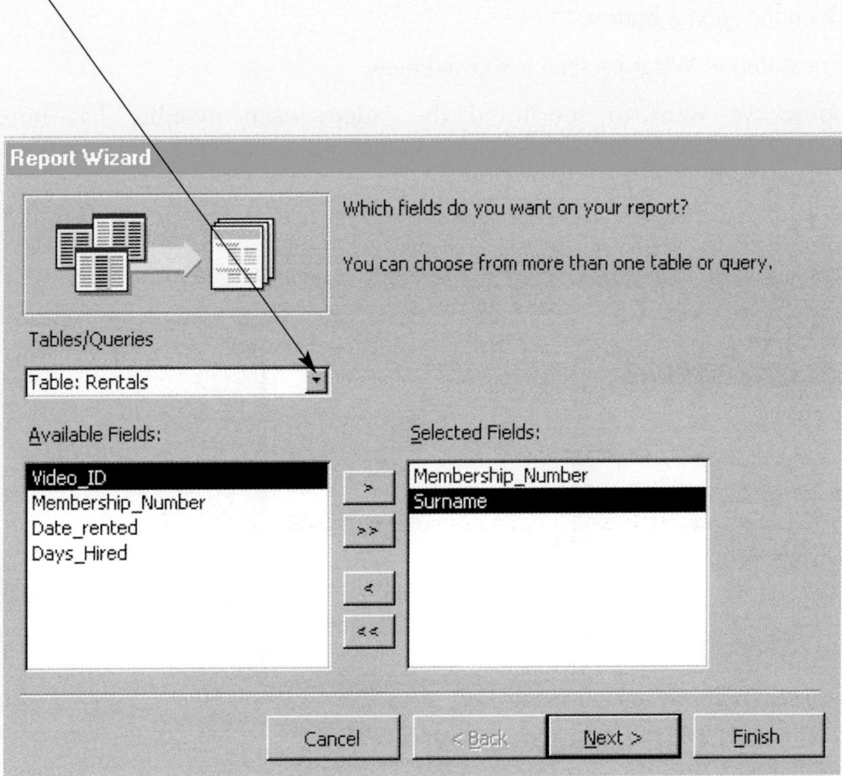

Notice that the fields now listed are found in the rentals table.

Add Video_ID from this list to the Selected Fields.

6 Now change the table to Videos by clicking here and selecting from the pull-down menu that appears.

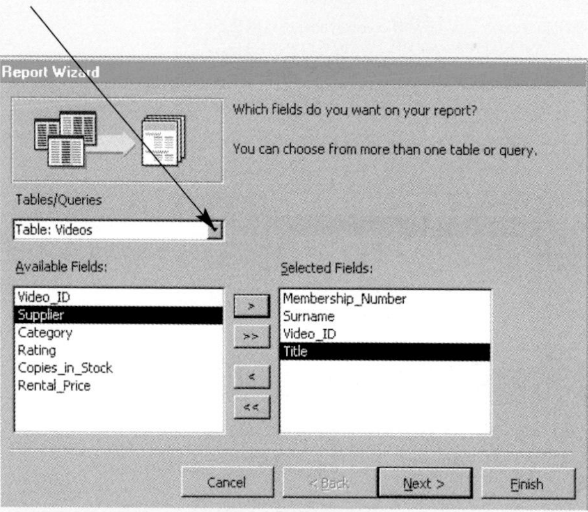

Add the field Title to the list of Selected Fields.

We have now added all the fields for the report.

Click on the Next> button.

7 The next Report Wizard screen is shown below.

Suppose we want to see listed the videos each member has hired out. The Membership_Number and the Surname appear at the start of each listing of the videos that they have hired.

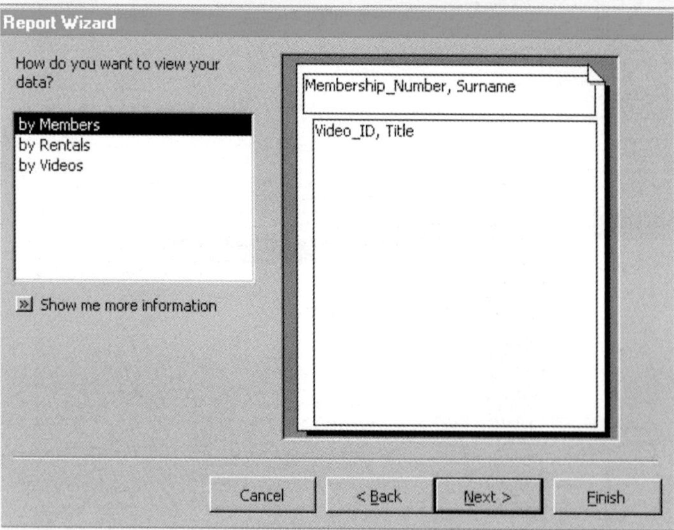

The settings shown are fine for what we want. Click on the Next> button.

When the next screen is shown, skip past it by clicking on the Next>button.

Exercise 19.1

8 The next Report Wizard screen appears (below). You can put either the Video_ID or Title into order by clicking here.

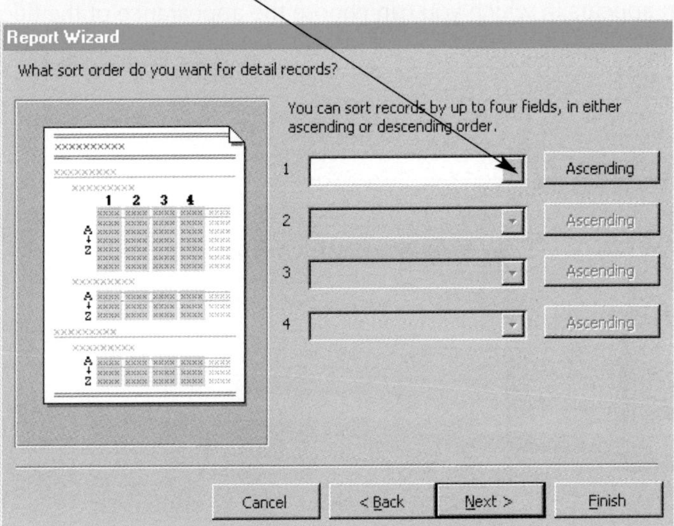

Select Title from the list. The section of the screen will now look like this:

You can sort records by up to four fields, in either ascending or descending order.
1 Title Ascending
2 Ascending
3 Ascending
4 Ascending

Click on the Next> button

9 The next screen is displayed:

Notice that on this screen you can:

- choose the page orientation
- fit all the fields on one page.

You can also select the layout.

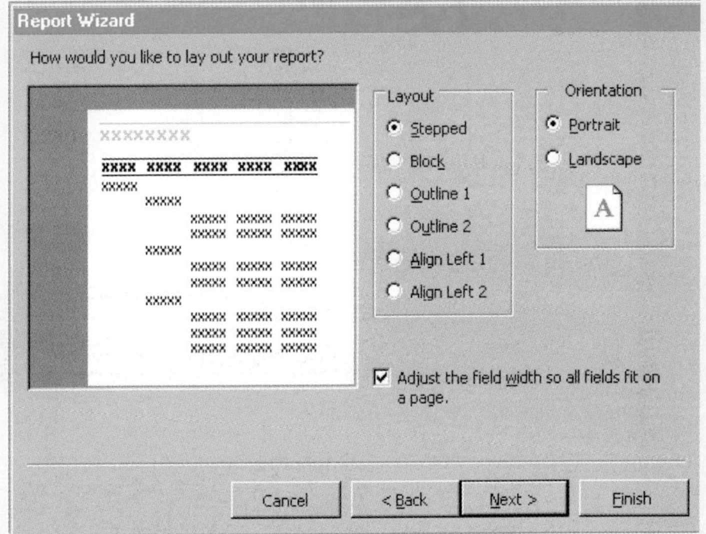

Make sure that your settings are identical to those shown in the previous screen. Click on Next>.

10 The following screen appears in which you can choose the appearance of the title.

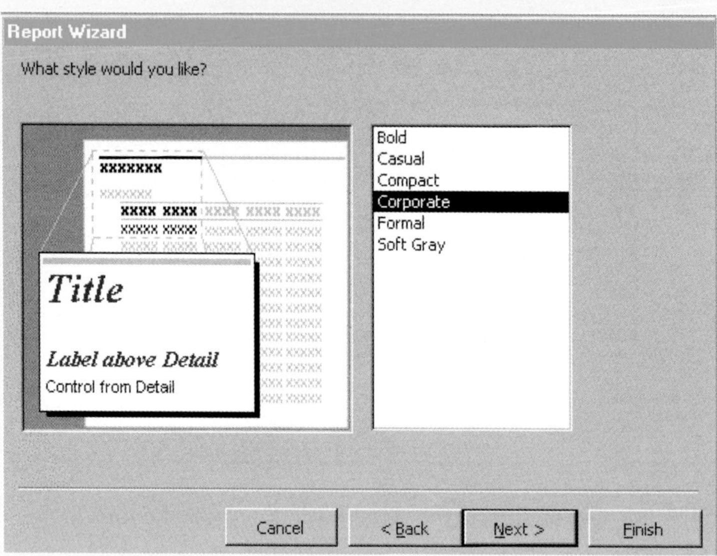

Select Corporate (this will probably be already highlighted) and click on Next>.

11 The final screen appears (below) in which a file name is given to the report.

Type in the name **Report showing the videos Members have hired**. It is much better to give the report a name like this rather than to use names like Report1, Report2.

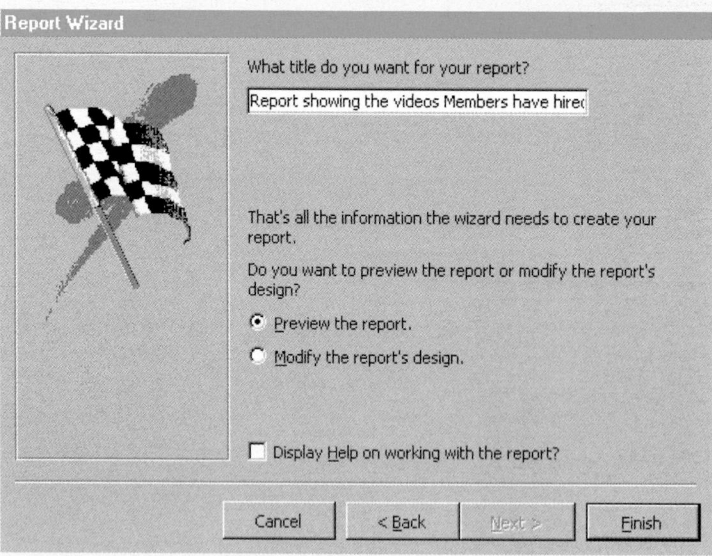

You have now completed the design of the report.

Click on the Finish button.

12 The report is saved and the results appear as shown here.

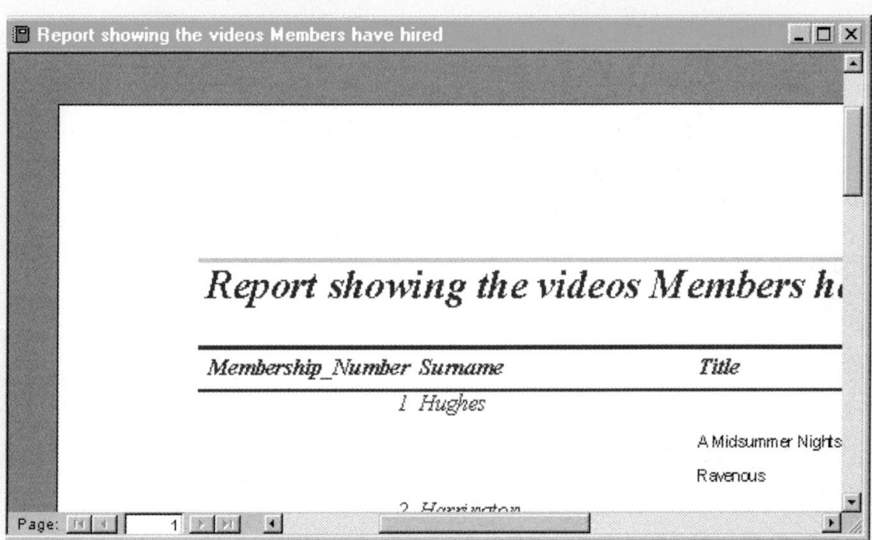

Click on the left mouse button and the report will appear as a single page:

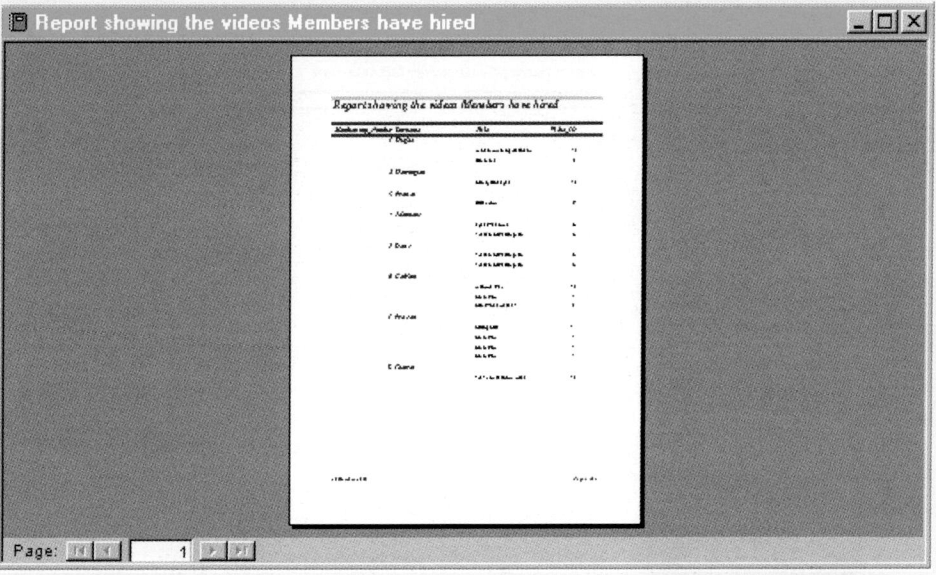

You can position the small magnifying glass on any particular part of the report you want to see in detail. Try it.

13 Close the screen and you will see the Database screen:

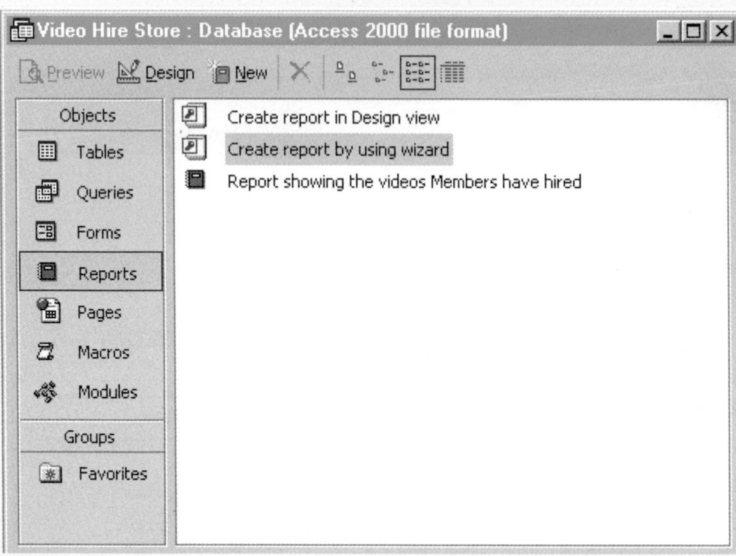

Notice that the report name has been added.

14 Open the report by double clicking on it. Make sure that your printer has paper and is on-line.

Click on the Print button to print out the report.

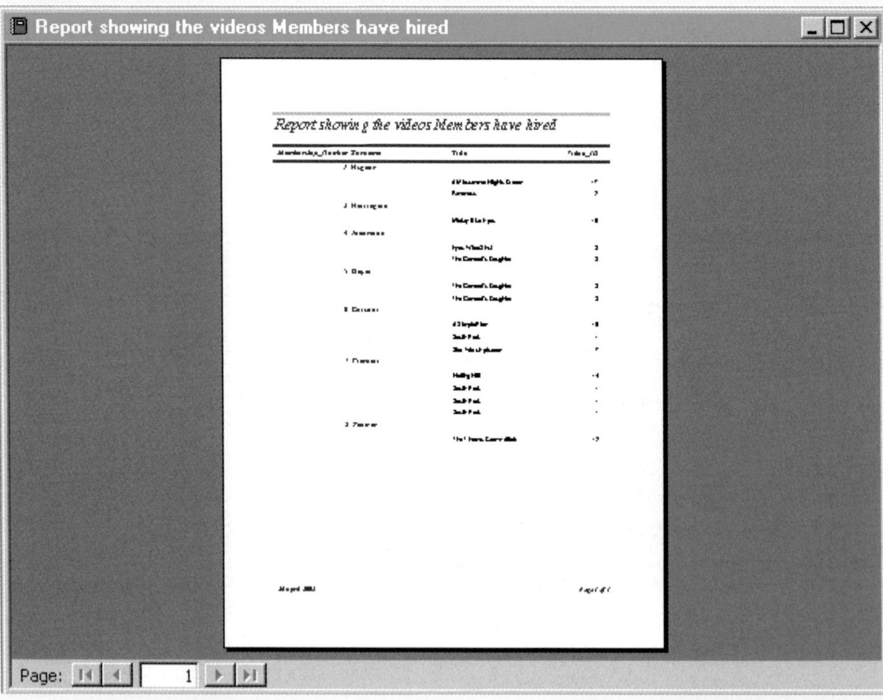

Notice how neat the report looks. It has the date on it and the pages are numbered so that you can be sure that nothing is missing.

Creating a report based on a query

In Chapter 18 we covered how queries could be constructed and how to get the computer to display the results. The results of queries are displayed on the screen and then printed out. Rather than do this, it is often better to use a report to print the results of the query. Using the report format gives a better appearance to the results.

Exercise 19.2

Printing the results of a query in report format

In the exercise you will learn how to:

- **select a query to be used as the basis of the report**
- **produce a report based on the results of the query.**

In this example we will be placing the query developed in Exercise 18.2 into report format.

1 Load Access and in the database screen, click on Reports. This screen appears:

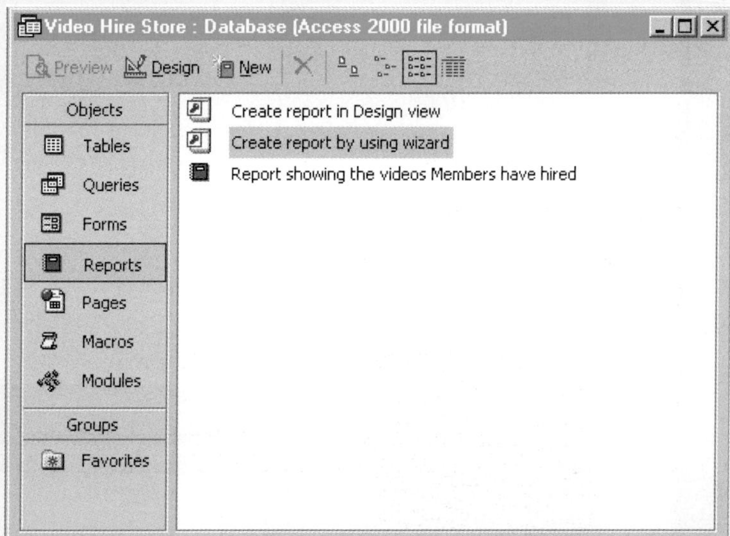

2 Click on Create report by using wizard.

In the Tables/Queries box here, click on the pull-down arrow and click on Query:An example of a calculation in a query.

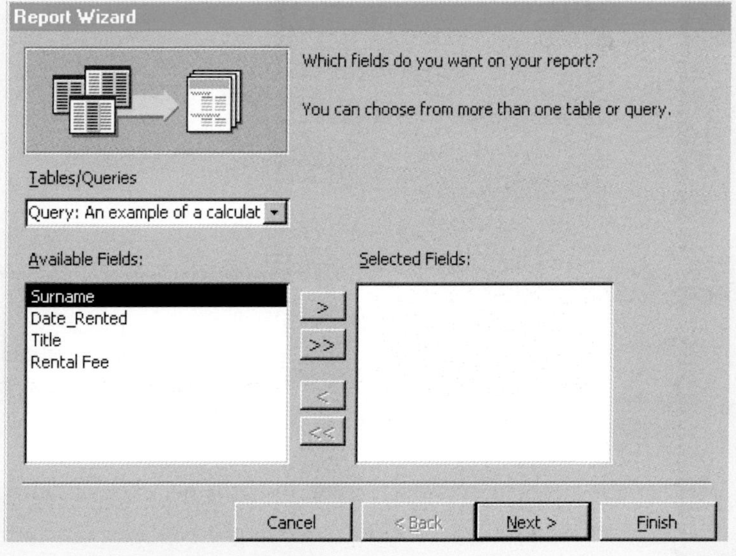

Exercise 19.2

3 We now add the fields to the list. Click on the button with the double arrows to add all the fields in the query to the report. After doing this your screen should look like this:

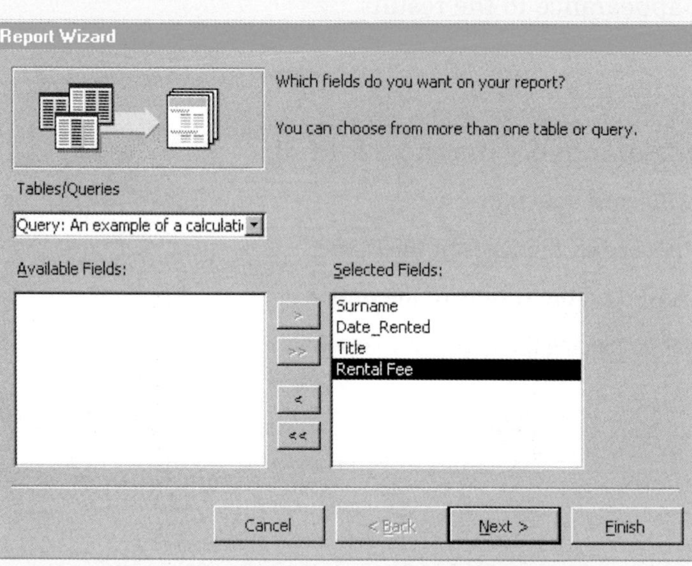

4 Click on the Next> button. The following screen will appear.

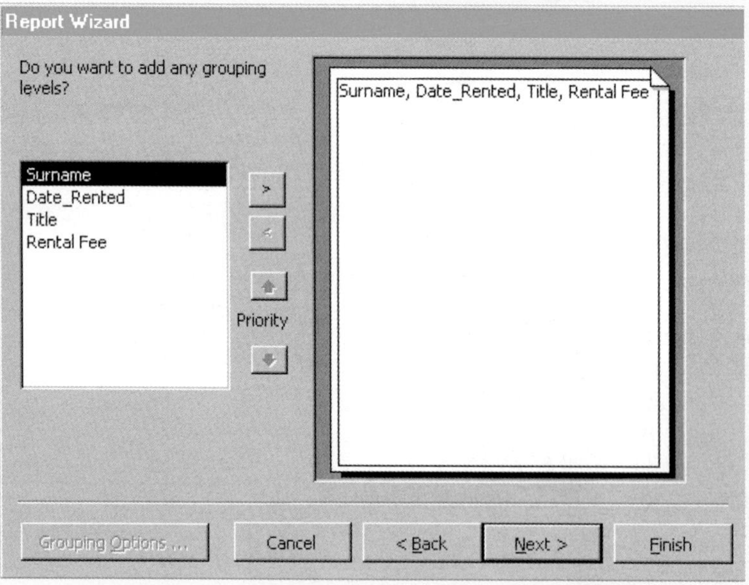

In order to group according to Surname, click on Surname in the list, then click on the add arrow (it looks like this >).

5 The screen will now look like this:

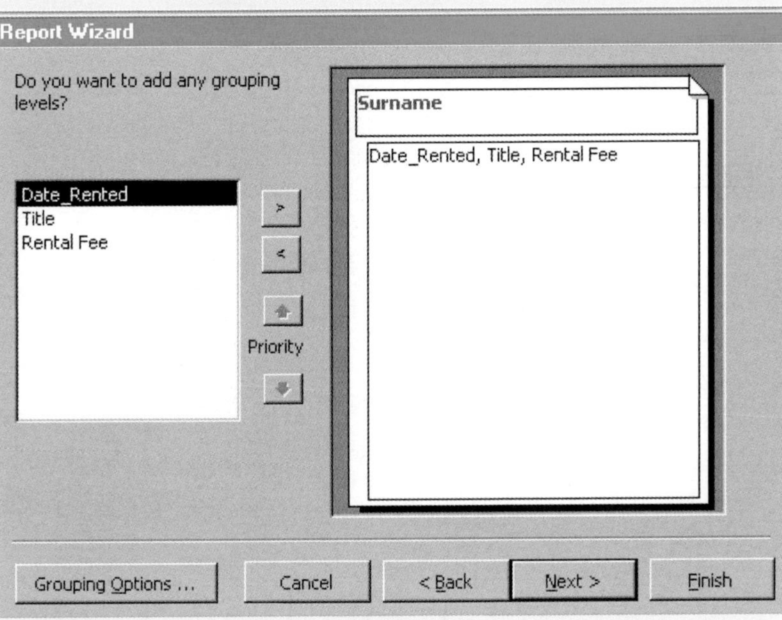

Click on the Next> button.

6 Click on the pull-down arrow and choose to sort by Date_Rented in Ascending order. Your screen will now look like this:

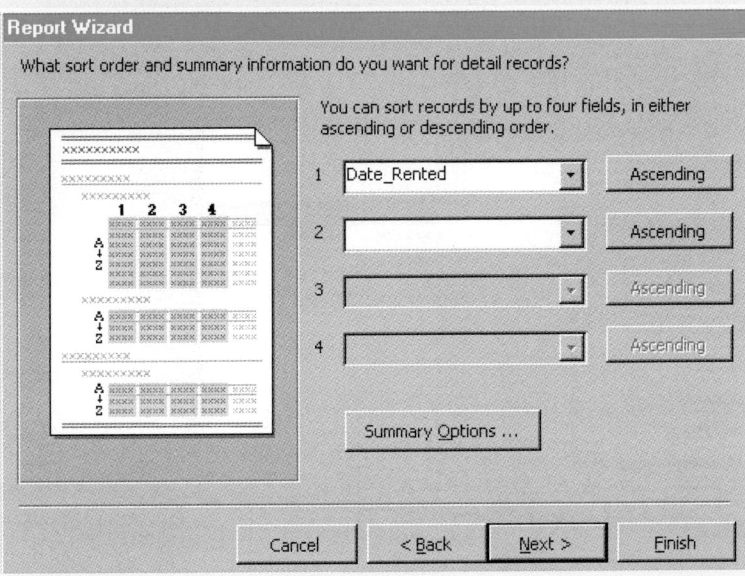

Click on the Next> button.

7 Select the following options from the screen below. Choose Block for the Layout.

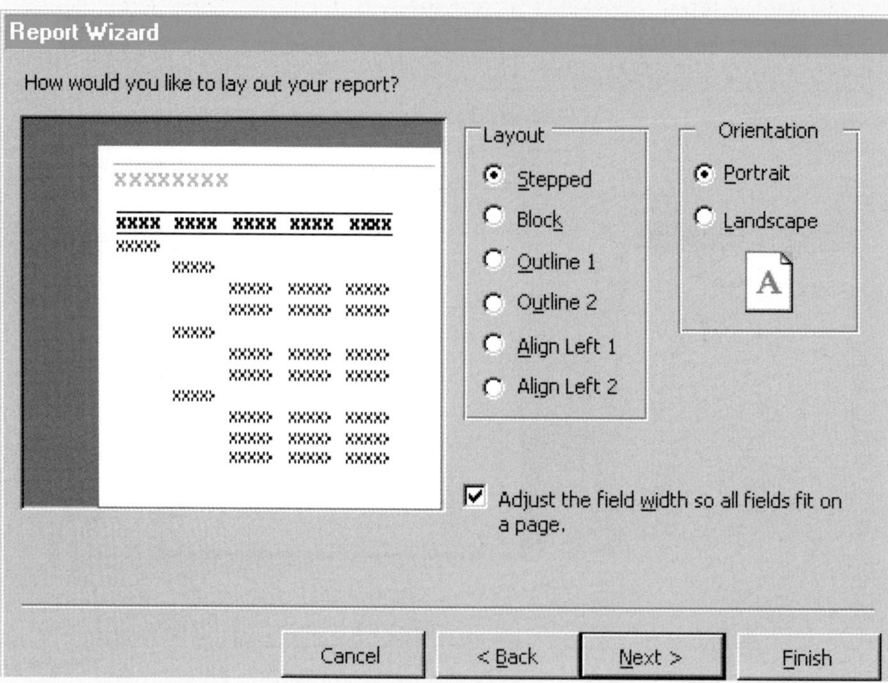

Notice that if you had a lot of fields to fit across the page, you could choose to print in landscape mode. There are not many fields here, so we will stay in portrait mode.

Click on Next>.

8 The screen below appears in which you can specify the style of the report.

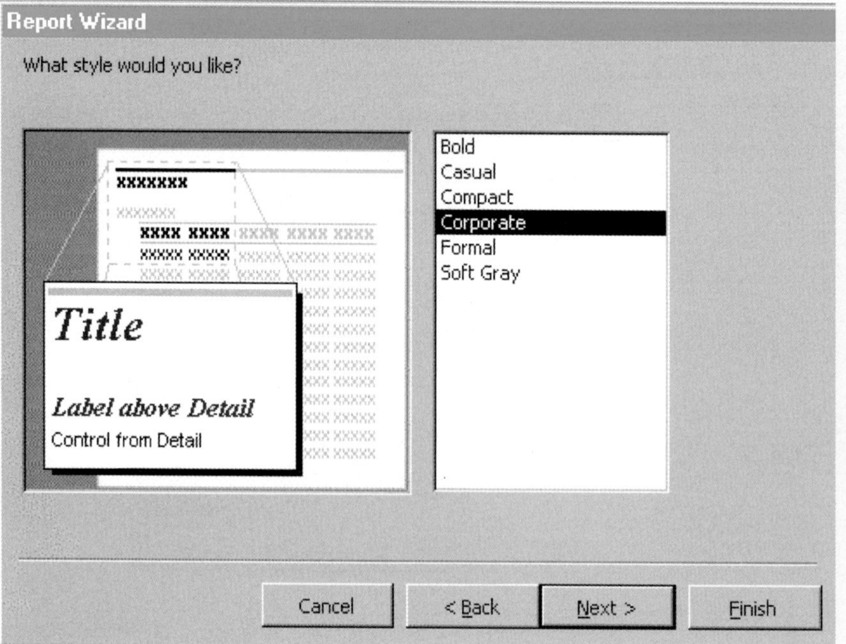

Select Corporate from the list and click on Next>.

9 You now have a screen in which you can enter a name for the report. The name of the query on which the report is based is already inserted. Keep this name. It will not become confused with the query, since the computer is able to distinguish between reports and queries even when they have the same name.

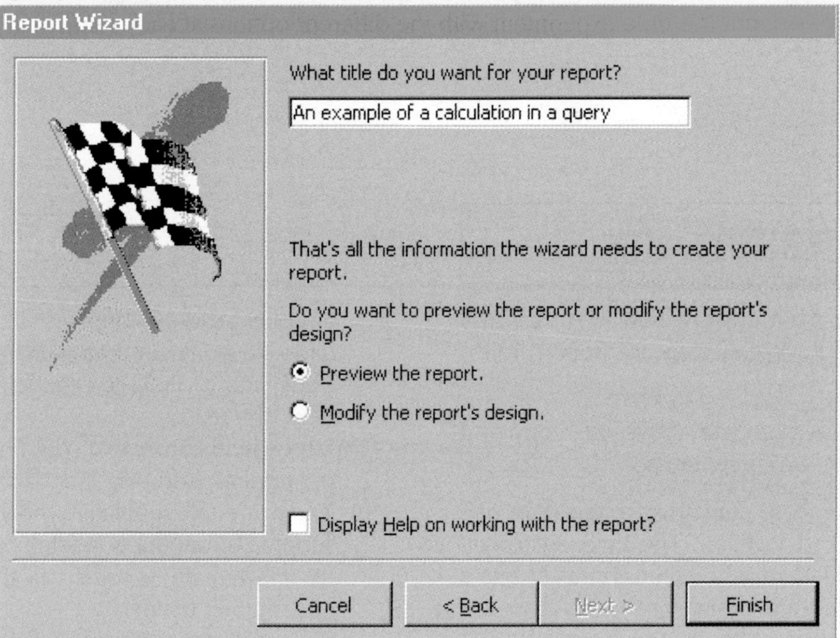

Click on Finish.

10 After a few moments, the following screen will appear.

An example of a calculation in a query

Surname	*Date_Rented*	*Title*	*Rental Fee*
Corkhill			
	03/12/2000	A Simple Plan	£1.50
	03/12/2000	Star Wars Episode 1	£3.50
	04/12/2000	South Park	£3.50
Doyle			
	01/12/2000	The General's Daughter	£2.50
	02/12/2000	The General's Daughter	£2.50
Harrington			
	05/12/2000	Mickey Blue Eyes	£1.50
Hughes			
	03/12/2000	Ravenous	£5.00
	04/12/2000	A Midsummer Nights Dream	£10.50
Johnstone			
	04/12/2000	Eyes Wide Shut	£3.50
	05/12/2000	The General's Daughter	£2.50

11 Click on the Print button to print out the report.

12 Close the window and this will return you to the database screen.

IT TASKS

Try experimenting with the format of the report in Exercise 19.2. Produce printouts and write a couple of sentences explaining what each report shows. You can go back to the beginning again and go through the steps using the wizard, but this time experiment with the different options at each step.

QUESTIONS

1 There are four main objects used in Access and other database packages. They are: report; form; query; table.

Using the words from the above list, copy and complete the following sentences.

A relational database consists of more than one _________ linked together. The links are called relationships. Data may be entered straight into a table, but if you are designing the database for others to use, it is better to use a _________. Once all the data has been entered, you can ask questions of the database using a _________. If the results need to be printed out, it is best to use a _________ since you have more control over the appearance of the printed page.

2 A database is to be set up to store details about suppliers and the products they sell. Rather than hold suppliers and product data together in the same table, it is decided to use two tables instead. Here are the two tables and the names of the fields that they contain.

Supplier table	**Product table**
Supplier_ID	Product_ID
Supplier_Name	Product_Name
Supplier_Address	Supplier_ID
Supplier_Tel_No	

(a) Supplier_Address appears in the Supplier table. It would be better if this was broken down into several separate fields. Why is this? Give one reason.

Give three field names that could be used instead of Supplier_Address.

(b) There are 20 suppliers who between them supply 200 products in total.
   (i) How many records will there be in the supplier table?
   (ii) How many records will there be in the product table?

(c) The Supplier_ID in the Supplier table can appear more than once in the Product table.
   (i) Why is this?
   (ii) What type of relationship will there be between the Supplier table and the Product table?

(d) Briefly explain why it was decided to use two tables rather than just one.

3 (a) Briefly explain the difference between a query and a report.

(b) The results of queries may be printed out in report format. Give one advantage of doing this rather than just printing out the answer to the query.

20 Coursework

There are two parts to any GCSE in IT: the final examination and the project/coursework. The final examination takes place in either May or June, but project work can be started at any time. You will be given a date on which the project work has to be handed in. This date is fixed so you must not miss it under any circumstances.

After working through this book you should be able to see how you can use hardware and software packages to solve IT problems for yourself.

Finding out about a real problem

To solve a particular problem using IT you have to be very clear about what the problem is and what the user wants.

You may be basing your GCSE project around a job that maybe your parents or other relatives need solving and you may know little about the problem itself. It will be easier to develop a really good project if you find out as much about the problem as possible. To do this it is a good idea to meet users and ask them a series of questions about the task. Make sure that you are prepared for this meeting. Produce a questionnaire containing a series of questions asking them about the problem and what they want to be able to get out of the new system.

You will need to tell your teacher about the project you intend to do, and they will advise you on the project's suitability. Above all they will look at how complex the problem is and whether it is suitable for you. They will also assess the timescale needed to complete the project and the resources required (whether your school/college has them).

Coursework

Coursework is work that you undertake on your own using the computer. It is extremely important, since in all the GCSE full courses it will contribute 60% to your final mark. If you are taking a short course, then the coursework will also contribute 60% to your final mark.

What you have to do as part of your course is outlined in a lengthy document called a specification. To obtain the specification you need to know the name of the examining board (i.e. Edexcel, AQA, OCR, CCEA, WJEC), whether you are taking the short or full GCSE and also which specification is required (if the exam board has more than one). You can then use the web address of the exam board to log on to their website where you will find lots of useful information, including the specifications. You can then download the documents you need.

There is a section later on in this chapter which outlines the coursework requirements for each of the specifications and for each of the examination boards.

The whole point of this book is to give you the skills in using popular software so that you can make an informed choice of the software to use for your project/coursework.

Important notes about project work

Here are some important notes about the project work.

1 Your project does not have to be complicated for you to get a good mark.
2 Documenting your project is very important. This supplies your teachers with evidence of your work and enables

them to give your project an accurate mark. Someone from outside your school (called the moderator) will want to look at samples of work from your class. They may ask to see your project to make sure that your teacher has given you a fair mark.

Unlike your teacher, the moderator will not know how much work you have put into your project unless you have written about it and provided evidence.

When you work on your project your motto should be 'evidence all the way'.

As soon as you do something, make sure you write about it or provide printouts with explanations.

3. It is much better if you think up the idea for the project yourself. Your teacher may have to let the exam board know if they have helped you pick one. Your mark may be lowered if they pick a project for you.
4. Always have a real user. They can give you feedback and advise you throughout the project. They can also evaluate your project at the end.
5. You must thoroughly describe your project. Make sure that someone who does not know anything about computers could understand what you have done. Show it to lots of other people to make sure that it is easy to understand. At the same time get them to check that the sentences all make sense.
6. Make sure that you check your work for grammatical and spelling mistakes. Do not just rely on the computer to do this. You should always proof read your work thoroughly.

What software can I use?

As this book covers the skills in Microsoft Office, you will be probably be using this package for most of your project work. Microsoft Office is an integrated package and this means that each part of the software has a similar look and feel to it and it is very easy to transfer data from one application to another. For example, it is very easy to import a spreadsheet into a wordprocessed document.

Discrete packages do just one particular job. You can buy all the parts of Microsoft Office separately.

Here is a list of the general software you should know about for your course:

- databases (relational or flat file)
- spreadsheets
- business graphics (this could also be looked at using database or spreadsheet software)
- wordprocessors
- desktop publishing (this could also be done using a wordprocessing package)
- modelling or simulation packages (you could also use spreadsheet software for this)
- data logging and control packages (there are numerous specialist packages for this).

There are other types of more specialist software which you can use to develop material for your project. Such software includes:

- computer aided design (CAD)
- multimedia
- website design software.

What help is allowed?

Your project must be all your own work. If your teacher suspects that you have had help they will have to let the examination board know. It is pretty easy to see if you have been helped, so it is not worth taking the risk. Cheating is regarded as a very serious matter by the examination boards.

Your teacher may give you some help, but they will prefer not to give you too much as this will have to be recorded and your project mark would be lowered. There may be times when you are struggling trying to get something to work with the software. Your teacher will help you in these circumstances.

If you have a real user (i.e. someone other than yourself or your teacher, who came up with the project) then it is OK to keep asking them advice along the way. Maybe you don't understand the problem or the way they want the output arranged. This kind of help is fine. You should involve your user as much as possible in your project.

What if I get stuck?

Everyone gets stuck at some stage with their project, so don't worry. If you and your teacher have agreed the project beforehand, it should not be too hard for you. Try not to change the project to another one or you might end up going round in circles.

This book only skims the surface of Microsoft Office. There are many features that you might find useful when doing your project. To find out about these you could use:

- computer magazines
- the Help facility provided by Office (this is good because it is free)
- guides/manuals for the software
- websites on the Internet.

You need to get into the habit of seeking help using all of the above. Things move so fast in computing and there isn't always someone around to ask, so get into the habit of finding out for yourself.

You can always ask your teacher but remember that they may not have used the feature you are interested in and will have to find out about features in exactly the same way as you should.

The project steps

Although all projects are very different, there are some steps that can be taken when developing a project. Some of these steps may not be appropriate for every type of project. If you find a step that you cannot do, then do not worry about it, just go on to the next step.

Identify the project

In many ways this is the hardest step. Coming up with the right kind of project is essential to getting a good mark. If it is too simple, you may find it hard to get a high mark. If it is too ambitious or complex then you may not be able to complete it in the time required. You have to be realistic in your choice. Try to choose a project that matches your capabilities.

What is the best way to choose a project?
Ask friends, neighbours and relatives what they do at work. Could you develop a computer system for them to make their job easier? You will have a real user and they can help you understand the problem. You can also get constant feedback from them.

At the start of the project you will need to describe the project. Your problem description could start something like this:

> My father works in a garage. Although the garage mainly sells and repairs used cars there is also a small car hire operation. There are around 20 cars to hire and this part of the business is expanding rapidly. My father would like a way of recording and storing the details about the cars, customers and rentals. At present all the details are stored manually on cards held in filing cabinets. This was fine when the garage only hired a couple of cars each week but with 20 cars, they need to obtain information quickly.
>
> I have decided to use …… software to …… etc.'

In this section it is a good idea to mention the scope of the project. This means how far-reaching the project will be. As well as saying specifically what the project will do, you can also mention what it will not do. If you make the scope of the project too wide, you may not have enough time to complete it or it may be too complicated.

Analyse the problem

If the job you intend to improve is being done at the moment, you could briefly describe how it is being done. You could produce a questionnaire to give to the user so that you can find out further information about the system. You can add this questionnaire and its response to your project documentation.

If the user wants you to develop something new to function in a way they have not done before, you can still use the questionnaire to find out more about what they want you to do. You can either get the user to fill in a questionnaire on their own or preferably sit with them and go through the questions and answers.

Find out where the data needed by your system comes from. For example, customer information for the car hire company would come from the customer. They are usually asked to fill in a form before they are allowed to hire a car.

Diagrams

Use diagrams to help explain the new system. If the new system is to replace an older system you could also use diagrams to help explain the old system. These diagrams could just show how the data flows around the system.

If you want, you could use the specialist diagrams that computer staff use to describe systems. Such diagrams include systems flowcharts, structure diagrams and data flow diagrams. All these diagrams are described fully in the companion book to this one, *Information Systems for You*.

Forms

You could design a data capture form such as an application form, enrolment form, membership form, or order form. Always consult the user whenever you are developing anything for them. Show them your form and ask 'Is this OK?' 'Have I missed anything out?' 'Is there anything I have included that is not really needed?'

Any coding systems you use to save time entering data need to be explained in this section.

Performance criteria

As part of the analysis you should include the performance criteria. The performance criteria are a list and explanation of those things by which your new system will be judged to have been a success. You can look at the requirements of the system and then check that your system meets them. As part of the performance criteria you will need to consider how to make sure that your solution meets the requirements exactly.

Explain your choice of software

If you are considering a project to store and manipulate data you need to look at the types of software you could use. You could use a spreadsheet if the database is simple or it might be better to use a specialist database. It is important to consider the two and decide which to choose. Again, you should write briefly about the alternative software choices and the reasons for your choice. If you reject a particular piece of software, you should state your reasons for doing so. If your choice has been restricted by the hardware or software your school has, you should mention this too.

The following systems may have to be evaluated and a choice made between:

- DTP or wordprocessor, since many wordprocessors also contain DTP features
- database using a database program or a database using a spreadsheet program
- graphics using a specialist graphics package or as part of wordprocessing or spreadsheet software
- modelling using specialist modelling software or using spreadsheet software.

If you are choosing a particular type of wordprocessor, such as Word XP, you should say why this was chosen, because there are many different wordprocessing products all doing a very similar job. It is fine to argue that you chose a particular one because you knew how to use it or because it was the only one available.

You should also say what features of the particular piece of software you intend to use for your solution (e.g. I will be using the mail merge facility in Microsoft Word XP).

If your solution involves calculations, you need to explain these calculations.

If your solution involves a relational database you must describe how you decided on the number of tables and the fields in each table. You would also need to describe your choice of primary key fields and the relationships between the tables.

During the analysis stage, you need to consider what output you are going to get from the system. Is this output going to be on paper or on screen? Remember you cannot output anything from your system that has not been input or calculated from the data input. Think also what data needs to be input to obtain the output. Where does the input data come from?

Finally, consider the validation and verification methods you will use.

Produce a testing strategy so that you can check when you come to the implementation/ testing stage that the results are correct. Think about what you can test for.

Finally, consider the criteria by which you can evaluate the project at the end.

Testing your solution

This is not proper testing

You need to identify a set of suitable data to be entered into the system for testing. Some of this data should be of the wrong type (i.e. letters where numbers should be entered and vice versa). Some of this data should be of the wrong size so that it fails the validation checks. It is important that both wrong and right data are entered.

Sometimes when a system is developed it does not do what the user wanted it to do. Maybe the person developing the system has not understood exactly what the user wanted. To prevent this from happening, the developer should agree with the user a list of things that the new system must be capable of doing. This is called the project specification.

During the testing it is important to make sure that all the items in the list have been included in the project. You could produce a table showing this and then place a tick and the date next to each item when it has been completed. This makes sure that there are no important parts missing.

Design the solution to the problem

Try not to approach the problem like this

Try to approach it like this

Start with a problem and then choose the best type of software for the job

In this section you have to describe how you have designed the solution to the problem. As part of the design of the system you need to mention briefly your choice of software and what hardware is needed to run it. Any peripheral devices (e.g. scanners, printers, digital cameras) should be mentioned.

If you have produced a database, you should supply a printout of the file structure. Also include details of any validation checks you have built into the database and say which types of errors these checks are capable of finding.

Examples of any user interfaces, such as forms to enter data into a database, should be included here. A good way to provide evidence is to produce screen dumps. You should make it clear that you have considered the user in your design. Maybe you changed the colours of the text and the background to make it easy on the user's eyes? You could also explain why you have positioned fields in a database in certain places on the screen.

Flowcharts can be used to help explain the design process as well as structure or systems diagrams.

If you have produced a control system where the production of printouts would not be evidence that the thing works, you can always video or photograph the equipment working.

Throughout the design process you may have some rough work such as draft designs. Include these in your documentation as your teacher/moderator will be able to see how your project has progressed.

Reusability

When you design a solution to a problem there are often situations where you need to change the data in the future. Maybe you have produced a spreadsheet to show the cash flowing into and out of a business for a particular year. This spreadsheet may be used at a later date with new figures: it could be next week, next month or next year. You would need to explain how this could be done. Many systems need to be designed to be re-usable and you can supply evidence of this in the user guide.

Use/implement

In this section you have to describe how the system was implemented. This means you describe how you got to the stage of actually using the system. You must show evidence that you have completed the system in a clear and methodical manner.

If the old system used paper files, the data on these files may have had to be input into your computer system before you could start to use the new system. How was this done and how long did it take? You could include a diary of events with the times and dates when each part of the project was completed.

As part of this section you should provide evidence of using the system to solve the problem. For example, in the car hire firm example you could include the following:

- a list of your customers sorted into surname order
- a list of cars sorted into order according to the date they were first registered
- a query to obtain the details of those cars that are due for a service or MOT test
- a report showing the models of cars hired by different customers over the last month.

You should include the printouts as evidence that your solution actually works. To make it easy for your teacher/moderator to understand the purpose of the printouts you should write on them why they were done and what they show. For example, if you have made a query using database software, you should add comments about the purpose of the query and also some information on how the query was produced.

Sometimes you may not be able to get the right output because your design did not cover it. You may therefore have to alter your design. An example of this might be leaving an important field out of a database and not finding the deficiency until you wanted the field in a query or report. It is OK to go back and make alterations to your design as long as you mention here why you did it.

Testing your solution is extremely important. You need to be sure that it is giving you the right answers. You will need to develop a testing plan. In this plan you must describe what tests you are going to perform and how you intend to perform them. You should include the results expected and those actually obtained. The results of tests can be tabulated.

In many projects you can prevent the user from entering wildly wrong data by using validation checks. These validation checks need to be described. If you include validation checks, make sure that they are tested by entering extreme data as well as allowable data.

If the testing reveals weaknesses these should be investigated further and corrections made.

Include a section that describes how to use your system. This is often called a 'user guide'. You could also include some training exercises for the user to familiarise themselves with the package.

It is perfectly permissible to make changes to your system to get it to work. Make sure that you include evidence to support the changes.

When you think you have completed the project ask yourself this: 'Is the project at the stage where others could successfully use it without any problems?'

Evaluate the solution to the problem

If you have developed a project for someone else to use, you should let them do so and note down their comments. Do not worry if the comments are not all positive. Given time you could use these comments to make improvements to the system.

In the evaluation section you need to comment on your solution. These comments need to refer back to the original problem. How effective was it? What difficulties did you encounter? If you had the time to start again would you still do it the same way? What limitations does the system have? Did you make any compromises along the way? What modifications had to be made? Most importantly, what did the user think of your solution to their problem? How satisfied were they?

To find out about the user's comments you could devise a short questionnaire and hand it to them. They may be more blunt in a questionnaire rather than a face-to-face meeting.

If there is more than one user you could include quotes of what exactly was said about your solution.

You should avoid any of your own comments which sound like this:

> 'I thought it worked well and really enjoyed doing the project'.

You are free to criticise your own work; you will not be marked down for doing so. It is important to be able to identify the shortcomings in your work and be able to spot improvements that could be made to the system if you had more time.

Project checklist

On the next page is a project checklist that will help you make sure that you have included everything you need for your coursework. You can photocopy this and tick each item off as you do it. Do not worry if you do not have ticks in every box as not all the parts can be included for every type of project. Tick the box and fill in the date as you finish each stage.

Spelling, punctuation and grammar

Since marks are offered for spelling, punctuation and grammar it makes sense to do all you can to get it right.

- Use a spellchecker.
- Obey all the rules of punctuation.
- Proof read anything you have written several times before handing it in.
- Use a grammar checker.
- Get other people to look through your work to see if it makes sense.

Project checklist

Stage	Description of documentation	Tick when completed	Date completed
Identify	Identified and defined the problem		
Identify	Defined the scope of the project (i.e. what it will cover and what it won't)		
Analyse	Collected facts from the user		
Analyse	Analysed the way the job is done now		
Analyse	Analysed the way it is proposed to do the job using the new system		
Analyse	Produced diagrams of old and new systems		
Analyse	Considered where the data used by the system comes from		
Analyse	Explained and justified the choice of software		
Analyse	Explained any alternative systems considered and mentioned reasons for their rejection		
Analyse	Described the features of the software packages that will be used		
Analyse	Explained the processing that needs to be performed		
Analyse	Considered the output required by the user		
Analyse	Looked at the validation and verification methods that could be used with the system		
Analyse	Described the criteria that will be used to evaluate the system		
Analyse	Described how the system will be tested		
Design	Identified the hardware and software needed to run the system		
Design	Explained how the system has been designed		
Design	Produced draft designs		
Design	Used diagrams/flowcharts to illustrate the design process		
Design	Produced screenshots/photographs to show the design		
Use/imp.	Explained how the system was implemented		
Use/imp.	Completed a diary of times for the implementation		
Use/imp.	Produced annotated printouts to show how the system can be used		
Use/imp.	Showed how the system was modified after user's comments		
Use/imp.	Produced results of the testing		
Use/imp.	Explained how the system was modified (if needed) due to test results revealing weaknesses in the system		
Use/imp.	Documented the system for others to use		
Evaluate	Evaluated the system using the evaluation criteria		
Evaluate	Sought the user's comments on the system		
Evaluate	Produced your own comments on the system together with mention of any improvements		

How do I get a really high mark?

To get a really high mark for your project work you have to make sure that the problem is sufficiently complex to allow you to demonstrate your skills.

Although you tend to learn your skills in sections (e.g. wordprocessing, spreadsheets, databases, graphics, etc.) you need to consider the full range of software to solve a problem.

For example, the overall problem you might be looking at could be producing a short magazine for a pop or football fan club.

You could just go ahead and concentrate on the magazine itself and get involved in the DTP package. But for a really high mark you might consider the following:

- Because the contributors to the magazine use wordprocessing packages you need to explain how their work on disk is incorporated into the DTP document.
- You may need pictures for your magazine (photographs of members of the pop group or football team). Where did you get them (you might need to get them off the Internet or scan them in or even use a digital camera)?
- You will need to keep records of your members. How are these kept? How will you know when their subscriptions are due? Is there an easy way to send letters to lots of people?
- When they join members are probably given a membership card. How is this card designed and produced?

As you can see, the problem can be expanded to give more tasks to attempt and document and hopefully this will get a much better mark.

Hints and tips for coursework

Here are some hints and tips to help you obtain the best mark you can for your coursework.

- Documentation is very important. Do not try to simply solve the problem. It is more important to show that you have carried out correct analysis, design and implementation.
- Annotate and explain any work you do. Do not simply produce printouts without any explanation.
- Make your solutions efficient. For example, in a database system, do not duplicate data.
- The user guide should be about using the software rather than how the solution to the problem was created. It is important to mention how the user would perform the day to day tasks.

Discussion

Here are a few project ideas. Discuss these among yourselves and with your teacher to see how you can expand the initial problem.

1. Produce of a range of letters your form teacher or year head could send to pupils' parents.
2. Design a spreadsheet to summarise and display examination results for the school, to be used by the headteacher and other senior staff.
3. See how hot different cups keep a hot drink.
4. Look at the relationship between the voltage, current and resistance in a circuit.
5. Develop a model to see how much change there would be in an electricity bill if low voltage bulbs were used throughout the house. How long would it take for the saving to cover the extra cost in the bulbs?
6. Organise the running of a school event (a play, disco, barbecue, sponsored walk, etc.)

Coursework for your examination board

Because the type of coursework you have to do differs so much from one examination board to another, it is impossible to look in detail at the requirements for each one. Your teacher/lecturer will give you details about what is expected.

There follows a brief summary for the main examination boards.

Edexcel Full Course

Coursework accounts for 60% of the total marks for the course and consists of four coursework problems of equal weighting. Two of the coursework problems have to be on:

- creation and manipulation of spreadsheets, or
- creation and manipulation of databases.

The other two coursework problems are to be chosen from the following list:

- Data logging and control
- Word processing
- Desktop publishing
- Website publishing
- Multimedia
- Programming
- Free choice 1
- Free choice 2.

If a really complex problem is tackled then it could be split into two smaller problems. For example, you could have a problem requiring the use of databases and mail merge. This would then count as two coursework problems.

For each of the four problems you have solved, you will need to keep notes to provide evidence for your solution. These notes should be structured under the following headings:

- Identify
- Analyse
- Design
- Use and/or implement
- Evaluate.

You may not always be able to put notes under each of these headings since the headings may not be suitable for certain solutions.

Edexcel Short Course

Coursework accounts for 60% of the total marks for the course and consists of two coursework problems of equal weighting.

At least one of these coursework problems has to be on:

- creation and manipulation of spreadsheets, or
- creation and manipulation of databases.

If you only choose one of the problems above, then the other task is to be taken from the following list:

- Data logging and control
- Word processing
- Desktop publishing
- Website publishing
- Multimedia
- Programming
- Free choice 1
- Free choice 2.

For each of the two problems you have solved, you will need to keep notes to provide evidence for your solution. These notes should be structured under the following headings:

- Identify
- Analyse
- Design
- Use and/or implement
- Evaluate.

You may not always be able to put notes for your solution under each of these headings since the headings may not be suitable for certain solutions.

CCEA Full Course

Coursework accounts for 60% of the total marks for the course. There will be six assignments set by CCEA, which are internally assessed (i.e. assessed by your teacher) and externally moderated. Some of the assignments will enable you to incorporate ICT-related work carried out in other subjects.

The emphasis on the coursework will be *quality* rather than *quantity*.

The topics for the coursework will change from year to year. Here are the ones chosen for first examination in Summer 2003.

A1 Design a multimedia presentation

A2 Produce a booklet or report

A3 Design a website

B1 Using the Internet

B2 Garden World (plants database and customer database)

B3 Mobile phones

CCEA Short Course

Coursework makes up 60% of the total assessment mark and consists of four assignments that are set by the exam board CCEA, assessed by your teacher and externally moderated. Some of the assignments will allow you to incorporate ICT-related work that you have carried out in other subjects.

The emphasis on the coursework will be *quality* rather than *quantity*.

The topics for the coursework will change from year to year. Here are the ones chosen for first examination in Summer 2003.

For the short course, you will be required to do one piece of coursework from A1, A2 or A3 and all the Section B coursework.

A1 Design a multimedia presentation

A2 Produce a booklet or report

A3 Design a website

B1 Using the Internet

B2 Garden World (plants database and customer database)

B3 Mobile phones

AQA Specification A

Full course

Coursework contributes 60% to the final assessment and consists of an assignment and a project.

AQA-set Assignment	*30% of total marks*

The AQA-set assignment consists of a situation where the appropriate use of ICT will solve some given problems. This will be described in a booklet that you will be given.

For this assignment you will have to produce a report that demonstrates your ability to analyse a problem in order to identify what the requirements are. You are also required to make use of ICT to provide solutions, which you will then design, implement, test and evaluate.

Project	*30% of total marks*

Candidates are required to submit a report on the solution to a problem that demonstrates their ICT capabilities. Wherever possible, you should select a problem from your own area of interest.

Short course

Coursework contributes 60% to the final assessment mark and consists of an assignment set by AQA.

AQA-set Assignment	*60% of total marks*

The AQA-set assignment consists of a situation where the appropriate use of ICT will solve some given problems. This will be described in a booklet that you will be given.

For this assignment you will have to produce a report that demonstrates your ability to analyse a problem in order to identify what the requirements are. You are also required to make use of ICT to provide solutions, which you will then design, implement, test and evaluate.

AQA Specification B

Full course

Coursework contributes 60% to the final assessment mark.

Candidates are required to submit reports on two coursework tasks, one from each of the following areas:

- Communicating and handling information
- Controlling, measuring and modelling

The tasks will:

- involve using ICT to solve a problem
- address a need (e.g. a third party may have asked you to design and implement a solution to a problem).

Short Course
Coursework contributes 60% to the final assessment.

Candidates are required to submit a report on one coursework task from either of the two following themes:

- Communicating and handling information
- Controlling, measuring and modelling.

The task will:

- involve using ICT to solve a problem
- address a need (e.g. a third party may have asked you to design and implement a solution to a problem).

WJEC Full Course

For the final assessment, 60% of the marks are based on coursework. The coursework consists of a portfolio and a project (30% for each).

The portfolio of work is assessed and it should demonstate your capabilities in: obtaining and interpreting different types of information; using, developing and communicating information to meet the purpose of your studies; and presenting the results of your work. This is achieved through tasks involving:

- information handling
- spreadsheet modelling
- communicating information.

The details of these tasks are summarised here.

Task 1: Information handling

- Identify information needed and suitable sources.
- Carry out effective searches.
- Select information that is relevant to your purpose.

Task 2: Spreadsheet modelling

- Enter and bring together information using formats that help development.
- Explore information needed for the purpose.
- Develop information and derive new information as appropriate.

Task 3: Communicating information

- Select and use appropriate layouts for presenting combined information in a consistent way.
- Develop the presentation to suit the purpose and the type of information.
- Ensure work is accurate, clear and saved appropriately.

The project involves submitting a report on the solution to a problem that demonstrates your information systems capability.

You must also make sure that your project is based on elements not covered by the portfolio.

There are four sections you have to include in your project and these are:

- the statement of the problem and its analysis
- the design of the solution
- the development of the solution
- an evaluation.

WJEC Short Course

For the final assessment, 60% of the marks are based on coursework. The coursework for the short course consists of a portfolio.

The portfolio of work is assessed; it should demonstate your capabilities in: obtaining and interpreting different types of information; using, developing and communicating information to meet the purpose of your studies and presenting the results of your work. This is achieved through tasks involving:

- information handling
- spreadsheet modelling
- communicating information.

The details of these tasks are summarised here.

Task 1: Information handling

- Identify information needed and suitable sources.
- Carry out effective searches.
- Select information that is relevant to your purpose.

Task 2: Spreadsheet modelling

- Enter and bring together information using formats that help development.
- Explore information needed for the purpose.
- Develop information and derive new information as appropriate.

Task 3: Communicating information

- Select and use appropriate layouts for presenting combined information in a consistent way.
- Develop the presentation to suit the purpose and the type of information.
- Ensure work is accurate, clear and saved appropriately.

OCR Specification A

Full Course

Coursework accounts for 60% of the total assessment marks. The specification for the full course consists of four units and two of these units are assessed by coursework. Unit 2 is assessed by two pieces of coursework called Project 1a and Project 1b. Unit 4 is assessed by a piece of coursework called Project 2. Projects 1a and 1b together carry the same number of marks as Project 2.

Here is what each project covers:

Title	Topic
Project 1a	Mostly communication and directly related to key skills.
Project 1b	A piece of work related to handling data, modelling, measurement or control.
Project 2	A piece of work related to systems design.

You are free to choose the tasks with the help of your teacher or your teacher may compose tasks for you to do.

Short Course

Coursework accounts for 60% of the total assessment marks.

The specification for the short course consists of two units and one of these units is assessed by coursework. Unit 2 is assessed by two pieces of coursework called Project 1a and Project 1b.

Projects 1a and 1b together carry equal marks.

Here is what each of these projects cover:

Title	Topic
Project 1a	Mostly communication and directly related to key skills.
Project 1b	A piece of work related to handling data, modelling, measurement or control.

OCR Specification B

Full Course

Coursework accounts for 60% of the total assessment marks. The specification for the full course consists of four units and two of these units (i.e. Units 2 and 3) are assessed by coursework.

Unit 2 coursework consists of a coursework task which is set by OCR. You will be given twelve hours to complete this task in semi-controlled conditions. You will have to log the time you spend at school/college and at home to complete the task. The twelve hours that you are given does not include time for research, investigation and practice.

For this task you will be required to explore the use of ICT systems, data handling and processing and explore hardware and software requirements. The portfolio will need to provide evidence and this evidence can be in the form of logs of time spent, photographs, taped and video evidence, supported witness statements or paper-based evidence.

Unit 3 coursework extends the coursework you have completed for Unit 2 and you will choose one area that you are interested in and develop it further. You will be given another twelve hours to complete this.

Short Course
Coursework accounts for 60% of the total assessment marks. The specification for the full course consists of two units and one of these units (i.e. Unit 2) is assessed by coursework.

Unit 2 coursework consists of a coursework task which is set by OCR. You will be given twelve hours to complete this task in semi-controlled conditions. You will have to log the time you spend at school/college and at home to complete the task. The twelve hours that you are given does not include time for research, investigation and practice.

For this task you will be required to explore the use of ICT systems, data handling and processing and explore hardware and software requirements. The portfolio will need to provide evidence and this evidence can be in the form of logs of time spent, photographs, taped and video evidence, supported witness statements or paper-based evidence.

Project choices

The following list gives you some ideas for projects. The idea of these lists is not to give you a project title because your project will be a lot better if you have a real user. Instead it is to show you a range of typical projects so that you can see the sorts of things you could do. Do not worry if your project is not listed.

Database software

- Car/van hire.
- Equipment hire companies (e.g. HSS).
- Video/games/DVD hire.
- Mail order companies (CDs, books, clothes, wine, household goods, cosmetics, gardening, etc.).
- Clubs (health, sports, football, fan, etc.).
- School library.
- Health centre.
- Estate agent.
- Music collection for a DJ in a club.
- Tool/equipment hire store.
- Appointments system for a hairdresser/beautician.
- Medical records.
- Keeping records of the computer hardware, software and peripherals in a school/college/company.
- Production of a stock control system.
- Flat rental agency.
- Temporary staff agency.
- Talent/model agency.
- Computer dating agency.
- Dress hire company.
- Database for places of interest in your area.
- Healthy eating database (research whether pupils in your year have a healthy lifestyle).
- Database for the running of a riding school.
- Fancy dress hire.

Wordprocessing software

- Produce a pack of information for students taking GCSE IT.
- Produce a range of leaflets to advertise weekend breaks in a hotel near to where you live (also include details of the local attractions).

Presentation software

- A presentation outlining the advantages of being a member of a health/fitness club.
- A presentation of a new product (e.g. toy, computer chip, computer software, etc.).
- A presentation opposing the development of a new housing estate on a wood inhabited by many wild animals.

Graphics design software

- Garden design for a landscape gardener.
- Designing a bathroom, bedroom, kitchen or conservatory.
- Production of network diagrams.
- Producing the design for an office.

Spreadsheet

- Managing a car park where the places are paid for annually.
- Producing a booking system for a school play.
- Finding the value of stock in a shop.

Modelling

- Modelling the throwing of two dice and seeing how the probability compares with the theoretical probability.
- Find the optimum area for a sheep pen given a particular length of fencing.
- A model of the queues at a supermarket checkout.
- A model of the traffic at a busy junction without traffic lights.
- A model to consider why buses always seem to arrives in threes.
- A model to look at how a pedestrian crossing affects the traffic flow along a busy road.
- A model of traffic flow along a busy road when there are roadworks so that vehicles in only one lane are able to pass along a quarter of a mile section of the road at the same time.
- A model to show how the population of tadpoles varies in a garden pond.
- A model of the money obtained from growing a crop in a field (potatoes, apples, vines, Christmas trees).
- A model of a flu epidemic using spreadsheet software.

Multimedia

- Produce a multimedia guide to your school.

Controlling and measuring

- Controlling the temperature and humidity in an art gallery where priceless paintings are housed.
- Controlling the temperature, humidity and watering in a greenhouse for growing tropical plants.
- Using Logo to produce patterns or shapes.
- Controlling a set of traffic lights.
- A computer controlled security system to protect a priceless exhibition of jewellery.
- The collecting and subsequent analysis of weather data.
- A burglar alarm system.
- Railway signaling/safety systems.

Can I use more than one piece of software for a single project?

You are not restricted to using a single package for your project. You could use several. For example, rather than create the data for a mail merge in Word, you could create the data in Access and use this data to perform the mail merge.

Here are a few projects where more than one software package would be needed.

Project 1

A database for secondhand vehicles

In such a database, customers could submit information about their vehicles. Customers would pay a small fee for the service and the details of each vehicle would be stored on a database.

This system could include some of the following:

- a data capture sheet created using wordprocessing software
- a digital camera system used to capture images of the vehicles for sale
- the creation of a database to contain the details of the vehicles for sale and their photographs
- use of the database for searching for vehicles matching the search criteria.

You could even try to develop a website for this company. Start by just advertising a couple of the best car bargains on it.

Project 2

Promotional material

Produce a set of promotional material for a new company.

To do this you might use the following:

- design software to produce a logo for the company
- a DTP package to produce a design for a business card
- a wordprocessing package to produce headed paper (you can import the logo you have designed)
- either DTP or wordprocessing to produce posters advertising the company's products and services.

Project 3

Designing cups

A company that manufactures cups for vending machines needs to conduct an investigation into the best types of cup to keep hot drinks hot.

You could:

- use sensors with data logging software to investigate the heat-keeping properties of certain types of cup
- enter the temperature measurements into spreadsheet software for analysis of the results. You could use the spreadsheet software to draw graphs.

Project 4

Monitoring heart rate

For this project, you could use

- data logging hardware and software to monitor heart rate before and after vigorous exercise (e.g. jogging, running up and down stairs, or using an exercise bike)
- a spreadsheet to show the effect of age and weight on the measurements
- wordprocessing software to produce a report, and import spreadsheets and charts into the report.

Examination Board websites

All the examining boards have their own websites. You will find the specification details here and some of the websites contain past examination papers and useful information such as sample projects.

AQA

www.aqa.org.uk

OCR

www.ocr.org.uk

Edexcel

www.edexcel.org.uk

CCEA

info@ccea.org.uk
www.ccea.org.uk/index.htm

WJEC

www.wjec.co.uk

21 The Example Project

The following project was submitted for the GCSE ICT examination. It is included here as an example showing what a project might look like. This project is not perfect, and after the project there is a section explaining what is good and bad about it. Each examination board has a different set of requirements so it is important to make sure that you meet the requirements of your own examination board.

You will see that this student has chosen to do a project based around a database and wordprocessing package. You are free to choose the most appropriate packages to solve your own problem.

The aim of the example project is to give you some idea of what is required. Most exam boards also supply specimen projects which your teacher may show you. Look at these closely but do not copy any part of them.

Example Project: Weight Watchers Slimming Club

GCSE ICT Project: Amy Hughes 2003

Identify section

The problem

Weight Watchers Slimming Club is a large company that helps people lose weight. They hold classes where people who want to lose weight get weighed and receive encouragement. The classes are held all around the country.

My mother, Mary Hughes, is an area organiser. She has people who organise the groups of slimmers at various venues in the city. Groups are organised by people called 'leaders'. My mother currently has 20 leaders working for her and each leader holds between one and ten classes.

My mother is responsible for all of the classes (currently 70) and all the leaders of all her groups. When a new member comes to the group they fill in an application form. The personal details of each member are written onto a card and then these cards are placed in a card box for that particular class. As some leaders have ten classes and classes can have as many as 60 members in them, there are a lot of details to hold.

My mother will supply me with any information I need and she is hoping to actually use the system when I have completed it. I will not have time to input everyone's details but I will type in a sample which will be sufficient to check whether it is working properly and to allow the user to evaluate it.

1

GCSE ICT Project: Amy Hughes 2003

Analyse section

The current system

At present the system uses small cards. Here is what goes on at the moment:

- Members fill in an application form when they join and the leader writes their details onto the cards.
- They are then allocated a class and a leader.
- The cards are stored in box files in alphabetical order according to surname.
- Each class is in a different section in the box file.
- There is also a box file containing cards with the personal details of the leaders on them. These cards are in alphabetical order according to surname.
- Letters have to be sent to members, and at present finding the data and then typing the letters takes a lot of time.

Problems with the current system

There are lots of problems with the manual system. Here are some of them:

- The details on the card are written by hand and often they are hard to read.
- Alterations are frequently made (change of address, change of name, etc.) and lots of crossing out makes the details on the cards hard to read.
- Members forget which class they are in so it means going through all the cards to find out.
- Searching for specific information such as the names of members who are over 60 is very time-consuming.
- Personal details about members are stored and the security of card boxes is not sufficient. We have to comply with the Data Protection Act.

The new system

Hardware

The following hardware is desirable for this system:

- PC with Pentium 4 processor. A superfast processor.
- 256 MB of RAM will make the system fast, especially when the mail merge is being performed.
- 15" TFT flat panel monitor. This will take up less space on the desk.
- 80 GB hard drive. Plenty of storage here for lots of programs and data.
- 56 K data/fax/voice modem. Needed in order to contact some members in the future by e-mail. Also needed to register the software and get upgrades.
- CD-RW (this could be used to back-up both programs and data).

A system like this would cost around £700 including VAT.

Additional hardware:

- A laser printer (black and white to produce fast and high quality printouts).

2

GCSE ICT Project: Amy Hughes 2003

Software

Microsoft Windows XP (the latest operating system from Microsoft).
Microsoft Office XP Professional. This package includes:

- Access (a relational database)
- Word (a wordprocessing package).

Also desirable would be:

- a virus-checking program and a web browser. (This could be provided by an Internet service provider.)

Inputs

There are currently around 1000 members in my mother's groups. Their details will need to be converted from the cards to computer records. It is suggested that new member details are put straight onto the computer. The other members can be added when time permits. It is essential that the details are added as soon as possible.

Outputs

My mother will be able to extract any data held in the table when producing queries and reports. It could be information about the members in each class, the personal details of leaders and so on. It is important to hold names and address details so that mail merges can be performed to enable personalised letters to be sent to members or leaders. Using queries, you can just send letters to certain members.

Process

The data is stored in tables so that further processing is made easy. Some of the data will be processed to produce queries, reports, sorts, searches, etc. Other data will be used to produce mail-merged letters to send to certain groups of people.

Backup/security

Backing up on a floppy disk is not feasible for this database as it is too big. Normally, the data will be stored on the hard drive. Backup will be stored on a CD, written using the CD-RW and the backup CD will be put into my mother's briefcase and taken home each night. She will have to remember to take the CD out of the machine in case the machine is stolen.

Security is ensured by using a password to gain access to the database. This will make the data more secure than the present manual system.

Scope of my project (i.e. what my project will and won't cover)

The new system will deal with the following:

- Recording details of members, leaders and classes.
- Searching for specific information for the benefit of leaders and the area organiser.

3

GCSE ICT Project: Amy Hughes 2003

- Sending personalised letters to the members.

The following are outside the scope of the system:

- The payments made by members for their classes.
- The payments made to the leaders and area organiser.
- Orders for products that Weight Watchers Slimming Club sell at their meetings.

Objectives of the new system

I have discussed the objectives for the new system with my mother. We came up with this list.

- The system must be easy to use as many leaders have little experience of ICT.
- The system must hold accurate information on members, classes and leaders.
- It must be able to supply the area organiser with information to help them manage their area.

Benefits of the new system

Area organisers and leaders are paid on the basis of the numbers enrolled. Any time saved on administration can be put into recruiting new members or retaining existing members. This will mean that the leaders and my mother will earn more money.

- It is much easier to chase up members who have not attended.
- Alterations such as changes of address, changes of phone numbers, etc., are made easier.
- There will not be the problem of having to decipher handwriting on the cards.
- Letters can be sent out using mail merge.

Performance criteria

We have agreed that the project should be judged against the following performance criteria:

- The system is designed to make learning the system easy.
- The system needs to reduce the time taken to process enquiries.
- The system needs to be more secure than the existing manual system.
- A reduction in the overall paperwork needed to do the job.
- Fast access to information.
- Forms are used to make data entry easy.
- Only relevant data is stored by the system.
- Checks are in place to make sure that invalid data is not entered into the system.
- Data duplication is to be minimised.
- Data is to be stored and reported in a logical order.
- It should be easy to produce letters using data from the database.

4

GCSE ICT Project: Amy Hughes 2003

Design section

Alternative ways I considered solving the problem

In school we learnt how to create a small database using a spreadsheet. This database would be limited to a single set of data. I need more than one set of data so this rules out the use of a spreadsheet. I need to hold details about the following:

- leaders
- members
- classes.

We learnt about how data can be stored in tables and these tables can be related to each other. This would be useful since we can combine data in any of the tables. I therefore decided to use a relational database. The one we use is called Microsoft Access and is part of the Microsoft Office XP package.

My mother wants to send letters to members so I needed to find out how this would be done. I could create the data for the mail merge using the wordprocessing package Word but as the data is already in the database, it would be easier to use this data. Also, having two sets of data about the same thing would be confusing and hard to keep up-to-date. I do not know how to do this, but I intend to use the Help facilities in the packages and books to find out. Using the data in the database to perform the mail merge has the advantage that if the data in the database is changed, then the mail merge will always use the latest version of the data. I have also heard that you can do searches and then send letters only to certain members, such as women over 12 stone, men over the age of 50, etc.

The first thing I need to create is a system data flow diagram. This will show the data which flows into and out of the system.

Data flow diagram

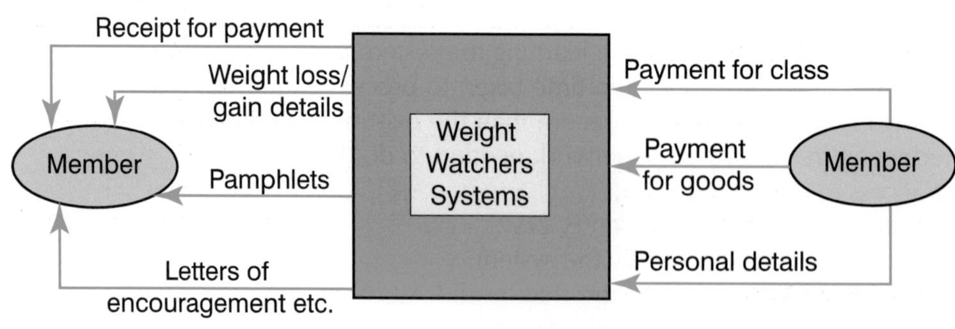

5

GCSE ICT Project: Amy Hughes 2003

I have discussed with my user what output is required from the system and I have used this to work out the various tables I will need to produce.

These fields are grouped according to whether they are data about members, classes or leaders.

Here is a list of the fields that would need to be held:

Name of field	Data type	Group (table)	Validation check
Leader no	Number	Leaders	>= 0 and <1000
Surname	Text	Leaders	None
Forename	Text	Leaders	None
Street	Text	Leaders	None
Town	Text	Leaders	None
Postcode	Text	Leaders	None
Telephone no	Text	Leaders	Input mask
Class number	Number	Leaders	> = 0 and < 80
Member number	AutoNumber	Members	None
Forename	Text	Members	None
Surname	Text	Members	None
Street	Text	Members	None
Area	Text	Members	None
Telephone no	Text	Members	None
Date of birth	Date/time	Members	None
Height	Text	Members	None
Starting weight (st & lb)	Text	Members	None
Class number	Autonumber	Class	None
Class venue	Text	Class	None
Class time	Date/time	Class	None

The database design

As can be seen from the above tables, I intend to store data about leaders, members and classes. Each of these will form a table in my database and I will need some primary key fields which will be unique to each table.

6

GCSE ICT Project: Amy Hughes 2003

The primary keys I will use are:

- leader number in the leaders' table
- member number in the members' table
- class number in the classes' table.

The mail merge design

I first considered creating the members' details as a data file in the wordprocessing package. This is because we had covered this already when we were taught about mail merges. Creating the data file would be duplicating the data held in the database. This would lead to two copies of similar data being held and it could cause problems when trying to keep both versions the same. Updates to the database would also have to be done on the data file in the wordprocessor.

I will use the members' table in Access along with the mail merge facility in Word to produce letters to be sent to each member or selected groups of members.

Implementation section

Here are three tables in the database created, which are based on the design in the design section:

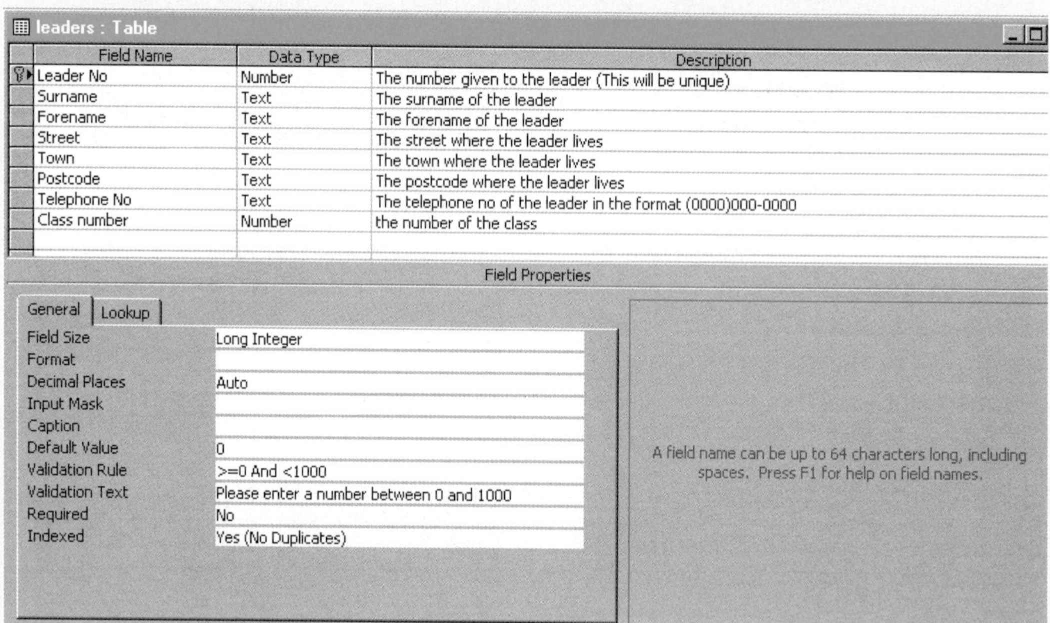

leaders : Table

Field Name	Data Type	Description
Leader No	Number	The number given to the leader (This will be unique)
Surname	Text	The surname of the leader
Forename	Text	The forename of the leader
Street	Text	The street where the leader lives
Town	Text	The town where the leader lives
Postcode	Text	The postcode where the leader lives
Telephone No	Text	The telephone no of the leader in the format (0000)000-0000
Class number	Number	the number of the class

Field Properties

General | Lookup

Field Size	Long Integer
Format	
Decimal Places	Auto
Input Mask	
Caption	
Default Value	0
Validation Rule	>=0 And <1000
Validation Text	Please enter a number between 0 and 1000
Required	No
Indexed	Yes (No Duplicates)

A field name can be up to 64 characters long, including spaces. Press F1 for help on field names.

Leaders' table: this shows details of all the leaders

It indicates a validation check for the leader number which insures the user inputs only numbers between 0 and 1000. This is the error message that is shown if the user enters the wrong data in the leader number field.

7

GCSE ICT Project: Amy Hughes 2003

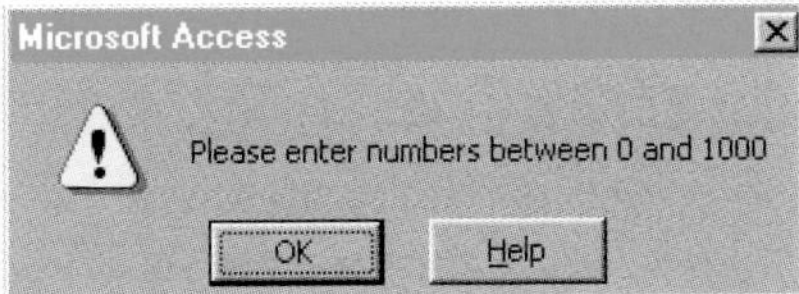

The table also indicates an input mask for the telephone number which indicates the format to be entered by user.

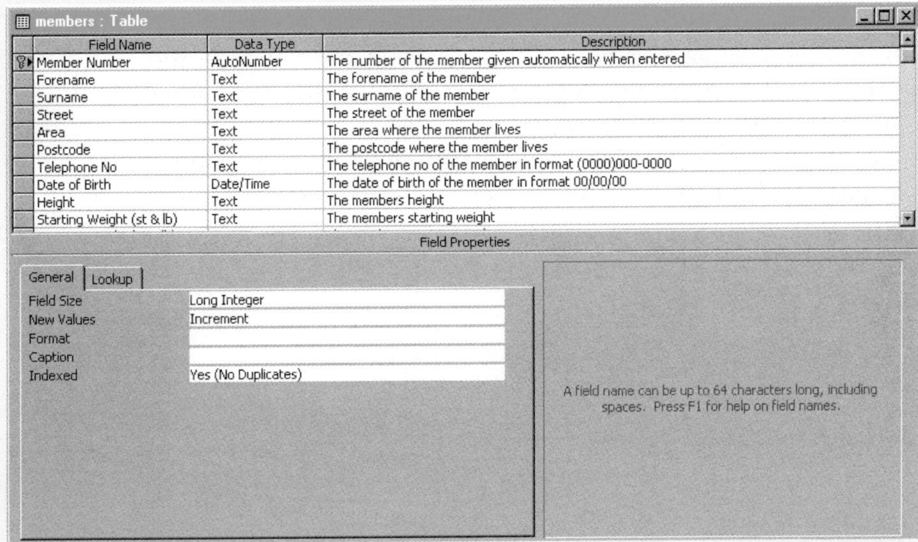

members : Table
Field Name
Data Type
Description
Member Number
AutoNumber
The number of the member given automatically when entered
Forename
Text
The forename of the member
Surname
Text
The surname of the member
Street
Text
The street of the member
Area
Text
The area where the member lives
Postcode
Text
The postcode where the member lives
Telephone No
Text
The telephone no of the member in format (0000)000-0000
Date of Birth
Date/Time
The date of birth of the member in format 00/00/00
Height
Text
The members height
Starting Weight (st & lb)
Text
The members starting weight
Field Properties
General
Lookup
Field Size
Long Integer
New Values
Increment
Format
Caption
Indexed
Yes (No Duplicates)
A field name can be up to 64 characters long, including spaces. Press F1 for help on field names.

Members' table: this shows details of all the members

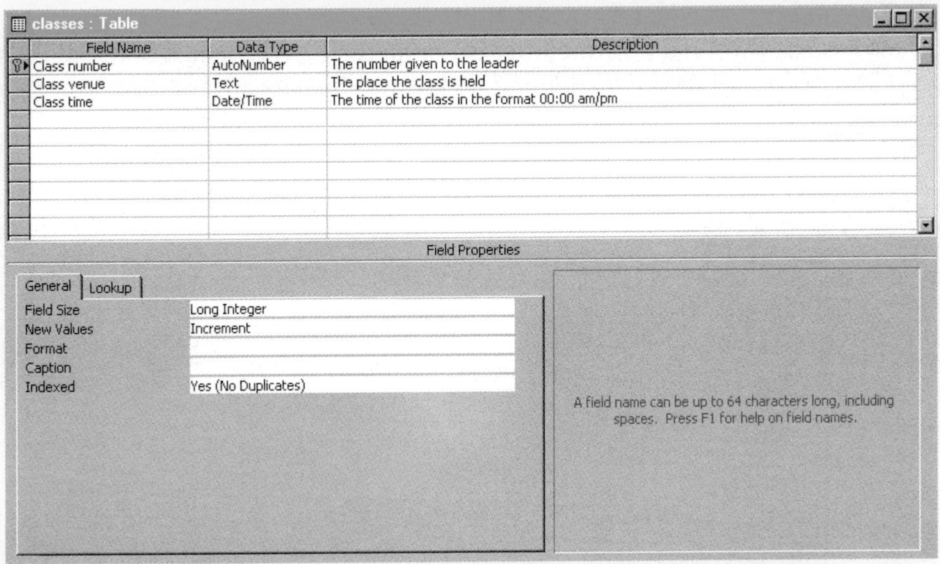

Classes' table: this gives details of the classes held

8

GCSE ICT Project: Amy Hughes 2003

Relationships

The screen shot below shows the relationships between the tables. It shows the one-to-many relationships between each table. The leaders will have many members, but the members will have just one leader. Also, the leaders will hold many classes, but the members will attend one class.

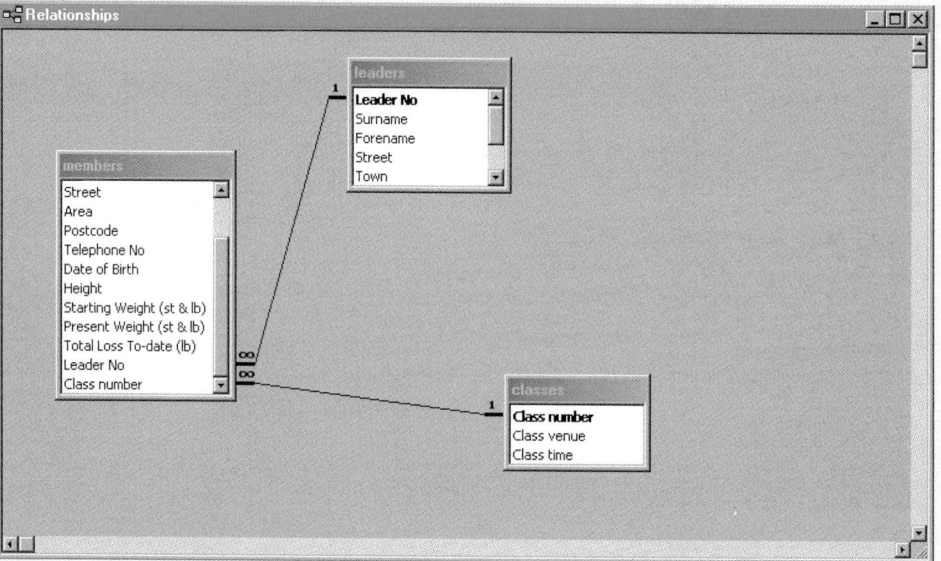

Forms

To enter data into the database I have designed some forms for each table so new information can be entered easily by the user.

This form is used when a new member is enrolled. The member is automatically allocated a number and then a leader and a class will be allocated by the person doing the enrolling.

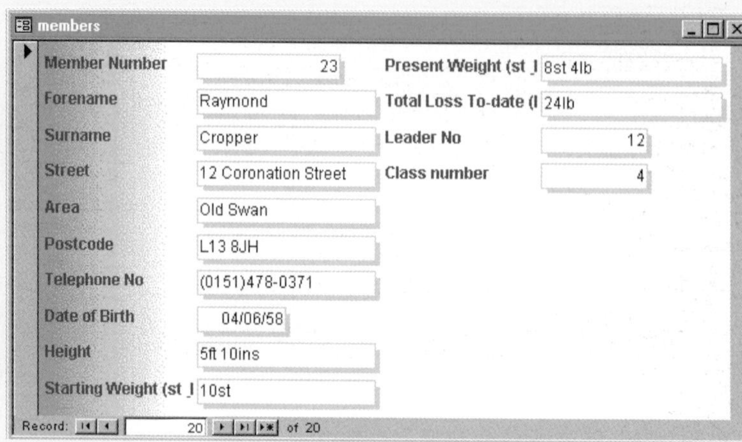

GCSE ICT Project: Amy Hughes 2003

Here is a form used to input leader details into the leaders' table.

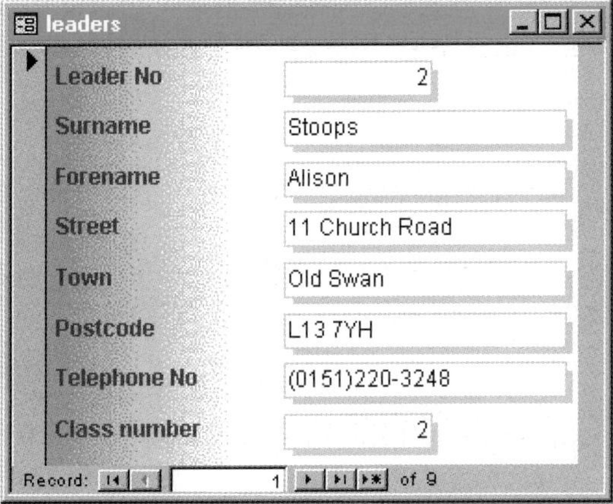

leaders

Leader No	2
Surname	Stoops
Forename	Alison
Street	11 Church Road
Town	Old Swan
Postcode	L13 7YH
Telephone No	(0151)220-3248
Class number	2

Record: 1 of 9

Here is a form to enter the class details into the classes' table.

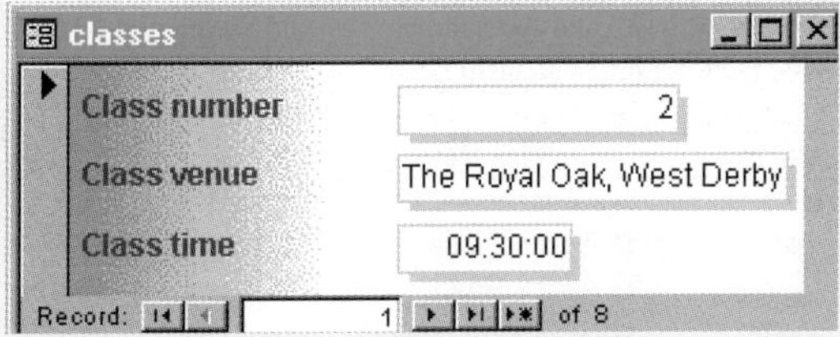

classes

Class number	2
Class venue	The Royal Oak, West Derby
Class time	09:30:00

Record: 1 of 8

I had to think about the order in which I filled the data into the tables. The classes' table is completed first, followed by the leaders' table and finally the members' table.

classes : Table

Class number	Class venue	Class time
2	The Royal Oak, West Derby	09:30:00
3	The Gabbage Breck Road	19:00:00
4	The George, Breck Road	10:30:00
5	The Stag and Rainbow	19:00:00
6	The Crown, West Derby	10:30:00
7	The Crown, Tuebrooke	20:00:00
8	The Red Lion, Huyton	19:00:00
9	The West Derby, West Derby	19:30:00
(AutoNumber)		

Record: 1 of 8

Data in the classes' table

10

GCSE ICT Project: Amy Hughes 2003

leaders : Table

	Leader No	Surname	Forename	Street	Town	Postcode	Telephone No	Class numb
▶ +	2	Stoops	Alison	11 Church Road	Old Swan	L13 7YH	(0151)220-3248	
+	3	Sumner	Gill	72 Garston Old Road	Gartson	L24 7TR	(0151)480-2694	
+	5	Sundell	Marie	9 Portelet Road	Old Swan	L13 6TS	(0151)426-8946	
+	8	Paula	Paula	13 Stoneville Road	Allerton	L34 7TY	(0151)727-7289	
+	12	Henderson	Jane	18 Camp Road	Woolton	L35 1WD	(0151)546-9193	
+	16	Price	Dawn	1 Ingoe Lane	Old Swan	L13 5ES	(0151)546-9878	
+	22	Quinn	Barbara	45 Buttermere Close	Woolton	L35 5WD	(0151)548-9502	
+	30	Apsley	Joanne	9 Holly Bank	Garston	L24 8YU	(0151)722-2481	
+	54	Parr	Sarah	1 Oak Leigh	Old Swan	L13 9GF	(0151)286-3813	
*	0							

Data in the leaders' table

I then used the members' form to input the member details into the members' table.

members : Table

	Member Number	Forename	Surname	Street	Area	Postcode	Telephone No	Date of Bir
▶	4	Dianne	Kennedy	49 Abbeyfield Drive	Old Swan	L13 7FR	(0151)547-1812	08/06/
	5	Ann	Hugh	93 Aspes Road	West Derby	L12 6FG	(0151)724-9880	09/07/
	6	Paula	Edwards	109 Pagemoss Lane	Old Swan	L13 4ED	(0151)228-3142	11/05/
	7	Fiona	Philips	3 Lake Avenue	Old Swan	L13 5FC	(0151)220-0861	01/10/
	8	Kirk	Kennedy	49 Abbeyfield Drive	Garston	L24 7HJ	(0151)547-1812	29/12/
	9	Joanne	Macmahon	18 Grassendale Court	Woolton	L35 6FD	(0151)426-9849	21/01/
	10	Barbara	Mckay	10 Crondoll Grove	Old Swan	L13 4GH	(0151)281-5074	30/03/
	11	Eamon	Holderness	111 Elmshouse Road	Garston	L24 7FT	(0151)280-6458	08/08/
	12	Irenee	Gant	34 Austin Close	Garston	L24 8UH	(0151)475-3351	29/12/
	13	Rita	Lynch	99 Astley Road	Old Sawn	L13 5DF	(0151)289-9300	09/01/
	14	Paula	Martin	34 Richmond Avenue	West Derby	L12 3DE	(0151)489-3805	15/09/
	15	Marie	Marshall	50 Fairfield Cresent	West Derby	L12 4SD	(0151)709-9207	18/10/
	16	Nicola	Metcalf	35 Aigburth Hall Lane	West Derby	L12 8HG	(0151)475-5225	19/03/
	17	Margaret	Thomas	139 Hollow Croft	Old Swan	L13 9KL	(0151)449-3123	12/12/
	18	David	Jones	35 Speke Hall Road	Garston	L24 5VF	(0151)480-4589	28/05/
	19	Angela	Gerrard	66 Clough Road	Woolton	L35 6GH	(0151)708-3445	15/06/
	20	Gill	Martin	8 Crofton Road	Old Swan	l13 5DF	(0151)336-5050	12/12/
	21	Amy	Cheung	18 Rycroft Road	West Derby	L12 5DR	(0151)427-2384	22/05/
	22	Maureen	Criddle	42 Lawson Drive	West Derby	L12 3SA	(0151)722-6899	19/03/
	23	Raymond	Cropper	12 Coronation Street	Old Swan	L13 8JH	(0151)478-0371	04/06/
*	(AutoNumber)							

Record: 1 of 20

11

GCSE ICT Project: Amy Hughes 2003

The rest of the data in the members' table is shown here.

members : Table

Date of Birth	Height	Starting Weight (st & lb)	Present Weight (st & lb)	Total Loss To-date (lb)	Leader No	Class numb
08/06/67	5ft 10ins	34st 3lb	8st 2lb	365lb	12	
09/07/82	5ft 6ins	12st 4lb	10st 3lb	29lb	30	
11/05/79	5ft 9ins	15st	12st 5lb	37lb	12	
01/10/80	5ft 4ins	14st 5lb	14st 2lb	03lb	22	
29/12/67	5ft 10ins	14st 3lb	12st	31lb	12	
21/01/56	5ft 8ins	10st 5lb	9st 8lb	11lb	30	
30/03/69	5ft 3ins	12st 9lb	10st 5lb	32lb	12	
08/08/74	6ft	16st 8lbs	12st 6lb	58lb	12	
29/12/78	5ft 8ins	11st 2lb	11st	02lb	22	
09/01/59	5ft 4ins	13st 5lbs	12st 11lbs	08lb	54	
15/09/61	5ft 7ins	13st 1lb	10st 6lb	37lb	12	
18/10/66	5ft 7ins	12st 12lb	11st	26lb	30	
19/03/62	6ft 1in	11st 5lb	9st 3lb	30lb	12	
12/12/59	5ft 9ins	10st 4lb	10st 1lb	03lb	22	
28/05/62	5ft 11ins	16st 5lb	14st 6lb	27lb	16	
15/06/59	5ft 8ins	10st 12lb	9st 1lb	25lb	12	
12/12/54	5ft 6ins	11st	10st 5lb	09lb	22	
22/05/58	5ft 3ins	10st 2lb	9st	16lb	30	
19/03/60	5ft 5ins	10st 1lb	9st 8lb	07lb	12	
04/06/58	5ft 10ins	10st	8st 4lb	24lb	12	
					0	

Record: 1 of 20

Queries

Queries have been set up to help the leader find certain members for a variety of reasons.

This screen shows a query to find the members of a certain class so that they can be notified of class information.

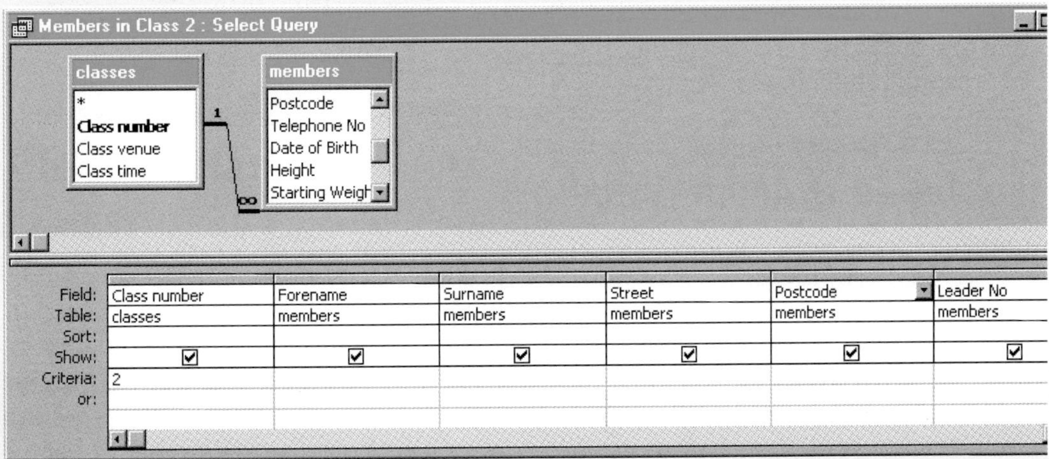

GCSE ICT Project: Amy Hughes 2003

This screen shows the results of the query.

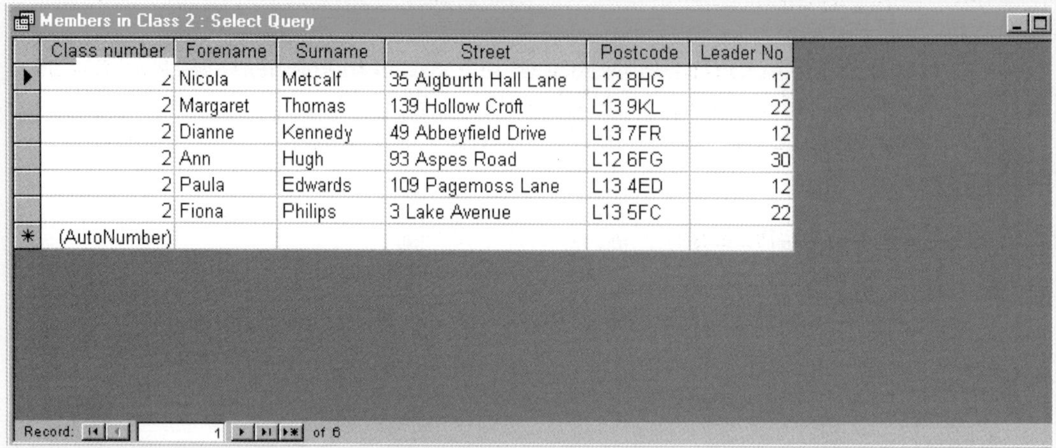

Members in Class 2 : Select Query

Class number	Forename	Surname	Street	Postcode	Leader No
2	Nicola	Metcalf	35 Aigburth Hall Lane	L12 8HG	12
2	Margaret	Thomas	139 Hollow Croft	L13 9KL	22
2	Dianne	Kennedy	49 Abbeyfield Drive	L13 7FR	12
2	Ann	Hugh	93 Aspes Road	L12 6FG	30
2	Paula	Edwards	109 Pagemoss Lane	L13 4ED	12
2	Fiona	Philips	3 Lake Avenue	L13 5FC	22
(AutoNumber)					

Record: 1 of 6

Implementation of the mail merge

The results from the above query were used to cut down on paperwork and time. A mail merge has been set up to contact all the members of the class, so if the leader needs to contact one or all of the members, then a letter(s) can be easily edited and printed, thus saving a lot of time.

Alison Stoops
11 Church Road
Old Swan
L13 7YH

«Forename» «Surname»
«Street»
«Area»
«Postcode»

Thursday, 08 August 2002

Dear «Forename»

Just a quick note to let you know that I am on holiday next week, from Monday 12th Aug till Sunday 18th Aug. I have a replacement, Gill Sumner, she is lovely and she holds a great class. Have fun and I will see you in a couple of weeks and keep up the good work.

Yours truly,

Alison

13

GCSE ICT Project: Amy Hughes 2003

First, I chose the members' table to see what happened; this worked well. However, I only needed to send letters to members of Class 2. I then found out that you can use the data from a query to supply the data for the mail merge. I then chose to use the data from 'Members in Class 2'.

I used my letter design to type in the above letter. Mail merge fields were added using data from the query called 'Members in Class 2'.

I used the mail merge wizard to guide me through the steps to complete the mail merge.

User guide for the mailmerge

The first step is to select Letters.

Then the letter is typed in and blanks are left where the recipient information is to go.

The third screen shows how you select where you want the recipient information to come from.

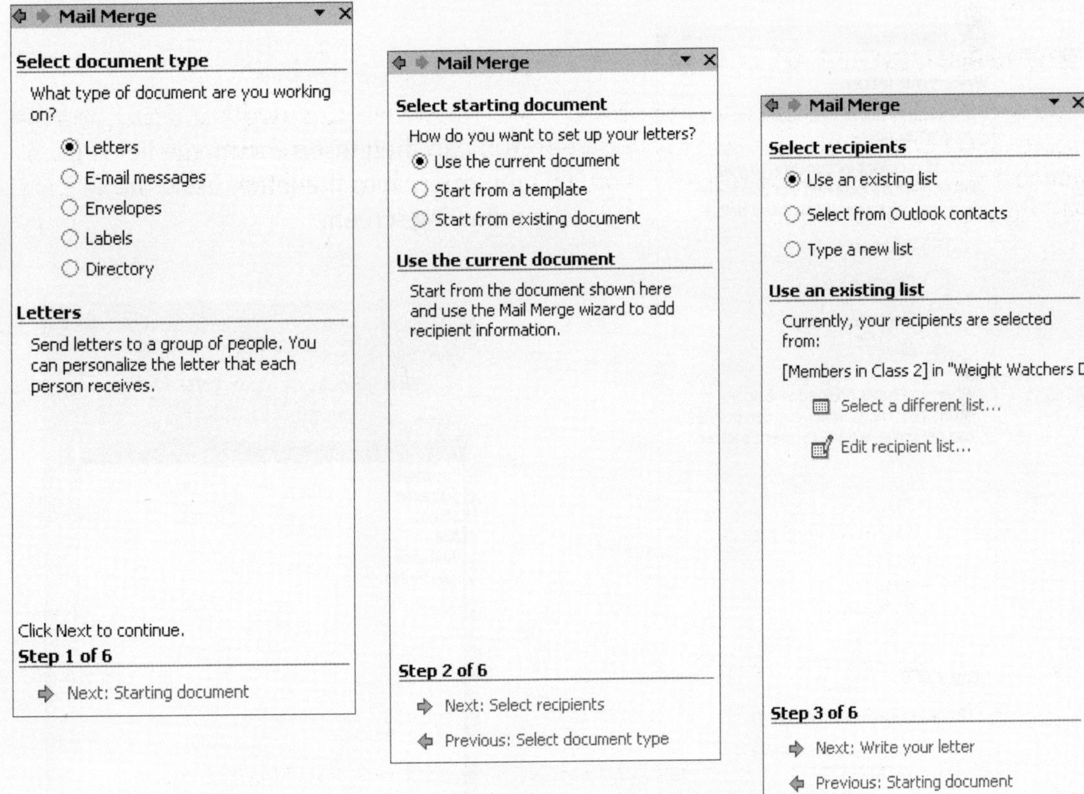

Click on 'Select a different list ...'. Then the following screen will appear, where you can choose where the data is to come from. Notice that it contains not just the tables but the queries as well.

14

GCSE ICT Project: Amy Hughes 2003

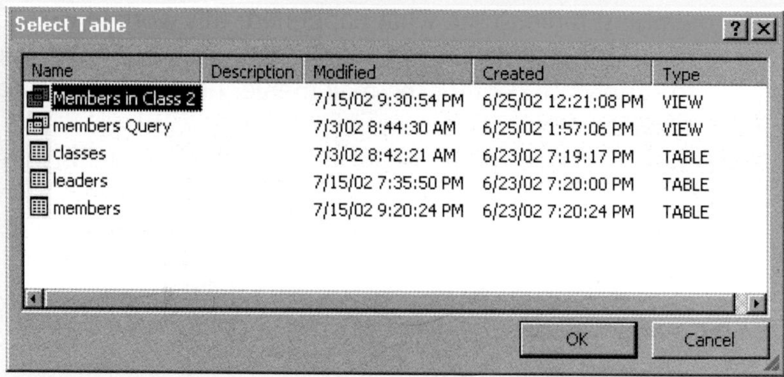

You now add the merge fields from the query. In this screen, More items... will give you a list of the fields in the query that you could add to your letter.

You can then insert the merge fields from the query into the letter, using the following screen.

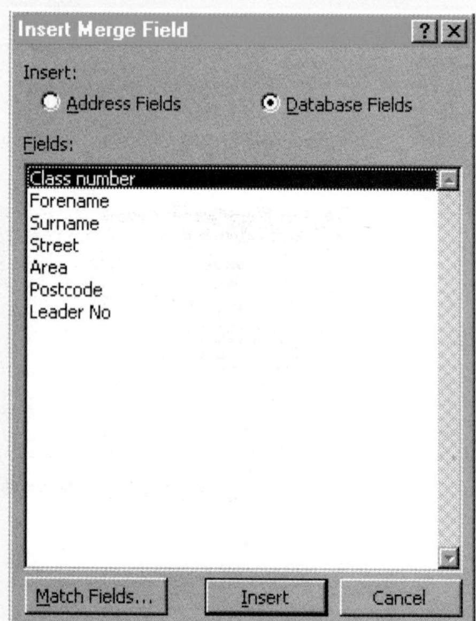

15

GCSE ICT Project: Amy Hughes 2003

Add the fields as shown in the following screen.

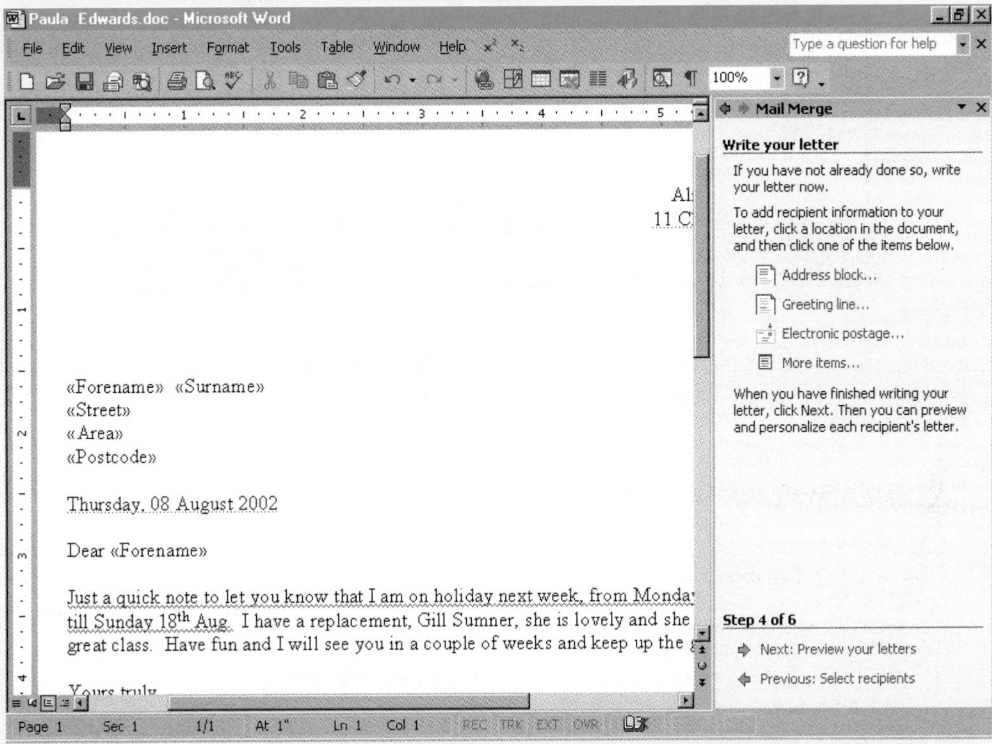

To test the mail merge look at the mail merge recipients' list to check that the letters are only being sent to those members in Class 2. Check this with the members' data in the members' table to see if the letters are being sent to the correct recipients.

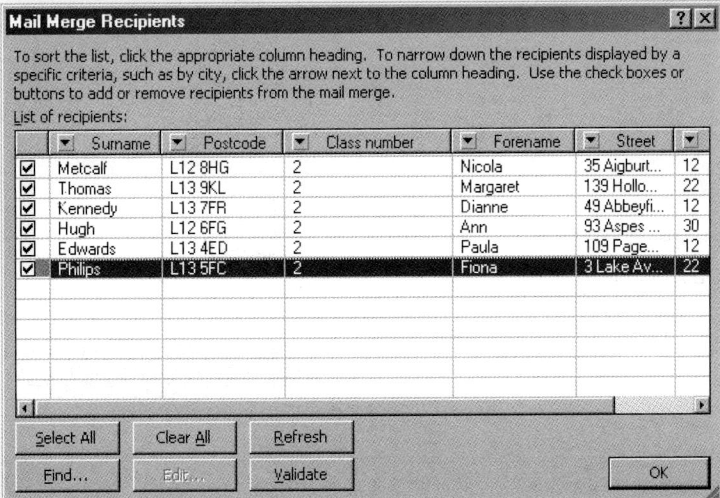

Mail Merge Recipients

To sort the list, click the appropriate column heading. To narrow down the recipients displayed by a specific criteria, such as by city, click the arrow next to the column heading. Use the check boxes or buttons to add or remove recipients from the mail merge.

List of recipients:

	Surname	Postcode	Class number	Forename	Street	
☑	Metcalf	L12 8HG	2	Nicola	35 Aigburt...	12
☑	Thomas	L13 9KL	2	Margaret	139 Hollo...	22
☑	Kennedy	L13 7FR	2	Dianne	49 Abbeyfi...	12
☑	Hugh	L12 6FG	2	Ann	93 Aspes ...	30
☑	Edwards	L13 4ED	2	Paula	109 Page...	12
☑	Philips	L13 5FC	2	Fiona	3 Lake Av...	22

Select All | Clear All | Refresh | Find... | Edit... | Validate | OK

16

GCSE ICT Project: Amy Hughes 2003

Before printing check each letter using Preview your letters. You can then click on Complete the merge.

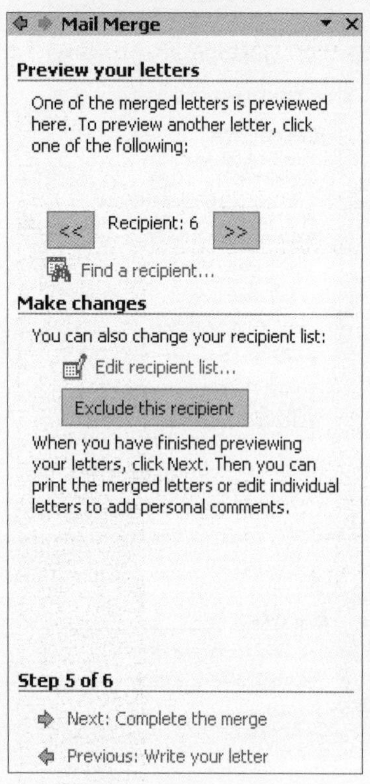

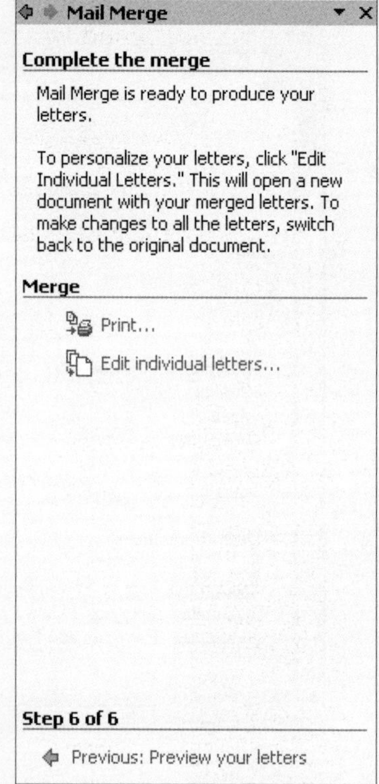

One of the merged letters is shown here. Other letters were viewed on the screen to check they were correct.

Alison Stoops
11 Church Road
Old Swan
L13 7YH

Nicola Metcalf
35 Aigburth Hall Lane
West Derby
L12 8HG

Thursday, 08 August 2002

Dear Nicola

Just a quick note to let you know that I am on holiday next week, from Monday 12th Aug till Sunday 18th Aug. I have a replacement, Gill Sumner, she is lovely and she holds a great class. Have fun and I will see you in a couple of weeks and keep up the good work.

Yours truly,

Alison

17

GCSE ICT Project: Amy Hughes 2003

Reports

Reports are produced to show a professional printout of any tables or queries that are produced from the database.

The following report was produced to show those members who had leader number 12.

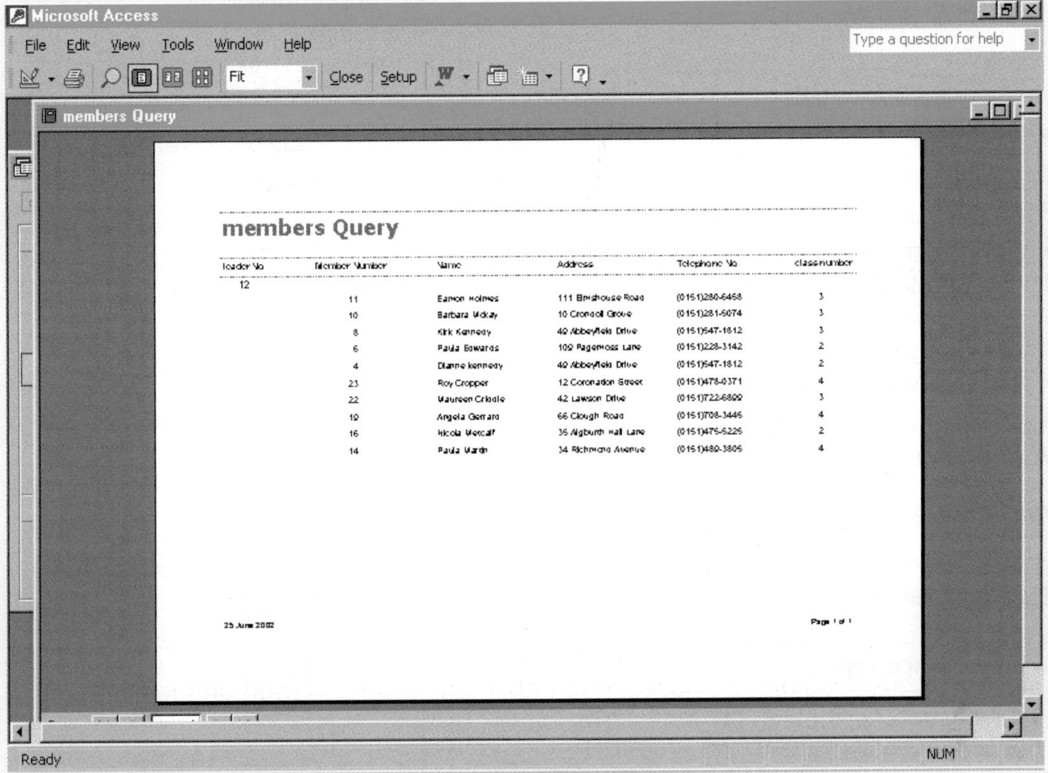

members Query

leader No	Member Number	Name	Address	Telephone No	classnumber
12					
	11	Eamon Holmes	111 Birchouse Road	(0151)280-6458	3
	10	Barbara Mckay	10 Cronaoll Grove	(0151)281-6074	3
	8	Kirk Kennedy	40 Abbeyfield Drive	(0151)547-1812	3
	6	Paula Edwards	109 Pagemoss Lane	(0151)228-3142	2
	4	Dianne Kennedy	40 Abbeyfield Drive	(0151)547-1812	2
	23	Roy Cropper	12 Coronation Street	(0151)478-0371	4
	22	Maureen Crisdle	42 Lawson Drive	(0151)722-6899	3
	19	Angela Gerrard	66 Clough Road	(0151)708-3446	4
	16	Nicola Metcalf	35 Aigburth Hall Lane	(0151)475-6225	2
	14	Paula Martin	34 Richmond Avenue	(0151)489-3806	4

25 June 2002 Page 1 of 1

The table below is a testing plan for the validation checks in this database.

Test number	Table/field being tested	Validation check	Input	Result	Pass/fail	Action taken
1	Leaders/leader no	> = 0 and < 1000	1001	Message: Please enter a number between 0 and 1000	Fail	None
2		> 0 and < 100	–30	Message: Please enter correct price	Fail	None

18

GCSE ICT Project: Amy Hughes 2003

The table below is a testing plan for the input masks in the database.

Test number	Input mask	Input	Result	Action taken
1	(0000)000-0000	(3459)876-5	Message: The value entered isn't appropriate for the input mask (0000)000-0000	Enter correct number format

User Guide

1 Open Weight Watchers Slimming Club database.
2 To enter information into database click on Forms button.
3 Then click on required form and enter details into required boxes.
4 To open tables click on Table button.
5 Then open required table.
6 To open reports click on report button.
7 Then click on required report.
8 To open queries click on query button.
9 Then open required query.

Verification

Here I looked at the performance criteria identified at the start of the project and I have ticked off the criteria that have been met.

Performance criteria	Verification	Comments
Designed to make learning the system easy	Yes	
Reduces the time taken to process enquiries	Yes	
More secure than the existing manual system	Yes	
Reduces the overall paperwork	Yes	
Fast access to information	Yes	
Forms are used to make data entry easy	Yes	
Checks are in place to make sure that invalid data are not entered	Yes	
It is easy to produce letters using data	Yes	

19

GCSE ICT Project: Amy Hughes 2003

Verification questionnaire

The purpose of this questionnaire is to find out the user's honest opinion of my solution.

1 Did you find the system easy to use?
2 Are you satisfied that the system holds all the information you need to successfully complete your work. If the answer is no, please explain what is missing.
3 Did you encounter any problems when using the system? If so, please describe the problems.
4 To what extent do you think the new system is an improvement of the old system?
5 Are the processes involved in doing your job speeded up by the new system?
6 Did you find the output from the system useful?
7 If you could change any part of the system how would you change it?
8 On a scale of one to ten (ten is the best), how do you rate the new system?

Evaluation

There were no problems setting up the Weight Watchers database. It is successful in giving the leaders of the classes all the necessary information about their members; it makes enrolling new members easier and updating records of weight loss or gain a lot more accurate. It gives easier access to all the member records and searches of members' details have cut down time greatly. It also gives the leader instant member details; for example, sending out personal messages to members who have had good weight losses is a lot easier and gives the members a more 'individual' feeling to their diet plan.

The only problem that may need to be overcome is the user access to the database, as a novice could become confused when trying to enter the database. It may be necessary to make the user interface more simple, with buttons that will take the user straight into the database.

20

The good and bad things about this project

It is hard to produce a perfect project and because the example project is a real project there are some good and bad things about it. We will start off with the good and then look at the bad.

Good things

- The student has used a real problem with a real user and has chosen suitable software, with reasons for solving it. The problem has enough breadth for the student to get a high mark (i.e. she has used a database and the mail merge facility of a wordprocessor).
- The student looked at alternative ways of solving the problem (i.e. she looked at producing a database using spreadsheet software) and gave a reason why this was rejected.
- Reusability has been thought of because the student has considered that the mail merge can be used with the changed data in the database.
- The structure of the project was good and followed this particular exam board's specification. Headers and footers were used to good effect.
- The design and implementation sections were good with good explanations and screen shots. The mail merge section was explained here and also as part of the user guide.
- Implementation was carried out well. There was evidence of testing but only a few tests were done. There was no evidence of any modifications that needed doing if the test did not work as planned. (Remember to test the results of any sorts, searches, queries and reports.)
- The evaluation section was good and it included a verification questionnaire where the user could check that the solution to the problem matched the performance criteria as set out in the analysis section.
- She has included some further enhancements in the evaluation section (i.e. things that she would do if she had been given more time to improve the solution).

Bad things

- Data capture forms such as the application form to become a member should have been included.
- In the analysis section, a questionnaire could have been included to give to the student's mother to find out about the administrative systems involved in running the club.
- The analysis mentioned the need for passwords. This wasn't implemented despite personal data being stored and therefore having to comply with the Data Protection Act.
- The dataflow diagram should have focused more on the part of the system being developed. This dataflow diagram gave an overall view of the system. One should have been drawn showing more detail with boxes for the processing and where data is stored being included.
- There were no hand-drawn designs for the forms being used.
- The user guide is brief. It needs to be divided into sections covering different areas such as entering new member details, searching for a member, etc. It is only a user guide for the solution that is needed and you should not include material on how to use the actual software since it is assumed that the user can do this. Reusability should be included here. For example, you can focus on the day-to-day changes that need to be made (e.g. changing member details, deleting members who have left, etc.).
- A report was included but there was no explanation about why this report was produced. For any sorts, queries (i.e. searches), reports, and so on, there needs to be a clearly stated reason for producing them. To save space, it is a good idea to annotate any printouts. This means that you should make notes and explanations on the printouts themselves.

- There is nothing to show how the solution was modified over time. It would be very unusual to produce something that was perfect first time. There needed to be evidence of how the solution was corrected.

Index

Page references in *italics* indicate illustrations